VB.NET Programming with the Public Beta

Billy S. Hollis
Rockford Lhotka

Wrox Press Ltd.

VB.NET Programming with the Public Beta

Published by Wrox Press Ltd,
Arden House, 1102 Warwick Road, Acocks Green,
Birmingham, B27 6BH, UK
Printed in Canada
ISBN 1-861004-91-5

Trademark Acknowledgements

Wrox has endeavored to provide trademark information about all the companies and products mentioned in this book by the appropriate use of capitals. However, Wrox cannot guarantee the accuracy of this information.

Credits

Authors
Billy S. Hollis
Rockford Lhotka

Technical Reviewers
Maxime Bombardier
Robin Dewson
Robert Dunaway
Brian Francis
Jacob Hammer
Scott Hanselman
Hope Hatfield
Rob Howard
Don Lee
Paul Morris
David Schultz
Rick Tempestini
Radomir Zarik

Technical Editors
Benjamin Egan
Gary Evans
Paul Jeffcoat
Gareth Oakley

Technical Architect
Kate Hall

Category Manager
Bruce Lawson

Author Agent
Sarah Bowers

Project Administrator
Cilmara Lion

Production Manager
Simon Hardware

Production Coordinator
Pip Wonson

Figures
Shabnam Hussain

Cover
Shelley Frazier

Index
Martin Brooks

About the Authors

Billy Hollis

Billy Hollis has also written many articles, reviews, and columns, appearing in such publications as the Visual Basic Programmers Journal, Unisphere, and Computer User Magazine. He is a frequent speaker at industry events such as the Visual Basic Insiders Technical Summit (VBITS) and Comdex. He presented two sessions at VBITS New York in June 2000 on *Getting Ready for Web Forms* and *A COM Component for Browser Independence*. His session at VBITS 99 in Chicago was the highest rated session at the conference. His most recent presentation was at the Wrox conference in Las Vegas (September 2000) on *What's new in VB.NET*. He is also currently writing the introductory chapter for the Wrox book (in production) previewing Microsoft.NET.

Billy is the Microsoft MSDN Regional Director for Nashville, Tennessee, and collaborates with Microsoft to put on Developer Days in Nashville. He is considered a Subject Matter Expert at Microsoft, and is on the content committee to develop the content for Developers Days 2000.

An opportunity like this book doesn't come along very often, and I owe a lot of gratitude to many folks for letting me take advantage of it.

My family received a lot less attention than they deserved during the holidays last year, so Cindy, Ansel, and Dyson are first in line for thanks. I promise I'll spend the next several weekends with them instead of with a computer running .NET. And I'm sorry I didn't have time to shop for proper Christmas gifts. Next year will be better.

Several folks helped me decode the intricacies of .NET, and I'd like to acknowledge their help. They include Jay Glynn, Gary Bailey, and Burt Harvey. I wish I knew as much as those guys.

Thanks to the folks at Wrox for asking us to do one of the very first books on VB.NET, and for working with us to find a way to make it all come together. Sarah Bowers, and Kate Hall especially deserve thanks. It's been intense, but well worth it.

Rockford Lhotka

Rockford Lhotka is the author of *Professional Visual Basic 6 Distributed Objects* and *Visual Basic 6 Business Objects* both published by Wrox Press and is a contributing author for Visual Basic Programmers Journal and DevX. He has presented at numerous conferences including Microsoft Tech Ed and VBITS. He has over 14 years experience in software development and has worked on many projects in various roles, including software architecture, design and development, network administration and project management. Rockford is the Principal Technology Evangelist for Magenic Technologies, one of the nation's premiere Microsoft Certified Solution Providers dedicated to solving today's most challenging business problems using 100% Microsoft tools and technology.

This book has been one of the most fun projects I've worked on in some time. VB.NET is a very exciting product and working with it, even in beta form, has been sheer joy!

As with all books, this one has been a lot of work, and I owe great thanks to my family for their love, patience, and support.

I also want to thank the various people who contribute to the msnews.Microsoft.com newsgroups. Whether positive, negative or just plain helpful, there are many people on these newsgroups who have influenced the content of the book.

My deepest thanks to the excellent team of reviewers and editors from Wrox Press. Their feedback and support have been outstanding and I appreciate them greatly!

Finally, thank YOU for purchasing this book. Hopefully it will help as you explore this exciting technology. I hope you will come to love VB.NET as much as I do!

Thanks, code well and have fun!

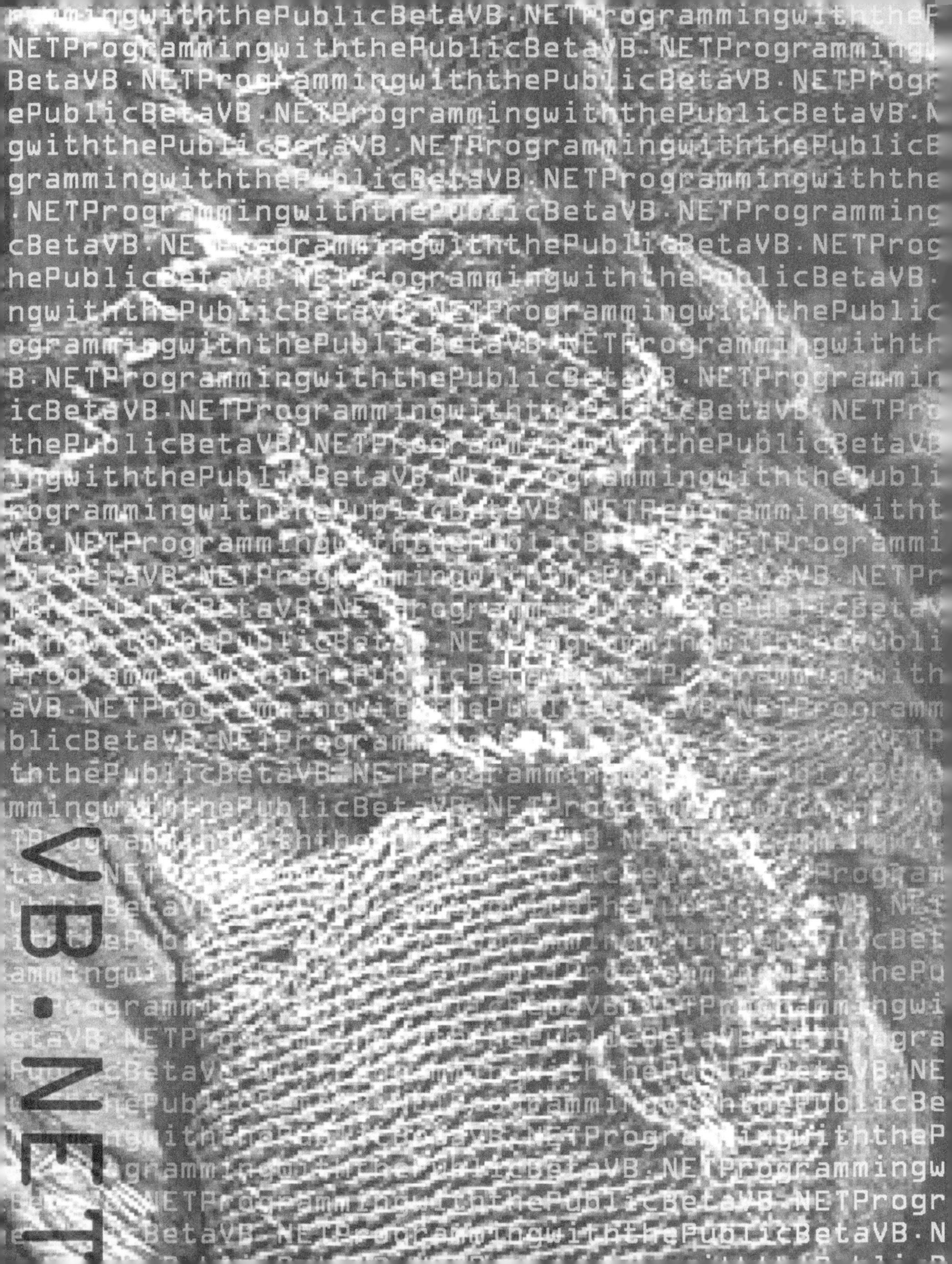
VB.NET
VB.NET Programming with the Public Beta

Table of Contents

Table of Contents

Table of Contents

Table of Contents

Table of Contents

Introduction

Microsoft has staked its future on the .NET Framework, and VB.NET is likely to be the most popular tool to develop on this framework for the next few years. That means hundreds of thousands of Visual Basic developers will need to make the transition, and it is a major one. VB developers need to quickly learn the most important details about VB.NET, and this book is targeted to satisfy that need.

By writing this book we intend to tell experienced VB developers the most important things needed to know in order to begin using VB.NET effectively. There are many new technologies in VB.NET which will be of interest to experienced VB developers, including:

❑ Full inheritance

❑ Other new object capabilities such as parameterized constructors and shared members

❑ Structured error handling

❑ New threading models

Documentation is sparse at this stage in the beta cycle and it is hoped that this book will save you many hours of confusion as you step up from VB6 to VB.NET.

What's Covered in this Book?

This book begins by covering the basic VS.NET environment, which provides a powerful common set of capabilities for all .NET developers. The first two chapters are devoted to an introduction to the .NET Framework, providing both an overview of its development and an introduction to the features seen in the VS.NET IDE.

Having introduced the new IDE, Chapter 3 then moves on to take a look at what new features lie within VB.NET, highlighting not only the introduction of the use of namespaces and full inheritance, but also changes in the error handling and garbage collection routines.

Chapter 4 looks at WinForms, and migration of older code to the VB.NET environment, as well as illustrating some of the new features unavailable to VB6 developers.

Chapter 5 takes a closer look at the new object-oriented capabilities available to VB.NET developers, giving a detailed analysis of the nature of inheritance and how this can be used in applications.

Having looked at the new full OO abilities, Chapter 6 moves on to look at the other new capability on offer to VB developers, Web Forms. After considering the structure and creation of Web Forms the chapter looks at Web Services with a worked example to show their means of deployment.

Chapter 7 examines at data access through the use of ADO and looks in more detail at the SOAP protocol and the use of XML, both from a client and server point of view.

In Chapter 8 we discuss advanced programming topics, including creating middle-tier components in VB.NET, threading in VB.NET, writing console applications, deployment, creating Windows services, monitoring the file system, and operations from the command line.

Chapter 9 covers interoperability with VB and migration to VB.NET. As such it covers using your COM objects from .NET, calling the Windows APIs, and using the Migration tool.

Chapter 10 has two development examples – one a Web Forms Payment Calculator and the other a query screen for the `Titles` table of the `pub` database in SQL Server. Both of these example applications use techniques and tools discussed earlier in the book and serve to consolidate what you will have learnt.

Finally, Chapter 11 wraps up the book by pointing you in the direction of further VB.NET resources and suggesting steps you can take now to ensure that the migration of your projects from VB to VB.NET is a smooth one.

Who is this Book for?

This book covers a product that is still under development and, as such, is aimed at developers with a good working knowledge of VB, or ASP and VBScript. No attempt is made at providing a tutorial about the VB language, other than some comparisons between VB6 and VB.NET code techniques – so a good familiarity with VB6 (or at least VBA or VBScript) is necessary to get the full benefit from this book.

This book is primarily targeted at experienced VB6 developers who are looking towards the future and the .NET platform, and want to learn how to use VB.NET quickly and effectively.

As VB.NET is positioned to be a prominent web development tool, this book will also appeal to web developers who are using ASP.NET (previously called ASP+) and intend to use the VB language when developing their ASP.NET sites. The level of integration between ASP.NET and VB.NET far exceeds that between ASP and VB6, and a comprehensive understanding of VB.NET will be a huge asset to any web developer using ASP.NET.

In fact, the Visual Interdev development tool provided by Microsoft for ASP development has been, in effect, replaced by the VS.NET environment itself. The functional equivalent to Visual Interdev in the .NET environment is the VS.NET IDE.

The .NET framework provides a powerful new way to program for both Windows and the Internet, and this may well attract experienced developers from other platforms and languages to the .NET platform and the VB.NET language. This book will appeal to these people as it provides discussion and examples of commonly performed programming tasks and techniques – allowing rapid transition from other platforms or languages to VB.NET.

What You Need to Use this Book

A full discussion of both the hardware and software required to run all of the example code in this book is provided in Chapter 1, but as a rough guide you should have a minimum of:

❑　A Pentium II, 450 MHz computer with 128 MB of RAM and 3 GB of hard disk space

❑　Windows 2000

❑　Internet Explorer 5.5

❑　IIS

❑　SQL Server 2000

And of course the VS.NET beta 1, available from http://msdn.microsoft.com/net.

Conventions Used

We've used a number of different styles of text and layout in the book, to help differentiate between different kinds of information. Here are some of the styles we've used and an explanation of what they mean:

> **These boxes hold important, not-to-be forgotten, mission-critical details that are directly relevant to the surrounding text.**

Background information, asides, and references appear in text like this.

❑　**Important Words** are in a bold font

❑　Keyboard strokes are shown like this: *Esc*

❑　Words that appear on the screen, such as menu options, are in a similar font to the one used on screen, for example, the Tools menu

❑　All object names, function names, and other code snippets are in this style:
`System.WinForms.Form`

Code that is new or important is presented like this:

```
Private Sub Button1_Click(ByVal sender As System.Object, _
                          ByVal e As System.EventArgs)

End Sub
```

Whereas code that we've seen before or has little to do with the matter being discussed, looks like this:

```
Dim lstNewListBox As New Listbox()
```

Feedback

We've worked hard to make this book as useful to you as possible, so we'd like to know what you think. We're always keen to know what it is you want and need to know.

We appreciate feedback on our efforts and take both criticism and praise on board in our future editorial efforts. If you've anything to say, let us know via e-mail:

feedback@wrox.com

or via the feedback links on our web site:

http://www.wrox.com

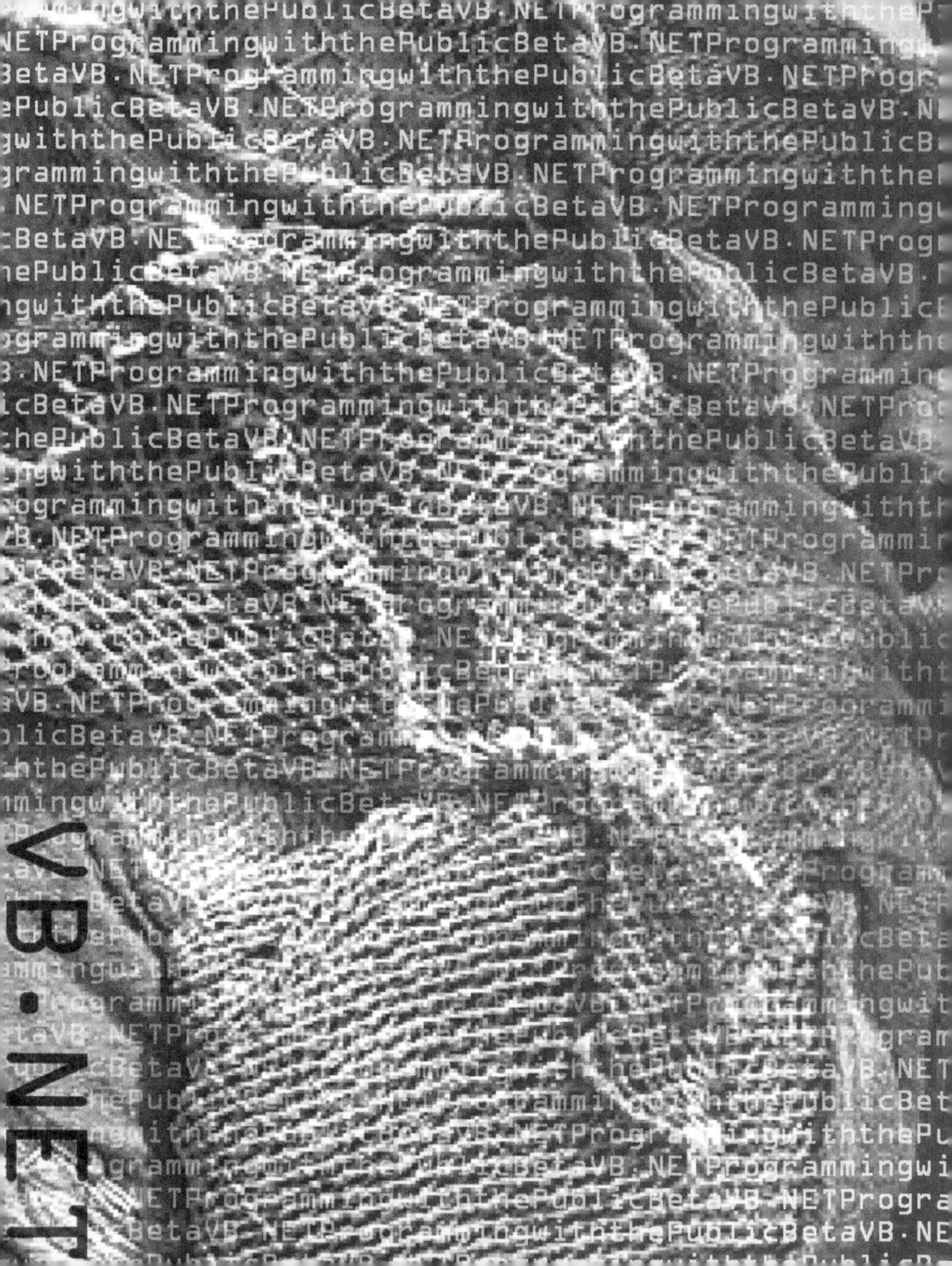
VB.NET
VB.NET Programming with the Public Beta

1

Getting Started

In July 2000 at the Professional Developers Conference (PDC), Microsoft announced the .NET initiative – a major shift in the technical direction of Microsoft, and a major shift for those engaged in developing software using Microsoft tools. Microsoft has staked its future on the .NET Framework, shifting away from the COM-based world of today toward a more distributed, open, and dynamic environment.

Today, Visual Basic (VB) is the most widely used programming language in the world. Not surprisingly, Microsoft is carrying VB forward into the .NET Framework in the form of Visual Basic.NET. VB.NET is the natural progression for existing VB developers as they move to the .NET environment, and so is likely to be the most popular tool to develop in this Framework for the next few years.

Microsoft has also introduced the new C# (pronounced "C sharp") language, with a lot of fanfare and hype. There is no doubt that C# will be used by many developers. However, for the typical VB developer it is likely that VB.NET will be the natural progression since it preserves the same basic language structure and syntax as VB has today.

The .NET Framework is a large change from the existing development environment, and VB.NET has some substantial changes from previous versions of VB. At the same time, most existing VB developers will probably have enough to learn without having to become familiar with a new language syntax and structure such as C#.

Perhaps even more important is the fact that the VB.NET and C# languages have the same basic capabilities, so neither offers a clear advantage over the other from an objective standpoint. C# offers a couple features that VB.NET doesn't (such as operator overloading), while VB.NET in turn offers a couple of features that C# doesn't (such as late binding syntax). The choice of language between C# and VB.NET really does come down to which one decreases the learning curve and makes us more comfortable and productive as developers.

.NET has been in development for more than three years. Parts of it have gone under the names COOL, Next Generation Windows Services (NGWS), Windows DNA, COM+ 2.0, and Visual Studio 7.0. All of these have now been consolidated within the .NET umbrella, thereby providing a level of consistency.

The Beta 1 software we have today, though still new by software standards, is not entirely new, having been in development for some time. Additionally, the .NET environment builds on a great deal of existing software, including the Windows 32-bit operating systems, COM, COM+, MSMQ, and previous versions of Visual Studio. The .NET Framework also builds on a number of new or existing standards such as HTML, CSS, XML, and SOAP.

.NET is arguably the biggest thing to hit the VB community since VB4, when the ability to create 32-bit applications, classes and COM components was introduced. In fact, .NET is a much bigger and broader-reaching change since it provides a whole new inter-object communication mechanism that doesn't rely directly on COM.

That means hundreds of thousands of existing VB developers will need to make the transition from VB6 to VB.NET, and this is a major leap. This book is intended to help smooth the transition by:

❑ Discussing the new capabilities of VB.NET

❑ Illustrating the important changes and differences from previous versions of VB

❑ And, most importantly, by providing experienced developers' understanding of the changes and, where possible, the reasoning behind them.

We feel that VB.NET and the .NET Framework are the most exciting and revolutionary technologies to come from Microsoft in many years. We hope that through this book we can share our enthusiasm and help developers rapidly come up to speed in this new environment.

The Eighty/Twenty Principle for Coverage of Topics

.NET represents a very substantial platform change for Microsoft developers. While most of the component-oriented concepts from COM carry forward to .NET, there are some very major changes and enhancements in the new environment.

Whereas today a developer may interact with the Win32 API, in .NET most interaction will be with the .NET system class library. In fact, any .NET program will make heavy use of this system class library to operate, thus requiring any developer who wishes to work in the .NET environment to learn the class library to a large degree.

On top of all these platform changes, there are the changes to VB itself. From a feature perspective, we now have inheritance and free-threading, to name just a couple. In addition to the feature changes, there are many syntax and coding changes that will impact upon day-to-day use of the language.

The VB IDE has now been merged into the Visual Studio.NET IDE, along with all the other .NET development tools. This integrated IDE is similar in some ways to the VB6 IDE, but there are some radical differences.

In fact, there are so many changes that a single book can't cover everything. Rather than trying to provide superficial coverage of every change, we've opted to apply the "80-20" rule originated by Pareto that says that "a minority of input produces the majority of results" – the idea being that if we cover 80% of the features we'll be providing a resource useful in most cases. In this book, we'll provide thorough coverage of the most common changes developers will face. We'll focus quite a lot on the IDE changes, the syntax changes, and the most important new features. To some degree we'll also cover the .NET system class library, but only as it pertains to the types of scenarios most commonly faced by VB developers today.

Overview of Changes in VB.NET and Where they are Discussed in this Book

There are many new technologies in VB.NET, which will be of interest to experienced VB developers, including:

- ❑ Full object oriented (OO) capabilities:
  - ❑ Code inheritance
  - ❑ Method/operator overloading
  - ❑ Parameterized constructors
  - ❑ Shared members
- ❑ Structured error (exception) handling
- ❑ New threading models

All of these are based on Microsoft's .NET Framework and we'll start Chapter 2 with an overview of .NET, emphasizing the details of importance to a VB developer. Then the new technologies discussed above will be covered, relating them to the .NET Framework as necessary.

While the .NET Framework offers the long-awaited new capabilities listed above, it also raises barriers to making the transition from older versions of VB to VB.NET. There are a significant number of syntactical differences and other incompatibilities. Fitting into the Microsoft.NET Framework required VB to make serious structural changes – including rationalization of data types and syntax to bring VB in line with other languages, and changing from traditional VB forms to **WinForms**. These pose difficulties which must be understood to allow developers to make a fast, efficient, and frustration-free leap to VB.NET. This is the focus of Chapter 3, which provides an overview of the new VS.NET IDE and explores the syntactic and coding changes to the language.

For years VB developers have worked with the Ruby forms engine. This forms environment is what allows VB developers to quickly and easily build applications with Windows user interfaces. The .NET Framework provides a common forms environment known as WinForms; VB.NET uses this, not Ruby. While WinForms offers the same powerful Windows GUI capabilities as the old VB forms engine, this is an entirely new environment, offering new capabilities and new ways to do the things that we've been doing for years. Chapter 4 tackles this new environment, demonstrating how to build the usual types of GUI interface and some of its exciting new capabilities.

With the introduction of version 4.0, VB developers gained the ability to use class modules to write OO programs and to create reusable COM components. Since then, it has become apparent that the lack of a complete OO environment – in particular the lack of **inheritance** – was a huge limiting factor when building complex systems in VB. Inheritance is the ability to create a new class that "inherits" the properties, methods *and code* from an existing class.

VB.NET addresses this issue head-on by providing full OO capabilities, including inheritance, method overloading, method overriding, and more. These capabilities are integral to the .NET environment in general, as well as being of great benefit to the VB developer. We'll explore these new capabilities in Chapter 5, illustrating how all the benefits of OO programming are now available to VB developers.

Besides changing traditional VB development, VB.NET will also open up the possibility of web programming to hundreds of thousands of developers who did not embrace Active Server Pages and its related technologies. Chapter 6 provides a quick look at the **ASP.NET** environment – giving us a glimpse of how, with VB.NET, the development of web-based screens and software will be quite similar to development of Windows screens and software with earlier versions of VB. ASP.NET makes it easy for VB developers to develop web systems.

The key technologies in VB.NET that simplify the transition are **Web Forms** and **Web Services**. While many of the features of these technologies will look familiar to VB developers, there are some significant differences and pitfalls to be avoided, such as the problem of using events extensively when communicating with a server. ASP.NET is a very large topic in itself, but Chapter 6 should provide a good start on the concepts from a VB developer's perspective.

Over the years Microsoft has developed a continual string of data access technologies, which have been available to VB developers. We've worked with DAO, then RDO, and most recently the various versions of ADO. It should be no surprise then that .NET comes with a whole new data access technology called **ADO.NET** (which was also named ADO+ for a time). While it is possible for VB.NET programs to continue to use older data access technologies through interoperability mechanisms, most VB.NET developers will be likely to use ADO.NET since it provides the easiest and most direct approach. Chapter 7 covers ADO.NET, demonstrating how to read, create, update, and delete data using the new technology.

The entire .NET platform, VB.NET included, is very reliant on XML technologies. Chapter 7 discusses how developers can use XML from VB.NET, both via ADO.NET and directly from VB itself.

One key goal of the .NET Framework is to simplify deployment and to eliminate "DLL Hell", a topic we'll enthusiastically cover in Chapter 8 since it has been one of the biggest headaches for VB developers. Not only does VB.NET fix most "DLL Hell" issues, but we are now provided with the most powerful and complete deployment technology ever included with Visual Basic – a huge step forward as compared to previous Setup Wizard or Package and Deployment Wizard technologies.

We'll also discuss some more advanced topics in Chapter 8, such as the creation of middle-tier and transactional components, the creation of console applications (VB.NET interacts easily with the standard console input/output mechanisms – `stdin` and `stdout`), and the set of very powerful external tools and utilities that come with the .NET Framework – including the VB compiler itself which can be run directly from the command line if needed. We'll also take a brief look at cross-language development with C#, how to write a program to monitor the file system for changes, and how to create a Windows NT service with VB.

Obviously, most existing developers have substantial applications based on COM and other existing technologies such as ADO. Chapter 9 will cover interoperability and migration, showing how VB.NET programs can make use of existing COM components, or can be used from COM components if necessary. We'll also take a quick look at Microsoft's migration wizard here. This wizard helps upgrade existing VB6 applications to VB.NET, but is far from complete in the Beta 1 release of VB.NET.

Chapter 10 shows how to build a sample application in VB.NET. We'll create an application with a standard Windows GUI user interface using the WinForms technology. Then we'll show how to build a web interface based on Web Forms and ASP.NET. Throughout the application, we'll demonstrate the use of inheritance and other OO features, as well as ADO.NET, Web Services, and other .NET technologies.

Finally we'll wrap up with Chapter 11, which lists some steps you can take now to learn more about the .NET Framework and VB.NET, and for smoothing the transition from VB6 to the new environment. In this chapter we'll also list some other resources that may be of value in coming up to speed with everything that is going on.

We'll now round off Chapter 1 with a look at installing Visual Studio.NET.

Installation of Necessary Technologies for a VB.NET Test Bed

The .NET Framework and VB.NET are two separate but related things. The .NET Framework includes the Common Language Runtime (CLR), the system class libraries, and other tools. VB.NET is part of the Visual Studio.NET (VS.NET) package and is a development tool and IDE for use by developers.

The Microsoft.NET Framework is required for VB.NET to function and even includes the VB compiler. It is possible to do VB development with just the .NET Framework SDK (Software Developer's Kit), though doing so means working without an IDE and all the integrated tools that come with it. However, for those who are comfortable programming in a text editor – perhaps coming from an ASP, Unix, or OpenVMS programming background – it is quite possible to develop applications without VS.NET and rely entirely on the .NET Framework SDK.

For the purposes of this book however, we'll focus primarily on the use of VS.NET as we build our VB.NET applications. VS.NET is a very powerful IDE, which makes the development process substantially easier and more productive. There are a great many little details and steps required to create and build a .NET application, things that we *can* do by hand but which are far more efficiently done for us by VS.NET.

To create a full VB.NET test bed we'll need to not only install VS.NET, but also the .NET Framework SDK. We'll also probably need to upgrade various components of our operating system and environment to meet the minimum requirements for the .NET environment and VS.NET.

Getting the Software

The .NET Framework SDK and VS.NET are widely available. They can be downloaded freely or ordered on CD for a nominal charge.

Making the software so widely available in beta form is quite a departure from previous Microsoft development software betas. Historically, such a widely available beta hasn't been seen until perhaps Beta 3, while with .NET many people had access to the product even prior to Beta 1. This offers us huge potential benefits as we can come up to speed on the new technology long before we are put in a position where we need to use it to build mission critical applications.

For information about ordering the materials on CD, go to http://msdn.microsoft.com/net.

Downloading the Software

Almost anyone (subject to export restrictions) can download the .NET Framework SDK from the MSDN web site at http://msdn.microsoft.com/net. This site also has a link to the download site for VS.NET, though that download is only available to MSDN Universal subscribers or MCSP organizations.

> **It is recommended that these betas are downloaded on to machines specifically set aside for testing purposes. Also note that the SQL Server 2000 pubs and Northwind databases can be overwritten by the installation.**

.NET Framework SDK

The .NET Framework SDK is a single download of around a 100 MB and can be installed on any Windows 32-bit operating system, including Windows 95. The downloaded file is a self-extracting installer – just run it to install the SDK on the computer.

Note that the .NET Framework SDK does have some dependencies – software that must be installed prior to running the Framework installer program.

> *The easiest way to install the .NET Framework SDK may be to simply download the WINUPD CD discussed below. This CD not only includes the SDK, but also includes all the required upgrade software to ensure that the computer meets the minimum requirements for the SDK to operate effectively.*

VS.NET

The VS.NET download, available at http://msdn.microsoft.com/vstudio/nextgen/beta.asp, is larger and more complex. If you don't already have the CDs, they are a three-part download:

❑　CD 1

❑　CD 2

❑　Windows Component Update CD (WINUPD)

CD 1, CD 2, and WINUPD CD are about 245, 121, and 358 MB in (compressed) size, respectively.

> **The WINUPD CD contains the .NET Framework SDK, so downloading the SDK separately is not required.**

These files are archives, which unpack into directory structures that can be used to create installation CDs. Alternatively (and more easily), we can install directly from the hard drive by simply unpacking the archives into directories there.

> **To install from the hard drive, both CD 1 and CD 2 must be unpacked into the *same* directory, otherwise the installer will be unable to find CD 2.**

To install from CD, unpack all three archives into separate directories, then use those directories to burn three CDs using a CD writer.

The CDs *must* be labeled properly for the CD-based installation to function:

VS.NET CD 1	vsentd1
VS.NET CD2	vsentd2
WINUPD CD	vswcud1

Either way, please read through the notes below as VS.NET has dependencies on the operating system and other software, which may require upgrades to the system. These upgrades are handled automatically by the WINUPD CD during the install process, but may impact upon the system in ways we need to be aware of.

Requirements of the Environment

There are specific hardware and software requirements for a VB.NET test environment, as well as optional software components that we'll need to install in order to take full advantage of all that VB.NET has to offer.

Hardware

VS.NET has the following system requirements:

	Minimum	Recommended
Processor	Pentium II-class, 450 MHz	Pentium III-class, 733 MHz
RAM	128 MB	256 MB
Available Hard Disk Space	3 GB	
Video	800x600, 256 colors	1024x768, High Color 16-bit
CD-ROM Drive	Required	

> *While Microsoft lists the CD-ROM drive as a requirement, it is perfectly possible to install the software by extracting the archives to a hard drive and installing from there. Not that this matters in most cases, since it is hard to find a computer without a CD-ROM these days.*

If there's one thing that will make a huge difference here it is memory. When running, the VS.NET IDE consumes around 90 MB of RAM at present, which can leave very little memory for anything else on a system with only 128 MB of RAM.

Also keep in mind that this is Beta 1 software, with lots of extra debug code and very little performance optimization. The performance we see in the product today is probably not indicative of the performance we should expect to see in the final product. At the same time, given the performance today, it is best to get the most powerful hardware possible when running the beta.

Operating Systems

VS.NET (which includes VB.NET) will run on Windows 2000, NT 4.0, Me, and 98.

> *Note that while VS.NET installs on all these platforms, Windows 2000 is required to use all the features of the .NET Framework. Some features, such as GDI+, are only supported in Windows 2000. Other features, such as MSMQ, will only be available if the underlying software is installed on the system – regardless of operating system.*

The .NET Framework SDK will also install on Windows 95, but the VS.NET development environment will not. Windows 95 is only supported for running .NET applications, not for creating them.

Upgrading the operating system after VS.NET is installed is not supported and will not work.

While VS.NET installs on several operating systems, all are not equal, and the installation process will vary somewhat between operating systems. We'll cover the key differences as we continue.

Requirements for the .NET Framework SDK

The installation of the SDK has some underlying requirements for the operating system and other software components. These are not automatically installed by the SDK installer, and it will not run to completion until the minimum requirements are met.

These minimum requirements include:

❑ Internet Explorer 5.5

❑ MDAC 2.6

In order to create applications that use Web Forms or Web Services we must have an installation of IIS on our network, and that machine must have the .NET Framework SDK installed. This machine may be our development workstation or another machine on the network.

> *Note that the installation won't complain or fail if we don't have IIS installed. After all, it is perfectly acceptable to have it installed on some other machine.*

Either way, FrontPage 2000 Server Extensions are required on the IIS installation. These must be installed *before* the .NET Framework SDK is installed.

This is as much as we'll cover on the .NET Framework SDK installation. For the rest of the chapter we'll stick to coverage of the VS.NET product, which includes the SDK via the WINUPD CD.

Requirements for VS.NET

At a basic level, the only thing required to start installing VS.NET is the operating system. However, the WINUPD CD will upgrade several operating system and other software components during the install. This process includes:

❑ Upgrade to Windows 2000 Service Pack 1

❑ FrontPage 2000 Server Extensions

- ❏ Setup Runtime Files
- ❏ Microsoft Office Shared Components
- ❏ Internet Explorer 5.5 and Internet Tools
- ❏ Internet Explorer Web Forms
- ❏ Microsoft XML Parser (MSXML) 3.0
- ❏ Microsoft Data Access Components (MDAC) 2.6
- ❏ .NET Framework SDK

As with the plain .NET Framework SDK installation, in order to create applications that use Web Forms or Web Services, we must have an installation of IIS on our network.

Mapped Drives

We cannot install VS.NET Beta 1 to a mapped drive. It must be installed to a physical local drive to operate.

The .NET applications we write must be stored on the local drive. Applications will not run properly if run from a mapped drive.

Optional Services

To fully explore the capabilities of VB.NET we'll need an environment that supplies a set of services. Not all of these services are required for basic applications, but they are required to gain the full benefit of the technology.

- ❏ Database. Many of the sample projects in .NET require a SQL Server database to operate. This will probably be true of most applications we create, since most business applications interact with a database. At a minimum we'll run the MSDE (Microsoft Data Engine) server, which is a subset of Microsoft SQL Server 2000. It is often nicer to have a full installation of Microsoft SQL Server 2000 available for use however. This server can run on our development workstation, or on a separate server as long as it is available for use by our applications.

- ❏ MSMQ (Message Queuing Services). The .NET system class libraries include the `System.Messaging` namespace. These classes provide support for queued messaging and they rely on an installation of MSMQ. We might install MSMQ directly on our development workstation, or it can be running on a server in our network, with only the MSMQ client software installed on our workstation. Either way, MSMQ is required to work with the `System.Messaging` classes.

- ❏ DTC (Distributed Transaction Coordinator). The .NET environment supports transactional components. These components rely on the DTC to provide transactional support. If we're going to build transactional components we'll need the DTC installed in our environment.

Preparation for Installation

It is strongly recommended that VS.NET Beta 1 be installed on a clean installation of the operating system, thus avoiding possible conflicts with existing software or configuration data. This is not a *requirement*, but it is a good practice.

Software

VS.NET is known to coexist on a computer along with Microsoft Office 2000 and Visual Studio 6.0. This is nice, as it means that we can have a computer with all three products installed and working – a much more productive environment than having a computer totally dedicated to just VS.NET.

VS.NET may coexist with other software as well, but Microsoft has not officially tested other configurations, and so they may or may not work properly. If you decide to go down that road, you're on your own – make lots of backups!

> *For example, on my system I also have installed Visio 2000 Professional, Microsoft Money, EditPlus, and the software to drive my camera, scanner, and CD writer. However,* winspool.exe *fails to start as I boot my system, so there's an unexpected conflict in there somewhere.*

The VS.NET IDE can be used via Windows 2000 Terminal Server, though debugging does not work properly in that environment. VS.NET does not work with Windows NT Terminal Server Edition.

Previous PDC Installation

Installations of the PDC Tech Preview of the .NET Framework SDK or VS.NET must be removed before installing the Beta 1 version of VS.NET.

> **It is recommended, in this case, that the operating system be reinstalled to ensure the older versions are removed.**

If the Beta 1 software must be installed without reinstalling the operating system, Microsoft supplies a set of instructions for removal of the older software. These instructions are in the readme.htm file at the root of CD 1.

> *In addition to the steps described in the* readme.htm *file, it may be beneficial to also delete the* WINNT\Assembly *directory and to manually remove all the registry keys containing the string "NGWS" prior to installing the Beta 1 software. Do these additional steps at your own risk, as they are not recommended by Microsoft, but may help increase the success of the Beta 1 installation.*

Order of Installation

Software is often somewhat sensitive to the order in which it is installed. This is typically truer of development software than commercial software, but it's a problem we've always faced to some degree. Most people have probably run into the problem where the installation of a software package required the *reinstall* of a service pack for the operating system because some key file was overwritten.

Beta software tends to be very sensitive to this sort of thing – after all, the setup process is in beta too. VS.NET Beta 1 is no exception. Installing components in the wrong order can lead to some very unexpected results.

Installation should occur in the following order:

❑   Operating system

- ❑ IIS (under Windows 2000 or Windows NT)
- ❑ FrontPage 2000 Server Extensions
- ❑ Windows 2000 SP1
- ❑ Microsoft Office 2000 (optional)
- ❑ Microsoft Visual Studio 6.0 (optional)
- ❑ Microsoft SQL Server 2000 (optional)
- ❑ Windows Compatibility Update (WINUPD)
- ❑ Visual Studio.NET

The last two steps are accomplished by running the VS.NET setup program from CD 1. It will automatically invoke the WINUPD setup program to update required operating system and software components.

Notes for Installing Operating Systems

Before installing VS.NET it is strongly recommended that the system has a clean installation of the operating system. In this section we'll walk through any notes that should be followed when performing this install.

Windows 2000 Server

IIS is installed under Windows 2000 Server by default. Make sure to leave this default alone, as IIS is required to use Web Forms and Web Services on the development workstation.

When installing IIS it is best to ensure that the FrontPage 2000 Server Extensions are installed. This step is also performed by the Windows Component Update process, but should be performed automatically during the IIS installation.

If the System.Messaging namespace is to be used, then MSMQ should be installed on the server during installation. Note that MSMQ only installs completely if the server will be joining an existing Windows 2000 domain. By default MSMQ is installed such that only private queues are available for use.

If the server is being installed in a standalone mode, then it will need to be upgraded to a domain controller using dcpromo.exe before a full installation of MSMQ can be completed – enabling the use of public queues. In such a case, it is better to leave the MSMQ option unchecked during the initial install, and then install it after promoting the server to a domain controller.

Windows 2000 Professional

IIS is *not* installed by default under Windows 2000 Professional. During the install process, make sure to check the IIS box, causing IIS to be installed along with the operating system. Alternatively, once the operating system is installed, use the Add/Remove Programs applet under Control Panel to add IIS to the system configuration.

When installing IIS it is best to ensure that the FrontPage 2000 Server Extensions are installed. Installation of the extensions is a sub-option beneath the IIS installation in the setup wizard. This step is also performed by the Windows Component Update process, but should be performed automatically during the IIS installation.

As with Windows 2000 Server, MSMQ must be installed to use the `System.Messaging` classes. Only the MSMQ client software can be installed under Windows 2000 Professional so, to use public queues, there must be an existing MSMQ server installation on the network. Otherwise, the installation will still allow the use of private queues on the workstation.

Windows NT 4.0

Before running the VS.NET installation program the Windows NT Option Pack *must* be installed on the computer. Part of the Option Pack includes IIS. Service Pack 6a should be installed after the Option Pack has been installed.

The Windows Component Update process will run to upgrade components under Windows NT 4.0 as well, including the installation of the FrontPage 2000 Server Extensions.

As with Windows 2000, MSMQ should be installed to use the `System.Messaging` classes. MSMQ is part of the Option Pack.

Windows Me and Windows 98

No preparatory work is required to install VS.NET on Windows Me or Windows 98. Just install the operating system and everything should be ready.

Note that .NET can't use the Personal Web Services in Windows Me or 98 to run Web Forms (ASP.NET) or Web Services. To develop these types of applications when VS.NET is installed on Windows Me or 98 requires that we also have a server machine running IIS with the .NET Framework SDK installed.

Installation of Visual Studio.NET

At this point we've got our development workstation set up with a supported operating system. We may also have installed IIS, MSMQ, and either MSDE or SQL Server 2000. Optionally, we might have installed Microsoft Office 2000 and Visual Studio 6.0.

Given all that, we're ready to move on to installing VS.NET itself. To do so, run the `SETUP.EXE` program from CD 1, or allow the auto-run to kick in from the CD. This will bring up a dialog similar to that shown in the following screenshot:

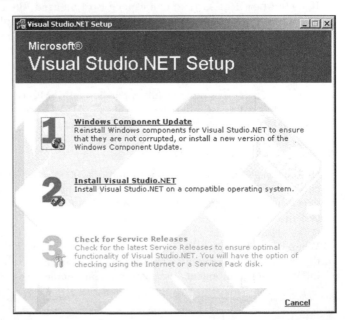

This diagram shows the installation after the Windows Component Update has been run. If the WINUPD step is not already complete, only option 1 will be available – which will be true in the typical case.

Just click on the option 1 link to begin.

Windows Component Update Install

Before the setup program will install VS.NET itself, we must run the Windows Component Update (WINUPD) installation to ensure that our operating system and software components meet the minimum requirements.

The WINUPD installation can also be run separately from the VS.NET install. This is done by running the SETUP.EXE program on the WINUPD CD itself. Doing this can be useful, as it is a great way to install the .NET Framework SDK with assurance that all required components are updated – even if we don't go on to install the VS.NET tool itself.

The WINUPD install is fairly simple, though it does a great deal of work. When it is run, we'll be presented with a dialog requesting that we agree with the license agreement. Assuming we agree and click Continue, we'll move on to the next step, where we are asked for a username and password to use as the system is restarted:

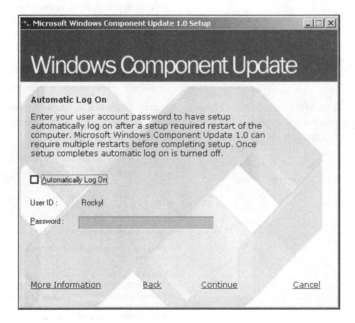

This is optional, but be aware – the WINUPD process reboots the machine a number of times. Allowing the setup program to automatically log back into the system after each reboot means it can run from start to finish without any help from us. On the other hand, this is beta software. If we check the Automatically Log On box we'll be presented with both a warning dialog and an extensive web page that spells out the risks we are taking. It boils down to this: if the install fails in the middle, it is possible that our machine will be left such that it will automatically log in on subsequent reboots and hence you could be leaving yourself open to a security breach.

This can be remedied by altering a registry key so it isn't a permanent issue but, in today's security-conscious world, Microsoft obviously felt that they needed to make the risk very clear.

> *In reality, my installs crashed on at least two computers, but on no occasion was my system left open in this way. There's no doubt that it could happen, but the risk isn't terribly great.*

If the install goes as planned, the setup program will remove the auto-login registry key and our system will be restored to normal operation.

Regardless of whether we choose to use auto-login or not, when we click Continue we're presented with a list of the actions the WINUPD process will perform. The following screenshot shows the typical list of actions for a Windows 2000 Server machine:

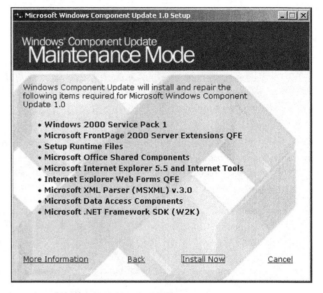

When we click Install Now, the process will begin – running from top to bottom until complete. If we chose to use the auto-login mechanism then no further intervention is required on our part. If we didn't choose that option, we'll need to log in after reboots one or more times during the process.

When the WINUPD installation is complete, we'll see a screen similar to the following:

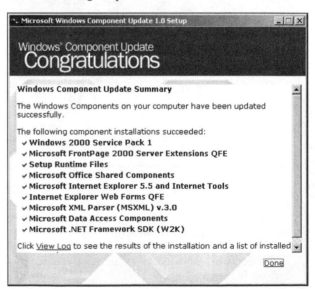

Just click **Done** to continue.

At this point, our system is ready to use the .NET Framework SDK. We can develop applications by hand using text editors, and we can deploy and run .NET applications to this machine – it is all ready to go. Now we're ready to move on to the VS.NET installation.

VS.NET Install

Once the Windows Component Update is complete, we'll be returned to the main installation start screen:

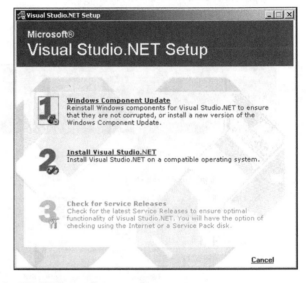

Click on the link next to option 2 to proceed with the VS.NET installation.

During most installations, we will be asked to accept a license agreement at this point. After accepting, we're presented with a dialog where we can choose what parts of VS.NET to install, which will look something like this:

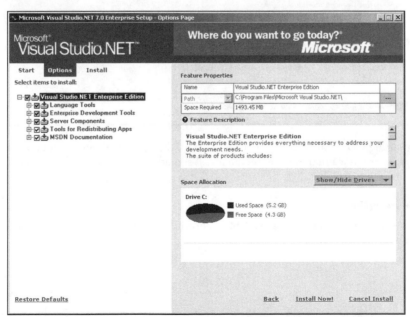

Keep in mind that this is beta software with a beta installer. There is no guarantee that unchecking different options will result in a correct installation.

> *For instance, on one install I unchecked the Visual FoxPro product and got a successful install with an error dialog. On another machine I unchecked the Visual FoxPro product and it installed without a hitch.*

It's probably best to install everything.

Click the Install Now! link. The install will take some time, during which the dialog will show some status information as well as a list of the major features available in VS.NET:

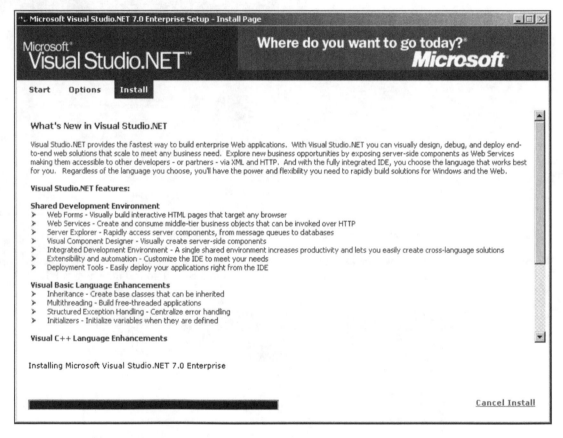

Other than inserting CD 2 (unless installing from the hard drive), no user intervention is required during the install process. After a few minutes or more, the install should complete. Click Done to finish the process and return to the main install dialog.

Updating the Installation

Now we can see that the third option is available – allowing us to have the installer check for any updates that may be available:

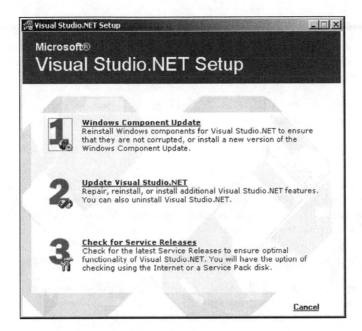

If we click the link next to the third option, we'll be presented with a dialog asking if we want to check for updates via the Internet, or to update from a CD:

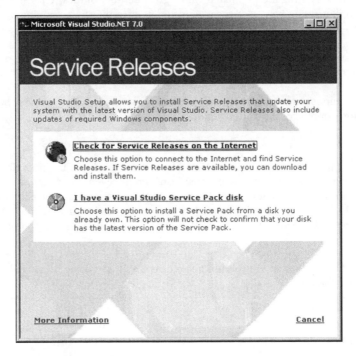

At the time this book was written there were no service packs or updates available, though clicking on the Internet link did appear to cause the installer to go out on the Internet to look for an update.

Installing and Configuring the Samples

When we installed the .NET Framework SDK, either directly or through the Windows Component Update process, a large number of sample applications were copied onto our system. Before these samples can be viewed or run however, they must be unpacked and configured.

On the desktop, subsequent to the SDK install, there should be a shortcut to a web page titled .NET Framework SDK Overview. When this page is opened, it will contain a link to The .NET Framework Samples.

Expanding the Samples

The Microsoft .NET Framework Samples page contains instructions and links for installing and configuring the samples. The samples are initially copied onto our system in a compressed format, requiring an installation process be run to unpack them and make them ready for use. When unpacked, the samples consume around 120 megs on the hard drive.

To run this installation process and unpack the samples, click on Expand the samples.

The installer will unpack the installation software first, then will ask where we want to unpack the samples themselves. The default is into the Program Files directory where the Framework SDK itself was installed. It is recommended that the default be used.

The unpacking process will take some time depending on the speed of the computer. Once it is complete, we'll have a large directory structure populated with a great number of files. These sample files are immensely useful in illustrating how to create a wide variety of applications ranging from simple to complex, from Windows GUI applications to Web Form applications.

While the samples are unpacked and can be viewed at this point, they are not ready to be run yet. First we need to configure them.

Fortunately, once the unpacking process is complete, our web page should automatically refresh, enabling two more installation options for the sample applications.

Install MSDE

Many of the sample applications require access to a SQL Server database. If our environment already has SQL Server 7.0 (or higher) installed we can use that installation – even if it is on a separate machine. However, if our environment does not currently have a SQL Server available, we'll probably want to install the Microsoft Data Engine on the development workstation. Do this by clicking the Install MSDE link by Step 2 on the web page. If we already have a SQL database available, this step can be skipped.

> **Installing MSDE in this way can corrupt or even remove the existing `pubs` and `Northwind` databases.**

Configuring the Samples

Before the sample applications can be run we must configure them. This process involves a number of steps:

❑   Setting up appropriate virtual roots

- ❑ Copying sample databases into the SQL Server data directory

- ❑ Modifying CONFIG.WEB

- ❑ Adding required registry keys

- ❑ Compilation of all sample code

> **Much of this process runs in a minimized DOS window – make sure the process is complete before moving on.**

The details of each step are described more fully in the web pages supplied by Microsoft along with the samples.

Setting up the Databases

Four databases are used by the sample applications. Two of them are normal default databases provided with SQL Server 7.0 and higher: pubs and Northwind. Two of them are new databases for use by the .NET samples: GrocerToGo and Portal.

If our SQL Server is on the same machine where we installed VS.NET, these databases should be automatically configured. However, if our SQL Server is on a separate machine we'll need to take some extra steps.

> **The sample programs make some assumptions about the database configuration. They assume that SQL Server is installed on the local development machine, and that the databases are accessible to the sa user account, which must have no password. If any of these assumptions are different in our environment, we'll have to update the connection strings in the samples for them to work.**

During the configuration process, the source files for the two new databases are copied into the SQL Server default data directory. To make them available for use we need to add them to our SQL Server installation by using the SQL Server Enterprise Manager.

To run the Enterprise Manager, choose Start | Programs | Microsoft SQL Server | Enterprise Manager. In the left-hand pane, expand the tree until the list of databases is visible. This should bring up a screen similar to the following:

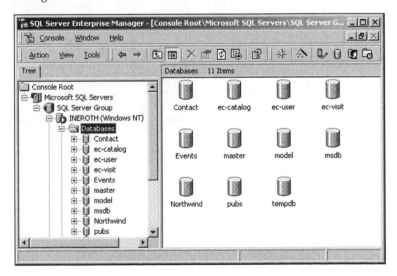

Now right-click on the **Databases** entry in the left-hand pane, and then from the context menu choose **All Tasks | Attach Database…** This will bring up a dialog asking us for information about the database to be attached:

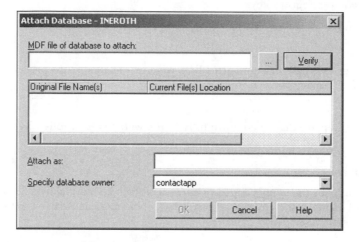

First we need to indicate the source file – which will have an MDF extension. In the default SQL Server data directories for SQL Server 7.0 and 2000, we'll find both `Grocer.mdf` and `Portal.mdf`, so we'll need to do this process twice.

Click on the […] button to select the file to be attached. In the following diagram we've chosen the `Grocer.mdf` file:

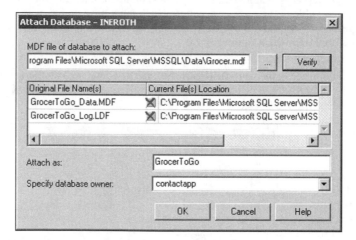

SQL Server provides some default values for our database files, which are incorrect and must be changed.

The **Current File(s) Location** must be updated for both the **MDF** (data) and **LDF** (log) files. Additionally, the database owner should be specified as being **sa** or some other appropriate owner account for the database. These changes are illustrated in the following diagram:

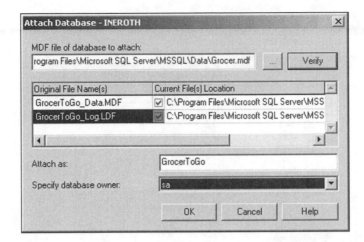

Notice that the red **X** marks have changed to green check marks to indicate that our file selections are now valid. Click the **OK** button to add the database to our server. Repeat the process for the `Portal` database and we should then be ready to go.

Running the Samples

Once the configuration process is complete, our web page will automatically refresh, now showing options for removing the sample applications and providing us with a list of links to run the samples.

To run a sample, click on the link for that sample. This will bring up a page describing the sample in more detail, including a sample overview, the location of the sample, and instructions for rebuilding and running the sample. Some samples can be run right from the browser, others require opening DOS windows or taking other steps.

For many of the samples to run as they stand, our machine must meet the following requirements:

❑ IIS 4.0 or higher (not **PWS**) must have been installed prior to configuring the samples

❑ SQL Server 7.0 or higher (or **MSDE**) must be available on the local machine (`localhost`)

❑ The SQL username `sa` must be valid and must have a blank password

> Having username **sa** with no password is a poor security practice. Be cautious when configuring a SQL Server in this manner.

If these conditions are not met, then coding changes may be required to run some of the sample applications.

Making the Web Samples Available

Once installed and configured, the samples are ready to run from our machine. However, we may want to access some of the web samples from other machines on our network or even on the Internet.

By default, the security setting on the virtual roots created for the web samples preclude running the samples on machines other than the server itself. For those samples that should be available to a wider audience, we'll need to update the security.

To do this, open up the Internet Information Services MMC console by choosing Start | Settings | Control Panel, then choosing Administrative Tools, then choosing Internet Services Manager:

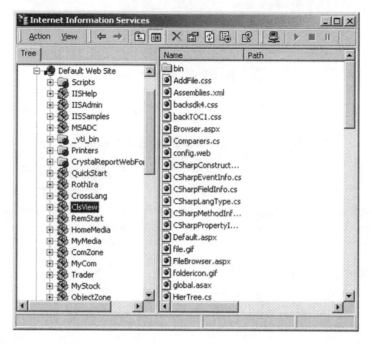

In the Internet Services Manager, expand the Default Web Site entry in the tree on the left. Locate the virtual root to be altered in the list of virtual roots – such as ClsView (you can find out which virtual root corresponds to which sample by looking through the .NET Framework SDK Samples section on the Microsoft .NET Framework Samples page accessible via your desktop). Right-click on this, and choose the Properties option:

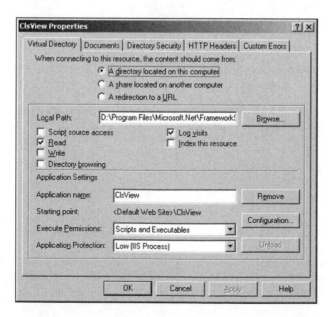

Switch to the Directory Security tab and click the Edit button in the IP address and domain name restrictions panel. This will bring up another dialog, which shows that this virtual root is restricted for use only by the local machine:

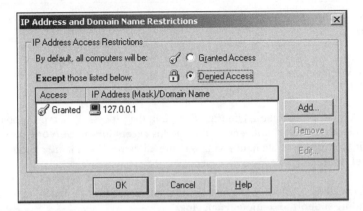

To make the root available to all other machines, simply click the Granted Access option, then click OK. This change removes the machine restriction from the virtual root, making it available to all machines on the network. If our machine is available via the Internet, the virtual root will now be available to anyone on the Internet.

> Configuring the virtual roots in this manner can cause a security issue. ASP.NET is beta software, and may have undetected security holes at this time. Be aware of the potential risks before opening these sites up for general Internet access.

Configuring a Remote IIS Server

To develop applications using Web Forms or Web Services, we must have access to a machine with an IIS installation. That machine might be our development workstation, in which case we're all set. However, it might be a separate machine – especially if our development workstation is running Windows Me or Windows 98.

If the web server is a separate machine, we need to configure that machine before it can be used for .NET applications.

Initial Configuration

The remote web server must be running IIS 4.0 or higher along with FrontPage 2000 Server Extensions, so it must be either a Windows 2000 or Windows NT 4.0 machine. Personal Web Server under Windows Me or Windows 98 is not supported. Additionally, under Windows NT Workstation some extra configuration is required.

Installing Required Components

Once you got the correct initial configuration sorted out, run the VS.NET installation by running setup.exe from CD 1.

Allow the installer to perform the Windows Component Update process – thereby upgrading all required components on the server and also installing the .NET Framework SDK.

> **As a bare minimum, the .NET Framework SDK is required for any machine to run .NET applications.**

At this point the server machine can run .NET applications, but is not fully configured to provide debugging support for VS.NET.

Continue with the VS.NET installation, choosing Step 2 in the process. When prompted for the various installation options by the installer, uncheck all the options except for the Server Components. Then expand the Server Components element and make sure all items within it are checked – in particular, the Remote Debugger option.

Continue with the installation, allowing the installer to configure the server machine with the server components, including support for remote debugging.

Configuring Windows NT 4.0 Workstation

If we're running Windows 2000 or Windows NT 4.0 Server, we are all done. However, if we are running Windows NT 4.0 Workstation with Peer Web Services (PWS), we have one more thing to do in order to make Web Services work properly on the server.

Web Services are discovered by referencing a link contained in the <HEAD> section of our site's root default web page. This page is not automatically updated in the Windows NT 4.0 PWS environment, so we need to make the change by hand.

The file we need to edit is the default web page for our server – typically this is `c:\inetpub\IISSAMPLES\Default\welcome.htm`, though it could be different if our server's default page has been changed. Edit this file with a text editor and add the following line somewhere between the <HEAD> and </HEAD> tags:

```
<link type='text/xml' rel='alternate' href='/Default.disco'/>
```

Once this is done, the Web Services discovery process should work properly, allowing dynamic discovery of the web services installed on the server.

Expanding the Samples

We may also want to expand and configure the sample applications on the server (following the process described earlier). Many of the samples are designed to run within the ASP.NET environment and therefore must run on a web server to operate.

At this point we can use this remote server from our development workstation to create web applications using Web Forms, ASP.NET, and Web Services.

Making Sure It Works: A Hello World Program

The best way to make sure that the .NET Framework SDK and VS.NET are correctly installed is to try them out. In this section we'll walk quickly through the process of building the traditional "Hello World" program.

We'll return to this program in Chapter 3 to explain everything that is going on. So, for now, let's just roll with it, even though there may be a number of things that look a bit odd to any VB6 developer. The goal here is to walk through the steps to make sure VS.NET works as planned.

To get started, open up the Visual Studio IDE by choosing Start | Programs | Microsoft Visual Studio.NET 7.0 | Microsoft Visual Studio.NET 7.0. This will bring up the IDE for the first time, as shown in the following diagram:

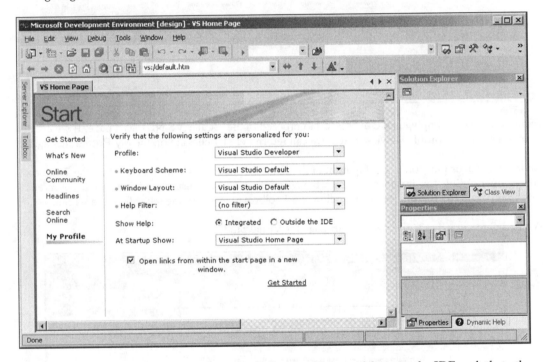

The VS.NET IDE is common across VB, C#, and C++, and Microsoft licenses the IDE such that other vendors can add languages to it as well. This could make it a very complicated place – just think about pressing *F1* for help on a keyword in VB and getting a description of that word for something like Modula-3.

To avoid this sort of issue, the IDE allows us to specify the profile we want to use within it. My Profile defines the keyboard shortcuts that apply, the default layouts of the windows, the default filter to be used when searching for help, along with some other configuration items.

For most existing VB developers the appropriate choice will be to select Visual Basic Developer from the list in the Profile dropdown. Choosing this will change the other options, causing the screen to appear as shown in the following diagram:

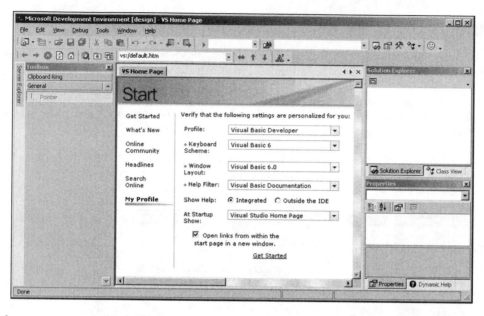

From here we can simply click **Get Started** to proceed to the regular VS.NET start page. If we ever feel the need to change the profile we've selected, we can return here by clicking on the **My Profile** link again.

Notice the tack or pin icon in the top right of the **Toolbox** pane. This icon indicates that the **Toolbox** is pinned open. While this is typical for the VB environment, it also consumes a large amount of screen space, so we may want to click the pin icon to allow the **Toolbox** to fold into the left side of the screen.

We now find ourselves at the default start page for Visual Studio:

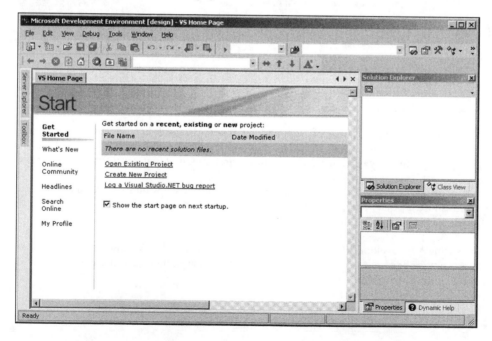

This is the screen we'll typically see when starting VS.NET from this point forward. From here we can open existing projects, start new projects, change our profile, search for help, and perform other useful operations.

In our case we'll want to choose the **Create New Project** option. This will bring up a new project dialog similar to the following:

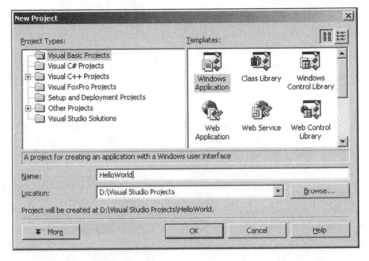

There are a lot of new and different options listed here – many of which we'll explore throughout the remainder of this book. For now, however, let's stay focused on creating a simple program. Choose Windows Application template from the Visual Basic Projects node – this is comparable to the regular Windows GUI applications we've created with previous versions of VB.

Change the Name to HelloWorld and click OK to set up the project. VS.NET will then set up a new Windows application project called HelloWorld in a solution of the same name. In VS.NET, a solution can hold many projects of different languages and types – even multiple executable (EXE) projects can be contained within a single solution. The screen will then appear as follows:

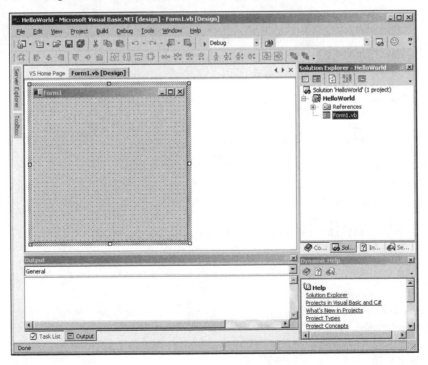

Again, we see a lot of enticing new features like the **Dynamic Help** window in the lower right-hand corner. We'll discuss many of these in Chapter 3, but for now, we'll finish our application.

There are obviously a variety of ways to create a "Hello World" program, but we'll make ours a little more complex than necessary to provide a decent introduction to VB.NET.

First off, move the mouse over the **Toolbox** on the far left. This will cause the **Toolbox** window to extend out over our form designer so we can choose the controls to be added to the form. Double-click on both a **TextBox** and a **Button** to add them to the form; alternatively, we can drag-and-drop them.

Arrange the controls so they don't overlap, then right-click the **Button** control and choose **Properties** from the menu. This will display the **Properties** dialog in the lower right of the IDE, just where we'd expect to find it in VB6. Change the **Text** property to **Show text** and press *Enter*.

Now double-click on the **Button** control in the form to bring up the code window and add a `Click` event.

So far things aren't a whole lot different than anything we've seen in VB in the past. The code we now see, however, does offer some interesting differences. Here's the default code we'll see in the window:

```
Imports System.ComponentModel
Imports System.Drawing
Imports System.WinForms

Public Class Form1
    Inherits System.WinForms.Form

    Public Sub New()
        MyBase.New

        Form1 = Me

        'This call is required by the Win Form Designer.
        InitializeComponent

        'TODO: Add any initialization after the InitializeComponent() call
    End Sub

    'Form overrides dispose to clean up the component list.
    Overrides Public Sub Dispose()
        MyBase.Dispose
```

```
        components.Dispose
    End Sub
```

Windows Form Designer generated code

```
    Protected Sub Button1_Click(ByVal sender As Object, _
      ByVal e As System.EventArgs)

    End Sub

  End Class
```

Overall, it looks very much like regular VB code but there are some striking differences, like the `Imports` statements, the fact that our form is a class, the use of the `Inherits` keyword, and the box indicating some **Windows Form Designer generated code**. Most of these changes will be covered in Chapters 3 and 4, with the `Inherits` keyword and associated OO features being discussed in Chapter 5.

To complete our application, let's make a message box pop-up to display the text in the textbox when the button is clicked. This is done by adding the following code:

```
    Protected Sub Button1_Click(ByVal sender As Object, _
      ByVal e As System.EventArgs)

      MsgBox(TextBox1.Text, MsgBoxStyle.Information, "Test")

    End Sub
```

In VB6, we could have achieved the same result like this:

```
    Private Sub Button1_Click

      MsgBox TextBox1, vbInformation, "Test"

    End Sub
```

Other than the two new arguments to the `Button1_Click` event and the parentheses around the `MsgBox` arguments there's not much different here from any VB code we might have written in the past. This will be generally true as we go through the rest of this book. Almost everywhere we look there are changes to the IDE or the language – but a great deal of those changes are trivial or beneficial and are easy to get used to.

Now just press *F5* (sound familiar?) to run the program. After the solution is compiled, our application will run – displaying our form with its two controls:

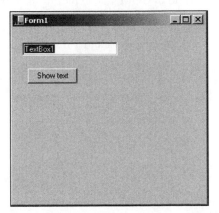

If we type Hello world into the text box and click the button, up pops our message box:

If this works we can have a reasonable level of confidence that our .NET Framework SDK and VS.NET have been installed correctly. We've also had an opportunity to configure VS.NET for use as a VB development environment and to get a quick look at the process of creating a simple VB.NET application.

Summary

Microsoft.NET is a very exciting and major technology change. While it builds on the concepts introduced by COM, it is quite different from anything we have today – promising to make us more productive as it merges the Windows GUI and browser-based Internet development environments closer together.

VB, the most popular development tool today, is fully supported in the .NET environment through VB.NET. VB.NET will likely be the most common development tool for the new .NET platform, since it offers the smoothest transition for existing VB developers, as well as being very accessible to developers who have used other languages and tools in the past.

At the same time, it is important to approach VB.NET for what it is – a substantially changed and enhanced language for a substantially changed and enhanced development environment. While a lot of VB.NET will seem familiar to existing developers, there are a great number of changes to the IDE, the language and features – providing a substantial challenge when moving to the new language and environment.

In this chapter we've seen how to locate, install, and configure the .NET Framework SDK and VS.NET. We now have a development workstation running VS.NET, possibly along with a web server running IIS and the .NET Framework SDK for web development.

In the next chapter we'll discuss the .NET Framework in more detail – comparing and contrasting it to the world of COM, and exploring all its new features and capabilities.

From there we'll dive into the features of VB.NET, including the IDE, the VB language changes, and how the .NET Framework and VB work together to create great applications.

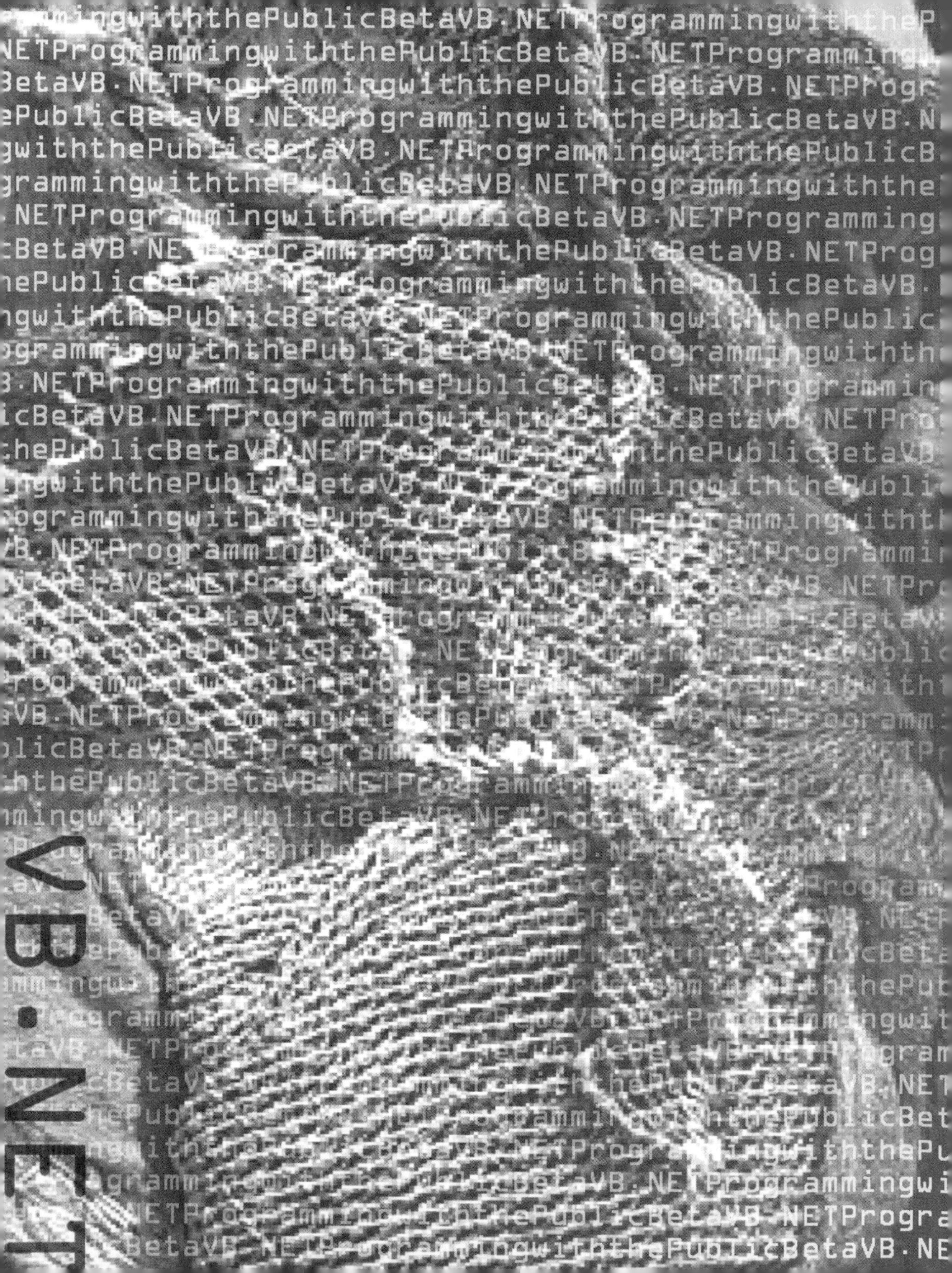
VB.NETProgrammingwiththePublicBeta
VB.NET

2

Introduction to the .NET Framework

When Microsoft introduced their Microsoft.NET initiative at the Professional Developers Conference (PDC) in Orlando, Florida in July 2000, most of us felt that we were present at a turning point in the world of Windows software for Microsoft platforms. We were given our first look at the .NET Framework, a new platform for development and implementation, one designed from the ground up for the Internet world.

Microsoft's .NET initiative is broad-based and very ambitious. It includes the .NET Framework, which encompasses the languages and execution platform, plus extensive class libraries providing rich built-in functionality. Besides the core .NET Framework, the .NET initiative includes protocols (such as the Simple Object Access Protocol, commonly known as SOAP) to provide a new level of integration of software over the Internet, and a family of server-based products called .NET Enterprise Servers that are the next generation of Microsoft's BackOffice.

In this chapter, we'll look at the .NET Framework from the viewpoint of a Visual Basic developer. Since the .NET Framework is the foundation of most of the changes in Visual Basic.NET, an introduction to the .NET Framework is an essential first step in assimilating the changes that will be presented in the chapters that follow.

The .NET Framework means changes for everyone who uses Microsoft technologies, and Visual Basic developers get more than their share. One goal Microsoft has for the .NET initiative is to bring together the best of all of their language platforms. In a broad sense, this means that other languages get many of Visual Basic's ease-of-use features, such as easy drag-and-drop generation of forms, while Visual Basic receives new dramatic capabilities, such as full object orientation, that take away many of the limitations Visual Basic developers have put up with in the past.

One of the first released products based on the .NET Framework is expected to be Visual Studio.NET, and indeed beta one of Visual Studio.NET became available in November of 2000. No firm dates are available for the full commercial release of Visual Studio.NET, but general expectation is for fall 2001 at the earliest.

How important is .NET to Microsoft? Their executives have stated publicly that 80% of Microsoft's R&D resources in 2001 are being spent on .NET. It is expected that, eventually, most Microsoft products will be ported to the .NET platform.

A Broad and Deep Platform for the Future

Calling the .NET Framework a "platform" doesn't begin to describe how broad and deep it is. It encompasses a virtual machine that abstracts away much of the Windows API from development. It includes a class library with more functionality than any yet created. It makes available a development environment that spans multiple languages. And it exposes an architecture that makes multiple language integration simple and straightforward.

At first glance, some aspects of .NET appear similar to previous architectures such as UCSD Pascal and Java. No doubt some of the ideas for .NET were inspired by these past efforts, but there are also many brand new architectural ideas in .NET. Overall, the result is a radically new approach to software development. This is the first development platform designed from the ground up with the Internet in mind. Previously, Internet functionality has been simply bolted on to pre-Internet operating systems like Unix and Windows. This has required Internet software developers to understand a host of technologies and integration issues. The .NET Framework is designed and intended for highly distributed software, making Internet functionality and interoperability easier and more transparent to include in systems than ever before.

The vision of Microsoft.NET is globally distributed systems, using XML as the universal glue to allow functions running on different computers across an organization or across the world to come together in a single application. In this vision, systems from servers to wireless palmtops, with everything in between, will share the same general platform, with versions of .NET available for all of them, and with each of them able to integrate transparently with the others.

But this does not leave out classic applications as we've always known them. Microsoft.NET also aims to make traditional business applications easier to develop and deploy. Some of the technologies of the .NET Framework, such as Windows Forms, demonstrate that Microsoft has not forgotten the traditional business developer.

An Important Caution

This book will preview the technology and structure of the .NET Framework and Visual Basic.NET. An early start at understanding this technology is important for enabling intelligent decisions about the role of Visual Basic.NET.

However, it's very important to remember that this book discusses unreleased products. There will no doubt be many changes during the development cycle. In particular, many of the changes relating to language syntax and features are subject to revision. Bottom line – don't bet the farm on the information presented here. Be prepared for changes as Visual Basic.NET and the .NET Framework move closer to actual production.

Avoiding Confusion – the Role of the .NET Enterprise Servers

Microsoft has already released several products, which they describe as being part of the .NET Enterprise Server family. More of these are coming, and most will be released by the time this book is published. Products in the .NET Enterprise Server family include

- ❑ SQL Server 2000 (discussed in *"Professional SQL Server 2000" from Wrox Press, ISBN 1861004486*)

- ❑ Commerce Server 2000

- ❑ BizTalk Server (discussed in *"Professional BizTalk" from Wrox Press, ISBN 1861003293*)

- ❑ Exchange 2000

- ❑ Host Integration Server (the successor to SNA Server)

- ❑ Internet Security and Administration (ISA) Server (the successor to Proxy Server)

Some of the marketing literature for these products emphasizes that they are part of Microsoft's .NET strategy. However, it is important that you understand the difference between these products and the .NET Framework upon which Visual Basic.NET is based. The .NET Enterprise Servers are *not* based on the .NET Framework. Most of them are successors to previous server-based products, and they use the same COM/COM+ technologies as their predecessors.

These .NET Enterprise Servers still have a major role to play in future software development projects. When actual .NET framework projects are developed, most will depend on the technologies in the .NET Enterprise Servers for functions like data storage and messaging. However, the first actual product based on the .NET framework will be Visual Studio.NET (which will contain Visual Basic.NET), and it is not expected before Fall 2001.

What's Wrong with What We Have Now?

Starting in late 1995, Microsoft made a dramatic shift towards the Internet. The company was refocused on marrying their Windows platform to the Internet, and they have certainly succeeded in making Windows a serious Internet platform as well as a platform for all the business-oriented software developed with the Windows DNA (Distributed iNternet Architecture) programming model.

However, Microsoft had to make some serious compromises to quickly produce Internet-based tools and technologies. In particular, Active Server Pages (ASP) has always been viewed as a bit clumsy. After all, writing reams of interpreted script is a real step backwards from structured and object-oriented development. Designing, debugging and maintaining such unstructured code is also a headache.

Other languages such as Visual Basic have been used in Internet applications on Microsoft platforms, but mostly as components that worked through Active Server Pages. Presently, Microsoft tools lack the level of integration and ease-of-use for web development that would be ideal. A few attempts were made to place a web interface on traditional languages, such as `WebClasses` in VB, but none of these gained wide acceptance.

Microsoft has attempted to bring some order to the chaos with their concept of Windows DNA applications. DNA paints a broad picture of standard three-tier development based on COM, with Active Server Pages (as well as Win32 clients) in the presentation layer, business objects in a middle layer, and a relational data store and engine in the bottom layer. Here is a typical diagram of a generic Windows DNA application:

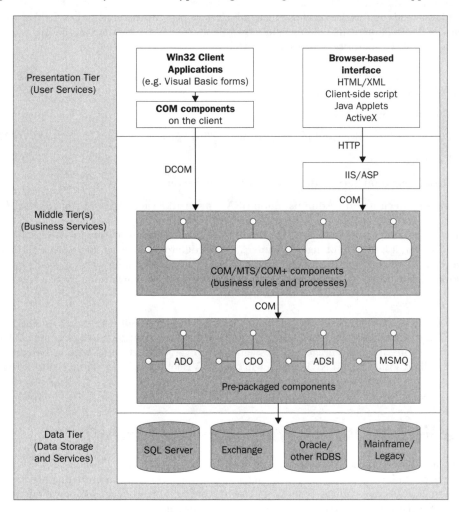

Presentation Tier

In Windows DNA, there are two major choices for user interfaces – Win32 clients and browser-based clients.

Win32 clients, most often produced with a visual development tool such as Visual Basic, are often the simplest to create, and offer a rich user interface. The drawback is that such client software is difficult to deploy and maintain, requiring an install on every client and a change to every client when an upgrade is needed. Besides the logistical difficulties of getting the software to the clients and maintaining/updating it, there is another serious issue. DLL conflicts on the client are frequent because of variations in the version of the operating system and other software installed on the client. These conflicts are difficult and expensive to diagnose and repair. You may have heard this referred to as "DLL Hell".

Browser-based clients are somewhat more difficult to create, and offer a more limited user interface with fewer controls and less control over layout of the screen and the handling of screen events. However, they are far easier to deploy. All the client needs is a compatible browser and an Internet or intranet connection.

Browser-based clients can use technologies such as client-side script or Java applets to make the user interface richer and more functional. These options work for most modern browsers. Applying these technologies adds additional development time, and they do not address all user interface issues.

There are some "in-between" options. If clients are restricted to certain browsers Dynamic HTML (DHTML) can be used to add further functionality to the interface. And if clients are restricted to Internet Explorer, ActiveX controls can be used to make an interface close to that available in a Win32 client. However, ActiveX controls add deployment issues of their own. Visual Basic can be used for ActiveX controls, but then deploying the controls requires lots of supporting Visual Basic DLLs on the client. ActiveX controls are typically written in C++ instead to make the install as lightweight as possible. This adds to development time and requires a higher level of development expertise.

One important factor that is often overlooked in the DNA model is that there may be a need to implement both Win32-based and Internet-based user interfaces. Or there may be a need to have different levels of user interfaces, say one for novice or occasional users and one for advanced users.

Middle Tier

The middle tier in a DNA application should encapsulate as much of the business processing as possible. Besides those rules needed to validate data on the client, most business rules should be in this layer.

The middle tier often breaks down into multiple sub-tiers. One tier may handle the interface to the client, another handles the business rules, and another the interface to the data repositories.

Visual Basic is the most common language used to write middle-tier components. This is a more sophisticated type of development than for typical forms-based Visual Basic programs, requiring a higher level of expertise in COM and object-oriented programming concepts. It is also important to understand how to create components that scale well, which often means developing components that are implemented using Microsoft Transaction Server on Windows NT or COM+ Services on Windows 2000. Such components typically use stateless designs, which can look very different from the stateful designs often used in client-based components.

Understanding the nuances of COM is important in constructing a middle tier because the components in this layer must work together. Versioning all the components properly so that they understand each other's interfaces can be a challenge.

Components in the middle tier may talk to a variety of protocols and components to communicate data to the data tier. The diagram shows examples such as HTTP, ADO, and CDO (Collaborative Data Objects), but that list is by no means exhaustive.

Data Tier

Most business applications must store information for long-term use. The nature of the storage mechanism varies with the installation. Usually a relational database system (RDBS) is required, with the most common options being Microsoft SQL Server and Oracle. If the information is more based around documents and messages, a messaging data store such as Exchange may be required. And many installations still depend on legacy mainframe systems.

Besides holding the data, the data tier may also have logic to process, retrieve, and validate data. Stored procedures, written in some variation of the SQL language, can be used in RDBS databases to do this.

Issues with the DNA Model

The concept behind DNA is reasonably sound, but actually making it work has many challenges. For example, there are many possible locations for programming logic in a DNA application. Some of them are:

❑ Visual Basic code in forms

❑ Visual Basic used in components on the client

❑ Visual Basic used in components on the server

❑ VBScript or JavaScript for server-side scripting in Active Server Pages

❑ VBScript or JavaScript for client-side scripting

❑ HTML, DHTML, CSS (Cascading Style Sheets)

❑ XML, XSL

❑ C++ in ActiveX components

❑ Stored procedures (Transact-SQL in SQL Server or PL-SQL in Oracle)

With this many options, inexperienced developers have a lot of opportunity for inappropriate choices, such as putting logic on the client that belongs on the server, or creating VB Script for formatting when Cascading Style Sheets might work better. Designing and constructing a complex DNA-based application calls for a high level of expertise with a number of different technologies.

DNA applications usually require COM components on the server, and sometimes on the client as well. Developing COM components requires a level of development expertise that takes a lot of time to reach, although some languages, such as Visual Basic, make it easier than others.

Another big issue with DNA apps is deployment. Getting a complex middle tier of COM components to work correctly and interface properly to the presentation and data tiers can be nightmarish. Many problems can arise from the versioning and installation of components, and the components that they rely on.

Microsoft realized that, while it was possible to write good Internet applications with Windows-based technologies, it was highly desirable to find ways to develop applications faster and make it far easier to deploy them. Other platforms (such as Unix) and other development environments (such as WebSphere) were continuing to raise the bar for developing Internet applications, making it essential that Microsoft address the limitations of the DNA programming model.

Limitations of Visual Basic for DNA Application Development

Visual Basic is easily the most popular language for developing applications with the DNA model. As noted above, it can be used in two major roles – forms-based VB clients and COM components (either on the client or the server).

There are other options, of course, including C++, J++, and various third-party languages such as Delphi and Perl. But the number of VB developers outnumbers them all put together.

That does not mean Visual Basic is without limitations in this environment. Some of the most serious limitations include:

❑   No capability for multithreading

❑   Lack of implementation inheritance and other object-oriented features

❑   Poor error-handling ability

❑   Poor integration with other languages such as C++

❑   No effective user interface for Internet-based applications

Lack of multithreading implies, for example, that VB can't be used to write an NT-type service. There are also situations in which the apartment threading used by components created in VB limits performance.

VB's limited object-oriented features make it unsuitable for development of object-based frameworks, and denies design options to Visual Basic developers that are available to C++ or Java developers.

VB's archaic error handling becomes especially annoying in a multi-tier environment. It's difficult in Visual Basic to track and pass errors through a stack of component interfaces.

Integration of multiple languages in a COM application is a challenge. Visual Basic's implementation of COM, although easy to use, causes problems with such integration. Class parameters in VB are "variant compliant", forcing C++ developers who want to integrate with VB to convert parameters to types more appropriate for their purposes. These varying data structures and interface conventions must be resolved before components in Visual Basic can be integrated into a multiple language project. Besides necessitating extra code, these conversions may also mean a performance hit.

But perhaps the biggest drawback to using Visual Basic became apparent when many developers moved to the Internet. While VB forms for a Win32 client were state-of-the-art, for applications with a browser interface Visual Basic was relegated mostly to use in components because of the difficulties (discussed above) with alternatives such as WebClasses and browser-based ActiveX components.

Microsoft tried to address this problem in Visual Basic 6 with WebClasses and DHTML pages. Neither caught on. WebClasses offered an obscure programming model, and limited control over visual layout. "DHTML Pages" in Visual Basic 6 must send a (usually large) DLL to the client, and so needed a high-bandwidth connection to be practical, limiting their use mostly to intranet applications.

All of these limitations needed to be addressed, but Microsoft decided to look beyond just Visual Basic and solve these problems on a more global level. All of these limitations are solved in Visual Basic.NET through the use of technology in the .NET Frameworks.

The Origins of .NET

At the beginning of 1998, a team of developers at Microsoft had just finished work on a new version of Internet Information Server (version 4.0), including several new features in Active Server Pages. While developers were pleased to see new capabilities for doing Internet development on Microsoft NT applications, the development team at Microsoft had many ideas for improvement. That team began to work on a new architecture implementing those ideas. This project eventually came to be known as Next Generation Windows Services (NGWS).

After Visual Studio 6 was released in late 1998, work on the next version of Visual Studio (then called Visual Studio 7) was folded into NGWS. The COM+/MTS team brought in their work on a universal runtime for all the languages in Visual Studio, which they intended to make available for third party languages as well.

The subsequent development was kept very much under wraps at Microsoft. Only key Microsoft partners realized the true importance of NGWS until it was re-christened Microsoft .NET and introduced to the public at the PDC. At that point, development had been underway for over two years, and most attendees were pleasantly surprised to see the enormous strides Microsoft had made.

The concepts in .NET are inspired from many sources. Previous architectures, from p-code in UCSD Pascal up through the Java Virtual Machine, have similar elements. Microsoft has taken many of the best ideas in the industry, combined in some great ideas of their own, and brought them all into one coherent package.

The .NET Framework – An Overview

First and foremost, .NET is a framework that covers all the layers of software development above the operating system. It provides the richest level of integration among presentation technologies, component technologies, and data technologies ever seen on a Microsoft, or perhaps any, platform. Secondly, the entire architecture has been created to make it as easy to develop Internet applications, as it is to develop for the desktop.

The .NET Framework actually "wraps" the operating system, insulating software developed with .NET from most operating system specifics such as file handling and memory allocation. This prepares for a possible future in which the software developed for .NET is portable to a wide variety of hardware and operating system foundations. (Beta one of Visual Studio.NET supports all versions of Windows 2000 plus Windows NT4, Windows 9x, and Windows Millennium Edition.)

A Common Substrate for all Development

The major components of the Microsoft.NET framework are shown in the following diagram:

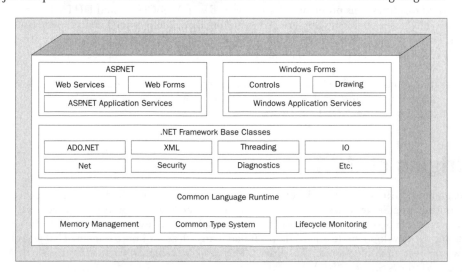

The framework starts all the way down at the memory management and component loading level, and goes all the way up to multiple ways of rendering user and program interfaces. In between, there are layers that provide just about any system-level capability that a developer would need.

At the base is the Common Language Runtime, often abbreviated to CLR. This is the heart of the .NET Framework: it is the engine that drives key functionality. It includes, for example, a common system of data types. These common types, plus a standard interface convention, make cross-language inheritance possible. In addition to allocation and management of memory, the CLR also does reference tracking for objects, and handles garbage collection.

The middle layer includes the next generation of standard system services such as ADO.NET and XML. These services are brought under control of the framework, making them universally available and making their usage consistent across languages.

The top layer includes user and program interfaces. Windows Forms (often just referred to as WinForms) is a new and more advanced way to do standard Win32 screens. Web Forms provides a new web-based UI. Perhaps the most revolutionary is Web Services, which provides a mechanism for programs to communicate over the Internet, using SOAP). Web Services provide an analog of COM and DCOM for object brokering and interfacing, but based on Internet technologies so that allowance is made even for integration to non-Microsoft platforms. Web Forms and Web Services, which comprise the Internet interface portion of .NET are implemented by a part of the .NET Framework referred to as ASP.NET.

For completeness, there is a console interface that allows creation of character-based applications. Such applications were very difficult to build with previous versions of Visual Basic. Chapter 8 discusses how these applications are written in VB.NET.

All of these capabilities are available to any language that is based on the .NET platform, including, of course, Visual Basic.NET.

The Common Language Runtime

We're all familiar with runtimes: they go back further than DOS languages. However, the **Common Language Runtime** (**CLR**) is as advanced over traditional runtimes as a machine gun is over a musket. Here's a quick diagrammatic summary of the major pieces of the CLR:

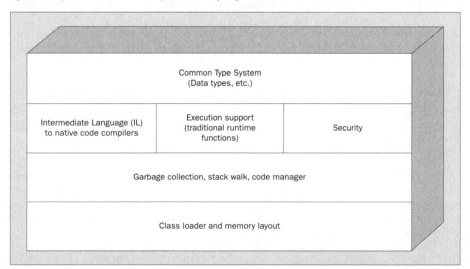

That small part in the middle called "Execution Support" contains most of the capabilities normally associated with a language runtime (such as the VBRUNxxx.DLL runtime used with Visual Basic). The rest is new, at least for Microsoft platforms.

Key Design Goals

The design of the CLR is based on the following goals:

❑ Simpler, faster development

❑ Automatic handling of "plumbing" such as memory management and process communication

❑ Excellent tool support

❑ Simpler, safer deployment

❑ Scalability

Let's look at each of these in detail.

Simpler, Faster Development

A broad, consistent framework allows developers to write less code, and reuse code more. Less code is possible because the system provides a rich set of underlying functionality. Programs in .NET access this functionality in a standard, consistent way, requiring less "hardwiring" and customization logic to interface to the functionality than is typically needed today.

Programming is also simpler in .NET because of the standardization of data types and interface conventions. As will be discussed below, .NET makes knowledge of the intricacies of COM much less important.

Getting Rid of Plumbing

A lot of programming infrastructure is either automatically handled by the CLR or rendered completely unnecessary. That is, some of it is hidden, and some of it is just not there any more.

Memory management is an example of hidden infrastructure. Visual Basic developers stopped worrying much about memory long ago. Developers in other .NET languages now have the same luxury.

Hiding this infrastructure simplifies many programming tasks. As we will see in the section below on memory management in .NET (*Details on .NET Memory Management*), this simplification does not come without a price.

A lot of the missing plumbing is replaced by metadata – standardized information about components, interfaces, and processes that can be accessed in a consistent way. A section below covers metadata in more detail.

Tool Support

Though much of what the CLR does is similar to operating system functionality, it is designed first and foremost to support development languages. It furnishes a rich set of object models that are useful to tools like designers, wizards, debuggers, and profilers. And since the object models are at the runtime level, such tools can be designed to work across all languages that use the CLR. It is expected that third parties will produce a host of such tools.

It's also important to note that Microsoft is not restricting use of the CLR to Microsoft languages. Third party language vendors are encouraged to re-architect their languages to use the CLR, which offers a host of benefits. Besides taking advantage of all the CLR functionality (and thereby not having to write it or support it), using the CLR enables never before seen levels of cross-language integration. More on that is below, in the section on multiple language support.

This capability of the CLR to work transparently with multiple languages has huge benefits for developers. Debuggers offer the best example. The CLR makes it possible to write a source-level debugger that treats all languages equally, jumping from one language to another as necessary. Visual Basic developers will benefit by having access to these more powerful tools.

Simpler, Safer Deployment

It's hard for an experienced Windows component developer to see how anything can work without registration, GUIDs, and the like, but the CLR does. Applications produced in the .NET framework can be designed to install with a simple XCOPY. That's right – just copy the files onto the disk and run the application. We haven't seen this since the days of DOS (and some of us really miss it).

This works because compilers in the .NET framework embed identifiers (in the form of metadata, discussed below) into compiled modules, and the CLR manages those identifiers automatically. The identifiers provide all the information needed to load and run modules, and to locate related modules.

As a great by-product, the CLR can manage multiple versions of the same component (even a shared component), and have them run side-by-side. The identifiers tell the CLR which version is needed for a particular compiled module because such information is captured at compile time. The runtime policy can be set in a module to use the exact version of a component that was available at compile time, to use the latest compatible version, or to specify an exact version. The bottom line is that Microsoft.NET is intended to eradicate "DLL Hell" once and for all.

This has implications that might not be apparent at first. For example, if a program needs to run directly from a CD (without first running an installation program) that was not feasible in Visual Basic after version 3. That capability will reappear with Visual Basic .NET.

Another significant deployment benefit in .NET is that applications only need to install their own core logic. An application produced in .NET will not need to install a runtime, for example, or modules for ADO or XML. Such base functionality will be part of the .NET Framework, which will be installed separately and only once for each system, and will eventually be included with the operating system and probably with various applications (Internet Explorer, perhaps?). Those four-diskette installs for a VB "Hello, world" program will be a thing of the past.

Making all of this work automatically requires a sophisticated security infrastructure. The .NET Framework captures the origin of a piece of code, and the publisher of a module can be identified with a public encryption key. The bottom line is that a system can be set up to not run untrusted software, which provides mechanisms to block viruses like the infamous ILOVEYOU. A method of a component, no matter how deep it is in the object model, can demand proof of authorization to run all the way back along the call chain that got to it.

Scalability

Since most of the system-level execution functions are concentrated in the CLR, they can be optimized and architected to allow a wide range of scalability for applications produced in the Microsoft.NET framework. As with most of the other advantages of the CLR, this one comes to all applications with little or no effort.

Memory and process management is one area where scalability can be built in. The memory management in the CLR is self-configuring and tunes itself automatically. Garbage collection (reclaiming memory that is no longer being actively used) is highly optimized, and the CLR supports many of the component management capabilities of MTS/COM+ (such as object pooling). The result is that components can run faster, and thus support more users.

This has some interesting side effects. For example, the performance and scalability differences among languages become smaller. All languages compile to a standard byte code called **Microsoft Intermediate Language** (**MSIL**), often referred to simply as **IL**, and there is discussion below on how the CLR executes IL. With all languages compiling down to similar byte code, it becomes unnecessary in most cases to look to other languages when performance is an issue. The difference in performance among .NET languages is minor – Visual Basic, for example, gives about the same performance as any of the other .NET languages.

There are early-stage plans for the CLR to be available on a wide range of devices. Eventually the vision is for .NET to be running at all levels, from smart palm-top devices all the way up to web farms. That means the same development tools should work across the entire range – news that will be appreciated by those who have tried to use Windows CE development kits. Of course, this is an ambitious plan and may be subject to changes and retractions.

Metadata

The .NET Framework needs lots of information about an application to carry out so many automatic functions. The design of .NET requires applications to carry that information around inside them. That is, applications are self-describing. The collected information that describes an application is called metadata.

The concept of metadata is not new. COM components use a form of it called a type library, which contains metadata describing the classes exposed by the component and is used to facilitate OLE Automation. Using the facilities of COM+ also requires supplying more metadata to specify, for example, whether a component supports transactions.

One of the drawbacks to metadata in COM and COM+ is that metadata is stored in different places, and outside the component. A component's type library may be stored in a separate file. The component's registration GUID (which would be considered metadata related to identification of the component) is stored in the Windows registry.

In contrast, the metadata in .NET is stored in one place – inside the component it describes. Metadata in .NET also contains more information about the component, and is better organized.

In .NET, the metadata is generated by a compiler and stored automatically in an EXE or DLL. It's in binary, but the framework offers an API to export metadata to and from an XML schema or a COM type library. An XML schema export might be useful, for example, in extracting version and compile information for a repository on components. Here are some of the items in the metadata defined for the .NET Framework:

- ❑ Description of a deployment unit (called an assembly)
  - ❑ Name, version, culture (which could determine, for example, the default user language)
  - ❑ A public key for verification
  - ❑ Types exported by the assembly

- Dependencies – other assemblies which this assembly depends upon
- Security permissions needed to run
- Base classes, and interfaces
- Custom attributes
  - User defined (inserted by the developer)
  - Compiler defined (inserted by the compiler to indicate something special about the language)

Some of these, such as the custom attributes, are optional – the tools manage all the required ones automatically.

The metadata is one of the ways the CLR can support a wide variety of tools. Here are some of the possible consumers of .NET metadata:

- Designers
- Debuggers
- Profilers
- Proxy Generators
- Other .NET IL compilers (to find out how to use a component in their language)
- Type / Object browsers
- Schema generators

Compilers are some of the most extensive users of metadata. A compiler can examine a module produced by a different compiler and use the metadata for cross-language type import. This would allow, for example, the VB compiler to look at components produced in C#, or a .NET version of COBOL, and expose those C# or COBOL components to a VB developer. The components would look the same way components developed in VB would look. And of course, a compiler can produce metadata about its own compiled modules, including such elements as flags that a module was compiled for debugging, or a language-specific marker.

The metadata data store is very flexible. Even information that might appear in a ToolTip can be embedded in metadata.

This extendable data store about a compiled module greatly facilitates the simpler deployment available under the .NET Framework. An API, called the Reflection API, is available for scanning and manipulation of metadata elements.

Metadata is key to the easy deployment in .NET. When a component is upgraded or moved, the necessary information about the component cannot be left behind. Metadata can never get out of sync with a .NET component because it's not in a separate file. Everything the CLR needs to know to run a component is supplied with the component.

Multiple Language Integration and Support

The most ambitious aspect of the CLR is that it is designed to support multiple languages and allow unprecedented levels of integration among those languages. By enforcing a common type system, and by having complete control over interface calls, the CLR allows languages to work together more transparently than ever before.

Previously, one language could instantiate and use components written in another language by using COM. Whilst at times, calling conventions were difficult to manage, especially when Visual Basic was involved, they could generally be made to work. However, subclassing (re-using an existing compiled component by adding some new functionality to it) was more difficult. Using VB to subclass a component written in a different language required writing a sophisticated wrapper, and only advanced developers did such work.

It is straightforward in the .NET Framework to use one language to subclass a class implemented in another. A class written in Visual Basic can inherit from a base class written in C++, or in COBOL for that matter. (At least one major vendor is at work on a COBOL implementation for .NET.) The VB program doesn't even need to know the language used for the base class, and we're talking full implementation inheritance with no problems requiring recompilation when the base class changes.

How can this work? The information furnished in metadata makes it possible. A class interface looks the same, regardless of the language that generated it. The CLR uses metadata to manage all the interfaces and calling conventions between languages.

This has major implications; mixed language programming teams become far more feasible than before. And it becomes less necessary to force developers who are perfectly comfortable in one language to adopt another just to fit in to a development effort. Cross-language inheritance promises to open up architectural options that have never existed before.

One Microsoft person summed this up by saying that, as far as they are concerned, with Microsoft.NET, the language used becomes a "lifestyle choice". While there will always be benefits to having programming teams use a common language, Microsoft.NET raises the practicality of mixed-language projects.

A Common Type System

A key piece of functionality that enables multiple language support is a common type system, in which all commonly used data types, even base types such as Long and Boolean, are actually implemented as objects. Coercion among types can now be done at a lower level for more consistency between languages. And, since all languages are using the same library of types, calling one language from another doesn't require type conversion or weird calling conventions.

This results in the need for some readjustment, particularly for Visual Basic developers. For example, what we called an Integer in VB6 and earlier, is now known as a Short in Visual Basic.NET. But the adjustment is worth it to bring VB in line with everything else. And, as a by-product, other languages get the same support for strings that VB has always had.

Reference Types vs. Value Types

There are two families of types in .NET. **Value types** are what Visual Basic developers would call data variables and user-defined types (UDTs). **Reference types** are basically classes.

One reason to understand this classification is that value types are tested for equality differently from reference types. Another major reason it is helpful to differentiate these types is that their memory management is handled differently. This will be described in the section below on how the CLR manages memory.

Notice that reference types and value types are also treated differently in assignment statements. Consider this code:

```
Dim nRooms As Integer
Dim nAvailableRooms As Integer
nAvailableRooms = 10
nRooms = nAvailableRooms
```

After this code is executed, there are two variables, nRooms and nAvailableRooms, which have the same value in them. From this point forward, changing the value in nRooms will not affect the value in nAvailableRooms – there is no implicit connection between the two variables. That's because Integer is a value type.

By contrast, consider the following code in Visual Basic 6:

```
Dim objRoom As clsRoom
Dim objAvailableRoom As clsRoom
Set objAvailableRoom = New clsRoom
Set objRoom = objAvailableRoom
```

In this case, there is a connection between objRoom and objAvailableRoom. Both point to the same underlying object. Changing the object with one of the references means the other reference will reflect the changes. That's because objRoom and objAvailableRoom are a reference type, namely the class clsRoom.

> *The VB6 code in the above example would not be the same in Visual Basic.NET. Instantiation is done somewhat differently and the Set statement is not used. Here is the equivalent Visual Basic.NET code:*

```
Dim objRoom As clsRoom
Dim objAvailableRoom As New clsRoom
objRoom = objAvailableRoom
```

> *Chapter 3 will discuss these changes in detail.*

A final difference between value types and reference types concerns how instances of a type are initialized. A variable declared as a reference type is initialized to Null and does not contain a reference to a valid object until assigned such a reference (by setting to a new instantiation of the class, or by assigning a reference from an existing valid object).

A variable containing a value type, on the other hand, always refers to a valid object. Note that all types, even native data types, are actually objects in .NET – see more on that below. A primitive type (a type supported natively by the compiler such as an Integer, a Boolean, a String, etc.) will be initialized to an appropriate value (0 for Integer, False for Boolean, etc.). A section below discusses more on primitive types in .NET.

Everything's an Object

As previously mentioned, every type supported by the Common Type System is an object. That means every type is derived from the System.Object class. This gives every type in .NET the ability to support the following methods:

Boolean Equals(*Object*)	Used to see if two objects are equal. For a reference type, the method returns True if the base object and the *Object* parameter both reference the same object. Value types should return True if the *Object* parameter has the same value as the base object.
Int32 GetHashCode()	Generates a number that is mathematically derived from the value of an object. If two objects of the same type are equal, then they must return the same hash code. The handling of collections by the .NET Framework depends on values from this method.
Type GetType()	Gets a Type object that contains useful information about the type. It is used, for example, in place of the VarType function in earlier version of Visual Basic.
String ToString()	For primitive types such as Integer, Boolean, and String, this returns a string representation of the type's value. For other types, the string returned varies. The default implementation of this method returns the fully qualified name of the class of the object. However, the method is usually overridden to output data that is more appropriate for the type, such as the value for primitive types mentioned above.

Primitive Types in the .NET Framework

As mentioned earlier, data types that are natively supported by a compiler are called primitive types. The .NET primitive types are:

Type	Referred to in VB.NET as	Description	Size
Boolean	Boolean	Boolean value of either true or false.	8 bits
Byte	Byte	A positive integer between 0 and 255.	8 bits
Char	Char	A Unicode character value.	16 bits
DateTime	Date	A date and time value.	64 bits
Decimal	Decimal	Positive and negative values with 28 significant digits, ranging from 79,228,162,514,264,337,593,543,950,335 to negative 79,228,162,514,264,337,593,543,950,335.	64 bits
Double	Double	Double precision, floating point number ranging from negative 1.79769313486231570E308 to positive 1.79769313486231570E308.	64 bits
GUID	GUID	Represents a globally unique identifier (GUID).	128 bits
Int16	Short	Signed integer value that can range from negative 32768 to positive 32767.	16 bits

Type	Referred to in VB.NET as	Description	Size
Int32	Integer	Signed integer value that can range from negative 2,147,483,648 to positive 2,147,483,647.	32 bits
Int64	Long	Signed integer value that can range from negative 9,223,372,036,854,775,808 to positive 9,223,372,036,854,775,807.	64 bits
Sbyte	Sbyte	Signed integer value that can range from negative 128 to positive 127.	8 bits
Single	Single	Single precision, floating point number that can range from negative 3.402823E38 to positive 3.402823E38.	32 bits

The set of primitive types supported by .NET has a lot of overlap with the primitive types supported by previous versions of Visual Basic. But the overlap is not complete. There are some new types, and some changes to old types in VB. Chapter 3, which summarizes changes in Visual Basic, discusses these data type changes.

Namespaces

One of the most important concepts in Microsoft.NET is **namespaces**. They help organize object libraries and hierarchies, simplify object references, prevent ambiguity when referring to objects, and control the scope of object identifiers.

Namespaces are discussed in more detail in Chapter 3. For now, it is useful to know that class libraries are normally referenced in each language before they are used. The reference allows the types to be used in the code with abbreviations instead of detailed library references. In VB, this is done with an `Imports` statement, and that this can be thought of as similar in concept to checking a box in the References dialog in Visual Basic 6. For example, a typical VB form module in .NET might have the following lines at the beginning:

```
Imports System.WinForms
Imports MyDebug = System.Diagnostics.Debug
```

The first line simply makes all of the standard form properties and methods available to the code in the form module. This second line illustrates the use of an alias. A branch of the object hierarchy can thus receive its own identifier, which is only valid in that code module. Instead of referring to the `System.Diagnostics.Debug` class object, the code in this module would refer to the `MyDebug` object.

The Structure of an Application in the .NET Framework

.NET functionality requires a new structure for applications. The way these applications are executed and the way memory is managed is also new.

Start with an Assembly, Build Up to an Application

The unit of deployment, as previously mentioned, is an **assembly**. It can consist of one or more files and is self-describing. It contains a "manifest" which holds the metadata describing everything exported from the assembly, and what's needed to deploy and run the assembly.

There really isn't a VB6 equivalent of an assembly. A compiled EXE or DLL file comes closest in concept, but the fact that a .NET assembly can contain more than one file makes the comparison inexact.

An assembly has its own version. Assemblies are combined to become applications.

An application has one or more assemblies, and also may contain application specific files or data. Applications may have their own private versions of assemblies, and may be configured to prefer their private version to any shared versions.

Assembly Structure

An assembly has the following general structure:

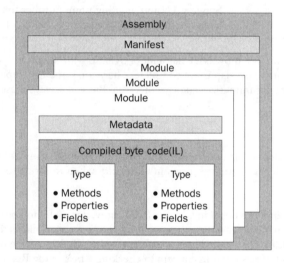

Here are details on the individual elements in an assembly.

Manifest – Every assembly must have a manifest. It may be a separate file in the assembly, or it may be contained in one of the modules. It contains the following information:

❑   Name and version number for the assembly

❑   Other assemblies that this assembly depends upon (including exact version numbers of those assemblies)

❑   Types (classes and members) exposed by the assembly

❑   Security permissions required by the assembly

Module – A module is either a DLL or an EXE in the Windows PE (Portable Executable) format. The compiled code in the module is in Microsoft Intermediate Language (IL), which is discussed below. A module also contains its own necessary associated metadata, and one module in an assembly may contain a manifest for that assembly.

Type – A type is a contained unit of data and logic affecting that data. It exposes information through properties, fields, and methods. Properties and fields look similar to a consumer of the type, and represent a piece of data. The difference is that properties have logic associated with them to verify or construct data, and fields are more like public variables. Methods, of course, are actions or behaviors of the type.

Deployment and Execution

With all the intelligence in the .NET framework, there is a lot more going on at execution time with the CLR than we are accustomed to. Programs or components can't just load and go – there are several things that must happen for the whole structure to work.

Execution

Source code modules for an assembly are compiled (at development time) into the CLR's Intermediate Language (IL). Then IL is compiled into native code before execution. That compilation can take place in several ways, and at various times. Normally, however, compilation into native code is done only once and the results are cached for future use.

The CLR contains a couple of just-in-time (JIT) compilers, which convert IL to native code (binary code targeted at a specific machine processor). One is called "Econo-JIT" and it has very fast compilation, but produces un-optimized code. It is useful when the code, such as script in a batch file, will likely be thrown away and regenerated.

The other is the standard JIT compiler, which operates a bit more slowly but performs a high level of optimization. It is used for most systems, including code generated by Visual Basic.NET

The JIT compilers produce code that is targeted at the specific processor on the machine. This is one of the reasons applications in .NET would normally be distributed in compiled IL, allowing processor-specific optimizations in native code to be done by the .NET compilers on a particular machine.

Code can be pre-compiled into native if appropriate. That is, an installation of a package can be set to pre-compile the IL code into native code during the installation.

Scripting also fits into this model, actually being compiled before it is used. In current systems interpreted script (in Active Server Pages or the Windows Scripting Host, for example) is never compiled. But in .NET, such script (which is not explicitly compiled by the developer) is automatically sent through a language compiler the first time it is accessed, and transformed into IL. Then the IL is immediately transformed into native code, and cached for future use. Scripts are created in .NET the way they are now, with any editor you like, and require no explicit compilation step. The compilation is handled in the background, and is managed automatically so that a change to the script results in appropriate recompilation.

The byte code in IL is very high level. There is a byte code for the action of inheritance, for example. Compilers for .NET languages don't have to understand how to make an inheritance work – that's the runtime's job. The compiler just places a byte code in a module indicating that the module inherits from another compiled class, and the runtime takes care of loading that class at execution and integrating it with the subclass.

With software compiled into a processor-independent intermediate language, Microsoft.NET makes it possible to achieve future platform independence. It is architecturally possible for a CLR to be produced for platforms based on other processors or other operating systems, which would enable applications produced on Windows 2000 to run on them. Microsoft has not emphasized this in their announcements, but the capabilities of the CLR in some respects parallel those of the Java virtual machine, which is designed for platform independence.

Details on .NET Memory Management

One of the strong points of the Common Language Runtime is the automatic memory management and garbage collection. The CLR takes care of loading components and laying out the memory for them, and then reclaims and cleans up the memory when the component is finished. That happens when the component has no more references pointing to it (such as when it falls out of scope).

Older versions of Visual Basic take care of these functions too. However, there is one critical difference in the way objects are de-allocated with the CLR vs. the old way objects are handled in VB6 and earlier. Older versions of VB did reference counting of object instances, and when the reference count reached zero, the object's Class_Terminate event was immediately called. In Visual Basic.NET, the CLR does garbage collection only when memory needs dictate that it is required. This implies that the equivalent of the Class_Terminate event, named the Dispose method of the object, does not necessarily get called immediately. It is called when the CLR decides that garbage collection is needed, which depends on when the area of memory reserved for object instances (called the "managed heap") gets full and needs compacting.

The old way, used by VB6 and earlier, is called **Deterministic Finalization**. This just means that it is possible for the developer to know with confidence when the finalization logic (in the Class_Terminate event) is run.

The .NET Framework does not have Deterministic Finalization. Since the CLR only does garbage collection as necessary, it is not possible to predict exactly when the finalization logic in a component (in the Dispose method) will be run. Once all references to an object are gone, the object may sit around in memory quite a while before the CLR decides to do anything about it.

This can lead to several development issues. Behavior of a program can vary with the memory needs of other programs on the system, leading to those dreaded intermittent program errors. Code converted from VB6 that depends heavily on Terminate events may need manual adjustment to work correctly in all cases in Visual Basic.NET.

Here's a typical example of a VB6 component that might be affected. It is a settings component, which is used to hold global application settings. The settings are loaded into the object from the Registry at instantiation (with logic in the Class_Initialize event), and any altered settings are stored back in the Registry in the Class_Terminate event. For simplicity, this example only uses two settings – LastReportRun, which is the name of the last report run by the user, and MaxPages, which is the maximum number of pages a report is supposed to print:

```
Option Explicit

' THIS IS VB6 CODE!!!

'local variable(s) to hold property value(s)
Private msLastReportRun As String    'local copy
Private mnMaxPages As Long           'local copy

' needed to get and set Registry values
Dim msAppName As String
Dim msSection As String

Public Property Let MaxPages(ByVal nData As Long)
    mnMaxPages = nData
End Property
```

```
Public Property Get MaxPages() As Long
    MaxPages = mnMaxPages
End Property


Public Property Let LastReportRun(ByVal vData As String)
    msLastReportRun = vData
End Property

Public Property Get LastReportRun() As String
    LastReportRun = msLastReportRun
End Property


Private Sub Class_Initialize()

' Get current values from Registry

Dim sKey As String
Dim sValue As String

' First set our application name and section name
' for the registry. These are member variables because
' they are also used in Class Terminate
msAppName = "MyVBApp"
msSection = "MySection"

' LastReportRun value - default is null string
sKey = "LastReportRun"
msLastReportRun = GetSetting(msAppName, msSection, sKey, vbNullString)

' MaxPages value - default is 100
sKey = "MaxPages"
sValue = GetSetting(msAppName, msSection, sKey, "100")
mnMaxPages = Int(Val(sValue))

End Sub


Private Sub Class_Terminate()
' Place current values into Registry

Dim sKey As String
Dim sValue As String

' The application name and section name were set in
' Class Initialize event

' Save LastReportRun value
sKey = "LastReportRun"
SaveSetting msAppName, msSection, sKey, msLastReportRun

' Save MaxPages value
sKey = "MaxPages"
sValue = Str$(mnMaxPages)
SaveSetting msAppName, msSection, sKey, sValue

End Sub
```

In a typical VB6 application, this design makes a lot of sense. Placing responsibility for management of the settings within the object means none of the other code has to worry about it. The component loads in its own registry values automatically at startup, and saves them automatically at termination.

However, in .NET, there is a major pitfall to this design. If the above component were migrated to .NET, the `Class_Terminate` code would be place in the `Dispose` method. It would not necessarily be run when the component was unloaded. If another instance of the component were created, it might be fetching old values out of the Registry because the updated values from the first instance had not yet been written back (because the CLR had not yet done garbage collection).

The preferred programming practice in the .NET Framework is for developers to take an increased level of responsibility for making sure that an object instance gets "cleaned up" when the program is through, usually with explicit calls either to a built-in `Dispose` method or to a custom method that takes care of finalization. This higher level of responsibility goes a bit against the grain of Visual Basic philosophy, and many VB developers are upset about it. It is not out of the question that Microsoft may make design changes that affect this issue, but at this point there's no reason to count on that.

The new memory management scheme does have some advantages. It is expected to yield better performance and remove many sources of memory-related bugs. It also solves the "circular reference" problem in Visual Basic, where Object A had a reference to Object B, and Object B also had a reference to Object A. In such a case, the reference count for neither object ever drops to zero, so the garbage collection algorithm in Visual Basic was unable to cope. The memory management algorithm in .NET detects such cases and manages them appropriately so that the objects can be deallocated when there is no reference to the objects from outside the circular loop.

The Next Layer – The .NET Class Framework

The next layer down in the framework provides the services and object models for data, input/output, security, and so forth. It is called the **.NET Class Framework**, sometimes referred to as the .NET base classes. For example, the next generation of ADO, called ADO.NET, resides here (though there will also be an updated version of regular ADO in Microsoft.NET to provide compatibility for older code). Also included is the core functionality to do things with XML, including the parsers and XSL transformer. There is a list below of additional functionality in the .NET Class Framework.

You might be wondering why .NET includes functionality that is, in many cases, duplication of existing class libraries. There are several good reasons:

❑ The .NET Class Framework libraries are implemented in the .NET Framework, making them easier to integrate with .NET-developed programs

❑ The .NET Class Framework brings together most of the system class libraries needed into one location, which increases consistency and convenience.

❑ The class libraries in the .NET Class Framework are much easier to extend than older class libraries

❑ Having the libraries as part of the .NET Framework simplifies deployment of .NET applications. Once the .NET Framework is on a system, individual applications don't need to install base class libraries for functions like data access.

What is in the .NET Class Framework?

The .NET Class Framework contains literally hundreds of classes and interfaces. Here are just some of the functions of various libraries in the .NET Class Framework:

❑ Data access and manipulation

❑ Creation and management of threads

❑ Interfaces from .NET to the outside world – Windows Forms, Web Forms, Web Services and console applications.

❑ Definition, management and enforcement of application security

❑ Application configuration

❑ Working with Directory services, Event Logs, Processes, Message Queues and Timers

❑ Sending and receiving data with a variety of network protocols

❑ Accessing metadata information stored in assemblies

Much functionality that a programmer might think of as being part of a language has been moved to the framework classes. For example, the Visual Basic keyword Sqr for extracting a square root is no longer available in .NET. It has been replaced by the System.Math.Sqrt method in the framework classes.

It's important to emphasize that all languages based on the .NET framework have these framework classes available. That means that COBOL, for example, can use the same function mentioned above for getting a square root. This makes such base functionality widely available and highly consistent across languages. All calls to Sqrt look essentially the same (allowing for syntactical differences among languages) and access the same underlying code. Here are examples in Visual Basic.NET and C#:

```
' Example using Sqrt in Visual Basic.NET
Dim dblNumber As Double = 200
Dim dblSquareRoot As Double
dblSquareRoot = System.Math.Sqrt(dblNumber)
Label1.Text = Cstr(dblSquareRoot)


' Same example in C#
Double dblNumber = 200;
Double dblSquareRoot;
dblSquareRoot = System.Math.Sqrt(dblNumber);
label1.Text = Double.ToString(dblSquareRoot);
```

Notice that the line using the Sqrt function is exactly the same in both languages.

> *As a side note, a programming shop can create their own classes for core functionality, such as globally available, already-compiled functions. This custom functionality can then be referenced in code the same way as built-in .NET functionality.*

Much of the functionality in the base framework classes resides in a vast namespace called System. The System.Math.Sqrt method was mentioned above. Here are just a few other examples of the subsections of the System namespace, which actually contains dozens of such subcategories:

Namespace	What it contains	Example Classes
System.Collections	Creation and management of various types of collections	Arraylist, Hashtable, SortedList
System.Data	Classes and types related to basic database management	DataSet, DataTable, DataColumn, SQLConnection, ADOConnection
System.Diagnostics	Classes to debug an application and to trace the execution of code	Debug, Trace
System.IO	Types which allow reading and writing to files and other data streams	File, FileStream, Path, StreamReader, StreamWriter
System.Math	Members to calculate common mathematical quantities, such as trigonometric and logarithmic functions	Sqrt (square root), Cos (cosine), Log (logarithm), Min (minimum)
System.Reflection	Capability to inspect metadata	Assembly, Module
System.Security	Types which enable security capabilities	Cryptography, Permissions, Policy

The list above merely begins to hint at the capabilities in the System namespace. Some of these namespaces are used in later examples in other chapters. For example, the System.Data namespace is covered extensively in Chapter 7.

User and Program Interfaces

At the top layer, .NET provides three ways to render and manage user interfaces (Windows Forms, Web Forms, and console applications), and one way to handle interfaces with remote components (Web Services).

User Interfaces

Windows Forms

Windows Forms (which, as previously mentioned, are often just called WinForms) is a more advanced and integrated way to do standard Win32 screens. Windows Forms is descended from the Windows Foundation Classes (WFC) originally created for J++, so this technology has been under development for a while.

All languages that work on the .NET Framework, including new versions of Visual Studio languages, will use the WinForms engine instead of whatever they are using now (MFC or direct Win32API calls in the case of C++, the VB forms engine in the case of Visual Basic). This provides a rich, unified set of controls and drawing functions for all languages, as well as a standard API for underlying Windows services for graphics and drawing. It effectively replaces the Windows graphical API, wrapping it in such a way that the developer normally has no need to go directly to the Windows API for any graphical or screen functions.

Windows Forms is actually part of the framework base classes – it's in the `System.Winforms` namespace. That makes it available to all languages that are based on the .NET Framework. Since Windows Forms duplicates the functionality of the VB forms engine, it gives every single .NET language the capability of doing forms just like Visual Basic. The drag-and-drop designer for Windows Forms (which is in Visual Studio.NET) can be used to create forms visually for use with any .NET language.

In Chapter 4 we will look at Windows Forms in more detail and note significant changes in Windows Forms versus older Visual Basic forms.

Changing the Tradeoffs for Client Applications Versus Browser-Based Applications

In the Windows DNA world, many internal corporate applications are made browser-based simply because of the cost of installing and maintaining a client application on hundreds or thousands of workstations. Windows Forms and the .NET framework have the potential to change the economics of these decisions. A WinForms-based application will be much easier to install and update than an equivalent Visual Basic client application today. With a simple XCOPY deployment and no registration issues, installation and updating become much easier.

That means that applications that need a rich user interface for a large number of users are more practical under Microsoft.NET than under Windows DNA. It may not be necessary to resort to browser-based applications just to save installation and deployment costs, thus extending the life of desktop-based applications.

Web Forms

A part of ASP.NET, Web Forms is a forms engine. It provides a web browser-based user interface. A user interface can also be rendered with the updated version of Active Server Pages, but Web Forms represent the next generation of web interface development, including drag-and-drop development.

Divorcing layout from logic, Web Forms consist of two parts – a template, which contains HTML-based layout information for all user interface elements, and a component, which contains all logic to be hooked to the UI. It's as if a standard Visual Basic form were split into two parts: one containing information on controls and their properties and layout, and the other containing the code. Just as in Visual Basic, the code operates "behind" the controls, with events in the controls activating event routines in the code.

To make this new UI concept work, Web Forms have lots of built-in intelligence. Controls on Web Forms run on the server but make their presence known on the client. This takes lots of coordination and behind-the-scenes activity. However, the end result is web interfaces that can look and behave very much like Win32 interfaces today, and the ability to produce such interfaces with a drag-and-drop design tool. These web interfaces can also have the intelligence to deal with different browsers, optimizing their output for each particular browser. Supported browsers cover a broad range. At the top end are advanced modern versions like Internet Explorer 5.5, which support DHTML. At the other end are simpler, less capable browsers on hardware such as wireless palmtop devices. Web Forms will render themselves appropriately on all of these.

As with Windows Forms, Web Forms will be available to all languages. The component handling logic for a form can be in any language that supports .NET. This brings complete, flexible web interface capability to a wide variety of languages.

Server Controls

Visual Basic developers are familiar with the idea of controls. They are the reusable user interface elements used to construct a form. The analogs in Web Forms are called **server controls**.

Server controls essentially create a proxy on the server for a user interface element that is on a Web Form or Active Server Page. The server-side control communicates with local logic as necessary, and then intelligently renders its own UI as HTML as necessary in any pages that are sent out containing the control. It also handles its own HTML responses, and incorporates the returned data.

Server controls need significant intelligence to render HTML for different levels of browsers, and to coordinate events with the client on which the page is running. A wide variety of controls are expected to ship with Visual Studio.NET, bringing web-based interfaces much closer to Win32 interfaces. Third parties are expected to add even more options for server-side controls. Tools vendors will have a brand-new market to attack.

One of the most important and amazing features of server-side controls is that they manage their own state. In ASP.NET, it is no longer necessary to write a lot of tedious code to reload state information into HTML controls every time a page is refreshed. Web Forms handle state by sending a tokenised (compressed) version of the state information to the client browser each time a page is sent. The page then posts that state information back to the server when changing the page. The server controls grab the state information, use or process it as necessary, and then send it out again with the next rendering of the page.

Chapter 6 introduces Web Forms in Visual Basic.NET. Server controls are discussed in detail, and an example application demonstrates how Web Forms are constructed. Other aspects of ASP.NET are extensively discussed in the book *A Preview of ASP+* (*Wrox Press, ISBN 1861004753*).

Console Applications

Though Microsoft doesn't emphasize the ability to write character-based applications, the .NET Framework does include an interface for such console apps. Batch processes, for example, can now have components integrated into them that are written to a console interface.

As with WinForms and Web Forms, this console interface is available for applications written in any .NET language. Writing character-based applications in previous versions of Visual Basic, for example, has always been a struggle because it was completely oriented around a GUI interface. Visual Basic.NET can be used for true console applications.

An introduction to console applications is included in Chapter 8.

Programmatic Interfaces

Web Services

Application development is moving into the next stage of decentralization. The oldest idea of an application is a piece of software that accesses basic operating system services, such as the file system and graphics system. Then we moved to applications, which used lots of base functionality from other, system-level applications, such as a database – this type of application added value by applying generic functionality to specific problems. The developer's job was to focus on adding business value, not on building the foundation.

Web Services represent the next step in this direction. In Web Services, software functionality becomes exposed as a service that doesn't care what the consumer of the service is (unless there are security considerations). Web Services allow developers to build applications by combining local and remote resources for an overall integrated and distributed solution.

In Microsoft.NET, Web Services are implemented as part of ASP.NET, (diagrammed at the top level of the .NET Framework in the first figure in this chapter), which handles all web interfaces. It allows programs to talk to each other directly over the web, using the SOAP standard. This capability requires very little additional work on the part of the developer compared to developing typical subroutines and functions. All that is needed is to indicate that a member should be included in the Web Services interface by marking it with a `<WebMethod>` attribute, and the .NET Framework takes care of the rest. This has the capacity to dramatically change the architecture of web applications, allowing services running all over the web to be integrated into a local application.

It is hard to over-emphasize the potential importance of Web Services. Consider, for example, the potential for Web Services to replace packaged software. A commercial software company could produce a Web Service that, for instance, calculates sales tax for every jurisdiction in the nation. A subscription to that Web Service could be sold to any company needing to calculate sales tax. The customer company then has no need to deploy the sales tax calculator because is it just called on the web. The company producing the sales tax calculator can dynamically update it to include new rates and rules for various jurisdictions, and their customers using the Web Service don't have to do anything to get these updates.

There are endless other possibilities. Stock tickers, weather information, current financial rates, shipping status information, and a host of other types of information could be exposed as a Web Service, ready for integration into any application that needs it.

Chapter 6 contains a detailed discussion of Web Services.

XML as the .NET "Meta-language"

Much of the underlying integration of .NET is accomplished with XML. For example, Web Services depends completely on XML for interfacing with remote objects. Looking at metadata usually means looking at an XML version of it.

ADO.NET, the successor to ADO, is heavily dependent on XML for remote representation of data. Essentially, when ADO.NET creates what it calls a **dataset** (a more complex successor to a recordset), the data is converted to XML for manipulation by ADO.NET. Then the changes to that XML are posted back to the datastore by ADO.NET when remote manipulation is finished. (Chapter 7 discusses ADO.NET and its use with XML in more detail.)

With XML as an "entry point" into so many areas of .NET, future integration opportunities are multiplied. Using XML to expose interfaces to .NET functions allows developers to tie components and functions together in new, unexpected ways. XML can be the glue that ties pieces together in ways that were never anticipated, both to Microsoft and non-Microsoft platforms.

The Role of COM

When the .NET Framework was first introduced, some uninformed journalists interpreted it as the death of COM. That is completely incorrect. COM is not going anywhere for a while. In fact, Windows will not boot without COM.

.NET integrates very well with COM-based software. Any COM component can be treated as a .NET component by native .NET components. The .NET Framework wraps COM components and exposes an interface that .NET components can work with. This is absolutely essential to the quick acceptance of .NET, because it makes .NET interoperable with a tremendous amount of older COM-based software.

Going in the other direction, the .NET Framework can expose .NET components with a COM interface. This allows older COM components to use .NET-based components as if they were developed using COM. (Chapter 9 discusses COM interoperability in more detail.)

No Internal Use of COM

It is important, however, to understand that native .NET components do not interface using COM. The CLR implements a new way for components to interface, one that is not COM-based. Use of COM is only necessary when interfacing to COM components produced by non-.NET tools.

Over a long span of time, the fact that .NET does not use COM internally may lead to the decline of COM. But that is for the very long term. For any immediate purposes, COM is definitely important.

The Role of DNA

Earlier in the chapter, we discussed the limitations of the current DNA programming model. These limitations are mostly inherent in the technologies used to implement DNA today, not in the overall structure or philosophy. There is nothing fundamentally wrong with the tiered approach to development specified by the DNA model. It was specifically developed to deal with the challenges in design and development of complex applications. Many of these design issues, such as the need to encapsulate business rules, or to provide for multiple user interface access points to a system, do not go away with .NET.

Applications developed in the .NET Framework will still, in many cases, use a DNA model to design the appropriate tiers. However, the tiers will be a lot easier to produce in .NET. The presentation tier will benefit from the new interface technologies, especially Web Forms for Internet development. The middle tier will require far less COM-related headaches to develop and implement. And richer, more distributed middle tier designs will be possible by using Web Services.

The architectural skills that experienced developers have learned in the DNA world are definitely still important and valuable in the .NET world.

Additional Benefits

The major benefits of Microsoft.NET discussed thus far can be summarized as:

- ❑ Faster development (less to do, the system handles more)
- ❑ Lots of built-in functionality through a rich object model
- ❑ More stable code through built-in, comprehensive memory management and use of prepackaged, widely-used functionality
- ❑ A variety of ways to interface and integrate with the outside world
- ❑ More reuse
- ❑ Easy to integrate different languages into one system
- ❑ Easier deployment

❑   Higher Scalability

❑   Easier to build sophisticated development tools

There are a couple of additional benefits that are worth mentioning.

Fewer Bugs – Whole Classes of Bugs will Hopefully Disappear

The architecture and capabilities of the CLR should wipe out whole classes of bugs. Memory leaks, failure to clean up at the end of execution, and other memory management related problems should become non-existent (assuming the developers of the CLR take care of their part). Instancing of classes is handled automatically, and they are managed throughout their lifecycle.

Potentially Better Performance

The built-in capabilities of the CLR are to be used almost universally. Microsoft knows that, for Microsoft.NET to succeed, these capabilities must be reliable and efficient, and they can invest the efforts of their very best architects and developers to make that happen.

This heavy investment in system-level code should have the result of speeding up performance for all but the most optimized applications. Critical and frequently used functions, no matter how ordinary, will usually be optimized to the hilt in the CLR.

Some Potential Downsides

Nothing comes completely for free. Here are a couple of ways in which there is a price to be paid to get the advantages of Microsoft.NET

Incompatibilities with Existing Code

Making languages work in this new framework usually means adjustment to the language syntax. This introduces compatibility problems in moving existing code into the .NET Framework. Visual Basic is a particular problem, as we shall see throughout this book.

Transparency of "Source Code"

The bytecodes in the Intermediate Language are much higher level than the processor instructions that programs are compiled into today. While we can disassemble a program in current environments, the assembler-based result is of limited use. .NET programs disassembled from IL, on the other hand, will more closely resemble actual source code. They will also contain the information needed to understand data structures. Such disassembled programs make algorithms and code processes more transparent than with current environments, making it more difficult to protect intellectual property. Microsoft may eventually build in some kind of encryption to remedy this problem, or perhaps third parties can introduce tools that "obfuscate" the code, but there are no known plans at this point.

The First Step – Visual Studio.NET

The first technology to be released in the Microsoft.NET framework will be the next generation of Visual Studio, which has been tagged Visual Studio.NET. It will include Visual Basic, Visual C++, and C# (the new language from Microsoft discussed below). Visual FoxPro is included in beta one of Visual Studio.NET, but the final status of Visual FoxPro as a .NET language is not known at the time this is being written.

Microsoft has been hinting for several months about what's going to be new in Visual Studio. Here are some of the confirmed changes and new features, as of beta one – keeping in mind that things can change before release.

Common IDE for All Languages

Microsoft has gradually been melding the Integrated Development Environment (IDE) for all their languages into one code base. In Visual Studio 6, Visual Basic was the last major holdout. That process is now complete, and the exact same IDE is to be used for all languages in the Visual Studio.NET suite.

However, a potentially bigger change is that Microsoft has completely opened up the IDE for other languages. Any third party language vendor can license the technology to place their language in the Visual Studio IDE and have the language work within the .NET framework. At least twenty languages are under consideration for such integration, including everything from Eiffel to COBOL.

Fully supporting a third party language in Visual Studio will require a lot of work. The vendor must create a compiler for the language that produces Intermediate Language bytecode instead of native machine code. The language's data types must be rationalized with the ones supported by the CLR. But the language vendor gets a lot in exchange, including arguably the most advanced development environment available anywhere, plus debugging tools and complete cross-language integration.

The Common Language Specification

Languages that fit into Visual Studio and Microsoft.NET must satisfy the **Common Language Specification** (**CLS**), which sets the constraints the languages must meet. If a language adheres to this spec, it gets an appropriate level of language interoperability.

All .NET Languages Are Not Created Equal

There are actually three categories of compliance to the CLS that .NET languages can subscribe to. They are:

- ❑ **Compliant producer** – The components in the language can be used by any other language.

- ❑ **Consumer** – The language can reuse classes produced in any other language. This basically means the ability to instantiate classes in the way that, for example, scripting languages can instantiate COM objects today, but no ability to create classes to be inherited by other code.

- ❑ **Extender** – Languages in this category can do more than just instantiate classes – they can also extend those classes using the inheritance features of Microsoft.NET.

All the confirmed languages in the Visual Studio suite (VB, VC++, C#) are expected to satisfy all three categories of the CLS. Third-party languages can select the combination of levels of compliance that make sense for them.

Management of Multiple Language Projects

Since any number of languages can now be used in a project, the Visual Studio IDE will now look at projects in terms of all the modules being used, no matter what language they are in. The project explorer (actually called the Solution Explorer) is the same no matter what combination of languages is used.

Absence of Visual Interdev

Visual Studio.NET does not have a separate piece identified as Visual Interdev. In effect, the functions of Visual Interdev have migrated into the IDE as a whole. There is an HTML editor, for example, which works across the whole IDE, and the new Solution Explorer bears a strong resemblance to the Resource window in Visual Interdev.

Also, Web Forms have basically taken the place of the drag-and-drop visual designer in Interdev, and they work with any language.

Impact on Visual Basic

We previously covered the limitations of Visual Basic in today's DNA programming model. To recap, they were:

- ❏   No capability for multithreading
- ❏   Lack of implementation inheritance and other object features
- ❏   Poor error-handling ability
- ❏   Poor integration with other languages such as C++
- ❏   No effective user interface for Internet-based applications

Since VB.NET is built on top of the .NET framework, all of these shortcomings have been eliminated. Visual Basic basically piggybacks on the stuff that was going to be implemented anyway for C++, C# and third-party .NET languages.

In fact, VB gets the most extensive changes of any existing language in the Visual Studio suite. These changes pull VB in line with other languages in terms of data types, calling conventions, error handling and, most importantly, object-orientation.

It is not yet definite what the new Visual Basic will be called, but the current favorite is Visual Basic.NET. This label will be used throughout this book, sometimes abbreviated as VB.NET.

Chapter 3 covers the changes to Visual Basic, especially the syntax changes, in detail. It will discuss several incompatibilities along with new features and capabilities. The last chapter of the book will cover some recommendations for preparing for Visual Basic.NET with programming conventions and design considerations in current VB6 code.

Microsoft intends to supply a conversion tool, which will assist in porting VB6 projects to .NET, but it will not do everything required. There will be some areas where the conversion tool merely places a note that indicates something needs to be done. And there are likely to be areas where it fails to realize a change is needed.

"How Does .NET Affect Me?"

One of the reasons you're probably reading this book is because you want to know how Visual Basic.NET will affect you. Here are some of most important implications.

A Spectrum of Programming Models

In existing Microsoft-based development tools, there are a couple of quantum leaps required to move from simple to complex. And sometimes the complex programming models are required to get more power. A developer can start simply with Active Server Pages and VB Script, but when those become cumbersome, it's a big leap to learn component-based, three-tier development in Visual Basic. And it's another quantum leap to become proficient in C++, ATL, and related technologies for system-level work.

A key benefit of Visual Basic.NET and the .NET Framework is that there exists a more gradual transition in programming models from simple to full power. Active Server Pages are more structured than before, and provide on-the-fly compilation to get better performance, and they use real Visual Basic code instead of VBScript. Visual Basic itself becomes a tool with wider applicability, as it becomes easy to do a web interface with Web Forms, and it also becomes possible to do advanced object-oriented designs. Even system-level capabilities, such as NT Services can be done with Visual Basic.NET. Old reasons for using another language, such as lack of performance or flexibility, are mostly gone. Visual Basic will do almost anything that other .NET languages can do.

This increases the range of applicability of Visual Basic. It can be used all the way from "scripts" (which are actually compiled on the fly) written with a text editor, up through sophisticated component and web programming in one of the most advanced development environments available.

Reducing Barriers to Internet Development

With current tools, programming for the Internet requires a completely different programming model than programming systems that will be run locally. The differences are most apparent in user interface construction, but that's not the only area of difference. Objects constructed for access by Active Server Pages, for example, must support Variant parameters, but objects constructed for access by Visual Basic forms can have parameters of any data type. Accessing databases over the Internet requires using technologies like RDS instead of the ADO connections that local programming typically uses.

The .NET Framework erases many of these differences. Programming for the Internet and programming for local systems are much more alike in .NET than with today's systems. Differences remain – Web Forms still have significant differences from Windows Forms, for example. But many other differences, such as the way data is handled, are much more unified under .NET.

A big result of this similarity of programming models is to make Internet programming more practical and accessible. With functionality for the Internet designed in from the start, developers don't have to know as much or do as much to product Internet systems with the .NET Framework.

Libraries of Pre-Written Functionality

The evolution of Windows development languages, including Visual Basic, has been in the direction of providing more and more built-in functionality so that developers can ignore the foundations and concentrate on solving business problems. The .NET Framework continues this trend.

One particularly important implication is that the .NET Framework extends the trend of developers spending less time writing code and more time discovering how to do something with pre-written functionality. Mainframe COBOL programmers could learn everything they ever needed to know about COBOL in a year or two, and very seldom need to consult reference materials after that. In contrast, today's Visual Basic developers already spend a significant portion of their time digging through reference material to figure out how to do something that they may never do again. The sheer expanse of functionality available, plus the rapidly changing pace, makes it a requirement that an effective developer also be a researcher. Microsoft.NET accelerates this trend, and will probably increase the ratio of research time to coding time for a typical developer.

Easier Deployment

A major design goal in Microsoft.NET is to simplify installation and configuration of software. With "DLL Hell" mostly gone, and with installation of compiled modules a matter of a simple file copy, developers should be able to spend less time worrying about deployment of their applications, and more time concentrating on the functionality of their systems.

Cautions

No one knows for sure if Microsoft.NET will live up to it's billing. Many of us were surprised at PDC to see how far Microsoft had progressed with this very ambitious effort, but there remains a lot to be done. We are even more optimistic after seeing the stability and completeness of beta one for Visual Studio.NET. But it's important to recognize that building in the intelligence that will be required for Microsoft.NET to work is a huge undertaking, and there are risks that some pieces of it might take another generation or two to be truly ready for prime time.

There is also lots of uncertainty in the time frames that will be required before the first .NET technology rolls into production status. In the meantime, it's important to understand enough about .NET to know when it makes sense to look seriously at using it, and to orient our current development practices in ways that will make eventual migration to .NET simpler and faster.

Summary

This chapter has provided some background to the whole development strategy regarding Microsoft's .NET framework, and in particular how this will affect VB developers. It is clear that this innovation will provide a raft of new challenges for such developers, but provides them with greatly enhanced functionality to work with, in particular the ability to develop web-based applications more easily. In the next chapter we move on to take a closer look at the VisualBasic.NET IDE and some of the key syntactical changes which VB developers need to grasp.

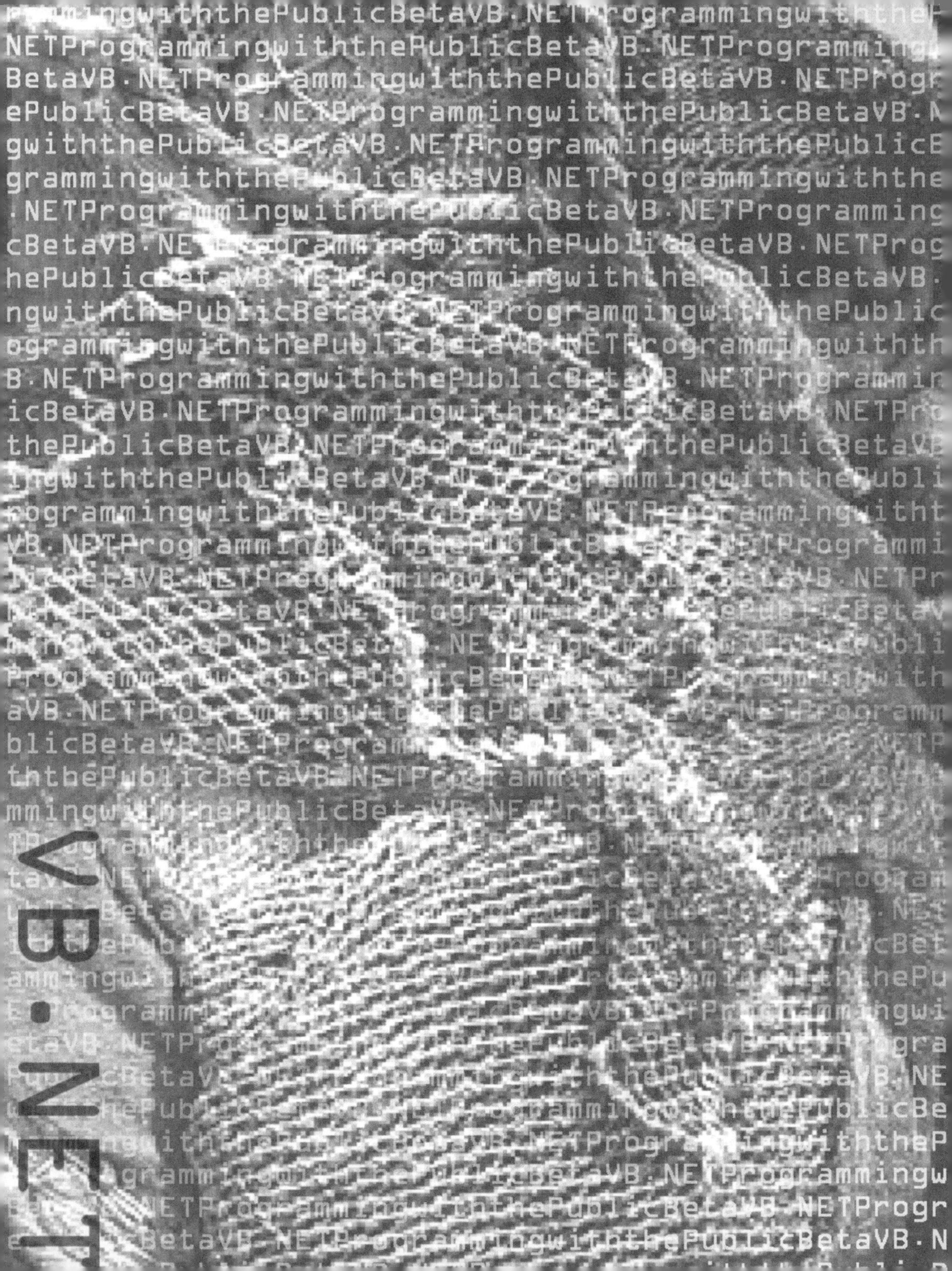
VB.NET
VB.NET Programming with the Public Beta

New IDE and Language Features of VB.NET

3

Visual Basic.NET preserves VB6's general approach to programming with a WYSIWYG development environment, click-through forms to get at the underlying code, and so forth. However, VB.NET introduces quite a number of exciting changes that help make VB a premier development tool for the .NET platform.

These include:

❑ New IDE features

❑ Full object-orientation

❑ Data type changes

❑ The introduction of namespaces

❑ Structured error handling

❑ A new threading model

❑ Various other syntactic changes to the language

In this chapter we'll discuss most of these changes, though we'll cover the new object-oriented features separately in Chapter 5.

It is also important to understand the close relationship between VB.NET and the .NET Framework that we discussed in Chapter 2. VB.NET applications always make heavy use of the .NET Framework, as it is this that compiles and runs our applications. Additionally, it is virtually impossible to create any application that does not make use of the .NET system class libraries – another key part of the .NET Framework.

In Chapter 1 we built a simple "Hello World" application with very little explanation. In this chapter we'll revisit that application, examining its composition in detail. In this way we'll be able to get a good understanding of the differences and similarities between a VB6 application and a VB.NET application. We won't get into too much detail regarding the GUI, however, as that topic will be covered thoroughly in Chapter 4.

Afterwards we'll move on to discuss the various new features of the VS.NET IDE. This new IDE supports all the .NET languages, including VB, C#, and C++, and offers a wide range of powerful capabilities for us as developers.

By that point we'll have a good understanding of a basic VB.NET application and the development environment, so we'll be ready to explore the language and syntax changes to the VB language itself. There are quite a number of changes and enhancements – some very useful and others that are less so, but which are necessary for operation in the .NET environment. In some cases we'll show both VB6 and VB.NET examples to better illustrate the differences and similarities.

So, without further ado, let's revisit the "Hello World" program from Chapter 1.

A Tour of the Hello World Program

Open up the VS.NET environment. At the start page we should be presented with the options to open a recent, existing or new project:

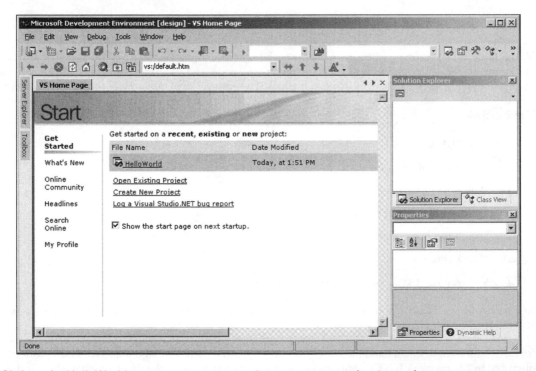

Click on the HelloWorld project to open it up in the environment and we're ready to go.

If you don't have the HelloWorld project, either return to Chapter 1 to recreate it, download the code from www.wrox.com, or just follow along with the code in the book. We'll cover everything pretty thoroughly, so it probably isn't critical to have the project right in front of you.

Let's walk through the code behind Form1. Bring up the code window by selecting Form1 in the Solution Explorer on the right side of the window and then clicking the View Code button at the top of the explorer window.

Declarations

Not surprisingly, at the top of the module we find a declarations section.

One thing to note is that there's no explicit declaration, such as `Option Explicit`, to force all variables to be declared. This is because `Option Explicit` is the *default* setting, finally. If, for some reason, we don't want to declare all our variables we can add a line such as:

```
Option Explicit Off
```

> This is not recommended as it will disable the mechanism that ensures variables are declared, allowing us to more easily introduce bugs due to misspelling our variables.

There are other options we might specify here as well, and these are discussed later in this chapter.

Namespaces

At the top of the code window we see the following lines of code:

```
Imports System.ComponentModel
Imports System.Drawing
Imports System.WinForms
```

As we mentioned earlier, all VB.NET programs make use of the .NET system class libraries. These statements import the **namespaces** for three of these libraries. Namespaces are a way of grouping related classes together for convenience and they are a key part of the .NET Framework since they provide organization to the huge number of classes in the system class libraries.

Namespaces are also an important tool for us to use in our applications. Creating namespaces allows us to organize our own classes, increasing the readability and maintainability of our code.

We'll discuss namespaces in more detail later in this chapter. For now it is enough to know that we've made the classes from the `System.ComponentModel`, `System.Drawing`, and `System.WinForms` namespaces available to the code behind Form1.

In reality, the classes from the entire system class library are available for our use. The `Imports` statement just allows us to avoid typing the entire path to each class. We'll discuss this in more detail later in the chapter.

Form Declaration, Initialization, and Termination

The remaining code is specific to our form – declaring the form, initializing it, and then making sure it can be properly destroyed.

Forms as Classes

The next line of code declares a class named `Form1`:

```
Public Class Form1
```

This is interesting. Since VB4 we've been able to treat a form module like a class, but form modules have never really *been* classes.

Now, in VB.NET, forms really are classes. They are just classes that happen to create a window and work with controls placed on that window. Since we've been able to treat forms as classes for some time now, this isn't a huge change.

On the other hand, up to now we've been able to refer to a form in two different ways. The first way is to use the form "directly", which would be done using the following VB6 code:

```
Form1.Show
```

This is referred to as interacting with the "default instance" of a form. We didn't explicitly create a `Form1` object – the VB runtime created the instance on our behalf behind the scenes. This was nice because it was simple, but this syntax is really a holdover from far earlier, since it originated with VB1 or thereabouts.

We could also *explicitly* create an instance of the form using the following VB6 code:

```
Dim MyForm As Form1

Set MyForm = New Form1
MyForm.Show
```

In this case, we've manually created an object of type `Form1`. Our code then interacts with this specific instance of the form. This type of syntax was required to support MDI forms, since an MDI parent could contain several child windows all of the same type and we needed some way to create more than one instance of a given form.

The unfortunate side effect of having these two ways of creating a form was the dreaded bug created by the following VB6 code:

```
Dim MyForm As Form1

Set MyForm = New Form1
Form1.Show
```

Notice how we create an explicit instance of `Form1`, then turn around and use the default instance to display the form. Of course the form that is displayed is the default instance – *not* the instance we explicitly created, and now we've got this extra form floating around in memory. This is one of the most common bugs in novice programmers' VB applications – all caused by the inconsistent treatment of a form module as both object and class.

VB.NET resolves this issue by always treating forms as classes. Now the only valid approach is to treat a form as a class and to create an instance of the form to interact with. This is illustrated by the following VB.NET code:

```
Dim MyForm As Form1

MyForm = New Form1()
MyForm.Show()
```

If we've typically created applications using the default instances of forms, this new approach will take a little getting used to. For those who regularly work with explicit instances of forms, there is no real change involved in the idea of a form being a class.

Forms Created by Inheritance

The next line of code uses the new keyword, `Inherits`:

```
Inherits System.WinForms.Form
```

This statement indicates that `Form1` is actually a subclass of the `System.WinForms.Form` class. This class is the root of all .NET GUI forms; any form we create in VB.NET will be inherited from this base class.

Many of the behaviors we expect from forms are actually implemented in this base class, meaning we don't need to implement them in our own forms. These behaviors include:

- ❑ Activation/deactivation
- ❑ Closing
- ❑ Detecting mouse clicks and mouse movements
- ❑ Drag and drop functionality
- ❑ Getting and losing focus
- ❑ Key press events
- ❑ Menu handling
- ❑ Form movement and resizing
- ❑ Managing the controls on a form

Also, this base form class implements the events that we typically associate with a Windows form, including:

- ❑ `Click` and `DoubleClick`
- ❑ `Resize`
- ❑ `LostFocus`

and many more.

Because our `Form1` class is a subclass of `System.WinForms.Form`, we automatically gain all these behaviors and events. We can use them as they are, or we can override them to alter their behavior as necessary.

Inheritance and overriding are discussed more thoroughly in Chapter 5.

77

The Constructor Method

Because `Form1` is actually a class, it has a **constructor** method. Constructor methods are also new to VB.NET. The constructor method is called as an instance of the class is created, somewhat like the `Class_Initialize` event in previous versions of VB.

In VB.NET, constructor methods are always named `New`. Here's the `New` method for `Form1`:

```
Public Sub New()
    MyBase.New

    Form1 = Me

    'This call is required by the Win Form Designer.
    InitializeComponent

    'TODO: Add any initialization after the InitializeComponent() call
End Sub
```

The first thing that all constructor methods *must* do is call the constructor in their base class. If we try to move this line of code later in the routine we'll get a syntax error.

> *Actually VB.NET will automatically call the base class constructor for us in many cases, so we don't need to write this line. This is discussed in more detail in Chapter 5.*

A class' base class is known by the keyword `MyBase` – just like the current instance of any class is known by the keyword `Me`. So to call the base class's constructor we have the line:

```
MyBase.New
```

The next line is very odd, since it appears to reference a `Form1` variable that is not declared:

```
Form1 = Me
```

The variable `Form1` is actually declared – it is just declared in a collapsed block of code as we'll see shortly. `Form1` is declared as type `System.WinForms.Form`, and is declared within our class module to make it possible to write code that *appears* to interact with the default instance of our form.

In other words, this line of code makes the keyword `Me` and the variable `Form1` both refer to the current form, so code like this is valid within the context of the form:

```
Form1.Text = "My caption"
```

and it does the exact same thing as:

```
Me.Text = "My caption"
```

This is just a nice touch to help increase the compatibility with existing VB code.

The constructor code then calls the `InitializeComponent` method – a call that is required for the form to work properly. Again the code for `InitializeComponent` is hidden inside a section of collapsed code, as we'll see momentarily.

Following this method call is a TODO comment, which marks the location where we can add our own code to do whatever we want as the form comes into being. Writing code here is very comparable to writing code in the Class_Initialize or Form_Load methods in VB6.

The TODO comment will also be listed in the Task List window. This is discussed in more detail later in the chapter.

The Dispose Method

If New is somewhat comparable to Class_Initialize or Form_Load, then it should come as no surprise that we also have a method, which is similar to Class_Terminate or Form_Unload. This method is named Dispose and it is called when the form is being destroyed, just like the Form_Unload method was in previous versions of VB:

```
'Form overrides dispose to clean up the component list.
Overrides Public Sub Dispose()
    MyBase.Dispose
    components.Dispose
End Sub
```

Again we see that this method interacts with the base class by calling its Dispose method. This is important, as it allows the code in the base class to perform any required clean-up before the form is destroyed. We also call the Dispose method on a variable named components. This is another variable that is declared in the collapsed code section, which we'll discuss next.

Windows Form Designer Generated Code

When the VS.NET IDE created our form, it automatically generated all the code we've seen so far. It also generated another section of code that we normally never need to see or interact with. This section of code is collapsed by default:

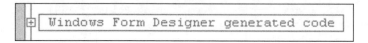

Clicking on the plus (+) symbol expands this collapsed block of code, which is called a **region**.

In fact, to the left of most of our class and method declarations, we see a minus symbol. Clicking on this will collapse our own code into a box similar to this one.

The code in this region is generated and maintained by the VS.NET IDE on our behalf.

> **Because this code is automatically created and maintained, we should never directly edit this code because this can cause unpredictable and undesirable side effects within the IDE.**

Typically we don't need to see this code or worry about what is going on within it. However, since we're in the process of learning how VB.NET works, it is worth walking through this hidden code once just to get a feel for what goes on inside.

As we look at this code it will become apparent that we could create a VB.NET form without the VS.NET IDE. Everything required to make the form work is entirely in code – nothing is hidden in a separate FRX file or anything like that. Of course the IDE makes development so easy it would be hard to give up, but it is interesting to consider that we could have created this entire application by just using Notepad.

Click on the plus symbol to expand this section of code. We can see how the code creates instances of the various controls on the form and sets their positions, initial values and so forth:

```
#Region " Windows Form Designer generated code "

    'Required by the Windows Form Designer
    Private components As System.ComponentModel.Container
    Private WithEvents Button1 As System.WinForms.Button
    Private WithEvents TextBox1 As System.WinForms.TextBox

    Dim WithEvents Form1 As System.WinForms.Form

    'NOTE: The following procedure is required by the Windows Form Designer
    'It can be modified using the Windows Form Designer.
    'Do not modify it using the code editor.
    Private Sub InitializeComponent()
        Me.components = New System.ComponentModel.Container()
        Me.Button1 = New System.WinForms.Button()
        Me.TextBox1 = New System.WinForms.TextBox()

        '@design Me.TrayHeight = 0
        '@design Me.TrayLargeIcon = False
        '@design Me.TrayAutoArrange = True
        Button1.Location = New System.Drawing.Point(24, 64)
        Button1.Size = New System.Drawing.Size(75, 23)
        Button1.TabIndex = 1
        Button1.Text = "Show text"

        TextBox1.Location = New System.Drawing.Point(16, 24)
        TextBox1.Text = "TextBox1"
        TextBox1.TabIndex = 0
        TextBox1.Size = New System.Drawing.Size(144, 20)
        Me.Text = "Form1"
        Me.AutoScaleBaseSize = New System.Drawing.Size(5, 13)

        Me.Controls.Add(Button1)
        Me.Controls.Add(TextBox1)
    End Sub

#End Region
```

Region Directive

The region of code is bounded at the top by a `#Region` directive and at the bottom by an `#End Region` directive. These directives allow the code editor to understand what code is to be included when this section is collapsed or expanded. The `#Region` directive also takes an argument – the text that is to be displayed in the box when the region is collapsed:

```
#Region " Windows Form Designer generated code "
```

The `Region` directive is a powerful tool that we can use to help make our code more manageable, or even to create an initial outline for our application.

Variable Declarations

Within the bounds of this region we find the declarations of those variables that were used earlier – `Form1` and `components`. Also declared as variables are the button and text box controls we placed on the form:

```
'Required by the Windows Form Designer
Private components As System.ComponentModel.Container
Private WithEvents Button1 As System.WinForms.Button
Private WithEvents TextBox1 As System.WinForms.TextBox

Dim WithEvents Form1 As System.WinForms.Form
```

Notice too that the `Form1` variable is declared using the `WithEvents` keyword. This ensures that any events that are raised by the form are echoed back into our code via the `Form1` variable just as they are with the `Me` keyword.

The same is true with the two control variables, `Button1` and `TextBox1`. These controls will very likely raise events and we want to be able to catch those events within our form so we can process them as needed.

InitializeComponent Method

In this section of code we also find the `InitializeComponent` method that we saw called earlier from the `New` method.

True to its name, this method initializes our form – first by creating instances of the constituent objects such as the button and textbox controls:

```
Me.components = New System.ComponentModel.Container()
Me.Button1 = New System.WinForms.Button()
Me.TextBox1 = New System.WinForms.TextBox()
```

It also has some special comments which act as directives for the IDE regarding where to position the form within the IDE:

```
'@design Me.TrayHeight = 0
'@design Me.TrayLargeIcon = False
'@design Me.TrayAutoArrange = True
```

Since these are not valid VB code, they are commented out. The `'@` marks the beginning of a special IDE comment – ignored by the compiler, but used by the IDE for display purposes.

From there, the initialization moves on to set the required properties on the `Button1` and `TextBox1` controls:

```
Button1.Location = New System.Drawing.Point(24, 64)
Button1.Size = New System.Drawing.Size(75, 23)
Button1.TabIndex = 1
```

```
Button1.Text = "Show text"

TextBox1.Location = New System.Drawing.Point(16, 24)
TextBox1.Text = "TextBox1"
TextBox1.TabIndex = 0
TextBox1.Size = New System.Drawing.Size(144, 20)
```

This really illustrates how forms created using the WinForms technology are entirely generated via code. While all this code is created for us by the IDE – it is pretty obvious that we could create a form in a simple text editor like Notepad if we wanted to. Pretty cool stuff!

Similarly, the form itself is also initialized:

```
Me.Text = "Form1"
Me.AutoScaleBaseSize = New System.Drawing.Size(5, 13)
```

Finally, the constituent controls are added to the `Controls` collection:

```
Me.Controls.Add(Button1)
Me.Controls.Add(TextBox1)
```

This collection is managed within the `System.WinForms.Form` base class and is available to all forms that inherit from that base class.

While all this code is generated and maintained on our behalf by the IDE, it's still good to have some basic understanding of what is going on behind the scenes. All of this sort of thing was also done in previous versions of Visual Basic, but it was entirely hidden within the VB runtime. Now we can, if we choose, see what is going on throughout the entire process of creating and initializing a form. This can make debugging much easier.

Event Handler Code

We're almost done with the code in our simple application. The only thing left is the code that we wrote to handle the `Click` event from `Button1`:

```
Protected Sub Button1_Click(ByVal sender As Object, _
                            ByVal e As System.EventArgs)
  MsgBox(TextBox1.Text, MsgBoxStyle.Information, "Test")
End Sub
```

While very similar to the type of event handler code we'd expect in VB6, there are some differences. In VB6 the code would have been as follows:

```
Private Sub Command1_Click()
  MsgBox Text1.Text, vbInformation, "Test"
End Sub
```

Of course, there's the obvious and trivial difference that, in VB6, our command button was named `Command1`, while in VB.NET the command button is `Button1`. Several control names have been changed from VB6 to VB.NET – this is something to be aware of, but also something that is pretty inconsequential.

More importantly, however, is the fact that the `Button1_Click` event handler accepts a couple of parameters. `Click` event handlers didn't accept parameters in VB6 – in fact *most* event handlers didn't accept parameters. In VB.NET, however, *all* event handlers accept two parameters:

Parameter	Description
`sender As Object`	This argument always contains a reference to the object that raised the event we are receiving. This means that our event handler may be called from more than one object – for instance, our `Click` event could be attached to more than one control – so we can use this parameter to tell which control raised the event.
`e As EventArgs`	This argument contains any arguments the sending object wanted to provide us. For a `Click` event there are no arguments, but for events such as `OnMouseMove` we'll be provided with the coordinates of the mouse pointer.

Things are actually a bit more complex than this. Sometimes `sender` *is declared as a specific type of object, and sometimes* `e` *is of a type that is a subclass of* `EventArgs`. *Still, the general formula of receiving two parameters is consistent throughout all of .NET.*

By having all event handlers accept two parameters, we gain a great deal of consistency in our code. Any event handler can count on knowing where the event came from – via the `sender` parameter, and if any further information is required we know it will be contained in the `EventArgs` object.

The other difference worth noting is that we called `MsgBox` like this in VB6:

```
MsgBox TextBox1, vbInformation, "Test"
```

While in VB.NET, the parameter passed to the `Show` property of `MsgBox` is within parentheses:

```
MsgBox(TextBox1.Text, MsgBoxStyle.Information, "Test")
```

The .NET system class libraries also include a new way to invoke a message box:

```
MessageBox.Show(TextBox1.Text, "Test", messagebox.IconInformation)
```

This is virtually identical to the `MsgBox` command from VB, but is not VB-specific.

The `MessageBox` class comes from the `System.WinForms` namespace, so that namespace must be referenced within the project for this to work. The VB `MsgBox` class comes from the `Microsoft.VisualBasic` namespace, which is automatically referenced by VB.NET projects and so is always available. We'll discuss referencing and importing libraries such as `System.WinForms` later in this chapter.

Throughout this book we'll use a little of each syntax. Neither offers a clear advantage over the other and there is some benefit in becoming familiar with both approaches.

Parentheses are now always required for procedure, method, and function calls that accept parameters. They are typically inserted by the IDE even when a method doesn't accept parameters.

While this is not a huge change, it is pervasive and it can take some getting used to before new habits form.

This quick tour through the code behind our simple "Hello World" application has shown some similarities and some differences between VB.NET and prior versions of VB. Next we'll take a look at the new VS.NET IDE.

New IDE Features

The development environment for VB.NET is Visual Studio.NET – an environment shared with the other major .NET languages, C#, JScript, and C++.

For many years now we've been hearing that the IDEs for the major development languages would merge together. In Visual Studio 6.0 we got closer, since the VID and J++ IDE was common and had a very similar look and feel to the VB IDE. Now, with VS.NET the promise of a unified development environment is finally a reality.

As we might expect, merging all these languages into the same IDE makes the IDE itself pretty complex. There are a lot of features and capabilities built into the environment – some are of more use than others. Fortunately, for the most part we only need to see or interact with the parts of the IDE that we find useful.

Home Page

Let's quickly go back to the home page by clicking on the VS Home Page tab:

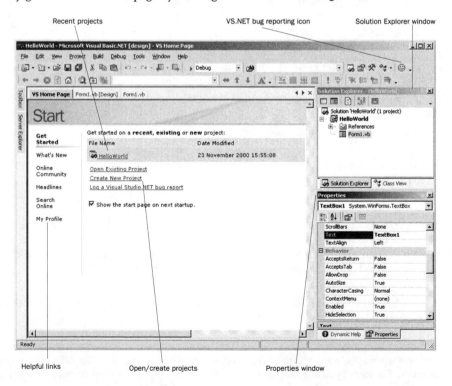

In the center of the display is the main window, which includes a list of helpful links, including the link to edit our profile. In this area we also find a list of recently opened projects, each one a link, which we can click on to quickly open that project and begin work. Below that list are links that allow us to open existing projects, create a new project, or log a VS.NET bug report (another way to do this is to click the smiley face icon in the toolbar in the upper right). All these links make the IDE much more like a browser.

Docking Windows

On the right-hand side we see both the Solution Explorer and Properties windows. We'll cover these in a bit, but first notice that both of these windows have tabs at the bottom. Along with the Solution Explorer we can also see a tab for a Class View, and along with the Properties window we have a tab for Dynamic Help.

This is a major feature of the VS.NET IDE – the ability to dock and arrange windows – including docking several windows in the same location such that they are displayed via tabs like we see here.

Using the mouse, we can click and drag the title bar for the Solution Explorer out into the main window, undocking it and making a free-floating window. Notice that the Class View tab comes along for the ride:

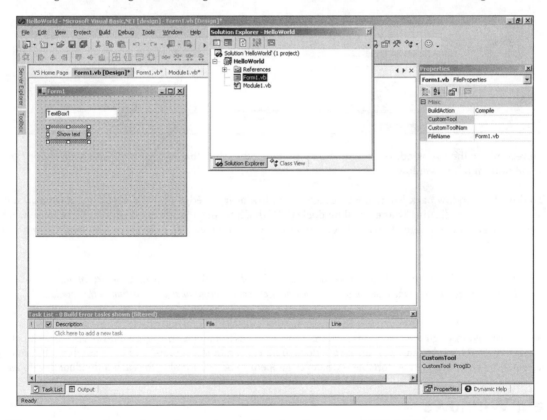

When we say free-floating here, the window really is free. It is not an MDI child window – so it can be dragged totally outside of the VS.NET main window.

To separate the Class View into its own window, click and drag the Class View tab away from the Solution Explorer window – now we have two free-floating windows:

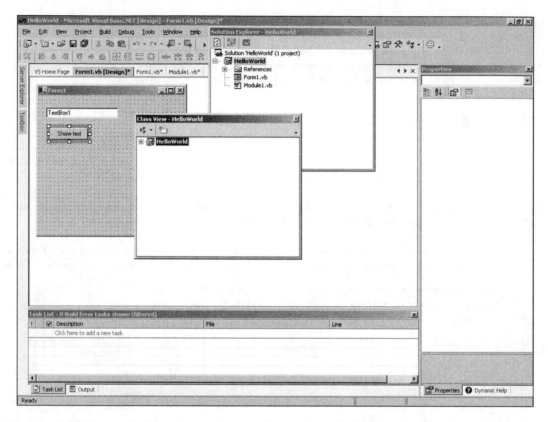

To recombine the two windows, drag one on top of the other such that they display with a tab-shaped outline at the bottom of the window.

To dock the window back where it was, drag the window near the edge of the VS.NET main window until an outline appears indicating where it will be docked. With a little playing it will be apparent that these windows can be docked and combined in a wide variety of ways. Even the tabs can be rearranged by dragging them to left or right.

It can take a bit of practice to get windows to dock and combine as desired. One tip is to keep in mind that the process keys off the location of the mouse pointer, not the original size or position of the window being dragged.

As we proceed through the rest of this section, we won't focus too much on *where* windows appear as much as what they do. This is because we can always dock, undock, combine, separate, and even autohide the windows to make the environment comfortable – whatever happens to be comfortable for each individual developer.

Main Windows

The VS.NET IDE provides us with access to a wide range of capabilities. Most of these capabilities have associated windows that can be docked and combined as we see fit.

To view any of the windows that are not visible, simply choose the View menu and then select the window to be displayed. All of them have default start locations, but can be moved as needed.

Graphical Designers

When we have a project open and are working with that project's files, we'll typically be focused on the large main window in the center of the VS.NET display. This is the area where the **designer** will be displayed for our particular file.

Designers were introduced in VB5 and were heavily used in VB6, but they really come of age in VS.NET. Any time we edit a file – be it creating a WYSIWYG form, editing code, or even creating a non-visual item like a regular class – we are presented with a designer appropriate for that type of file.

One of the most commonly used designers is the graphical Windows Forms designer, which allows us to drag and drop controls onto a form. However, there are several other types of designer that we'll encounter when working on projects in VB.NET. These include:

❑   Windows Forms designer – for creation of GUI interfaces

❑   Web Forms designer – for creation of web interfaces

❑   Component designer – for creation of non-visual components

❑   XML designer – for creation of XML documents

> *The Web Forms designer is used for creating ASP.NET applications. Such applications can be created in many languages, including VB.NET; hence two different groups of people use it – the ASP developer moving to ASP.NET and the VB developer moving to VB.NET to do web development.*

And ,of course, the regular code designer where we author our code. This understands a great many types of code, including:

❑   Visual Basic

❑   C#

❑   C++

❑   HTML and DHTML

❑   CSS files

❑   XML

Each of these file types gets automatic color-coding, and most get auto-formatting, auto-completion, and IntelliSense functionality.

Tabbed Navigation

Along the top of the designer window we'll find a row of tabs:

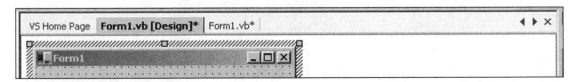

We've used these before – they let us easily navigate through all the open designer windows to find the one we need. Additionally, we can press *Ctrl-Tab* and *Shift-Ctrl-Tab* to cycle back and forth through the open designers.

Component Tray

In previous versions of VB we had the concept of an "invisible" control – an ActiveX control (or VBX if we go way back) that is visible on a form at design time but is invisible at runtime.

VB.NET formalizes and generalizes this concept through the use a new designer feature – the **component tray**. The component tray is a separate region in each graphical designer (WinForms, Web Forms, Component, etc.) where invisible controls are displayed.

We can see this in our `HelloWorld` application by adding a `Timer` control. Double-click on Form1 in the Solution Explorer to bring up the form designer. Then hold the mouse over the Toolbox tab on the far left until the Toolbox expands. Locate the Timer control and double-click on it.

> *The Toolbox may be pinned out as well, in which case we don't need to expand it. Given the immense flexibility of the IDE in terms of positioning and configuration of windows it is impossible to know for sure that any description of window access will apply to every developer's environment as they may have changed windows around in many ways.*

The result is that a `Timer` control is added to our form – but not directly on the form as it was in the past. Instead, it is displayed in a new region at the bottom of the designer:

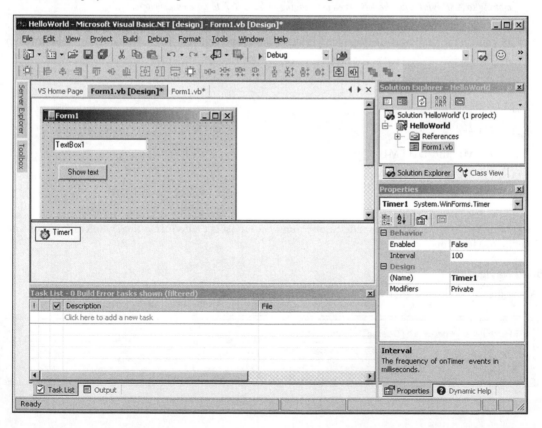

`Timer1`, the new control, is now part of our form just as much as the `Button` and `TextBox` controls. The only difference is where it is displayed in the designer. Notice how the Properties window to the right is displaying the control properties – allowing us to view and manipulate them just like any other control.

The component tray is a particularly nice feature when working with invisible controls, since we don't need to worry about them being obscured behind other controls – they are always available for our use.

This is even more important when using the **component designer**. This designer is geared towards the creation of non-visual components (somewhat comparable to COM DLLs), and so there's no WYSIWYG concept. However, the graphical designer *does* provide the component tray, so it is possible to drag and drop controls or other components onto the designer and thus make them available for use by the code within the component.

Solution Explorer

By default, on the right-hand side of the main VS.NET display we have the Solution Explorer, which is similar to the Project Explorer in previous versions of VB. The Solution Explorer is a bit more advanced, however, since it allows us to construct solutions out of several different projects – including those written in different languages. This makes it very easy to debug and jump between components.

In VB6 we had the concept of a **project group**, which was a group of related projects that could all be opened in the IDE at once. A **solution** is similar in concept, but is more advanced since it allows many different types of project, in many different languages – and even allows us to include arbitrary miscellaneous files that aren't in a formal project at all.

Notice how the Solution Explorer displays our HelloWorld solution, with the HelloWorld project inside:

The HelloWorld project itself is composed of some References and our Form1.vb code module, which contains our `Form1` class.

Files and Extensions

The Form1 file has a vb extension. In VB6 this would have had an `frm` extension instead, indicating it is a form. However, we now know that all forms in VB.NET are just classes, so there's no need to distinguish between various types of VB source files. In fact, all source files containing VB code will end in a vb extension regardless of whether they contain forms, classes, or general code.

> **All VB.NET code modules end in a vb extension, and any code module can contain more than one class.**

Another new feature of VB.NET is the ability to have more than one class in a code module. In previous versions of VB, physical files could only contain one code module – one class, one form, etc. In VB.NET, a physical file can contain several classes, forms or a mix of different types of code – as long as it is all written in the same language.

Technically it is possible to create an entire application in a single code file, including classes, forms and modules all in that one file. This approach is probably not ideal since it makes navigating through code more difficult.

References

The Solution Explorer shows a References entry under our project. This is where we manage the assemblies or components referenced by our project – much like the Project I References menu option in VB6. In fact, there is still a Project I Add References menu option in VB.NET.

To add a reference to our project, we can either right-click on the References item in the Solution Explorer, or we can choose the Project I Add References menu option. Either way, we'll be presented with a references dialog:

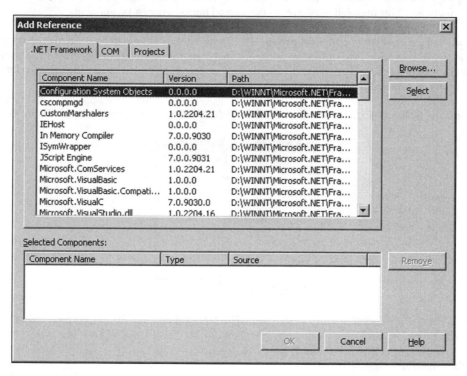

This dialog allows us to add references for .NET Framework components, COM objects, or other projects we're working on.

Once a reference has been added, it will be listed in the Solution Explorer under the References entry. To remove a reference, simply right-click on the reference to be removed and then choose the Remove option.

Adding a reference makes the namespaces and classes within the assembly or component available for use by our code. Namespaces and how they are used are discussed later in this chapter.

Properties Window

Beneath the Solution Explorer on the right-hand side of the VS.NET main window is the Properties window. This is very similar to the Properties window in previous versions of VB. It displays the properties for the currently selected object in the main window, allowing us to alter these properties at design time in a graphical fashion. The properties may be sorted or organized in different ways by clicking on the icons in the mini-toolbar within the Properties window.

In the Solution Explorer, double-click on Form1 to bring up its designer and then click on Button1, the Show text button. This will cause the Properties window to display the properties for that object:

As this window is very, very similar to its VB6 counterpart we'll forgo further discussion of it; other than to point out that changes to properties in this window cause the IDE to alter the code in the collapsed region where the generated code is kept, as we discussed earlier.

Class View

The Class View window is somewhat similar to the Solution Explorer, in that it provides a view into our solution and project. However, the Class View gives us a view of classes, methods, and properties rather than a view of files. This is a very powerful tool in the object-oriented world of .NET.

If we open the Class View window and expand the HelloWorld and Form1 items, we'll get a display similar to the following:

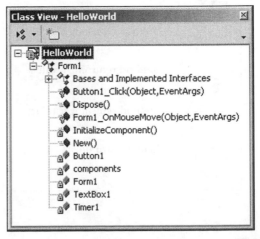

Double-clicking on an element in this display will bring up the code window for that element – making this a convenient way to move through the code in our project.

In this very graphical display, the icons to the left of each item give meaning:

Icon	Meaning	Scope
	class	public
	class	protected (key)
	class	private (padlock)
	class	friend (envelope)
	interface	public
	module	public
	module	private (padlock)
	module	friend (envelope)
	method	public
	method	protected (key)
	method	private (padlock)
	method	friend (envelope)
	method returning a value	public or friend (which does not have an envelope in this particular instance)
	method returning a value	protected (key)
	method returning a value	private (padlock)
	field or attribute	public

Icon	Meaning	Scope
	field or attribute	protected (key)
	field or attribute	private (padlock)
	field or attribute	friend (envelope)
	property	any scope
	event	public
	event	protected (key)
	event	private (padlock)
	event	friend (envelope)
	structure	public
	structure	protected (key)
	structure	private (padlock)
	structure	friend (envelope)

So **Form1** is marked as a public class, **New** is marked as a public method, and **Button1** is marked as a private attribute.

Since **Form1** is a subclass of another class, we see an item named **Bases and Implemented Interfaces**. This element appears anytime a class is a subclass or implements another interface, and it allows us to drill up into the base class or interface definition. Through this mechanism we can see virtually everything there is to see about our class and its ancestors.

There are two buttons in the window's toolbar. The leftmost button allows us to change the sort order of the display, while the right-hand one allows us to create a new folder. This new folder is really a specialized view into which we can drag-and-drop elements from the main display. The elements remain in the primary list as well, but within our folder we can have a narrower view of just those elements of interest.

Dynamic Help

One of the nicest new features of the VS.NET IDE, at least for beginning programmers or those getting used to the new environment and language changes, is the Dynamic Help window. This is a context-sensitive help system, so the window is constantly being updated with links to help on whatever is appropriate.

For instance, with the Timer1 control selected in our HelloWorld project, the Dynamic Help window appears as:

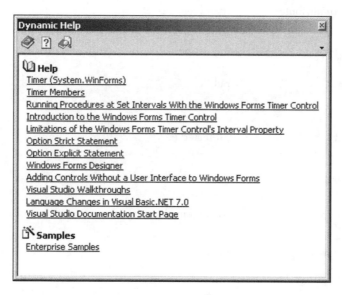

As we click on different controls or move our cursor into different keywords within our code, the list of topics will change to show help appropriate to that control, component, or keyword.

There is a performance implication to having this window open. The process of monitoring our context, searching for appropriate topics, and displaying the list takes memory and processor time. If your development workstation is nearer the minimum hardware requirement the performance hit may be more than it is worth.

Toolbox

The Toolbox, found by default on the left-hand side of the display, is a powerful window. It is where we find the controls to create our forms, but it is also a place to find non-graphical components such as database connections and code fragments that we can drag directly from the Toolbox into our code window.

Tabs

The Toolbox is organized into different tabs; each containing related components, controls, or code. We can add our own tabs to the Toolbox by right-clicking and choosing the Add Tab option.

The default tabs will vary depending on the type of project we are currently building, but some tabs are consistent across all project types:

Tab	Description
Data	Contains components that provide access to data and data sources.
Components	Contains various components such as reporting, message queuing, etc.
Clipboard Ring	Contains a list of the most recent items copied to the system clipboard. This is somewhat comparable to the clipboard ring found in Microsoft Office 2000.
General	Empty by default, this is a place for us to store general controls, components, and code fragments.

When we are building a Windows Forms project such as our HelloWorld example, an additional Win Forms tab will be available, containing Windows Form controls for use as we create our forms.

When we are building a Web Forms project, two additional tabs become available. The first is a Web Forms tab, containing server-side Web Form controls that we can use to create our web pages. The second is an HTML tab, containing controls that correspond to the standard HTML tags. The WinForm controls are substantially more sophisticated than their HTML counterparts and offer extra capabilities. We'll discuss this more in Chapter 6.

Many other tabs are available and will appear as appropriate. To see all the tabs, right-click on the Toolbox and select the Show All Tabs option. The list is quite extensive and covers a wide range of capabilities for the different tools found within the VS.NET IDE. Many of the options may appear disabled – either due to the current project type, or because the features are not yet implemented in the beta.

> *As we noted in Chapter 1, this is a very large and complex product – and there is far more here than can be covered in a single book. As such, we will stay focused on the concepts and tools that are most useful when developing a typical application with VB.NET.*

Working with the Clipboard Ring

The Clipboard Ring tab always lists the last few items copied to the system clipboard. This includes items copied to the clipboard from other applications, such as Word.

> *In the beta software, the Clipboard Ring appears to be somewhat quirky and doesn't always work in a predictable fashion.*

We can drag and drop items from the tab into our code or other designers where appropriate. This can be a very nice way to grab code or HTML fragments from various locations and quickly integrate them into our application.

Working with Code Fragments

Somewhat similar to the Clipboard Ring is the capability to grab fragments of code from a VS.NET code window and store a copy of that code in the Toolbox. Typically these fragments are stored on the General tab, though we can create our own tab for the purpose if we so desire.

To store a code fragment on the General tab, simply open up a code window – say for the Form1 module of our HelloWorld application. Highlight some text in the code window, then drag and drop that highlighted text onto the General tab.

This will add the code and expand the General tab. We'll see an entry like the following:

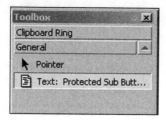

Just as with the items in the Clipboard Ring, these items can be dragged back into a code window at any point and the appropriate text will be added.

This is a great way to keep common code templates and routines quick at hand – just drag them into the code window and away we go.

Server Explorer

By default there's another tab to the far left of the VS.NET display – the Server Explorer. This is an exciting new feature of VS.NET – as it allows us to explore and access server components in a nice graphical environment.

In the following display we see the explorer showing a database connection to the pubs database and listing two servers:

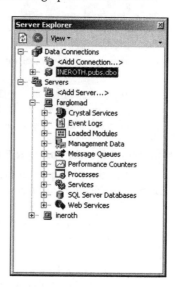

The elements displayed in the Server Explorer are more than just for show. Most can be dragged directly onto a designer (Windows Forms, Web Form, Component, etc.) making them available for use from our application.

For example, we can drag a stored procedure from the display onto a designer and VB.NET will automatically add the appropriate connection and command objects to make the stored procedure available via code. This is a very powerful capability.

This means that gaining access to a database, a message queue, or a Windows 2000 performance counter is as easy as drag-and-drop. When an element is dropped onto a designer, the IDE automatically adds code into the code region for automatically generated code. This code, in general, declares and instantiates an object of the appropriate type and sets its properties so the object ends up representing the item we selected from the explorer window. At that point the object is available for use by our code – all set up and ready for our use.

The Task List

One nice feature from Visual Interdev was the task list. This feature has been carried over and developed for VS.NET – providing a quick list of all the current build and syntax errors in our application. If it's not visible already, click on View | Show Tasks | All.

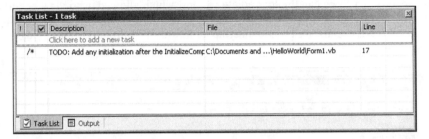

As we program, the automatic syntax checker is constantly checking our code for errors – just like in previous versions of VB. However, now the errors are not only indicated in the code window with a wavy underline – they are listed conveniently in the Task List window too.

Double-clicking on an error listed in the window will take us right to the troublesome point in our code. To see this in action, go into the code of a project and intentionally create a syntax error. The error will be displayed in the window and double-clicking the error will return us to the code window to fix the error.

The tasks shown in this window can be filtered by various criteria. To set the filtering, right-click on the window and choose the Show Tasks menu option. Then choose the appropriate option to filter for the tasks of interest.

TODO Comments

In addition, we can add special TODO comments to our code and they too will be displayed in the task list. In code the comments appear as:

```
' TODO: here is my comment
```

This is a great feature since it is quite common to leave bits of programming for later and using this technique allows us to easily mark and find places where further work is required.

Custom Comments

Better still, we can have the task list display comments based on other tokens of our choice. To configure this, choose the Tools | Options menu and go to the Task List option:

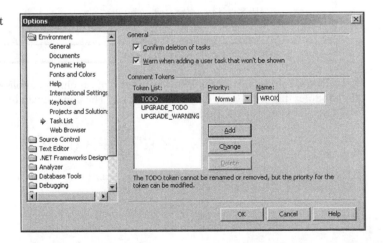

In the diagram we are in the process of adding a normal priority token named **WROX**. If this is added, then any comments starting with WROX will be listed in the task list just as TODO comments are by default.

Output Window

In previous versions of VB we had the Immediate window which allowed us to view debug output from our application, and to interact with the environment by entering bits of code or even calling procedures within our code. VS.NET splits this functionality up a bit, with the output portions being handled within the Output window:

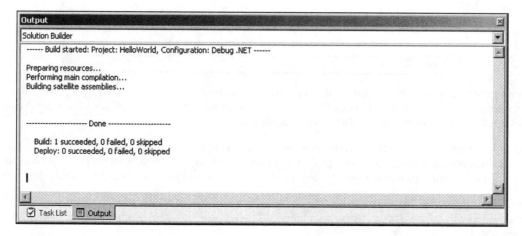

In this diagram we can see the output from a build process, indicating that the program has succeeded.

This is also the window in which debug output is displayed, as shown in the following diagram:

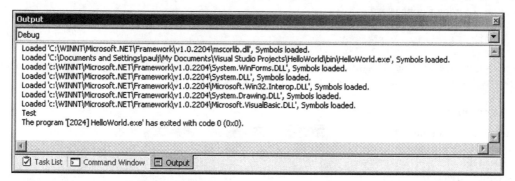

This diagram shows the output from the process of running an application in the debugger, including a list of the modules that were loaded into the debugger. The penultimate line is generated from code using the `System.Diagnostics.Debug` class:

```
System.Diagnostics.Debug.Write("Test" & Chr(10))
```

This is the VB.NET equivalent of the `Debug.Print` command in VB6.

Command Window

The Command window provides us with command-line access to the VS.NET environment and IDE. Through this window we can enter commands to manipulate the IDE, execute macros and macro commands, and so forth.

To view this window, go through View | Other Windows | Command Window. It may be convenient to drag the title bar of the new Command window onto the tab bar of the existing Task List and Output window.

If we enter a command such as:

```
File.AddNewProject
```

The IDE will respond by displaying the Add New Project dialog.

This window is not a direct replacement for the Immediate window familiar to experienced VB developers, since it does not allow us to directly enter and execute VB code during design time. However, like VB6's Immediate window, it can be used to interact with our application itself at runtime and evaluate lines of code.

Macro Support

While we're discussing IDE commands and macros, we should take a quick look at the macro capabilities of the VS.NET environment. *Macro*, in this context, means a macro to control the VS.NET environment – not a development environment for macros for use in other tools such as Microsoft Office.

Previous versions of VB have had some degree of macro programming support, since much of the IDE was exposed through COM. Until now, however, we've never had the ability to record and playback a simple set of actions, nor the total access to the environment that is provided by VS.NET.

Under the Tools | Macros menu are a number of options that allow us to record and play temporary macros, as well as create, explore, and run stored macros.

These quick macros can be an immense time saver when we are applying repetitive changes to a lot of code. We might record a macro to find some specific text, change it and then do a couple other code fixes in the surrounding code before moving on to find the next instance of the text. There are many other examples of repetitive code changes that can be quickly streamlined by recording a quick macro to play back.

Integrated Debugging

One of the strengths of VB ever since version 1 has been its integrated debugging capabilities. Few other tools have ever approached the ease with which VB applications can be debugged.

The VS.NET IDE provides a comparable integrated debugger, continuing to provide us with the same capabilities. The debugger is invoked by pressing *F5* to run an application from within the IDE – just as it has been for a decade.

The debug commands are available via the Debug menu. This includes an option to run our application from the IDE without invoking the debugger – a convenient feature.

As we edit our code we can set breakpoints by pressing *F9* or left-clicking in the left margin area at the line where we want to set the breakpoint. Alternatively, we can right-click in the code to get a full list of options.

When running a program in the debugger, right-clicking in the code provides an expanded list of options, including one that lets us add a watch for variables – much the same as in VB6.

F8 is used to step through code line-by-line.

> *Keep in mind that the specific keys used for these purposes can vary depending on the profile chosen for the VS.NET IDE. The keys described here are for the VB.NET profile, but may be different for other language profiles.*

We've already discussed the Output window and its role in providing output from the debugger and from our application via the `System.Diagnostics.Debug` class. However, there are a number of other windows directly related to the debugging capabilities of VS.NET.

Call Stack Window

The Call Stack window displays the current location of execution in our application, and the entire call stack that brought us to this point:

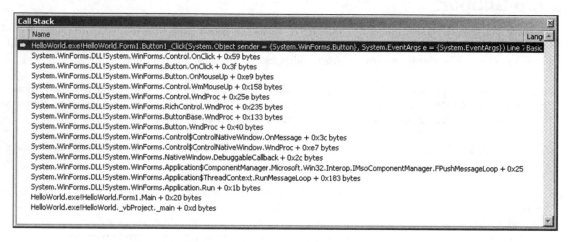

While more complex than the VB6 Call Stack window, this display is more complete; showing not only our code, but also all the various methods that were called that eventually led us to the current method.

Breakpoints Window

Another window available while debugging is the Breakpoints window. This window lists all the breakpoints currently set in our application. Double-clicking on a breakpoint in this window will take us to the location of the breakpoint in the code – making it very easy to move from point to point.

Also, each breakpoint has a checkbox to the left – allowing us to quickly enable or disable breakpoints. Unchecking a breakpoint doesn't remove it from the code, it just temporarily disables it – a very nice feature when debugging within loops.

Watch and Value Display Windows

Several other windows are at our disposal, including a Watch window that displays information about variables we've marked for watching.

There's also an Autos window and a Locals window, which display valuable information about the state of our application's variables.

Obviously, there's a lot more to the VS.NET IDE than we've discussed here. There are some other windows and designers available, and some other capabilities that may be very useful. However, we've covered the features and capabilities that are most likely to impact upon us on a day-to-day basis as we use the tool. Some other features are specific to the development of WinForms, which are covered in Chapter 4, or to developing Web Forms, which are covered in Chapter 6.

Let's move on now, and take a look at the language changes.

Language and Syntax Changes and Features

VB.NET is obviously still Visual Basic, sharing the same basic syntax, keywords, and programming approach. However, VB.NET does have a large number of new features, new or different keywords, and some new syntax and data types.

Before launching into the new language and syntax features, it is important to understand a new concept – **namespaces** – that are used throughout the .NET Framework and VB.NET.

Namespaces

"Namespaces" is a naming scheme that helps organize the various classes available to our application so they are more easily found. All code in .NET, VB or otherwise, is contained within a namespace.

This is true of code in the .NET system class libraries. For instance, the WinForms classes are in the `System.WinForms` namespace and the classes that support collections are in the `System.Collections` namespace.

All of the code in our applications is also contained in namespaces.

In VB6 much of our code was contained within a form of namespace as well. Any code in a COM component was addressed as *componentname.classname* – otherwise known as the PROGID. This technique was somewhat limited however:

❑ The address of a class was tied directly to the component in which it was contained

❑ Classes not in COM components were not in a "namespace"

❑ PROGID naming is only one level deep

❑ Component naming is always global to the entire computer

Namespaces in .NET overcome these limitations.

Several assemblies can be in the same namespace, meaning that classes from more than one component can be found in the same namespace. This also allows for multi-language namespaces, where a class written in VB can be in the same namespace as a class written in C#, for instance.

Likewise, a single assembly can contain multiple namespaces. Typically each assembly has a namespace for all of the classes it contains. Often, however, we'll subdivide those classes into sub-namespaces using namespace nesting – a concept we'll discuss shortly.

> *An assembly is roughly the .NET equivalent of a COM component. All code in .NET is contained in assemblies. Assemblies were explained more thoroughly in Chapter 2.*

In .NET, all code is in a namespace – whether that code is in an official component or a regular WinForms client application. If we don't provide an explicit namespace for our code, a namespace is generated for us based on the name of our assembly/application (the project name in VB.NET). This means that our code is always accessible via a consistent naming scheme.

Namespaces can also be nested, allowing for a great deal of clarity and readability when using them to organize classes. For example, if we were building a comprehensive manufacturing application, we might create a high level namespace `MyMfgApp`. Within that namespace we might have namespaces for various parts of the application:

```
MyMfgApp.Accounting.GL

MyMfgApp.Accounting.AP

MyMfgApp.MRP

MyMfgApp.Inventory
```

And so forth. So we've defined a base `MyMfgApp` namespace, with other namespaces contained within it – each one possibly containing classes, modules, enums, structures and other namespaces.

Each of these namespaces would contain the classes appropriate to that part of the overall application, but due to the namespace addressing it is always clear where the class belongs.

Class names only need to be unique within a namespace. This means that, even though WinForms has a `Form` class, we can create our own namespace that has a `Form` class – perhaps for a data entry application where the data is entered on forms. This helps reduce the number of reserved words that we are prevented from using effectively in our applications.

Unlike COM components, which are always global to an entire computer, namespaces come in two flavors – local and global. Local namespaces are visible only to the current application, while global namespaces are visible to the entire machine.

Local and Global Namespaces

By default, namespaces are visible locally – i.e. visible only to the specific application to which they belong. This is a feature of .NET that helps address the "DLL Hell" issues of COM.

If we create a set of classes for our application's use, in COM these classes are made available to the entire computer – all applications on the computer can see and interact with the classes. This can cause some nasty side-effects, since there's nothing to ensure that a class in one application is named differently to a class in another application.

In .NET on the other hand, most classes are local to each application. This means that two applications can have the same class names – even the same namespace names – without any fear of conflict. Each application has its own private set of namespaces and classes.

Of course there are times when we *do* want to create a set of classes that are available to all applications on a machine. .NET supports this concept through global namespaces or global assemblies. Global assemblies, and the namespaces they contain, are available to all applications on a computer – potentially leading us back down the road to "DLL Hell".

To help avoid this, global assemblies and namespaces must meet some stringent naming and versioning requirements, they must also be digitally signed, and must also be registered with the .NET runtime so they are available in the global assembly cache.

These extra steps help ensure unique naming of namespaces and classes across applications, and also act as an extra hurdle that we must overcome to create global assemblies – thus encouraging the use of the safer local namespace that we get by default.

Using Namespaces

It is impossible to create a .NET application without using namespaces. While this is true, namespaces are so well integrated into the environment that we may often use them without thinking – it becomes second nature.

We can use namespaces explicitly through direct addressing or implicitly through the Imports keyword.

> **Either way, our application must reference the assembly that contains the namespace we wish to use. This is done with the Project | Add References menu option.**

Direct Addressing

Any namespaces contained by assemblies referenced by our application are available for use in our code. For instance, if we want to read or write from stdio (the console input/output stream) the System.Console namespace is required. We can access any class in this namespace directly by providing its fully qualified name. For example:

```
System.Console.WriteLine("This is a test")
```

This line of code invokes the WriteLine method in the System.Console namespace – using it to print a line of text to an Output window.

This is true of any namespace available to our application, but it is somewhat lengthy to type. Fortunately, IntelliSense kicks in and helps to auto-complete the text on our behalf.

Imports Keyword

Another way to avoid typing quite so much, and to make our code more concise, is to use the Imports keyword. This statement allows us to implicitly address namespaces by making them available to our code – somewhat like a shortcut.

If we want to make all the classes in a given namespace available to our code without the need to type the entire namespace each time, we can use the Imports statement. For example:

```
Imports System.Console

Some code...

WriteLine("This is a test")
```

By importing the namespace at the top of our code module, we avoid having to explicitly reference the namespace each time we use a class within that namespace. This can save typing since we don't always need to use the fully qualified name – including namespace.

The only exception to this is where a given class name is used within two namespaces. If we import both namespaces we will still need to explicitly use enough of the fully qualified name when using that class, or the name will be ambiguous.

For instance, say we have two namespaces – `MyMfgApp.Inventory` and `MyMfgApp.Sales` – which both have a `Product` class. Then the following code would have trouble:

```
Imports MyMfgApp.Inventory
Imports MyMfgApp.Sales

Public Sub DoSomething()
  Dim obj As New Product()
End Sub
```

There's no way for the compiler to tell *which* `Product` we are referring to from the context. To avoid this problem, we can change the code to:

```
Dim obj As New Sales.Product()
```

Thus removing the ambiguity around the `Product` class.

Aliasing Namespaces

At first glance it seems that having the same class name in more than one namespace should be fairly rare. Unfortunately it is pretty common – meaning that we can find ourselves typing explicit namespace addresses quite often.

To help avoid typing quite so much, we can provide an alias for a namespace. One of the more common namespaces used by VB developers – especially when converting code from VB6 to VB.NET – is the `Microsoft.VisualBasic.Compatibility.VB6` namespace. This namespace happens to have a lot of classes that are ambiguous in many cases, and it is a lengthy namespace to type over and over.

To alias this namespace, we can use a variant syntax for the `Imports` keyword:

```
Imports vb6 = Microsoft.VisualBasic.Compatibility.VB6
```

With this line of code at the top of our code module, we can use `vb6` as a shortcut to get to the classes in that namespace. For instance:

```
vb6.Format(5, "00")
```

This is much easier to type than the long version.

Creating Namespaces

Any code we create using VB.NET will be contained within a namespace. We have control over how the namespace is named, though VS.NET does provide a default – the name of our project.

Setting the Root Namespace

Every project in VS.NET has a **root** namespace, which is set in the project's Property page. For example, our `HelloWorld` project's namespace is `HelloWorld` by default. Highlight the HelloWorld node in the Solution Explorer and then select View | Property Pages from the main menu, you should then see a form like this:

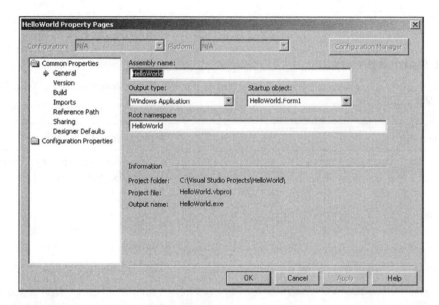

Notice the Root namespace field where the namespace is set. We can override this value if we desire, causing all the classes in our project to belong to a different namespace. If we want the classes from multiple projects to coexist in the same namespace we'd need to override this field in all the projects, to ensure that they have the same value.

In our `HelloWorld` project, we have a `Form1` class that is more properly named:

```
HelloWorld.Form1
```

Within our project we don't need to use this full name, but if we were to make `Form1` or some other class from our project available to other applications, this is the address that would be used.

Namespace Keyword

While VS.NET provides our code with a root namespace via the project properties, we know from earlier that namespaces can be nested so we can further organize our classes.

This is where the `Namespace` keyword comes into play. In a VB.NET project, a class will always be contained within the root namespace. However, if we want it to be in a more specific namespace, we can put the class within a `Namespace` block:

```
Namespace MyNamespace

Class MyClass
End Class

End Namespace
```

This class will now have the address of:

```
MyRootNamespace.MyNamespace.MyClass
```

Using this technique, we can be very specific in the naming of our classes – allowing us to organize our code as we so desire.

Useful VB Namespaces

There are a number of namespaces that exist to support the VB environment, or for backward compatibility with older VB applications.

Namespace Name	Description of Contents
Microsoft.VisualBasic	Provides access to most common VB keywords, such as Asc, Beep, Chr, Ubound, etc.
Microsoft.VisualBasic.ControlChars	Provides access to the common VB constants for character values, such as Cr, Lf, CrLf, etc.
Microsoft.VisualBasic.Helpers	Data type helper code and utilities.
Microsoft.VisualBasic.Compatibility.VB6	Provides access to depreciated VB6 keywords, such as Open, Close, CreateObject, etc. Use of these keywords is not recommended as there are replacements for them in the .NET system class libraries.

Obviously the .NET system class libraries contain many other namespaces that are very useful within the typical VB application, but these namespaces are specific to VB and thus it is important to become familiar with them.

Language and Syntax Changes

Now that we've got a basic understanding of namespaces and how they are used to organize and address our code, we can move on to discuss the various language and syntax changes we'll encounter in VB.NET.

Option Statements

VB has had Option statements for some time – allowing us to control the behavior of the compiler and thus affect how we code. VB.NET continues this tradition, using the Option keyword to allow us to override default behaviors as we desire.

Our options are:

Option Statement	Value	Description
Option Explicit	On	Requires declaration of all variables before they are used (default).
	Off	Variables may be used without being declared.
Option Compare	Binary	Strings are compared using a binary comparison algorithm (default).
	Text	Strings are compared using a text comparison algorithm.
Option Strict	On	Automatic type coercion will not take place (default). We must explicitly convert types when desired – for example, we must use CLng() to convert an Integer to a Long data value.
	Off	Automatic type coercion will take place much as it did in VB6, where data of one type will be automatically converted to other types without warning or error.

These options can be set within the project's properties so they are global to the entire project. Right-click on the project and choose **Properties** from the menu and select the **Build** tab. Here we can define the default options for this project. Any option default set in the properties window can be changed on a per-file basis through the use of explicit Option statements in the code – just like in previous versions of VB.

Option Explicit works largely as it did in the past. With this option turned On, we are not forced to declare variables before using them. Any undeclared variables are of type Object.

Notice that Option Base is no longer available. This option was used to indicate whether arrays should begin with a 0 element or a 1 element. In VB.NET all arrays are zero based, starting with a 0 element.

Also, Option Strict is new. One of the most controversial features in the recent versions of VB has been the liberal way in which VB would convert data from one type to another. In VB6 we could have code such as:

```
Dim MyLong As Long
Dim MyInt As Integer

MyLong = 5
MyInt = MyLong
```

While convenient, this code could be viewed as unsafe or unclear. Hidden in the assignment of MyLong to MyInt is a type conversion – changing the value 5 from an Integer to a Long. With Option Strict On in VB.NET this code will not run and must be changed to:

```
Dim MyLong As Long
Dim MyInt As Integer

MyInt = 5
MyLong = CLng(MyInt)
```

Depending on your view, this is either a nice new feature or a serious step backward. It should certainly reduce the potential for coding errors. Regardless, it is important to be aware of the new general type coercion statement, CType(), which we'll discuss in this chapter.

Data Type Changes

VB.NET introduces a number of data type changes – something that can be disconcerting at first. Some of these changes have been introduced to provide new capabilities, others to support future systems such as the 64-bit processors that will be supported by 64-bit versions of Windows 2000 and the new operating system code-named Whistler.

A common underlying change to the data types is that they are all now technically derived from type Object. This means that a simple Integer is of type Object and can be treated like any other object. Normally this has little impact on us as developers, but it is important to keep in mind, since any method parameter of type Object can not only accept 'real' objects, but can also accept native data types, since they too are objects.

Integer Type Changes (Byte, Short, Integer, Long)

Perhaps the most striking changes in data types are those to the integer data types:

Data Type	Size	Range
Byte	8-bit	0 to 255 (unsigned)
Short	16-bit	-32,768 to 32,767
Integer	32-bit	-2,147,483,648 to 2,147,483,647
Long	64-bit	-9,223,372,036,854,775,808 to 9,223,372,036,854,775,807

Integer and Long are the most commonly used data types in VB, and both have changed sizes. Integer used to be 16-bit and is now 32-bit, while Long used to be 32-bit and is now 64-bit.

This means that those people who used Long to achieve optimal performance on 32-bit processors will want to switch to using Integer, while those who used Integer as a general rule need to be aware that their favorite data type will contain values higher than 32767.

These changes also bring the VB data types more in line with their counterparts in SQL Server, which can help reduce bugs for those people interacting with databases on a regular basis.

Floating-Point Division

VB.NET still has the same basic Single and Double data types, though we'll see some different behaviors when it comes to division. **Floating-point** numbers are often designed to conform to the specifications from the IEEE standards body. Conformance with this specification leads to some interesting results from the following code:

```
Dim d1 As Double
Dim d2 As Double

d1 = 1
d2 = 0
System.Diagnostics.Debug.WriteLine(d1 / d2)
```

Where we'd expect to get a division by zero error, the output instead is the word `Infinity`.

Likewise, the following does not cause an error:

```
Dim d1 As Double
Dim d2 As Double

d1 = 0
d2 = 0
System.Diagnostics.Debug.WriteLine(d1 / d2)
```

This prints the text result of NaN.

These results, while a bit surprising, conform to the IEEE standard governing floating-point numbers.

Replacing Currency with Decimal

Previous versions of VB had a `Currency` data type that was used to represent large floating-point values. The idea was to provide support for large currency values.

VB.NET has no `Currency` data type, but does have a 128-bit `Decimal` data type, which provides support for very large values that can be scaled by powers of 10. It is divided into two parts – a 96-bit integer and an associated 32-bit integer. These allow representation of very large values. This means that the `Decimal` data type can act as a decent replacement for the `Currency` data type.

`Decimal` values can have anywhere from 0 to 28 digits to the right of the decimal point. The more digits to the right of the decimal point, the higher our precision, but the lower the overall range of values can be.

Char Type

VB.NET has both a `Byte` and a `Char` data type.

`Byte` contains a numeric value in the range 0-255 and consumes 1 byte of space and is a numeric value, not a character value. On the other hand, it is often used to store ASCI character values in numeric form.

`Char` contains values from 0-65535 and consumes 2 bytes of space. This is a Unicode value, meaning it directly supports international character sets.

The `Char` data type is intended for use in manipulating single character values or for creating arrays of character values. This can be confusing at first, since `Byte` is useful in working with characters as well.

However, `Byte` is only useful for simple ASCI characters, and we live in a Unicode world – which is where `Char` comes into play. Unicode characters are 2 bytes in length, and so the `Char` data type exists to support this 2 byte character scheme.

String Type

The `String` data type in VB.NET is different from that found in previous versions of VB. The VB.NET `String` data type flows from the .NET system class library, where we find namespaces devoted to dealing with text and `String` data.

The `String` data type comes from the `System.String` class, and is designed as an immutable string of text. This means it cannot be changed – so any attempt to change a `String` results in a new `String` being created to store the changed value, while the original is destroyed.

This is not all that different from the behavior in previous versions of VB, since even then any increase to a string's length would cause the same effect. However, in VB6 we could alter a string in-place:

```
MyString = "Hello"
Mid$(MyString, 5, 1) = "X"
```

In VB.NET this code causes a new String to be created. While the code continues to work transparently, there are obviously performance implications to be considered.

Another change to the String data type is that there is no longer the concept of a fixed-length string. In VB6 we could declare a variable as:

```
Dim MyString As String * 50
```

This variable is a String of exactly 50 characters and is fixed at that length – no longer, no shorter. In VB.NET this syntax is invalid and there is no fixed-length String concept – all String variables are of dynamic length.

Other namespaces with important string-handling classes and methods include:

❑ System.String

❑ System.Text

❑ System.IO

While the built-in VB functions for dealing with strings remain available, sometimes there are utilities available that can make life easier. For instance:

Replacing Variant with Object

One of the most powerful, flexible, and dangerous data types in previous versions of VB is the Variant data type. A variable of type Variant could hold virtually any value – automatically adjusting its internal data type to accommodate the value so it could be stored. The price of this flexibility was a serious loss of performance and the substantial potential for unintentional bugs due to automatic type coercion.

VB.NET does not have a Variant data type, thus avoiding some of the negatives that came along with it – but what about the positives?

VB.NET *does* have the Object data type. In fact, at least conceptually, all data types in .NET are technically objects – and so the Object data type is somewhat comparable to Variant in that a variable of type Object can hold virtually any value.

This means that Object is somewhat of a replacement for Variant, in that it provides comparable functionality. However, it is worth noting that the implementation of Object behind the scenes is not the same as the implementation of Variant in previous versions of VB.

Also, Option Strict comes into play here, changing the way code is typically written. For instance, in VB6 we might have code like:

```
Dim x1 As Variant
Dim x2 As Variant
```

```
x1 = 5
x2 = "10.5"
Debug.Print x1 + x2
```

But in VB.NET, with `Option Strict On` (the default), our code would appear as

```
Dim x1 As Object
Dim x2 As Object

x1 = 5
x2 = "10.5"
System.Diagnostics.Debug.WriteLine(CInt(x1) + CSng(x2))
```

While we have the flexibility of the `Variant`, we have greater clarity in this code because the type conversions are explicit rather than automatic.

CType Statement

One common use of both the `Variant` and `Object` data types in VB6 was to store object references. Methods and properties on those objects could then be called by using the variable. For example, in VB6 we might have:

```
Dim x As Object

Set x = New Customer
Debug.Print x.LastName
```

While VB.NET does continue to have the `Object` data type, and a variable of type `Object` can hold any object reference – just like in VB6 – things are a bit more complex due to `Option Strict`. Because of `Option Strict`, a variable of type `Object` can't be automatically coerced into any specific object type – we must do this explicitly by using the `CType()` statement. For example:

```
Dim x As Object

x = New Customer
System.Diagnostics.Debug.WriteLine(CType(x, Customer).LastName)
```

The `CType()` statement converts a value of one type into a value of another type. The new type is supplied as the second parameter to the statement – providing a lot of flexibility.

It can be argued whether this code is more or less readable than its VB6 counterpart. However, we could certainly declare another variable of type `Customer` and set our generic `Object` value into that variable to make the code more clear.

Changes in Declaration of Variables

Along with the data type changes, VB.NET also enhances the way that we declare and work with variables.

Declaring Multiple Variables

In VB6 we could declare several variables on one line:

```
Dim x, y, z As Integer
```

The deceptive result of this statement is that x and y are declared as type Variant, while z is declared as Integer. VB.NET alters this behavior so all three variables are declared as type Integer – a result that is arguably more intuitive.

Declaring Initial Values

Frequently, when declaring a variable, we also want to set its initial value. In VB6 we would do:

```
Dim x As Integer
x = 5
```

In VB.NET we can shorten this to:

```
Dim x As Integer = 5
```

This is shorter and more concise.

Declaring Constants

Constants in VB.NET must be declared with a specific type:

```
Public Const MY_CONSTANT As String = "The constant value"
Private Const MAX_VALUE As Integer = 42
```

While a small change, it is important to recognize.

Dim As New

In VB6 we could use the New keyword while declaring an object variable:

```
Dim x As New Customer
```

This was not recommended, however, due to the way VB6 implemented this functionality. While it appears that a new Customer object was created by this code, no object is created until the variable x is actually used in code. This deceptive behavior was the cause of some bugs, which were very hard to find in many applications.

Additionally, the way this was implemented behind the scenes meant that the VB compiler inserted code before *any* use of the variable x – code to check and see if the object already existed or if it needed to be created. All this extra code reduced the performance of our application.

VB.NET addresses these concerns by making the syntax work as we might expect, by creating the object immediately. This means the following line:

```
Dim x As New Customer()
```

will cause a new Customer object to be created immediately – the variable x represents the object right away – avoiding many of the bugs and performance issues from VB6.

We'll cover the instantiation of objects in far more detail in Chapter 5 when we discuss objects and the object-oriented features of VB.NET.

Scoping Changes

Variables declared in VB.NET may be subject to some different scope restrictions than those declared in previous versions of VB. In particular, VB.NET introduces the concept of block-level scope, where variables can be declared within specific blocks of code, such as an `If...End If` block.

In VB6, we could write code such as:

```
If True Then
  Dim x As Integer
  x = 5
End If
x = 15
```

In VB.NET, however, this code is invalid, since the variable x is not valid outside of the `If...End If` block. The same is true for any type of block structure, including `Do...Loop`, `While...Wend`, `For...Next`, and so forth.

For most people, who declare variables at the top of routines, this won't be an issue. For those who declare variables throughout their code as the variables are needed, this will require some changing of habits.

Changes to Arrays

In previous versions of VB, arrays were a native data type of the language itself. In VB.NET, arrays flow from the .NET system class libraries and are common across all .NET languages, including VB.

This means that arrays can be easily passed around within the .NET environment from component to component regardless of the language used to create each component, but this does represent a change from what we are used to as VB developers. Fortunately the basic syntax for using arrays remains relatively consistent and so, for the most part, the changes are transparent in day-to-day coding.

Zero-Based Arrays

Perhaps the biggest change is that all arrays are now zero-based, meaning that the lowest array element of any array is 0 rather than 1. In VB6 we had the `Option Base` statement, which allowed us to specify whether arrays were zero-based or one-based. In VB.NET this statement is gone and all arrays are zero-based.

This also means we effectively lose the topmost array element of any array as compared to a typical one-based array in VB6. In VB.NET we can declare an array as:

```
Dim myarray(10) As Integer
```

The result is an array with subscripts that range from 0 to 9 rather than from 1 to 10.

Another side effect of this change is that the `To` syntax is no longer supported, so we can no longer declare an array as:

```
Dim myarray(1 To 10) As Integer
```

This will cause an error.

LBound and UBound

In the past, the LBound statement would return the lowest valid index value for an array. This functionality remains intact, though obviously, since all arrays are zero-based, the LBound statement will always return the value 0.

The UBound statement also continues to work – returning the highest valid index value for an array. Again, due to the zero-based arrays, UBound will always return one less than the declared number of elements in the array:

```
Dim myarray(5) As String

MessageBox.Show(CType(UBound(myarray), String))
```

This code will display a message box with the value 4, the highest valid array index for this array.

Declaring Arrays

As with previous versions of VB, we can declare arrays with explicit sizes such as:

```
Dim myarray(5) As String
```

Or we can declare them with no explicit size, relying on the use of a ReDim statement to size the array later:

```
Dim myarray() As Decimal
```

VB.NET allows us to preload an array with data as it is being declared. This is conceptually the same as initializing any other variable as it is being declared, but with arrays the syntax is a bit different since we are supplying a list of values instead of a single value:

```
Dim myarray() As Integer = {1, 3, 6, 2}
```

This has the effect of sizing the array to hold the data elements we provide, as well as placing those values into the array. To use this feature we can't explicitly define the size of the array.

ReDim

The ReDim statement remains valid in VB.NET. This statement can be used to change the number of elements in an array, though it cannot be used to change the number of dimensions. This means we can write code such as:

```
Dim myarray() As String

ReDim myarray(5)
```

This declares an array and then changes the number of elements in the array to 5.

We can also redimension more complex arrays such as:

```
Dim myarray() As String

ReDim myarray(5)
```

Notice that the ReDim statement doesn't alter the number of dimensions, just the number of elements in each dimension.

ReDim Preserve

When using the ReDim statement, all existing data in the array is lost. To avoid losing this data, we can use the Preserve keyword. Use of this keyword places an additional restriction on the ReDim statement. In particular, when using the Preserve keyword, only the last dimension can be resized, so the following code is valid:

```
Dim myarray(0, 0) As String

ReDim myarray(5, 5)

ReDim Preserve myarray(5, 10)
```

This is valid because only the last (right-most) dimension is resized using the ReDim Preserve statement.

> *We can write code to use* ReDim Preserve *that changes any dimension in the array without causing a build error. This code appears valid in the IDE, but will cause an error at run-time.*

Changes to User-Defined Types

The concept of a user-defined type, or UDT, is a powerful one. It allows us to group a set of values together to form a more complex type. In VB6 this was done using code such as:

```
Public Type mytype
   Name As String
   Age As Integer
End Type
```

VB.NET preserves this functionality, but changes the syntax somewhat. Instead of using the keyword Type, we now use the keyword Structure:

```
Public Structure mystruct
   Public Name As String
   Public Age As Integer
End Structure
```

We have the same basic functionality, with just a slight change to syntax.

Notice that the individual elements of the structure are declared with a scope. This means that we can create a structure with some Public elements (the default), which are visible to other code, and also with elements that are more restrictive in their scope.

Changes to Collections

In previous versions of VB, the Collection type was native to the language. In VB.NET, support for collections, and similar functionality such as a Dictionary class, comes from the .NET system class libraries.

VB6 Style Collections

Functionality directly comparable to the VB6-style `Collection` object is depreciated, though still available from the `Microsoft.VisualBasic.Compatibility.VB6` namespace. This means we can write code such as:

```
Imports VB6=Microsoft.VisualBasic.Compatibility.VB6

Public Sub DoSomething()
  Dim col As New VB6.Collection()

  col.Add("some data")
End Sub
```

This `Collection` object works in the same way as the `Collection` objects that we are used to working with in previous versions of VB. However, this is not the recommended approach for new code, as it relies on the compatibility namespace.

System.Collections Namespace

The new collection functionality provided in the .NET system class libraries flows from the `System.Collections` namespace. This namespace not only provides support for the concept of a simple collection (or hash table) as we've had in the past, but it also provides support for a `Dictionary`-style collection such as that provided by the Windows Scripting Host Library. Other types of collections are available as well. The following is a list of commonly used items:

Collection	Description
ArrayList	Implements a single-dimension array that grows dynamically as elements are added.
BitArray	Implements a single-dimension array of `Boolean` values which are stored internally as single bits, providing a very compact way to manage a list of `Boolean` values.
Dictionary	Implements a collection of key-value data pairs that can be stored and retrieved within the `Dictionary` object.
Hashtable	Implements a collection of key-value pairs that are organized based on the hash value of the key. This allows very fast and efficient storage and retrieval of data based on the key value.
ObjectList	Implements a collection of arbitrary objects. Since all data types can be represented by `Object`, this collection can hold virtually any data.
Queue	Implements a FIFO (first in, first out) queue structure.
SortedList	Implements a sorted list of key-value pairs.
Stack	Implements a LIFO (last in, first out) stack structure.
StringCollection	Implements a collection of `String` values.

The variety of classes available can seem overwhelming when compared to the simplicity of a single `Collection` data type. However, we are now presented with substantially more options that we've had in the past, along with classes such as `Hashtable` and `ObjectList`, which provide functionality quite comparable to the `Collection` object with which we are familiar.

For instance, for `Collection`-style functionality where we don't care about the order of the elements, we might use the `Hashtable` class:

```
Imports System.Collections

Public Sub DoSomething()
    Dim ht As New Hashtable()
    Dim entry As DictionaryEntry

    ht.Add(1, "item 1")
    ht.Add(2, "item 2")

    For Each entry In ht
       System.Diagnostics.Debug.WriteLine(entry.Value)
    Next
End Sub
```

As with all the key-value collection implementations, the elements of the collection are represented by `DictionaryEntry` objects, which provide us with access to the key and value data for each element.

While slightly different from a VB6 `Collection` object, this code is quite similar, and is generally consistent with the type of code we'd write to work with any of the other collection classes available in the `System.Collections` namespace.

Creating Custom Collections

There are many cases where we need to create custom collections – most frequently because we want a collection that only contains a certain data type or type of object. Creating a custom collection in VB6 was somewhat of a black art, since it required us to implement the mysterious `NewEnum` property, along with setting its `Procedure ID` to the not-entirely-self-explanatory value of –4.

Things are much more clear in VB.NET, where we can use the object-oriented concept of inheritance to create a new collection that is based on one of the existing collection types provided in the system class library. In fact, we can base a new collection object on one of the base classes from the `System.Collections.Bases` namespace – they are designed for this purpose. Though we'll cover inheritance thoroughly in Chapter 5, it is worth showing how a custom collection can be created while we're discussing collection functionality.

Suppose we have a simple `Structure`:

```
Public Structure MyStruct
   Public Name As String
   Public BirthDate As Date
End Structure
```

And suppose we want a collection that only contains data in this structure. We can simply implement a subclass of the `TypedCollectionBase` class – a pre-built class designed to allow us to create collections that are strongly typed. The following code implements such a collection:

```
Imports System.Collections.Bases

Public Class MyCollection
  Inherits TypedCollectionBase
```

```
Default Public Property Item(ByVal Index As Integer) As MyStruct
   Get
      Return CType(List(Index), MyStruct)
   End Get
   Set
      List(Index) = Value
   End Set
End Property

Public Function Add(ByVal Value As MyStruct) As Integer
   Return List.Add(Value)
End Function

Public Sub Remove(ByVal Value As MyStruct)
   List.Remove(Value)
End Sub
End Class
```

Notice that we don't need to re-implement any of the base functionality – all of that is provided through the inheritance mechanism, which we'll discuss in Chapter 5. All we need to do is provide our own implementation of the Add, Item, and Remove methods so they accept and return only the MyStruct type.

New Arithmetic Operators

VB.NET introduces some new arithmetic operators – shortcuts for existing syntax. The following table illustrates the new syntax.

Arithmetic Operation	Existing Syntax	New Shortcut
Addition	X = X + 4	X += 4
Subtraction	X = X – 10	X –= 10
Multiplication	X = X * 2	X *= 2
Division	X = X / 13	X /= 13
Integer division	X = X \ 13	X \= 13
Exponent	X = X ^ 3	X ^= 3
String concatenation	X = X & " text"	X &= " text"

The existing syntax continues to work; we just have more options now than before.

Boolean and Bit Level Operators

In VB6 the And, Or, Not, and Xor statements were all bit level operators. In other words, rather than doing a Boolean operation, these operators worked with numeric values at a bit level.

In VB6 we could have this code:

```
MsgBox(2 Or 4)
```

The result would not be `True` or `False`, but rather would be 6. Unfortunately, it would also be implicitly `True` since any non-zero value in VB6 was considered to be `True`.

In VB.NET the `And`, `Or`, `Not`, and `Xor` statements are Boolean, not bitwise, so we get a syntax error when trying to enter the VB6 code shown above. This is because the `Or` statement expects to be working with values of type `Boolean` rather than values of some numeric type.

On a somewhat trivial side note, the numerical value of `True` in VB6 was –1, while in VB.NET it is 1.

To get the same functionality as we had in VB6, we need to use a new set of operators that operate at the bit level:

Operator	Meaning
BitAnd	bit level And
BitOr	bit level Or
BitNot	bit level Not
BitXor	bit level Xor

With these new keywords we now have the best of both worlds – full support for `Boolean` operators and for bit level operators.

Short-Circuited If...Then Statements

One change that may be the source of confusion is that, unlike in VB6, VB.NET `If...Then` statements are short-circuited. In VB6, all the code in an `If...Then` statement was processed – even if part of it returned `False` early on and hence caused the entire statement to be false. For example:

```
Dim myInt As Integer

myInt = 0
If myInt <> 0 And 17 \ myInt < 5 Then
```

The first part of this comparison (`myInt <> 0`) returns `False`. In VB6 the second part of the expression is evaluated anyway, resulting in a division by zero error.

In VB.NET this behavior is changed, so the evaluation is stopped as soon as the outcome is known. In this example, the entire expression is guaranteed to be `False` as soon as we know that `myInt` is zero and so evaluation stops. This means we won't get the division by zero error since that portion of the expression is not evaluated.

This has some positive benefits in terms of performance, and allows the `If...Then` structure to be used to proof against division by zero or other similar errors. On the other hand, if we are used to writing our code such that we count on the entire expression to be evaluated as it was in VB6 then we'll have to adjust.

Using Reserved Words as Procedure Names

There are many times when it would be nice to name a method or procedure using a word that is reserved by the language. For instance, we might want a method named `Compare` to compare two values:

```
Public Function Compare(ByVal v1 As Integer, ByVal v2 As Integer) As Short
   If v1 > v2 Then
      Return 1
   ElseIf v1 < v2 Then
      Return -1
   Else
      Return 0
   End If
End Function
```

Unfortunately `Compare` is a reserved word, and so this won't work. However, we can place the reserved word within square brackets and still use it, so this is valid:

```
Public Function [Compare](ByVal v1 As Integer, ByVal v2 As Integer) As Short
```

This should be used with care however, since any code that calls the method will also need brackets:

```
MsgBox([Compare](i1, i2))
```

If widely used, this can lead to some very obscure and hard to read code.

No Set Statement

One of the most confusing syntax elements of previous versions of VB is the use of the keyword `Set` when assigning objects to variables. This is confusing since it tends to set objects apart from any other data type.

In VB6 we might have statements such as:

```
Set x = New Customer
Set y = x
```

In VB.NET the `Set` statement is gone, simplifying our code, and so in VB.NET we have statements such as:

```
x = New Customer()
y = x
```

The result of this change is that object variables are treated the same as any other variable – simplifying the language syntax overall, and reducing much confusion, especially for new programmers or those coming from other languages.

Notice that you can still type `Set`, but VB.NET will automatically take it out once you have finished typing in the line!

Changes to Property Routines

Since we no longer have a `Set` statement, it should come as no surprise that the meaning of `Property Set` and `Property Let` are affected as well.

The concept of a `Property Set` doesn't exist as it did in VB6. Beyond this, however, there are other substantial syntax changes that affect how `Property` routines are built. In VB6 we might have code in a class module such as:

```
Private mstrName As String

Public Property Let Name(Value As String)
  mstrName = Value
End Property

Public Property Get Name() As String
  Name = mstrName
End Property
```

In VB.NET things are quite different. The same code is written in a VB.NET class as follows:

```
Private mstrName As String

Public Property Name() As String
  Set
    mstrName = Value
  End Set

  Get
    Name = mstrName
  End Get
End Property
```

There are a few things to note here. First off, all the code for the entire property is contained within one `Property` routine, and this routine is subdivided into two blocks – a `Set` block and a `Get` block. Though the `Set` statement for assignment of object references is gone, we still use `Set` within `Property` routines. There is no longer a `Property Let` – this is included in the functionality of the `Set` block we see in the above code.

Also notice that the `Set` block uses a `Value` variable – even though that variable isn't declared anywhere. In VB.NET, `Value` is now a keyword that automatically contains the value provided to the `Set` block. This is quite a change from VB6, but lends a lot of consistency to the structure and implementation of a `Property` method.

Consistent Scoping

One consequence of consolidating both the assignment (`Set`) and accessor (`Get`) functionality into the same `Property` routine is that they both have the same scope. In VB6 we could have scoped these differently, such as:

```
Friend Property Let Name(Value As String)
  mstrName = Value
End Property

Public Property Get Name() As String
  Name = mstrName
End Property
```

Thus restricting which code could change the value of `Name`, while allowing any code to read the value. We can't implement this the same way in VB.NET, since the entire `Property` routine is scoped the same.

To achieve similar functionality in VB.NET we need to implement two separate properties – each with the appropriate scope – or use methods rather than properties.

ReadOnly Properties

In VB6, implementing a read only property was as simple as writing a `Property Get` routine without a corresponding `Property Set` or `Property Let`. In VB.NET this remains true, but the syntax is more explicit – lending clarity to our code:

```
Public ReadOnly Property Age() As Integer
  Get
    Age = 3
  End Get
End Property
```

Notice the use of the `ReadOnly` keyword, which causes the compiler to ensure that we only supply a `Get` routine for this `Property`.

WriteOnly Properties

If we have a `ReadOnly` keyword, it only makes sense that there would be a `WriteOnly` keyword for declaring write only properties:

```
Public WriteOnly Property Data() As Integer
  Set
    mintData = Value
  End Set
End Property
```

This has the same general effect as the `ReadOnly` keyword, but the `WriteOnly` keyword ensures that we have a `Set` routine with no `Get` routine for this `Property`.

Default Properties

VB.NET changes the way we create default properties. In VB6, creating a default property involved using the **Procedure Attributes** dialog to change the **Procedure ID** to **(default)**. This had no visible impact on our code and generally seemed to be quite obscure.

VB.NET improves this process by making the creation of a default property something that is declared directly in our code through the use of the `Default` keyword:

```
Default Public Property Name(ByVal Index As Integer) As String
```

VB.NET also imposes an extra restriction on default properties – they *must* have at least one required parameter. It is no longer legal to have a default property that accepts no parameter.

Structured Error Handling

One area where VB has long been criticized is its lack of structured error handling.

Certainly we were able to do a lot with `On Error Goto` and `On Error Resume Next`, but these global error handlers lacked control and didn't lend anything to our program's readability. They also involved a huge amount of work.

> The older error handling options still exist in VB.NET, though a given procedure can use *either* the old or the new error handling capabilities, but not both in the same procedure.

VB.NET incorporates new structured error handling capabilities, addressing these concerns head-on. The structured error handling in VB.NET is quite similar to that found in many other languages, including:

- ❑ C++
- ❑ Java
- ❑ VAX Basic (from the OpenVMS world)

It provides us with a block structure that can be nested, controlled, and easily understood. This means we can implement very robust error handling that actually increases the readability of our code.

Additionally, VB.NET introduces exception handling – including an Exception class to augment the existing Err object we've had in previous versions of VB.

The Try...Catch...Finally Structure

The error handling is accomplished via a basic block structure. For example, we could create a bit of code that divides two values and traps any possible division error (such as division by 0):

```
Try
   intResult = intValue1 \ intValue2
Catch
   intResult = 0
Finally
   System.Diagnostics.Debug.WriteLine(intResult)
End Try
```

When using a Try block, at a minimum we must provide a Catch or a Finally block or we'll get a syntax error.

Let's take this apart to see what is going on.

The first part of our block structure is the Try section:

```
Try
   intResult = intValue1 \ intValue2
```

All code in the Try block is contained within an error trap. While this example shows just one line of code, it is possible to have many lines of code within a Try block – including nested Try...Catch blocks. If an error occurs in a Try block, the Catch block is invoked to handle the error:

```
Catch
   intResult = 0
```

This code is *only* run in the case that an error occurs in the Try block. If no error occurs, this code is entirely skipped and does not run. If we get here, we know that an error has occurred and so this code exists to handle the error as appropriate. Again, this example shows just one line of code, but the Catch block may contain many lines of code if needed.

We may also want some code to run regardless of whether there was an error or not. In many cases we need to perform cleanup or take other actions in any case. This is where the `Finally` block comes into play:

```
Finally
    System.Diagnostics.Debug.WriteLine(intResult)
End Try
```

The `Finally` block is optional – we don't need to have one if it doesn't make sense in a given scenario. However, any lines of code that are contained in a `Finally` block are run after the code in the `Try` block if there is no error, or after the code in the `Catch` block if there is an error.

Catch Statement Variations

The `Catch` statement can be more sophisticated than shown in our simple example. In particular, we can have more than one `Catch` statement in a `Try...End Try` block, each one set up to handle a specific error. For example:

```
Try
    ' our code goes here
Catch When Err.Number = 5
    ' handle error 5
Catch
    ' handle all other errors
End Try
```

In this way we can have separate error handling blocks to handle different errors that may occur.

Another variation is to assign a specific variable to hold the error exception information within the `Catch` block:

```
Catch e As Exception
    MessageBox.Show(e.ToString)
```

This example code would display a dialog showing a text description of the error that has occurred.

The two syntax variations can be combined as well:

```
Catch e As Exception When Err.Number = 12
```

These variations on the `Catch` statement provide us with a great deal of power to handle errors.

Exit Try

As with any block structure it is very nice to be able to jump out of the structure when needed. This is the purpose of the `Exit Try` statement. This statement can exist within the `Try` block of our overall structure, and causes the flow of execution to jump to the first line of code following the `End Try` statement:

```
Try
    ' protected code goes here
    If MyFlag = True Then Exit Try
    ' more protected code goes here
```

```
Catch
   ' error handling goes here
End Try
' execution resumes here
```

If we have a `Finally` block, that block of code must still be run before the `Try` block is exited:

```
Try
   ' protected code goes here
   If MyFlag = True Then Exit Try
   ' more protected code goes here
Catch
   ' error handling goes here
Finally
   ' execution resumes here
End Try
```

Based on the flow of our code, we can jump out of the protected region at any point with the `Exit Try` statement.

Note that the on-line help shows using `Exit Try` from within a `Catch` block. This doesn't work in practice, as it is a syntax error and prevents building the project.

Exception Objects

From a general syntax or coding level, the only real change to VB error handling is the introduction of the `Try...End Try` structured error handling. However, behind the scenes, VB.NET uses a substantially more sophisticated and capable error handling mechanism than was available in previous versions of VB. This new error mechanism is based on the concept of exceptions, which can be "thrown" to raise an error and "caught" when that error is handled.

The `Err` object now has a `GetException` method that will return the `Exception` object containing the details of the underlying exception that caused the error.

While largely hidden from day-to-day VB programming, this underlying exception mechanism will be a welcome addition to programmers from other languages that are used to dealing with exceptions and having access to that information.

Converting from On Error Goto

While the older `On Error` statements still exist in VB.NET, we may want to convert to the newer, more structured alternatives. Let's take a look at two different examples that cover the most common ways `On Error` is used within VB6.

First, we may have an `On Error Goto` statement, with an error handler later in our routine:

```
Sub DoSomething()
   On Error Goto Handler

   ' protected code goes here
   Exit Sub
```

```
Handler:
   ' error handling code goes here
End Sub
```

In VB.NET this code would appear as:

```
Sub DoSomething()
   Try
      ' protected code goes here
   Catch
      ' error handling code goes here
   End Try
End Sub
```

The result is pretty similar, but is somewhat easier to read and understand.

However, keep in mind that there's no Resume equivalent for Try blocks. If our current error handler resumes the protected code, then in some cases things get more complex. For instance, in VB6 we might have:

```
Sub DoSomething()
   On Error Goto Handler

   ' protected code goes here
   Exit Sub

Handler:
   ' error handling code goes here
   Resume
End Sub
```

The Resume statement will cause us to re-run the line that originally cause the error – jumping back into the normal flow of execution. This functionality doesn't exist within the context of a Try block. We cannot call Resume from within a Catch block to re-enter the Try block.

This is a major limitation of the structured error-handling scheme, and requires a bit more work on our part. Typically, the Resume statement is used when we are handling an "expected" error within our code – meaning it is an error that we can fix in the handler and thus allow the original code to continue as planned.

This scenario is now covered through the use of nested Try blocks. For instance, perhaps we expect that we might have a division by 0 error in one line of our code, but the rest of our code would work if the result was just forced to be a zero rather than an error. Our VB.NET code might appear as:

```
Sub DoSomething()
   Try
      ' protected code goes here
      Try
         x = x / y
      Catch
         x = 0
      End Try
      ' more protected code goes here
```

```
      Catch
        ' error handling code goes here
      End Try
    End Sub
```

This addresses the typical use of `Resume`, and potentially adds a great deal of clarity to our code, since we can see exactly what lines of code are *expected* to cause an error.

Converting from On Error Resume Next

Another very common error handling approach in VB6 is to use `On Error Resume Next`, and then to simply check the `Err.Number` value to see if an error has occurred. While we can continue to use this technique in VB.NET, we may want to change our code to use a `Try` block.

In VB6 we might have code such as:

```
    Sub DoSomething()
      On Error Resume Next
      ' protected code goes here
      If Err Then
        ' error handling code goes here
      End If
      On Error Goto 0
      ' unprotected code goes here
    End Sub
```

This type of error handling code is typically directed at catching a specific error that we expect to occur within our code. For instance, many applications use `On Error Resume Next` immediately prior to attempting to open a file that may or may not exist – providing a relatively readable technique for catching that error and handling it inline.

Structured error handling is a much better way to handle these scenarios. We can convert this VB6 code to VB.NET as follows:

```
    Sub DoSomething()
      Try
        ' protected code goes here
      Catch
        ' error handling code goes here
      End Try
      ' unprotected code goes here
    End Sub
```

We achieve the same end result – trapping and handling the potential error in our protected code – but structured error handling is much easier to read and thus to maintain.

Changes to Procedure Syntax

VB.NET introduces a number of changes to the way procedures (`Function`, `Sub`, and other methods) are called and the way in which they are created or declared.

Parentheses Required on Procedure Calls

One striking syntactical difference in VB.NET is that all method calls require parentheses unless the method accepts no parameters. In the past, parentheses were only required when calling a Function – a method that returns a value – with parameters, such as:

```
x = DoSomething(y, z)
```

Now, however, parentheses are required for any method that accepts parameters – whether the method returns a result or not. This means that many methods declared as Function and methods declared as Sub, with or without parameters, require parentheses. So, method calls now appear as:

```
x = DoSomething(x)
x = DoSomethingElse(y, z)
```

In fact, the IDE will often automatically insert parentheses even for those methods that don't accept parameters, even though the parentheses are technically optional:

```
DoMoreStuff()
```

While more consistent overall, this change in syntax does take some getting used to. And for consistency, it is probably best to get used to just putting parentheses after all method calls – parameters or not.

Though we'll discuss this more in Chapter 5, it is also worth noting that object creation also requires parentheses in VB.NET:

```
x = New Customer()
```

This is because any creation of an object causes an implicit call to the constructor method for that class – and all method calls require parentheses.

ByVal Default for all Parameters

When creating procedures (either Function or Sub) it is important to note that VB.NET changes the way parameters are passed into the procedure.

In VB6, most parameters were passed ByRef, meaning that the procedure gained a reference to the variable and any changes to the value of a parameter within a procedure would be carried back to the original calling code. Even though the ByRef keyword wasn't required, it was implicit in all parameter declarations. For us to pass a variable by value, we had to use the ByVal keyword.

In VB6 we could have code such as:

```
x = 5
DoSomething x
Debug.Print x

Private Sub DoSomething(value As Integer)
  value = 10
End Sub
```

The value printed as a result of this code is 10 rather than 5. This is because the variable x was passed by reference to the procedure – allowing the procedure to change the value at will.

VB.NET changes this default behavior, passing all parameters ByVal – by value. Converting the above code to VB.NET we have:

```
x = 5
DoSomething(x)
System.Diagnostics.Debug.WriteLine(x)

Private Sub DoSomething(value As Integer)
  value = 10
End Sub
```

The value printed as a result of this code is 5, since the variable x is passed by value – meaning the procedure can't cause the original value to change.

Obviously, the ByRef and ByVal keywords can still be used when declaring parameters for a procedure – meaning we can have whichever behavior we require. However, it is important to note that the *default* behavior has changed.

Optional Parameters Require Default Value

Another change to the way parameters are handled deals with optional parameters. One thing that hasn't changed is that optional parameters must be the last parameters in the parameter list – and that remains true.

However, it used to be that optional parameters had to be of type Variant, and we could use the IsMissing statement to find out if the optional parameter was supplied or not. In more recent versions of VB this behavior changed, as we were allowed to have optional parameters of other data types. IsMissing remained valid, but only for Variant parameters.

In VB.NET we no longer have the Variant data type, and so the IsMissing keyword has also been eliminated. Optional parameters still exist, but now must be declared with default values – making it easy for us to determine if a specific value was provided by the calling code since it would vary from the default value we have set.

The new syntax for declaring an optional parameter is:

```
Public Sub DoSomething(Optional ByVal param1 As String = "")
```

When using the Optional keyword for a parameter, we must also supply a default value for the parameter by adding an assignment after the type declaration.

Return statement

VB.NET enhances how we return result values from Function procedures. Long ago, we had to create our functions along this line:

```
Public Function GetCustomer(ID As Long) As Customer
  Dim objCust As Customer

  Set objCust = New Customer
```

```
    objCust.Load ID
    Set GetCustomer = objCust
End Function
```

More recently, we were able to use this syntax:

```
Public Function GetCustomer(ID As Long) As Customer
    Set GetCustomer = New Customer
    GetCustomer.Load ID
End Function
```

This syntax is highly disturbing for those programmers used to recursion, since it appears to be a recursive bit of code. I do not know why this was ever made to work as it does!

Now, in VB.NET, we can use the Return keyword to return our value:

```
Public Function GetCustomer(ID As Integer) As Customer
    Dim objCust As New Customer(ID)

    Return objCust
End Function
```

The Return keyword sets the result value of the Function to the value provided as a parameter.

For those curious about the object creation process shown here, we'll cover this in more detail in Chapter 5.

Apart from making obvious what is being returned, Return also facilitates changing the function name without having to run through all the code within the function to change the lines that set the return value.

Changes to Event Handling

VB.NET preserves the basic functionality of events as provided in VB6. In fact, raising events is unchanged, although handling events has been enhanced.

Raising Events

This means we continue to have event declarations in a class:

```
Public Event MyEvent()
```

Our events can also have parameters – values that are provided to the code receiving the event:

```
Public Event MyEvent(ByVal Info As String)
```

Within the class, our code can raise the event with the RaiseEvent statement:

```
Public Sub DoSomething()
    RaiseEvent MyEvent("Some info")
End Sub
```

So far this is all the same as VB6 code.

Handling Events

Where things get a bit different is in the code that handles the events. In VB6, an event handler was created using what can only be described as a weird syntax. If we had an object variable named myObject that raised an event, we might have a routine such as this:

```
Private WithEvents myObject As MyClass

Private Sub myObject_MyEvent(Info As String)
  Debug.Print Info
End Sub
```

While the WithEvents keyword is pretty clear, the rest of this syntax was far from intuitive to new developers, as it doesn't explicitly indicate what the routine is for. To clarify this, VB.NET uses the Handles keyword instead, allowing us to create the following code:

```
Private WithEvents myObject As MyClass

Private Sub OnMyEvent(ByVal Info As String) _
    Handles myObject.MyEvent

    System.Diagnostics.Debug.WriteLine(Info)
End Sub
```

Note how the procedure is declared with the Handles keyword – indicating the event that it will be handling. The procedure can be scoped as desired, and can be called directly if we want, but it will also be automatically called when the event is raised.

This is not only much more clear than the VB6 equivalent, but it is more flexible, since the procedure that handles an event can be named anything – the only requirement is that its parameter list match that of the event being raised.

The VB.NET IDE will create event handler methods for us – just like the VB6 IDE did. Simply select the object in the class name dropdown in the upper-left of the code window, and then select the event to be handled in the method name dropdown in the upper-right. The resulting method will appear as:

```
Public Sub myObject_MyEvent(ByVal Info As System.String) _
    Handles myObject.MyEvent
```

This is a pretty similar naming convention to what we're used to in VB6. If we don't like this name we can change it as desired – as long as the Handles statement remains to link the method up to the event.

Handling Multiple Events

The Handles keyword offers even more flexibility. Not only can the method name be anything we choose, but a single method can also handle multiple events if we desire. Again, the only requirement is that the method and all the events being raised must have the same parameter list.

> *As an aside, this explains why all the standard events raised by the .NET system class library have exactly two parameters – the sender and an EventArgs object. By being so generic, it is possible to write very generic and powerful event handlers than can accept virtually any event raised by the class library.*

One common scenario where this is useful is where we have multiple instances of an object that raises events:

```
Private WithEvents myObject1 As MyClass
Private WithEvents myObject2 As MyClass

Private Sub OnMyEvent(ByVal Info As String) _
    Handles myObject1.MyEvent, myObject2.MyEvent

  System.Diagnostics.Debug.WriteLine(Info)
End Sub
```

Notice that we've now declared two different object variables based on `MyClass`. They both raise the event `MyEvent`, and we've changed the `Handles` clause to indicate that the method will handle the events from *both* objects.

This technique can be used to consolidate a lot of code in some cases. Many VB6 programs have a large number of event handling routines that all simply call into a single, central routine to do the actual work. With VB.NET, all those events can be directly routed to a single handler where they can be processed.

Depreciated, Obsolete, and Unsupported Visual Basic Syntax

By now it has probably become apparent that there are a number of functions, keywords, and statements from previous versions of VB that are either unsupported in VB.NET or are at least considered depreciated and should not be used as they may be removed in future versions. In this section of the chapter we'll list these, as they stand at present. We must keep in mind that we are still working with beta software, and so the final list of unsupported or depreciated syntax may yet change.

Microsoft.VisualBasic.Compatibility.VB6 Namespace

The `Microsoft.VisualBasic.Compatibility.VB6` namespace contains quite a lot of items – all of which are considered depreciated and exist for the purpose of migrating older VB code into VB.NET. These include:

Class	Depreciated keywords	.NET replacement
Collections	`Collection`	`System.Collections`
Color	`QBColor`, `RGB`	`System.Drawing.Color`
Constants	All the `vb` constants such as `vbCr`, `vbLf`, etc.	`Microsoft.VisualBasic.ControlChars`
Conversions	`Hex`, `Oct`, `Str` functions	VB keywords
Date and Time	`DateAdd`, `DateDiff`, `DatePart`, `DateSerial`, `DateValue`, `TimeSerial`, `TimeValue`	`System.DateTime`
File system	`Close`, `EOF`, `FileAttr`, `Get`, `Put`, `FreeFile`, `Input`, `Line Input`, `Loc`, `Lock`, `LOF`, `Open`, `Print`, `Print Line`, `Rename`, `Reset`, `Seek`, `SPC`, `TAB`, `Unlock`, `Width`, `Write`, `Write Line`	`System.IO`

Class	Depreciated keywords	.NET replacement
Objects	`CreateObject, GetObject`	New keyword
Math	`Randomize, Rnd, Round`	`System.Random, System.Math`
Strings	`Format, LSet, RSet`	Individual data type classes

Though there are quite a number of depreciated keywords, there are corresponding new features either in VB.NET or in the .NET system class libraries that support the same, or more often, enhanced functionality.

In general, it is recommended that the functionality included in the `Microsoft.VisualBasic.Compatibility.VB6` namespace be avoided in favor of the functionality found in other namespaces. It is never wise to base software on depreciated keywords and functions, as most vendors eventually remove those features over time. While we don't know that Microsoft will remove them, it is a risk we are better off not taking.

Gosub

The `Gosub` keyword and related functionality has been entirely removed from VB.NET. Code that currently uses `Gosub` will need to be rewritten. For example:

```
Public Sub DoSomething()
  Dim x As Integer

  ' do some work
  Gosub Mysub
  ' do some more work
  Exit Sub

Mysub:
  ' do work in the subroutine using x
  Return
End Sub
```

We might re-write this code in a variety of ways. The most direct is to do something along this line:

```
Public Sub DoSomething()
  ' do some work
  Mysub(x)
  ' do some more work
End Sub

Private Sub Mysub(ByRef x As Integer)
  ' do work in the subroutine
End Sub
```

By passing the variable `x` as a `ByRef` parameter, we preserve the behavior where code in a `Gosub` routine could alter the value of variables in the main procedure.

DefType Statements

The little-used `DefType` statement has been a long-time holdover from the days when BASIC shared some commonality with FORTRAN. This statement allowed us to declare all variables starting with certain letters to be certain data types.

This has long been discouraged as a declaration mechanism, as it leads to code that is hard to read and maintain.

VB.NET removes support for this keyword and this concept.

Delegates

There are times when it would be nice to be able to pass a procedure as a parameter to a method, a concept known as function pointers or callbacks. The classic case is when building a generic sort routine, where we not only need to provide the data to be sorted, but we need to provide a comparison routine appropriate for the specific data.

VB6 had the AddressOf operator, which would return the address of a procedure in a BAS module. This approach had two limitations. First off, the code had to be in a BAS module. Second, and more important, there was no way to *call* the method based on its address from VB.

While VB.NET preserves the AddressOf operator, it extends its functionality to include methods of objects as well as procedures in code modules. More importantly, through the mechanism of **delegates**, we can call these methods from within our VB code.

The concept of a delegate formalizes the process of declaring a routine to be called and calling that routine. In our code we can declare what a delegate procedure must look like from an interface standpoint. This is done in a class by using the Delegate keyword:

```
Delegate Function IsGreater (v1 As Integer, v2 As Integer) _
   As Boolean
```

Once a delegate has been declared, we can make use of it within our code:

```
Public Sub DoSort(ByRef theData() As Integer, GreaterThan As IsGreater)
   Dim outer As Integer
   Dim inner As Integer
   Dim temp As Integer

   For outer = 0 To UBound(theData)
     For inner = outer + 1 To UBound(theData)
       If GreaterThan.Invoke(theData(outer), theData(inner)) Then
         temp = theData(outer)
         theData(outer) = theData(inner)
         theData(inner) =  temp
       End If
     Next
   Next
End Sub
```

Note the use of the Invoke method, which is the way a delegate is called from our code. All that remains is to actually create the implementation of the delegate routine and call our sort method. Typically this would be done in a separate code module or class.

The only requirement of the method providing the delegate implementation is that its parameter list must exactly match those in our Delegate statement above:

```
Public Function MyIsGreater(v1 As Integer, v2 As Integer) As Boolean
   If v1 > v2 Then
      Return True
   Else
      Return False
   End If
End Function
```

We can then use this implementation when calling the sort routine with code such as:

```
Dim myData() As Integer = {3, 5, 2, 1, 6}
```

```
DoSort(myData, AddressOf MyIsGreater)
```

This is where the AddressOf operator comes into play. We can use it to gain the address of a regular procedure in a code module, a method of an object, or a shared method of a class – a concept we'll discuss in Chapter 5. Any procedure or method is valid as long as the parameters match the Delegate declaration.

Attributes

One major new addition to the VB syntax in VB.NET is the introduction of **attributes**. Attributes can be applied to classes, methods, and other code. They provide an extensible mechanism by which we can add tags to instruct the .NET runtime or other code to alter its behavior as it interacts with our code.

The .NET runtime supports a number of attributes that are very useful to VB developers. Additionally, we can use attributes as a mechanism to build advanced frameworks of our own, if we desire. In this book we'll stick to a discussion of attributes as they pertain to the .NET Framework and typical VB development.

Most attributes are instructions for some portion of the .NET Framework or for the VS.NET IDE itself. We'll use and explain quite a number of them throughout the remainder of the book, as a lot of the functionality we'll explore will require their use.

We specify an attribute on a class using the following syntax:

```
Public Class <theAttribute()> MyClass
```

Some attributes can also accept parameters, for example:

```
Public Class <Description("My useful class")> MyClass
```

Often attributes accept named parameters, in which case we use the standard VB named parameter assignment of : = in the call:

```
Public Class <AnAttribute(SomeParam := theValue> MyClass
```

Another common place where attributes are used is on methods or procedures:

```
Public Sub <Description("My useful procedure")> DoSomething()
```

Attributes are defined as a type of class. This means they are syntax checked by the IDE and offer benefits such as IntelliSense. This also means that we can define our own attributes by creating an attribute class, and then we can use reflection to interrogate a class or object about its attributes – a powerful mechanism for building frameworks.

Attributes are an integral part of the .NET Framework, so we'll get to see lots of common examples of their use throughout the rest of this book.

Summary

VB.NET is most definitely still Visual Basic, providing the same syntax and coding style to which we are accustomed. At the same time, VB.NET has some language and syntax changes that allow it to fit very well into the .NET Framework – ensuring that it is a first-class .NET language.

While the syntax and language changes in VB.NET can take a little getting used to, we can use the `Microsoft.VisualBasic.Compatibility.VB6` namespace to ease the transition as needed.

There are a number of other language and syntax changes in VB.NET pertaining to objects and object-oriented programming – these are covered in Chapter 5.

Many of the other exciting new capabilities offered by VB.NET flow from the .NET system class libraries rather than from VB.NET itself. Some of these are explored in Chapter 8 where we take a look at some more advanced concepts.

Before we explore the object changes, however, Chapter 4 will cover the creation of Windows GUI user interfaces using the .NET Framework's WinForms forms technology.

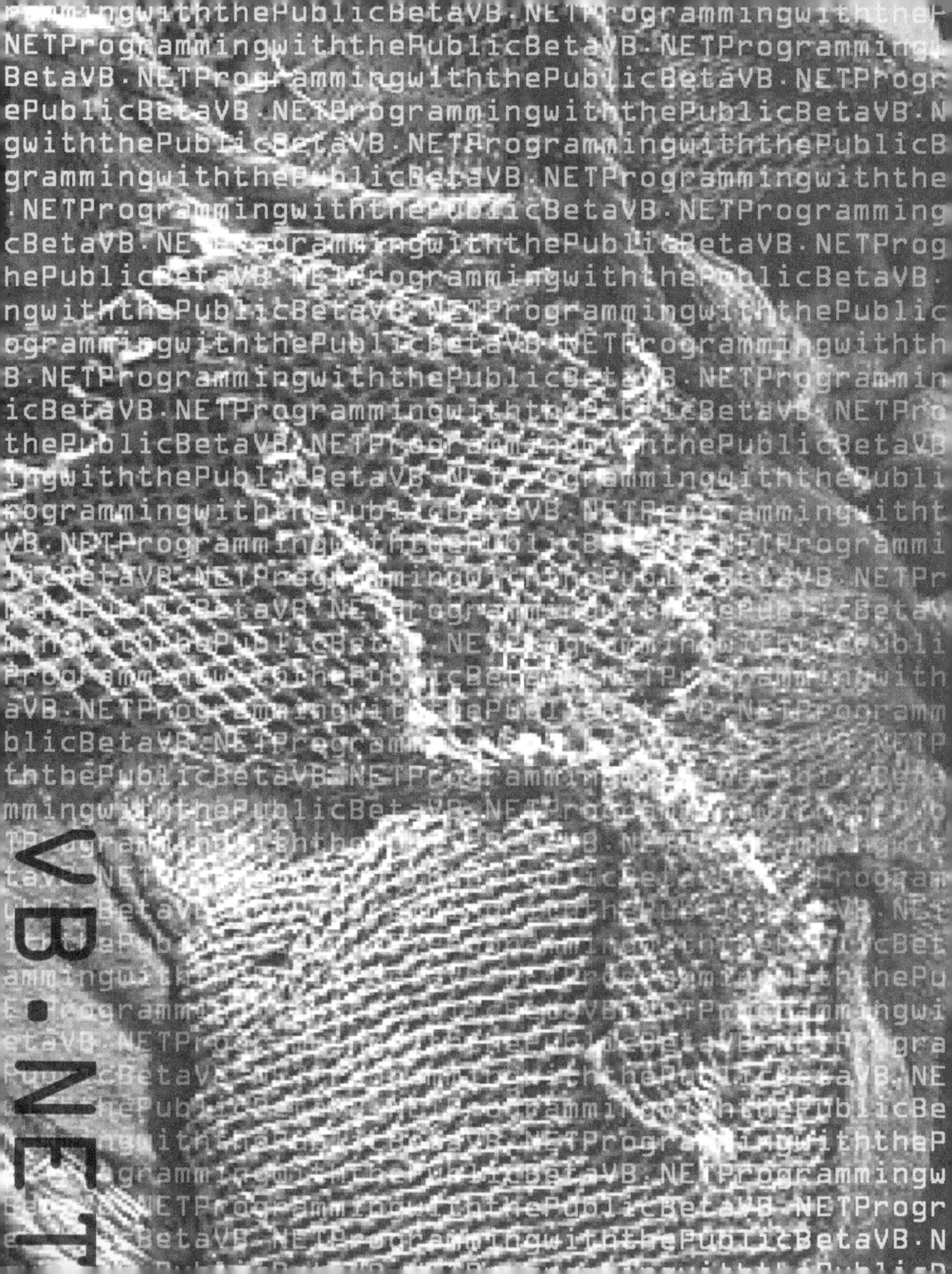
VB·NETProgrammingwiththePublicBeta
VB·NET

New Windows UI Capabilities of VB.NET

The .NET Framework provides three ways to render and manage user interfaces – Windows Forms, Web Forms, and console applications. In this chapter, we'll look in detail at Windows Forms, and compare and contrast with the VB forms used in previous version of Visual Basic.

Web Forms are covered in Chapter 6, and console applications are covered in Chapter 8.

The term "Windows Forms" is expected to be temporary. Microsoft's original naming choice for this functionality (WinForms) was subject to trademark issues, so they are still considering what they will use for a replacement. It is hoped that Windows Forms will have a permanent name by beta two of Visual Studio.NET.

What Are Windows Forms?

Windows Forms (sometimes abbreviated in the early .NET documentation and elsewhere as WinForms) is a more advanced way to do standard Win32 screens. The technology behind Windows Forms was originally created for the Windows Foundation Classes (WFC), which were developed for Visual J++ (Microsoft's implementation of Java). That means that the technology has been under development for a while, which accounts for its surprising maturity in a beta product.

As we will see in this chapter, Windows Forms includes some very robust and sophisticated functionality for developing Win32-type screens. Forms and controls in Windows Forms have considerably more functionality than Visual Basic developers are accustomed to.

All languages in the .NET Framework will use Windows Forms instead of whatever they are using now for graphical forms. For Visual Basic.NET that means that Windows Forms replaces the VB forms engine, and in fact the basic architecture of Windows Forms is very similar to the VB forms used in existing versions of Visual Basic. The expertise of Visual Basic developers in doing forms with Windows Forms translates over to any language based on the .NET Framework. Windows Forms provides a rich, unified set of controls and drawing functions for all languages, as well as a standard API for underlying Windows services for graphics and drawing. With Windows Forms, it is mostly unnecessary to use the native Windows graphical API for any graphical or screen functions.

Windows Forms is actually part of the .NET Framework base classes. The namespace used by Windows Forms is `System.WinForms` and will be examined in detail below.

The Importance of Windows Forms

When looking at the hype around .NET, it's easy to get the idea that Windows Forms is just an afterthought. Web Forms and Web Services tend to get more attention in the press. This seriously underestimates the importance of Windows Forms, and their applicability for developers going forward.

The need for client-based applications with a rich, flexible, and responsive user interface is not going away. In fact, as was mentioned in Chapter 2 in the overview of the .NET Framework, such applications may be more feasible than ever under .NET. Presently, many applications are made browser-based, in spite of the higher cost of development and a weaker user interface, just to get away from the deployment costs of client apps. With the XCOPY deployment of a Windows Forms-based application, the deployment and support costs are reduced. This may tip the scale towards a Windows Forms interface in the .NET world in situations that today would lean toward using a browser-based user interface.

In fact, the multi-tier programming model that we call Windows DNA today still applies in the .NET world, and that model leaves open the possibility that an application may have both a local Win32 interface *and* a web interface. For projects in the .NET Framework, that means that it will be desirable in some cases for an application to have one interface done with Windows Forms and another with Web Forms or Active Server Pages in ASP.NET. Both interfaces would sit on top of the same middle-tier components. For example, an ordering system might have a Win32 interface for telephone operators to enter orders using an interface optimised for speed, while another web interface allowed customers to enter orders directly into the same system.

It is possible to produce applications with both Win32 and web interfaces today, but it becomes much easier using .NET. The .NET Framework makes it easier to integrate components among tiers by providing a consistent component interface model for all .NET languages, including scripting languages. This means, for example, that it is unnecessary in .NET to have special versions of components that use `Variant`s in their interface the way today's Active Server Page interfaces require (and in fact, Chapter 3 mentioned that the `Variant` type is not even available in .NET).

It is also just as easy to integrate Windows Forms with Web Services as it is to integrate Web Forms to Web Services. Rich, Win32 interfaces based on Windows Forms can access and manage data on remote Internet servers through Web Services just as Web Forms can. While Visual Basic forms also had the ability to do web access through special controls, that functionality is much more integrated and accessible in Windows Forms, courtesy of the .NET Framework.

Basics of Windows Forms

Chapter 3 covered a "Hello World" program that was created in Windows Forms. Here's a summary of the main points made in that example:

- ❑ A Windows Form program is actually a class. There is no separate "form module" syntax in VB.NET.

- ❑ Since a form is actually a class, it cannot be implicitly loaded. That is, simply referring to a form to get it to load is not valid syntax. It is necessary to instantiate the form and then show it, the way classes are done in VB6.

- ❑ The class inherits the capability to be a Windows Form by inheriting from the `System.WinForms.Form` class.

- ❑ As with all classes in the .NET Framework, Windows Forms have constructors and destructors. The constructor, named `Sub New`, is a rough equivalent of `Form Load` in previous VB versions. The destructor, named `Sub Dispose`, is roughly equivalent to `Form Unload`.

- ❑ The visual forms designer inserts a lot of code in the class to instantiate and manage the form and the controls it contains. This designer code takes the place of the beginning section of a VB6 `.frm` file (which contains definitions and settings for controls in VB6 and earlier).

- ❑ Events are handled somewhat differently, and are more flexible than in VB6 forms. Events contain more information in their arguments, for example, and using advanced techniques a single event routine can be applied to multiple controls.

A program with a Windows Form interface is initially created by selecting File | New | Project..., which brings a dialog box similar to the following one:

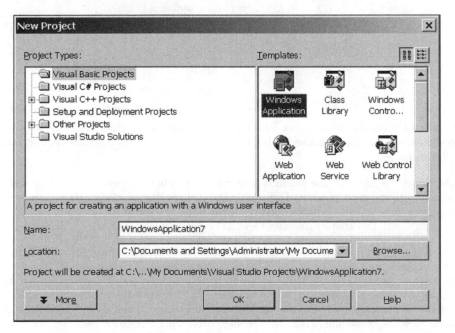

The Windows Application template should be selected for a Windows Forms project, and an appropriate name should be entered. Then, upon pressing the OK button, a project is created with a blank form named Form1, just as in VB6.

The construction of Windows Forms is very similar to the construction of forms in VB6 and earlier. Controls reside in a toolbox, and are placed on the form surface through drag-and-drop. Double clicking on a control activates the code window and places the cursor in an event handler for the control. The underlying actions are quite different, with the designer creating VB code instead of the header of a .frm file, but the actions from the developer's point of view are quite similar.

Architecture of Windows Forms

As with so many of the class libraries in the .NET Framework, the base classes concerned with Windows Forms are in the System namespace. There are several classes in that namespace that form an object hierarchy. That is, the namespace contains a base class, and another class which inherits from the base class and adds more functionality, and then another class which inherits from the second class and again adds more functionality, and so on. Here are the classes in the hierarchy, shown in diagrammatic form:

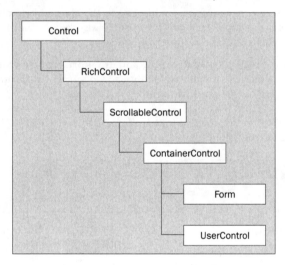

Of course, these classes ultimately inherit from the Object class (as all classes in .NET do), and there are some intermediate classes in the hierarchy, but these represent the classes important in understanding how Windows Forms work.

From a developer's perspective, the two most important classes in this hierarchy are Form and UserControl. All standard Windows Forms ultimately inherit from the Form class. Controls that appear on a Windows Form inherit from the UserControl class, or from some chain of classes that ultimately inherit from UserControl. This chapter contains a section below on inheritance in Windows Forms and controls.

Most of the properties and methods of forms and controls that Visual Basic developers will find familiar are actually not implemented in the Form class. They are implemented in classes above Form in the class hierarchy. Each of the classes in the hierarchy has its own set of members that it implements, and those are then available to all classes below that class in the hierarchy. For example, the Control class implements a Left property that works exactly like the Left property of a form or control in Visual Basic. All of the other classes in the hierarchy then inherit the Left property from the Control class.

The Control Class

Let's examine the hierarchy starting at the top. The `Control` class contains the basic functionality to define a rectangle on the screen, provide a handle for it, and process routine operating system messages. This gives the class the ability to perform such functions as handling user input through the keyboard and mouse. The `Control` class serves as the base class for any component that needs a visual representation on a Win32-type graphical interface. Application developers normally have no reason to inherit directly from this class because there are subclasses of it that are typically more suitable, and they are discussed later in the chapter.

The complete list of members of the `Control` class is too long to list here, but it is available in the help files for Visual Studio.NET. Here are some of the most important members of the `Control` class from the perspective of a VB developer:

Properties	
CanFocus	A read-only property that indicates whether the control can receive focus.
CausesValidation	A new property of forms and controls that indicates whether entering the control causes validation on the control itself or on controls contained by this control that require validation.
Controls	A collection of child controls which this control contains.
Enabled	Property indicating whether the control is currently enabled.
Handle	The HWND handle that this control is bound to.
Top, Left, Height, Width, Bottom, Right, Location, Size	Properties that relate to the size and position of the control. The Top, Left, Height, and Width properties are similar to their counterparts in VB6 and earlier.
Visible	Property that indicates whether the control is currently visible on the screen.

Methods	
BringToFront	Brings this control to the front of the Zorder.
Focus	Attempts to set focus to this control.
Hide	Hides the control by setting the Visible property to False.
Refresh	Forces the control to repaint itself, and to force a repaint on any of its child controls.
Show	Makes the control display by setting the Visible property to True.
Update	Forces the control to paint any currently invalid areas.
WndProc	A very important method that allows access to Windows messages. Since this is implemented in the Control class, all Windows Forms classes can have easy access to Windows messages.

Events	
Click, DoubleClick, GotFocus, KeyDown, KeyPress, KeyUp, MouseDown, MouseEnter, MouseMove, MouseUp, Resize	Same as corresponding events in Visual Basic 6 and earlier.
Leave	Occurs when the control is left (focus is lost).
MouseHover	New mouse event to determine when the mouse cursor has hovered over the control.
PropertyChanged	Occurs when a property of the control has changed

Many of these members, and the ones summarized for the other classes in the hierarchy below, will be discussed in detail in some of the sections that follow in this chapter. Especially for capabilities that are new, examples will be shown to illustrate usage.

RichControl class

The RichControl class inherits from the Control class. (Chapters 3 and 5 both have discussions of inheritance, if you are unfamiliar with that concept.) It takes care of much of the visual nature of the control. The members of the RichControl class include such visually related properties as Font, ForeColor, BackColor, and BackGroundImage. Many of these will be familiar to Visual Basic developers because these are also members of the standard VB form. Some new capabilities of this control are properties that affect layout, such as docking and anchoring the control.

Here are significant members of the RichControl class:

Properties	
AllowDrop	If set to True then this control will allow drag and drop operations and events to be used.
Anchor	Determines which edges of the control are anchored to the container's edges. Covered in detail below in the section on positioning and layout of forms and controls.
Dock	Controls to which edge of the container this control is docked to. Covered in more detail below in the section on positioning and layout of forms and controls.
BackColor, Font, ForeColor	Visual properties which are the same as corresponding properties in VB6 and earlier.

Methods	
DoDragDrop	Begins a drag operation.

Events	
DragDrop, DragEnter, DragLeave, DragOver	Events relating to drag and drop operations.
Paint	Occurs when the control is forced to repaint itself to the screen

Most of the controls in the WinForms namespace derive from RichControl. Microsoft expects that the RichControl class could be used by Visual Basic developers in rare cases. For example, the RichControl class could be used directly to create lightweight controls for display. However, as previously mentioned, Visual Basic developers will use the Form and UserControl classes almost exclusively.

ScrollableControl Class

As the name suggests, the ScrollableControl class adds support for scrolling the client area of the control's window. It is typically not used directly. Almost all the members implemented by this class relate to scrolling. They include AutoScroll, which turns scrolling on or off, and controlling properties such as AutoScrollPosition, which gets or sets the position within the scrollable area.

ContainerControl Class

The ContainerControl class derives from ScrollableControl, and adds the ability to support and manage child controls. It manages the focus and the ability to tab from control to control. As with the ScrollableControl class, ContainerControl is not usually inherited from directly. Here are the most significant members of the ContainerControl class from a VB perspective:

Properties	
ActiveControl	An object reference pointing to the currently active child control, that is, the child control that has the focus.
ParentForm	Indicates the form that a container control is assigned to. This allows, for example, controls on a form to indicate what form their container is (which could be the form, or a control on the form which can serve as a container).

Methods	
ActivateControl	Activates a child control. A parameter indicates the control to activate.
Validate	Validates the last unvalidated control (the most recently changed control that has not had its validation event fired) and its ancestors up through, but not including, the current control.

Form Class

Finally, we get to a class that VB developers will actually use a lot. However, keep in mind that the Form class is inherited from all the classes discussed above, and so it has all of the properties, methods, and events for those classes.

The Form class adds the ability to display caption bars and system menus, so that a form based on this class can look like a normal Windows form. However, the Form class can be used to create windows that are borderless or floating, or modal forms such as a dialog box. It also implements the capability to have default controls for pressing the *Enter* key and pressing *Esc* to cancel.

The new members of the Form class are discussed throughout this chapter in detail, but here is a quick listing of some of the most important members implemented by the Form class:

Properties	
AcceptButton	An object reference to the button control (the VB.NET equivalent to the command button) that will be activated (by having its Click event fired) when the *Enter* key is pressed. The *Enter* key only activates the AcceptButton control if the current control does not handle the *Enter* key. Editing controls, for example, process the *Enter* key themselves, and so pressing *Enter* in one of these controls does not activate the button referenced by AcceptButton.
ActiveMDIChild	If this form is a Multiple Document Interface (MDI) form, then this property indicates the active (MDI) child window. See the IsMDIContainer property below, which set a form to become an MDI form.
CancelButton	Similar to AcceptButton (above), but works with the *Esc* key instead of *Enter*. This property points to the button control that is activated (the Click event is fired) when the user presses the *Esc* key.
ClientSize	Gets or sets the size of the client area of the form (the area exclusive of borders, title bar, etc.).
DesktopBounds, DesktopLocation	Properties affecting the size and location of the form on the Windows desktop – discussion on these properties is in the section below entitled *New Layout Properties for Forms*.
DialogResult	Gets or sets the dialog result for the form. An example of the new techniques for dealing with dialog boxes is discussed below in the section *Differences in Dialog Boxes*.
HelpButton	Gets or sets a value indicating whether a help button is displayed in the title bar of the form.
IsMDIChild	Gets a value indicating whether the form is a multiple document interface (MDI) child form. Equivalent to the MDIChild property in VB6.
IsMDIContainer	Gets or sets a value indicating whether the form is a container for multiple document interface (MDI) child forms. This replaces the VB6 construct of a separate type of form for an MDI parent. Any form can be set as an MDI parent by setting this property. There is a section below on changes with MDI forms.

Properties	
MaximizeBox	Gets or sets a value indicating whether the maximize button is displayed in the title bar of the form. Equivalent to the MaxButton property in VB6.
MDIChildren	If the form is set to be an MDI container (with the IsMDIContainer property above), then this property references an array of forms that represent the multiple document interface (MDI) child forms that are contained by this form.
MDIParent	If the form is an MDI child form, then this property indicates the MDI parent form of this form.
Menu	Points to the MainMenu control which contains the main menu (the menu appearing below the title bar) for this form. There is a section below that discusses menus in Windows Forms.
MinimizeBox	Gets or sets a value indicating whether the minimize button is displayed in the title bar of the form. Equivalent to the MinButton property in VB6.
Modal	A read only property that indicates whether this form is displayed modally.
OwnedForms, Owner	Properties related to form ownership. A section below discusses this concept and explains these properties.
BorderStyle, ControlBox, Icon, KeyPreview, ShowInTaskBar, Size, StartPosition, WindowState	Similar to corresponding properties in Visual Basic 6.

Methods	
Close	Closes the form. Used instead of the VB6 Unload keyword.
ShowDialog	Displays this form as a modal dialog box. A section below discusses new techniques for dealing with dialog boxes in VB.NET.
Activate, Show	Similar to corresponding methods in VB6.

Events	
Closed, Closing	Events that occur when a form is being closed. Closing is roughly equivalent to Form QueryUnload. Closed is more like Form Unload, though you should compare the standard Dispose constructor, which also compares in some sense to Form Unload.
MDIChildActivate	For a form set to be an MDI form, occurs when an MDI child form becomes activated.
Activated, DoubleClick	Similar to corresponding events in VB6.

As this list indicates, Windows Forms are not radically different from standard VB forms in VB6 and earlier. Many of the same properties, events, and methods are available. Some of the new members replace equivalent members in VB6. And some members, such as the Menu property which points to MainMenu control, offer new ways to access old functionality.

UserControl Class

An original innovation of Visual Basic was to have an extendable set of visual form elements, called controls. Controls in VB.NET are getting quite a facelift, but the concept is still similar. The UserControl class is the base class for the controls Visual Basic developers are most familiar with. It provides an empty container to implement visual controls.

The UserControl class can contain other child controls, but the interface of UserControl is designed to present a single, unified interface to outside clients such as forms or container controls. The external interface of the UserControl class consists exclusively of members inherited from other classes.

Consistency with Web Forms

As we will see in Chapter 6 on web functionality in VB.NET, Windows Forms functionality and naming conventions are fairly consistent with Web Forms. There are no UI classes that are used in both, but the naming of the corresponding classes in each namespace is reasonably consistent. For example, both namespaces have a Button class with a Text property and an OnClick event. There is a UserControl class in both hierarchies which both serve as a container for visual form elements.

Comparison of Windows Forms to VB6 forms

Now that we understand the general architecture of Windows Forms, we can compare them to the forms we've all used in VB6 and earlier.

Differences in Using the Visual Designer for Windows Forms

While creating Windows Forms in VB.NET is basically similar to creating VB forms in VB6, there are some differences.

Invisible Controls Go in their Own Pane

In VB6, even controls that had no visible manifestation at run time were still located on the form surface at design time. The most common control used this way in VB6 was the timer control.

In VB.NET, there is a separate pane of the design surface for such invisible controls. This is a nice improvement, because there are more of these controls in VB.NET. It also ensures that such controls are neither in the way nor hidden on the form at design time. The sections below on Provider controls and Menu controls go into more detail on some of them.

To see how the extra pane works, pull up a Windows Form in VB.NET, and drag a Timer control (from the Toolbox | Components menu) and a PrintDocument control on to the form. You will see the extra pane appear below the normal form design surface. Here is a typical screen showing this extra pane, with a Timer control and a PrintDocument control added:

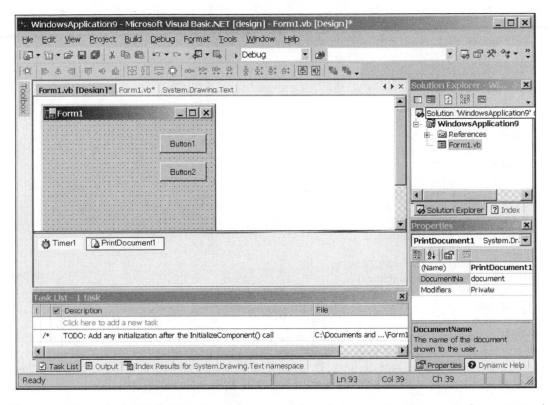

These controls can be highlighted in the extra pane, and then their properties show up in the properties box just as you'd expect. The sample screen above shows the PrintDocument1 control's properties in the Properties window.

Not All Controls Have to Be Locked

In VB6, there is a Lock Controls option on the Format menu. When this option is selected for a form, all controls are locked. Even new controls placed on the form are locked in place as soon as they are on the design surface.

In VB.NET, the Lock Controls menu option (still on the Format menu, and also available by right-clicking on the form) locks all controls currently on the form, but new controls remain unlocked until the option is selected again. This allows you to create some of the controls on the form, lay them out exactly as you would like, and then lock them in place while you lay out the rest of the controls.

Differences in Dialog Boxes

In VB6 and earlier, dialog boxes were ordinary forms that were displayed with the vbModal parameter (or a hardcoded 1) after the form's Show method. This caused the form to be the only active form in the application until it was exited.

A dialog box form needs a way to communicate with the form that called it. In VB6, this was often done by placing a read-only property on the form to communicate the user action. I normally called such a property Action, so my dialog boxes in VB6 would have code like this in them:

```
' This is VB6 code!!!!
Public Enum enuAction
    actionOK = 1
    actionCancel = 2
End Enum

Dim mAction As enuAction

Public Property Get Action() As enuAction
    Action = mAction
End Property

Private Sub cmdOK_Click()
    mAction = actionOK
    Me.Hide
End Sub

Private Sub cmdCancel_Click()
    mAction = actionCancel
    Me.Hide
End Sub
```

Notice the enumerated type enuAction, which has two values, actionOK and actionCancel. The Action property is set to be of this enumerated type. The command buttons set the Action property to an appropriate value and then hide the form. The form must be hidden and not unloaded, since the calling form will need to access the Action property to see what the user did in the dialog box.

Suppose such a dialog box form was named DialogForm. To call this form from another form requires (in VB6) code like this:

```
' This is VB6 code!!!
Dim frmDialogForm As DialogForm
Set frmDialogForm = New DialogForm
frmDialogForm.Show vbModal
```

But it's not enough just to call the form. To know what action the user took, it is necessary to examine the Action property of the dialog box, which can be done by adding the following lines to the above code:

```
' This is VB6 code!!!
Dim frmDialogForm As DialogForm
Set frmDialogForm = New DialogForm
frmDialogForm.Show vbModal

'When control returns, we assume the frmDialogForm
'is hidden but still loaded.

' Code to get information from frmDialogForm goes here
'. . .
Select Case frmDialogForm.Action
    Case actionOK
        ' code goes here for normal processing
```

```
      Case actionCancel
            ' code goes here for user canceling
   End Select
   Unload frmDialogForm
```

There are two significant changes in VB.NET that change the way this kind of logic is written. Let's examine the differences and compare the above code in VB6 to the equivalent code in VB.NET.

ShowDialog Instead of Show vbModal

The vbModal argument for the Show method of a form is not supported in VB.NET. In its place, a Windows Form has a ShowDialog method instead. Here's the comparison of equivalent code.

VB6 code:

```
   Dim frmDialogForm As DialogForm
   Set frmDialogForm = New DialogForm
   frmDialogForm.Show vbModal
```

VB.NET code:

```
   Dim frmDialogForm As New DialogForm
   frmDialogForm.ShowDialog
```

In the VB6 code, there's one line to Dim the form variable, and another line to instantiate the form. This is done to force an explicit instantiation instead of allowing an implicit instantiation when the form is first referenced. Since there is no implicit instantiation in VB.NET, it's not necessary to have both the Dim and Set, so those lines are replaced by one line which both declares and instantiates the form.

The last line in each example shows the switch from using the Show method with a vbModal parameter to using the ShowDialog method.

DialogResult

We saw above how it was common to create a custom form property to find out the user's action in a dialog box. Such homegrown properties, and their states, are usually not necessary in Windows Forms because a replacement is available. When a form is shown with the ShowDialog method, the form has a property already present, called DialogResult, to indicate its state.

The DialogResult property can take the following enumerated results:

- ❑ DialogResult.Abort
- ❑ DialogResult.Cancel
- ❑ DialogResult.Ignore
- ❑ DialogResult.No
- ❑ DialogResult.None
- ❑ DialogResult.OK
- ❑ DialogResult.Retry
- ❑ DialogResult.Yes

When the `DialogResult` property is set, as a by-product, the dialog is hidden.

The `DialogResult` property of a dialog box can be set in two ways. The most common way is to associate a `DialogResult` value with a button. The `button` control has a property to do just that, so that it is unnecessary to set the `DialogResult` in code. Here is an example that uses this technique.

In Visual Studio.NET, start a new Visual Basic Windows Application. On the automatic blank form (named `Form1`) that comes up, place a single button and set its `Text` property to `Dialog`.

Now, insert a new Windows Form using the **Project |Add Windows Form** menu, and name it `DialogForm`. Note that in Visual Studio.NET beta one, you cannot do this in the property box, but should instead go to the line that declares the class:

```
Public Class Form2
```

and change that to:

```
Public Class DialogForm
```

Place two buttons on `DialogForm`. Set the following properties for the buttons:

Property	Value for First Button	Value for Second Button
Name	btnOK	btnCancel
Text	OK	Cancel
DialogResult	OK	Cancel

Do not put any code in `DialogForm` at all.

On the first form (`Form1`), place the following code in the `Click` event for `Button1`:

```
Protected Sub Button1_Click(ByVal sender As Object, _
                       ByVal e As System.EventArgs)

Dim frmDialogForm As New DialogForm()
frmDialogForm.ShowDialog()

' We're back from the dialog - check user action.
Select Case frmDialogForm.DialogResult
    Case DialogResult.OK
        MsgBox("The user pressed OK")
    Case DialogResult.Cancel
        MsgBox("The user pressed cancel")
End Select

frmDialogForm = Nothing

End Sub
```

Now, run and test the code. When a button is pressed on the dialog form, a message box should be displayed (by the calling form) indicating the button that was pressed.

This code is the equivalent of the VB6 code shown earlier to instantiate a dialog box and check the result. Notice that the code that was needed inside the dialog box in VB6 (to define and set the `Action` property) has been rendered completely unnecessary. Because the form class inherits and implements the functionality to expose and manage the `DialogResult` property, the VB developer does not have to create any code for this functionality.

The second way to set the `DialogResult` property is in code. In a `Button_Click` event, or anywhere else in the dialog form, a line like this can be used to set the `DialogResult` and simultaneously hide the dialog form, giving control back to the calling form:

```
Me.DialogResult = DialogResult.Ignore
```

This line sets the dialog result to `DialogResult.Ignore`, but setting the dialog result to any of the permitted values will also hide the dialog form.

Owned Forms

As flexible as VB6 is, there are some programming situations that are difficult to handle with it. One example is working with a form that floats above the application, but does not interfere with using the application. Examples would be a search-and-replace box, or a tutorial help box. It is possible to get a window to do this in VB6 with Windows API calls, but it is much easier in Windows Forms using the concept of **owned forms**.

When a form is owned by another form, it is minimized and closed with the owner form. Owned forms (sometimes called slave forms) are also never displayed behind their owner form. But they do not interfere with allowing the owner form to get the focus and be used.

There are two ways to make a form owned by another form. It can be done in the owner form, or in the owned (slaved) form.

AddOwnedForm Method

In the owner form, another form can be made owned with the `AddOwnedForm` method. Here is code to make `Form2` become owned by `Form1`. This code would reside somewhere in `Form1`.

```
Me.AddOwnedForm Form2
```

Owner Property

The relationship can also be set up in the owned form. This is done with the `Owner` property of the form. Here is code that would work inside `Form2` to make it owned by `Form1`:

```
Me.Owner = Form1
```

OwnedForms Collection

The owner form can access its collection of owned forms with `OwnedForms` property. Here is code to loop through the forms owned by a form:

```
Dim frmOwnedForm As Form
For Each frmOwnedForm In Me.OwnedForms
    Debug.Write(frmOwnedForm.Text)
Next
```

The owner form can remove an owned form with the RemoveOwnedForm property. This could be done in a loop like the one above, with code like this:

```
Dim frmOwnedForm As Form
For Each frmOwnedForm In Me.OwnedForms
    Debug.Write(frmOwnedForm.Text)
    Me.RemoveOwnedForm(frmOwnedForm)
Next
```

This loop would cause an owner form to stop owning all of its slaved forms. Note that those de-slaved forms would not be unloaded – they would simply no longer be owned.

TopMost Property of Forms

Another way to get "always-on-top" functionality is to use the TopMost property of a form. Setting the TopMost property to True will create a form that is always displayed in your application. A top-most form is a form that overlaps all the other forms, even if it is not the active or foreground form. Top-most forms are always displayed at the highest point in the application.

The difference in using the TopMost property instead of making a form an owned form is that TopMost makes a form top-most for all forms of the application. An owned form is always on top of its owner form, but is not necessarily on top of other forms in the application. Also, a top-most form does not get minimized or closed when other forms in the application are minimized or closed.

Form Properties for Cancel Button and Default Button

In VB6, it is possible to set the button that is automatically activated (clicked) when the user presses the *Esc* key. It is also possible to set the button automatically activated by the *Enter* key. This is done by setting properties of the button. Setting the Cancel property of a button to True causes it to become activated when the user presses *Esc*. Setting the Default property of a button to True causes it to become activated when the user presses Enter, as long as the control with the focus is not already handling the *Enter* key.

The same functionality is available in VB.NET, but it is accessed differently. Now the *form* has the properties to determine the cancel and default buttons, rather than the button properties being used.

The properties of the form are named CancelButton and AcceptButton. They are normally set in the Properties window. When one of these properties is accessed, the property displays a drop-down with all of the buttons on the form. Setting a button in the CancelButton property allows it to be activated by *Esc*, and setting a button in the AcceptButton property allows it to be activated by *Enter*.

The button assigned to this property must be a button that is on the current form or located within a container on the current form. The property can only be set to a button, and not to any other type of control.

Though the cancel and accept buttons would typically be set in the Properties window and stay the same for the lifetime of the form, it is possible to set `CancelButton` and `AcceptButton` properties dynamically at run time. This might be done, for example, if a form had both a "normal" and an "advanced" mode, and it was desirable for the form to use different buttons for the cancel and accept functions in the different modes. The following code changes the cancel and accept buttons to two buttons named `btnCancel2` and `btnAccept2`, respectively, assuming that these buttons already exist on the form:

```
Me.CancelButton = btnCancel2
Me.AcceptButton = btnAccept2
```

Differences in Positioning and Layout for Forms and Controls

VB.NET has similar functionality for positioning and layout as VB6, but various actions are performed differently. Here are the new ways that VB.NET allows control over the positioning and layout of forms and controls.

Location Property

In place of the traditional `Left` and `Top` properties in VB6, forms and controls in VB.NET have a `Location` property. The `Location` property returns or accepts a `Point` structure, which contains X and Y coordinates that correspond to the old `Left` and `Top` properties. Point structures are useful in many of the drawing methods discussed in the section below on GDI+ in .NET.

The `Top` and `Left` properties are actually still there for forms and controls, and can be manipulated in code. But `Top` and `Left` do not show up in the property window for a form or control.

Size Property

The `Size` property is similar in concept to the `Location` property, except that it corresponds to the `Height` and `Width` properties. It returns or accepts a `Size` structure, which allows the height and width to be set at once instead of setting the properties individually.

As with `Top` and `Left`, `Height` and `Width` can still be manipulated as properties of forms and controls in code, but they do not show up in the Properties window.

BringToFront, SendToBack Methods

In VB6, the layered ordering of controls on a form is controlled by the `ZOrder` method, which could set the `ZOrder` for a control or form. For example, if two controls overlapped on the screen and `ControlA` has a `ZOrder` of 2 while `ControlB` had a `ZOrder` of 3, then `ControlB` would appear to be under `ControlA`. The control with the lower `ZOrder` number appears on top.

`ZOrder` is still available in VB.NET and is used to set a control to any desired layer, but alternatives are available to place a control at the top or bottom of the order. The `BringToFront` method of a control or form causes it to appear on top of any other controls or forms. Similarly the `SendToBack` method causes a control or form to be "beneath" any other forms or controls that overlap it.

New Layout Properties for Forms

For a form, there are some additional properties affecting size and layout. These include `DesktopBounds`, `DesktopLocation`, `MaxTrackSize`, and `MinTrackSize`.

DesktopBounds returns or sets a Rectangle the determines that size and location of the form on the current desktop. A Rectangle in .NET is similar to a RECT structure from the Win32 API, but much more flexible. A Rectangle in .NET is a structure in the System.Drawing namespace, which is discussed in detail in the section on GDI+ below. Setting up a Rectangle and passing to the DesktopBounds property sets both the size of the form and its location on the desktop all at once.

To just set the location, you can use the DesktopLocation property. It sets and gets a Point structure, just as the Location property above does. The difference in the DesktopLocation property is that it takes the Windows Task Bar into account, so that if the Task Bar is on top of the screen, for example, the form's position will be automatically adjusted downward by the height of the Task Bar.

MaxTrackSize and MinTrackSize both get or set a Size structure, the same as the Size property discussed above. These properties have the effect of determining how large and small, respectively, a form can be. If you want to have a form that is always exactly 500 x 500 pixels, then you could create a variable of type Size, set the height and width property of that variable both to 500, and then set the form's MaxTrackSize and MinTrackSize properties to the same Size structure.

Resizing Multiple Controls

In the Windows Forms designer, there is a new capability to resize multiple controls simultaneously. Just select several controls at once, by clicking and dragging a rectangle around them, or by holding down the *Ctrl* key to select multiple controls by clicking on them. The last control selected will have white resize handles, while the rest have black resize handles. Resizing the control with the white handles will cause all the other controls to resize proportionately.

New Properties of Controls

There are some new properties that are shared by all controls in Windows Forms. Here is a summary of some of the most significant.

Anchor and Dock

It is common in VB6 to have code in a form's Resize event to reposition and resize controls. For example, a grid control may need to be at the bottom of a form, and to always use the full width of the form. When the form is resized, the grid control's properties for size would need to be adjusted, and the code to do that would have to manually calculate distances on the form to work.

Such code is unnecessary in VB.NET. Every control has two properties that can be used for that kind of manipulation.

The Anchor property forces one or more borders of a control to remain at a constant distance from the closest border of the form. The Anchor property specifies which borders are to be controlled this way. For example, suppose we have a form with a list box that looks like this:

Now suppose I would like to make the `list box` stay at the same distance from the form's edge on the left, right, and bottom whenever the form is resized. To do that I set the `Anchor` property to `BottomLeftRight` in the Properties window. The `Anchor` property is set by clicking on a diagram containing the borders that can be used for anchors. Here's an example of a Properties window setting the `Anchor` property for the `list box` above:

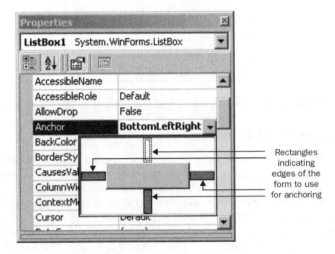

The dark gray rectangles indicate that the control is to be anchored to the left border, the right border, and the bottom border of the form. When this property diagram setting is accepted, the property value will show up as BottomLeftRight.

Once the `Anchor` property is set, the `list box` will resize as needed when the form resizes. Here is another look at a resized version of the form, and the new resized `list box`:

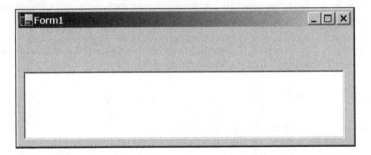

The `Dock` property provides resizing functionality also, but it is more akin to the `Align` property of certain controls in VB6. `Dock` allows a control to "stick" to one edge of the form. For example, if I replace the `list box` in the example above with rich text box, and set its `Dock` property to `Right`, when the form is displayed, the rich text box will be right against the form's right border, and it will extend from the top of the form to the bottom, like this:

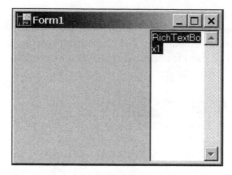

The Dock property can also be set to Fill, which makes a control fill the entire client area of the form.

Accessibility Properties of Controls

All controls inherit several members from the RichControl class relating to accessibility. All controls will show these properties (AccessibleDescription, AccessibleName, AccessibleRole) in the Properties window. Beta one of Visual Studio.NET does not contain documentation on using these properties. However, it is presumed that they will allow Windows Forms to work in Microsoft Active Accessibility framework. In Active Accessibility, client programs can be created for users with special accessibility needs, such as poor vision. These client programs (such as a program to use speech recognition to access menu options) need information about a forms-based interface. The accessibility properties are expected to provide that information.

Adding New Controls at Run Time

Visual Basic has had the capability to add controls to forms at run time, with the functionality increasing with various versions. Using the complete object-oriented capabilities of VB.NET, there is even more flexibility. However, the syntax for adding new controls is changing as a consequence of moving to the object-oriented paradigm for this capability.

The new syntax is simple. For example, if a button's Click event needed to cause a new list box control to be added, the Click event would contain code like this:

```
Private Sub Button1_Click(ByVal sender As System.Object, _
                         ByVal e As System.EventArgs)
    Dim lstNewListBox As New Listbox()
    lstNewListBox.Size = New Size(150, 200)
    lstNewListBox.Location = New Point(50, 50)
    lstNewListBox.Items.Add("First listbox item")
    lstNewListBox.Items.Add("Second listbox item")

    Me.Controls.Add(lstNewListBox)
End Sub
```

As this code shows, a control is just a class that needs to be instantiated and have its properties set. In most cases, we need to set the control's size and location. Also, since it's a list box in this example, some items are added to it.

The only logic that is special for adding a control rather than an arbitrary class is adding the control to the form's control collection, and the line just above the End Sub does that. The form's controls collection can be accessed in any form with Me.Controls (because Me refers to the current instantiation of any class, including a form). Then the Add method takes a control as an argument and adds it to the controls collection. Once the control is in the controls collection, it is managed the same way a control added at design time would be.

Note that there is a display issue with beta one. If no controls of that type have been displayed in any form yet, the new control added at run time may not appear on the form. If you have trouble getting the new list box to display in the example above, just add another list box to the form from the toolbox, run the program once, and then delete the list box you added. Then rerun the example code above.

Summary of Important Controls

In this section, we'll overview the controls available in Windows Forms, and highlight differences in controls and usage from VB6 to VB.NET.

Control Hierarchy

The class hierarchy for the standard controls included with Visual Studio.NET looks like this:

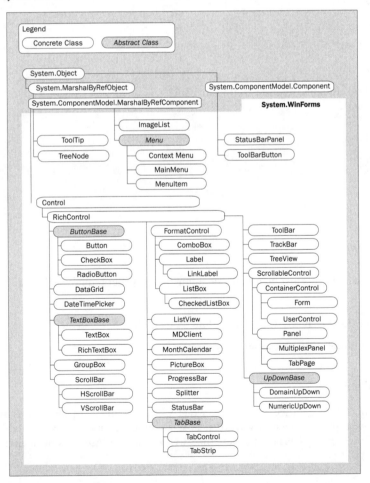

The abstract classes in the diagram cannot be instantiated directly. They are used to derive other classes that can be used directly.

Controls which have VB6 Equivalents

Many of the controls in Windows Forms have almost exact equivalents in VB6 (either in the standard VB6 controls or the Windows common controls). While some properties are changed in name, and additional properties are present, the following controls are similar enough to their VB6 equivalents that detailed discussion is unnecessary:

- ❑ Button (called Command Button in VB6)
- ❑ CheckBox
- ❑ ComboBox
- ❑ HScrollBar
- ❑ ImageList
- ❑ Label
- ❑ ListBox
- ❑ ListView
- ❑ PictureBox
- ❑ ProgressBar
- ❑ RadioButton (called Option Button in VB6)
- ❑ RichTextBox
- ❑ StatusBar
- ❑ TextBox
- ❑ Toolbar
- ❑ Trackbar (called Slider in VB6)
- ❑ TreeView
- ❑ VScrollBar

There are also some controls that offer equivalent functionality, but require slightly different usage in code. These include:

- ❑ Common Dialog Boxes (File Open, File Save, Color, Font, Print)
- ❑ Tab (combines VB6 SSTab and TabStrip)

New Controls

The remaining controls to be discussed have no exact VB6 equivalents. In some cases, such as the menu controls, these new controls are a new way to encapsulate functionality that was available in VB6. In these cases, while the functionality has not changed, the way in which it is used has been altered.

Other new controls, such as the DateTimePicker, have no equivalent functionality in the standard set of VB6 controls, but third-party controls could be used in VB6 to do some or all of the same things. And some controls, such as the provider controls, are new in concept, with no major third-party controls that have provided that functionality in the past.

Menu Controls

VB6 has the ability to specify standard Windows menus that appear at the top of a form. It contains a menu editor specifically to design these menus. VB6 then associates menu options with events, so that when a menu option is chosen, an event is fired.

VB6 also provides the ability to do pop-up menus (typically activated with a right mouse click). Such menus are designed with the same menu editor as the one used for standard Windows menus. A portion of such a menu can be popped up with the `PopUpMenu` method of a VB6 form.

In VB.NET, there are two controls that provide equivalent functionality. The MainMenu control allows a form to have a standard Windows menu at the top of the form. The ContextMenu allows creation of pop-up menus.

The MainMenu control contains a collection of `MenuItem` objects, which describe individual menu options. Properties can be set separately for each `MenuItem` object, which allows menu items to be made visible or invisible, enabled or disabled, etc.

Creating a menu with a MainMenu control is easy. There is a visual menu editor that appears at the top of a form containing a MainMenu control, and it's much easier to use than the old menu editor in VB6.

To create a standard menu on a form, first drag a **MainMenu** control (from the **WinForms** group in the Toolbox) on to the form from the toolbox. The MainMenu control does not appear on the form surface, since it has no visible manifestation there. It appears in a separate pane below the design surface for the form (this extra pane was discussed earlier in this chapter).

When the MainMenu control is highlighted in the separate design pane, a visual menu designer appears close to the title bar of the form. Here is an example of a form with a MainMenu control dragged onto it, showing the visual menu designer:

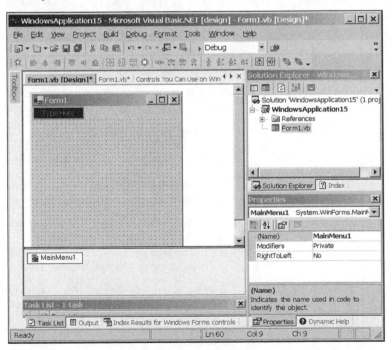

The visual menu designer is the shaded box close to the top of the form that says Type Here. Suppose we click on that box and type in the word File for the top-level File menu that usually begins a standard Windows menu. Then the area around the visual menu designer looks like this:

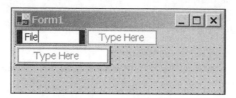

Now there are new areas to type in – one to the right of File that can accept the next top-level menu item and one under File that is for a submenu item inside the File menu when it is pulled down. Creating menu items is as easy as clicking on the appropriate box and typing them in. Double-clicking on a menu item brings up the event routine associated with the menu item, just as clicking on a control brings up the control's Click event routine. Also like VB6, entering an ampersand (&) character in the menu option text results in a short-cut key for the option.

Menu items are given default names just like other controls, and their names can be changed in the Properties window as described below. The default name for the first menu item added (typically the top-level "File" menu item) is MenuItem1.

To change the properties for a menu item, just click on the menu item and change its properties in the Properties window. Here are the properties available for a MenuItem object:

Property	Usage
Checked	If True, the menu item has a checkmark beside it. If False, item is not checked.
DefaultItem	Indicates whether this item is the default item for the next higher menu in the hierarchy. If so, it becomes automatically selected if the user pressed *Enter* for that next higher level.
Enabled	True if the menu item is currently available for selection, False if not. Items with the Enabled property set to False are grayed out on the menu.
MDIList	Only applicable for MDI parent forms. Allows a menu to contain as submenu items a list of the currently loaded MDI child forms. There is an example later in chapter. True uses this property.
MergeOrder	When this menu is merged with another menu, the MergeOrder determines the order in which the merged items are displayed.
MergeType	When this menu is merged with another menu, the MergeType property determines how this item is treated in the merged menu. This property can be used to add the item to a merged menu, have it replace an equivalent item from the merged menu, or to be left off a merged menu.
RadioCheck	If True, instead of using a checkmark to indicate that an item is checked, a radio button is used beside the item instead.
Shortcut	Allows any of the non-ASCII keys on the keyboard (such as function keys, *Insert, Delete*, etc.) to directly access this menu item.

Property	Usage
ShowShortcut	If True and the Shortcut property is set to a key, then the shortcut key is shown in the menu.
Text	The text in the menu item.
Visible	Determines whether the menu item can be seen.

Any of these properties can be manipulated at run time to dynamically affect the behavior of the menu.

Menu items can be added dynamically with code like this:

```
Dim mnuNewMenuItem As New MenuItem()
mnuNewMenuItem.Text = "New menu item"
MenuItem1.MenuItems.Add(mnuNewMenuItem)
```

This creates a new item and places it under the menu item identified as MenuItem1. For the example above, this would mean that the menu item would appear under File.

Pop-up menus are created with the ContextMenu control. It is also dragged onto the form and appears in the extra pane below the form's design surface. When the ContextMenu control is highlighted in the extra pane, the visual menu editor at the top of the form is used to design the popup menu.

To use one of these menus, it should be associated with a form or a control on the form. Highlight the form or control that will use the pop-up menu, and set the ContextMenu property on the form or control to the ContextMenu control that was previously defined.

A form only needs one MainMenu control, but it can have any number of different ContextMenu controls, which may be associated with various other controls on the form or with the form itself. A context menu is associated with a form or control using the ContextMenu property of the form or control.

LinkLabel Control

A LinkLabel is a new control that looks like a hyperlink in a web page. It displays text in hyperlink format, and provides a way to link to another window in the application, or to a web site. It is similar to a label control with different screen cosmetics. The linking action is actually accomplished in code in the control's Click event. The LinkLabel control can also display an image instead of text.

Here is a Windows Form during execution with both types of LinkLabel controls, and with examples of the UpDown controls discussed immediately below:

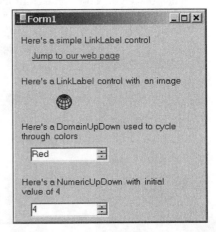

UpDown Controls – DomainUpDown and NumericUpDown

In VB6, an UpDown control (sometimes called a Spinner) is available. It has two common uses:

1. To cause numeric items in a text box to increment or decrement

2. To allow items in a combo box to be rotated through

The associated control in VB6 (text box for function 1, combo box for function 2) is called the **buddy control**.

In VB.NET, there are separate controls for these two different functions. The first function is performed by the NumericUpDown control. The second is performed by the DomainUpDown control. Both are pictured in the sample screen above.

The biggest difference from VB6 is that the UpDown controls in VB.NET include both the control holding the values and the control providing the up-down navigation. The NumericUpDown control has a place for the number to be displayed and the up and down arrow keys to increment and decrement the number. No separate buddy control (such a text box) is required. Similarly, the DomainUpDown control has a text area that holds the items being cycled through. Those items are loaded into the control the same way they would be loaded into a combo box. No separate buddy combo box is needed.

CheckedListBox

The VB6 list box can be set to place checkmarks beside items to indicate that they are selected. This is done by setting the `Style` property to `Checkbox`.

In VB.NET, such a list box is a separate control, called a CheckedListBox. It works like an ordinary list box (and is in fact derived from it), but adds the cosmetics to handle checkboxes beside each item.

DateTimePicker

Third party controls have long been used for choosing dates and times in Visual Basic, but VB.NET includes its own sophisticated date/time control called the DateTimePicker, which can be found in the Win Forms group in the Toolbox. It is similar to the DTPicker included in the VB6 common controls, and is easy to use compared to many third party equivalents.

When placed on a form, the control looks like a combo box, and contains a date. When the drop-down arrow is pressed, a monthly calendar is displayed for choosing a date. Here are screens showing these two states:

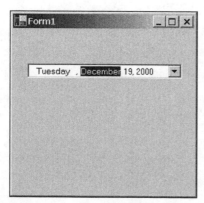 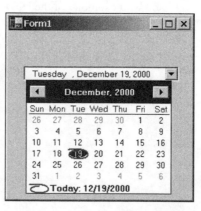

Properties control various options such as the date range that is available, the format of the date or time that is being selected, and the option to use a built-in UpDown control instead of the drop-down to change the date or time in the control. Here is a sample screen with the control's Format property set to Time (to make the control work with a time instead of a date), and with the ShowUpDown property set to True:

Panel and GroupBox Container Controls

In VB6, a frame control can be used as a container to group controls. A set of option buttons placed in a frame control automatically becomes related as one option group. Frames are also often used in VB6 to separate areas of a form into functional areas, or to group controls for showing and hiding. If a frame is hidden, all the controls in it are hidden. Sometimes frames in VB6 are used with a border (with or without a title for the frame), and other times without a border.

The functionality in the frame control for VB6 is divided into two controls in VB.NET. They are called the GroupBox control and the Panel control.

Each is like the VB6 frame control in the following ways:

❑   They can serve as a container for other controls

❑   If they are hidden or moved, the action affects all the controls in the container

The GroupBox control is the one that most closely resembles a frame control visually. It acts just like a VB6 frame control, with one significant exception. There is no way to remove its border. It always has a border, and it can have a title if needed. The border is always set the same way. Here is a form with a GroupBox control containing two RadioButtons:

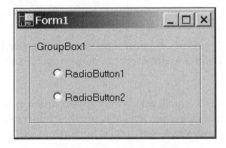

The Panel control has three major differences from GroupBox:

❑ It has options for displaying its border in the `BorderStyle` property, with a default of no border.

❑ It has the capability to scroll by setting its `AutoScroll` property to `True`.

❑ It has no ability to set a title or caption (it has no `Text` property).

Here is a form containing a Panel control with its border set to `FixedSingle`, with scrolling turned on, and with a list box which is too big to display all at once (which forces the Panel to show a scroll bar):

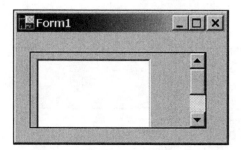

TrayIcon Control

Here's a new control that is really nifty. The TrayIcon control allows a form to display an icon in the Windows System Tray, which is the small tray of icons that is normally positioned on the right-hand side of the Windows Task Bar. Dragging a TrayIcon control onto the form places the control in the extra pane for controls with no visual manifestation on the form. When the control is highlighted, its `Icon` property can be set to associate the icon that will appear in the System Tray.

The TrayIcon's `Click` event is the event that is fired when the icon is double-clicked in the System Tray. This can make the icon in the tray take any action you wish. A pop-up menu can also be associated with the icon in the tray by setting up a ContextMenu control (discussed above) and setting the TrayIcon control's `ContextMenu` property to point to the ContextMenu control. Below is a System Tray with an icon (the one that looks like a CD) and its associated pop-up menu, all set up by a Windows Form:

Provider Controls

There is a new family of controls in Windows Forms that can only be used in association with other controls. Each of these controls, called **provider controls**, causes new properties to appear for every other control on the form.

Provider controls have no visible manifestation, so they appear in the extra pane below the normal design surface. The three provider controls currently available are the HelpProvider, the ToolTip and the ErrorProvider. All three controls work in a very similar fashion.

HelpProvider and ToolTip Controls

In VB6, context-sensitive help was supported with the `HelpContextID` and `ToolTipText` properties of controls. Neither of these is present in Windows Forms controls. Provider controls must be added to a form to get equivalent functionality in VB.NET.

The HelpProvider control allows controls to have associated context-sensitive help available by pressing *F1*. When a HelpProvider control (named `HelpProvider1` by default) is added to a form, all controls on the form get these new properties, which show up in the controls' Properties window:

Property	Usage
`HelpString on HelpProvider1`	Provides a pop-up tooltip for the control when *F1* is pressed while the control has the focus.
`HelpTopic on HelpProvider1`	Provides a topic to use in a help file for context-sensitive help for this control (the `HelpProvider1` control has a property that indicates the help file to use).
`ShowHelp on HelpProvider1`	Determines whether the HelpProvider control is active for this control.

Filling in the `HelpString` property immediately causes the control to have tooltip help when pressing *F1* while the control has the focus. The HelpProvider control has a property to point to a help file (either an HTMLHelp file or a Win32 help file), and the help topic in the `HelpTopic` property points to a topic in this file.

The ToolTip control works similarly, but is simpler. It just adds one property to each control, named `ToolTip on ToolTip1` (assuming the ToolTip control has the default name of `ToolTip1`). This property works exactly the same way the `ToolTipText` property works in VB6.

ErrorProvider Control

The ErrorProvider control presents a simple way to indicate to a user that a control on a form has an error associated with it. The added property for controls on the form when an ErrorProvider control is used is called `Error on ErrorProvider1` (assuming the ErrorProvider has the default name of `ErrorProvider1`). Setting this property to a string value causes the error icon to appear next to a control, and for the text to appear in a tooltip over if the mouse hovers over the error icon.

Here is a screen with several text boxes, and an error icon next to one (with a tooltip). The error icon and tooltip are displayed and managed by the ErrorProvider control:

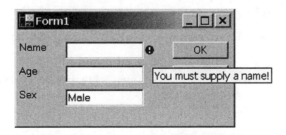

The ErrorProvider control's default icon is the red circle with an exclamation point. A property of the ErrorProvider control allows the icon to be changed.

Working with Provider Controls in Code

To get or set the properties added by provider controls, it is necessary to use syntax like this:

```
HelpProvider1.SetHelpString(TextBox1, "A new help string")
```

Each of the provider controls has specific methods to set the properties that are associated with individual controls. The above line sets the `HelpString` property for the `TextBox1` control.

PrintDocument Control

The new PrintDocument control is another control that does not appear on the form, but just adds functionality. When one is added to a form, it appears in the extra pane below the form's design surface.

The PrintDocument control has properties to set a document to be printed, and to control the way the document is printed. The `Print` method of the PrintDocument control causes the printing to take place. More details on this can be found in Chapter 8.

DataGrid Control

The new DataGrid control in Windows Forms is conceptually similar to previous grid controls such as the FlexGrid control. However, it is specifically written to support hierarchical datasets such as those used in ADO.NET. Chapter 7 (*Data Access in Visual Basic.NET*) discusses the DataGrid control.

Changes to Existing Controls

The changes that have occurred to existing controls fall into six groups:

- ❏ Some properties have been renamed
- ❏ Some controls receive different default names
- ❏ The `Name` property is not available at run time
- ❏ The `Tag` property no longer exists
- ❏ One entire control, the Image control, no longer exists
- ❏ Controls cannot be associated into control arrays

Let's take each of these changes in turn.

Renamed Properties of Controls

Some properties of controls have been renamed for consistency with .NET naming conventions.

> The most significant change has been that all properties that get or set text in a control are now called **Text**.

In VB6, some controls, such as command buttons, labels, and forms, had a `Caption` property that was used to set their text. These controls now have a `Text` property instead.

In the `list box` and `combo box`, the old `ListIndex` property has been replaced with a `SelectedIndex` property. Also, the old `List` collection of items in the controls has been replaced in VB.NET with an `Items` collection.

Different Default Names

The default names that controls receive when dropped on to the form's design surface have changed for a few controls. Since the command button in VB6 is now just called Button, the default name for a typical control of this type placed on the form has changed from `Command1` to `Button1`. Other renamed controls, such as option button (now RadioButton), and Slider (now Trackbar) similarly have default names changed.

In addition, one control has a change in default naming even though there the control's class name has not changed. The text box control used default names such as `TextBox1` in VB6, but the equivalent default name in Visual Basic.NET is `Text1`.

Name Property Not Accessible at Run Time

In VB.NET, the `Name` property of controls and forms is no longer available at run time. This means, for example, that it is no longer possible to loop through a collection of forms or controls looking for one with a particular name.

Tag Property no longer Available

Controls in VB.NET no longer have a `Tag` property. However, a HelpProvider control can be used for a work-around, allowing the tag to be placed in the `HelpString` property that the HelpProvider adds to controls. Perhaps a specific "TagProvider" control will be implemented in the future.

Image Control Gone

The Image control has traditionally been used in VB6 and earlier as a lightweight alternative to the PictureBox. Saving system resources is not the priority it once was, so the Image control is being retired. All of its functions can be fulfilled by the PictureBox control in Windows Forms.

No Control Arrays

In VB6, controls can be associated into control arrays, in which all the controls have the same name, but they vary by index. Control arrays are not available in VB.NET. However, controls can be placed into arrays and various types of collections using code, providing a work-around.

Differences in Multiple Document Interface (MDI) Forms

There are several minor differences in working with an MDI interface in VB.NET. Here's a summary. An example at the end of this section illustrates most of the changes, including sample code.

Creating an MDI Parent Form

In VB6, an MDI parent form is created with an option on the Project menu called Add MDI Form. MDI forms are considered completely different from forms with a regular layout.

In VB.NET, a regular form is converted to an MDI parent form by setting the `IsMDIContainer` property of the form to `True`. This should normally be done in the Properties window. While a form can be made into an MDI parent at run time by setting the `IsMDIContainer` property to `True` in code, the design of an MDI form is usually too different from that of a normal form.

Differences in MDI Parent Forms

In VB6, an MDI parent form automatically has a top-level menu, just like all forms do. It is only necessary to go into the menu editor and add options to the menu.

In VB.NET, a form never has a top level menu automatically, as discussed in the section on menu controls (above). A MainMenu control must explicitly be dragged on to an MDI parent form (as with any form in VB.NET) to give it a top-level menu.

In VB6, an MDI parent form can only contain controls that have a property called `Align`. This property determines to which side of the MDI parent form the control is supposed to be docked. Typical controls like buttons and text boxes cannot be added directly to an MDI parent form. They must be added to a container control, such as a PictureBox, which has an `Align` property.

In VB.NET, an MDI parent can contain any control that a regular form can contain. Buttons, labels, and such can be placed directly on the MDI surface. Such controls will appear in front of any MDI child forms that are displayed in the MDI client area.

It is still possible to use controls like PictureBoxes to hold other controls on a VB.NET MDI parent, and these controls can be docked to the side of the MDI form. In fact, every control in VB.NET has the equivalent of the `Align` property, called `Dock`. The `Dock` property was previously discussed above in the section on changes to controls in VB.NET.

Differences in MDI Child Forms

In VB6, an MDI child form is created by setting a form's `MDIChild` property to `True`. Such a form can then only be used as an MDI child form, meaning it can only be loaded when an MDI parent is available for the form to use for display. Also, the `MDIChild` property can only be set at design time. A form cannot be made into an MDI child at run time.

In VB.NET a form becomes an MDI child at run time by setting the form's `MDIParent` property to point to an MDI parent form. This makes it possible to use a form as either a stand-alone form or an MDI child in different circumstances. In fact, the `MDIParent` property cannot be set at design time – it must be set at run time to make a form an MDI child.

As with VB6, it is possible to have any number of MDI child forms displayed in the MDI parent client area. And, as with VB6, the currently active child form can be determined with the `ActiveForm` property of the MDI parent form.

Arranging Child Windows in the MDI Parent

In VB6, child windows in an MDI parent are arranged into a specific layout with the `Arrange` method. This method accepts values to tile the child windows horizontally or vertically, or to cascade them into a regular overlapping pattern.

In VB.NET, the same functionality is available with the `MDILayout` method.

An MDI Example in VB.NET

In this exercise, we will go through the steps and show code relating to creation of an MDI parent, and allowing it to display an MDI child form.

1. Create a new Windows Application. It will have an empty form named Form1.

2. In the Properties window, set the IsMDIContainer property for Form1 to True. This designates the form as an MDI container for child windows.

3. From the Toolbox, drag a MainMenu control to the form. Create a top-level menu item with the Text property set to File and with submenu items called New and Close. Also create a top-level menu item called Window. The first menu will create, show, and hide menu items at run time, and the second menu will keep track of the open MDI child windows. (For more information on working with MainMenu controls, see the section on menu controls above. Basically all you need to do it to type in the menu options on the bar that appears at the top of the form.)

4. In the menu option editor at the top of the form, right-click on the Window menu item and select Properties. In the Properties window, set the MDIList property to True. This will enable the Window menu to maintain a list of open MDI child windows with a checkmark next to the active child window.

5. Now we need to create an MDI child form to use as a template for multiple instances. To do this, select Project | Add Windows Form and then Open in the Add New Item dialog box. That will result in a new blank form named Form2.

6. To make the child form more interesting, we will put a RichTextBox control in it to simulate a word-processing app. (Of course, the child form template could have any controls desired.) Drag a RichTextBox control on to Form2. In the Properties window for the RichTextBox, set the Anchor property to All and the Dock property to Fill. This causes the RichTextBox control to completely fill the area of the MDI child forms, even when the form is resized. (See the section above on control layout for more discussion of the Anchor and Dock properties.)

7. Now go back to Form1 (the MDI parent form). In the menu editing bar, double-click on the New option under File. The code editor will appear, with the cursor in the event routine for that menu option. Place the following code in the event:

```
Protected Sub MenuItem2_Click(ByVal sender As Object, ByVal e As System.EventArgs)

    Dim NewMDIChild As New Form2()
    'Set the Parent Form of the Child window.
    NewMDIChild.MDIParent = Me
    'Display the new form.
    NewMDIChild.Show()

End Sub
```

8. Now go back to Form1 (the MDI parent form). In the menu editing bar, double-click on the Close option under File. The code editor will appear, with the cursor in the event routine for that menu option. Place the following code in the event:

```
Protected Sub MenuItem3_Click(ByVal sender As Object, _
                             ByVal e As System.EventArgs)
   End
End Sub
```

9. Now run and test the program. Use the File | New option to create several child forms. Note how the Window menu option automatically lists them with the active one checked, and allows you to activate a different one.

Using Custom Properties and Methods

It has been possible since Visual Basic 4 for forms to have custom properties and methods. These members were simply added as code to the form's code module. For, example, a form could have a `Clear` method that would clear out all of its text boxes, implemented by placing a public subroutine named `Clear` in the form module.

Custom members for forms are even more important in VB.NET because of changes in the way controls on form should be accessed. A common technique in VB6 and earlier is to call a control on a form directly to get a value out of it. Controls are always considered "public" in all existing versions of VB, so code like this works fine (although it is not considered good object-oriented programming practice):

```
' code executed from a .BAS module in VB6 or earlier
strNewEmployee = frmEmployee.txtEmployeeID.Text
```

This syntax does not work in VB.NET if the control still has its default definition. The error message indicates that the control is now considered private. It is possible to force the control to be public by changing the code produced by the Windows Form Designer, but this is not recommended. It is not consistent with good object-oriented principles for controls to be public (which is why the default is for them to be private in VB.NET).

There are good alternatives to this technique. Custom properties are typically the best choice. That is, to fix the example above for VB.NET, `frmEmployee` would have a property procedure that looked like this:

```
Public Property EmployeeID As String

   Get
      EmployeeID = txtEmployeeID.Text
   End Get

   Set
      txtEmployeeID.Text = EmployeeID
   End Set

End Property
```

The code in the `.BAS` module would then become:

```
' code executed from a .BAS module
strNewEmployee = frmEmployee.EmployeeID
```

This technique has other advantages. One is the capability to change controls on the form without affecting the calling logic in other routines. That is, if the employee ID in the form were moved to a label instead of a text box, the code in the .BAS module would not need to change. Only the code in the form's property procedure would need to change to work with the label instead of the text box.

Another advantage is that this technique provides more control over what information goes into controls. By placing additional logic in the Property Set, any invalid entry for the control can be rejected. Alternatively, controls can be set to read-only or write-only from outside the form, by making the property read-only or write-only.

Visual Inheritance in Windows Forms

Finally, VB gets full inheritance in VB.NET. While Chapter 5 covers inheritance in depth, there is one aspect of it that relates to Windows Forms, and that is visual inheritance from one form to another.

If you are unclear on the concept of inheritance, you may want to read Chapter 5 before reading this section. But it's simple enough to follow if you have a basic understanding of the inheritance concept.

The basic syntax for inheritance is simple, and in fact you've already seen it several times, starting with the "Hello World" program in Chapter 2. To quickly review, a class indicates the base class using the INHERITS keyword. The base class is referred to inside the subclass's code with a reference to MyBase.

We've already discussed the fact that a form in Windows Forms is really a class module, and that it inherits the capability to be a form from the .NET Framework classes. Here is an example of the code at the top of a WinForms class:

```
Imports System.ComponentModel
Imports System.Drawing
Imports System.WinForms


Public Class Form1
    Inherits System.WinForms.Form
```

By inheriting from System.WinForms.Form, the class representing the form automatically gets all the properties, methods, and events that a form based on WinForms is supposed to have. This is similar to the way that a form in VB6 or earlier automatically gets standard form properties and methods, but in VB.NET the inheritance of those members comes specifically because the class has inherited from System.WinForms.Form.

However, a class does not have to inherit directly from System.WinForms.Form to become a Windows Form. A class can also become a form by inheriting from another form, which itself inherits from System.WinForms.Form. Here's an example: suppose we create a form which looks like this in the visual designer:

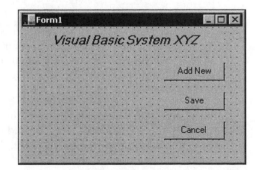

Now let's create a new form, Form2, which will have a visual layout like this:

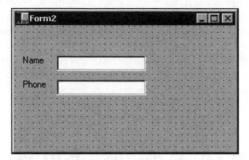

When Form2 was created, it had the following code close to the top:

```
Imports System.ComponentModel
Imports System.Drawing
Imports System.WinForms


Public Class Form2
    Inherits System.WinForms.Form
```

Suppose we change the last line of that code to look like this:

```
Imports System.ComponentModel
Imports System.Drawing
Imports System.WinForms


Public Class Form2
    Inherits System.WinForms.Form1
```

Now, if we instantiate Form2, it looks like this:

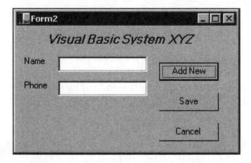

Notice that Form2 now has two sets of controls. The first set is those controls that were placed on Form2 by the visual designer. The second set of controls were originally placed on Form1 in the designer, and then inherited onto Form2. There are options to make inherited controls fixed in size and position, or to make them configurable by Form2.

And it's not just the visual appearance of the controls that is inherited. Any code which is behind the controls in Form1 is inherited by Form2. If the **Add New** button, for example, had some processing logic in Form1, then when that button is pressed in Form2, the logic in Form1 is executed.

Using inheritance this way has major implications for the architecture of VB form-based projects. It is possible to create a base form with logic and visual elements needed by all forms, and then have other forms inherit to get that functionality. The logic and visual elements are encapsulated into one location, so that changing the base form causes all the forms inheriting from it to change automatically.

There are a couple of additional items it is helpful to know about regarding inheritance in Windows Forms.

The Inheritance Picker

The example above was a quick illustration of how visual inheritance in forms works, but it's not the way that you would normally set a form to inherit from another form. The environment has something called the **Inheritance Picker** that provides that functionality.

However, a form must be compiled into an executable file, or a DLL with the Build command, before it can be used by the Inheritance Picker. Once that is done, the menu option Project | Add Inherited Form allows the addition of a form that inherits from another form in the project. To see this in action, do the following:

1. Open a new Windows Application project in VB.NET.

2. On the empty Form1 that is created for the project, place three buttons Add Now, Save, and Cancel, similar in layout to the screen for Form1 earlier in this inheritance section. The buttons should be close to the right-hand portion of the screen.

3. Build the project with the menu option Build | Build.

4. Select the menu option Project | Add Inherited Form. The dialog that appears will look roughly like this:

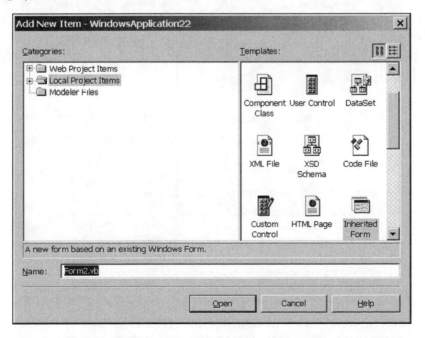

5. Select the Open button, and a dialog will appear that shows the forms that can be used as a base form for inheritance. It looks like this:

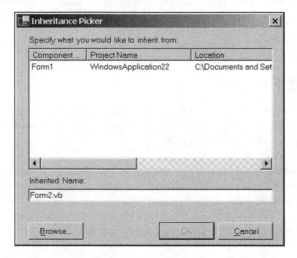

6. Choose Form1, and press OK. Then display the new Form2 in the visual designer. It will look something like this:

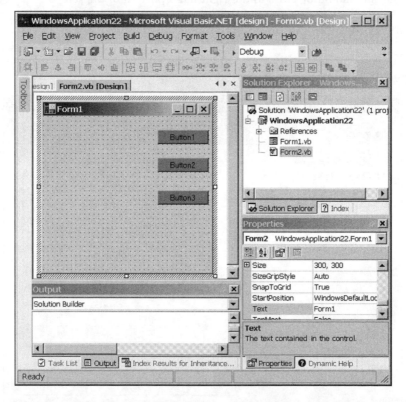

Notice the controls inherited from Form1 are in dark gray. These controls cannot be moved, nor can they be double-clicked to put code in their Click event routines (their event routines are actually in Form1).

It is also important to note that changes to `Form1` will not be displayed on `Form2` until a Build is selected and a successful build of `Form1` is performed. At this point, any changes to `Form1` will show up on `Form2`.

GDI+

Another part of the `System` namespace that is important for Windows Forms is **GDI+**. This is the new version of the old GDI (Graphics Device Interface) functions provided by the Windows API. GDI+ provides a new API for graphics functions, which then takes advantage of the Windows graphics library.

GDI+ functions are in the `System.Drawing` namespace. Some of the classes and members in this namespace will look familiar to developers who have used the Win32 GDI functions. Classes are available for such items as pens, brushes, and rectangles. Naturally, the `System.Drawing` namespace makes these capabilities much easier to use than the equivalent API functions.

Some of the things that can be done with classes in the `System.Drawing` namespace are:

- ❑ Bitmap manipulation
- ❑ `Cursors` class, including the various cursors that you would need to set in your application such as an hourglass or an insertion "I-beam" cursor
- ❑ `Font` class, including capabilities like font rotation
- ❑ `Graphics` class – this contains methods to do routine drawing constructs, including lines, curves, ellipses, etc.
- ❑ `Icon` class
- ❑ Various structures for dealing with graphics, these include `Point`, `Size`, `Color`, and `Rectangle`
- ❑ The `Pen` and `Brush` classes

This list is by no means exhaustive.

System.Drawing Namespace

The `System.Drawing` namespace includes many classes, and it also includes some subsidiary namespaces called `System.Drawing.Drawing2D`, `System.Drawing.Imaging`, and `System.Drawing.Text`. An overview of these namespaces is included below. First let's look at important classes in `System.Drawing`.

System.Drawing.Graphics Class

Many of the important drawing functions are members of the `System.Drawing.Graphics` class. Methods like `DrawArc`, `DrawEllipse`, and `DrawIcon` have self-evident actions. There are over forty methods that provide drawing related in functions in the class.

Many drawing members require one or more points as arguments. A `Point` is a structure in the `System.Drawing` namespace. It has X and Y values for horizontal and vertical positions, respectively. When a variable number of points are needed, an array of points may be used as an argument. The next example below uses points.

One odd thing about the `System.Drawing.Graphics` class that you should know is that it cannot be directly instantiated. That is, you can't just enter code like this to get an instance of the `Graphics` class:

```
Dim grfGraphics As New System.Drawing.Graphics()
```

That's because the constructor (`Sub New`) for the class is private. It is only supposed to be manipulated by objects that can set the `Graphics` class up for themselves. There are several ways to instantiate a `Graphics` class, but one of the simplest is with a Windows Form method called `CreateGraphics`. That technique is used in the next example.

Using GDI+ Capabilities in a Windows Form

Here is an example of a form that uses the `System.Drawing.Graphics` class to draw some graphic elements on the form surface. The example code creates a `Graphics` object for the form, and then uses it to draw an ellipse, an icon (which it gets from the form itself), and two triangles, one in outline and one filled.

Start a Windows Application project in VB.NET. On the `Form1` that is automatically created for the project, place a command button close to the bottom of the form. Change the button's `Text` property to the word **Draw**.

Then double-click the button to get to the code editor. In the button's `Click` event, insert the following code:

```
Protected Sub Button1_Click(ByVal sender As Object, _
                            ByVal e As System.EventArgs)

    ' Need a graphics object to use for the drawing.
    ' The form has a method to do that called CreateGraphics
    Dim grfGraphics As System.Drawing.Graphics
    grfGraphics = Me.CreateGraphics

    ' Need a pen for the drawing. We'll make it violet.
    Dim penDrawingPen As New _
        System.Drawing.Pen(System.Drawing.Color.BlueViolet)

    ' Draw an ellipse and an icon on the form
    grfGraphics.DrawEllipse(penDrawingPen, 30, 150, 30, 60)
    grfGraphics.DrawIcon(Me.Icon, 90, 20)

    ' Draw a triangle on the form.
    ' First have to define an array of points.
    Dim pntPoint(3) As System.Drawing.Point

    pntPoint(0).X = 150
    pntPoint(0).Y = 150

    pntPoint(1).X = 150
    pntPoint(1).Y = 200

    pntPoint(2).X = 50
    pntPoint(2).Y = 120

    grfGraphics.DrawPolygon(penDrawingPen, pntPoint)

    ' Do a filled triangle.
```

```
' First need a brush to specify how it is filled.
Dim bshBrush As System.Drawing.Brush
bshBrush = New SolidBrush(Color.Blue)

' Now relocate the points for the triangle.
' We'll just move it 100 twips to the right.
pntPoint(0).X += 100

pntPoint(1).X += 100

pntPoint(2).X += 100


grfGraphics.FillPolygon(bshBrush, pntPoint)

End Sub
```

Then start the program, and when it comes up, press the button. The resulting screen should look similar to this one:

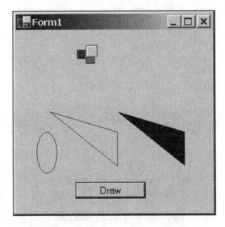

As you can see, the graphics functions are not difficult to use. The hardest part is figuring out how to initialize the objects needed, such as the `Graphics` object itself, and the necessary brushes and pens.

The example above is just to illustrate syntax. The problem with using it will be familiar to any VB6 programmer who has used `Form.Print`, `Form.Circle`, `Form.Line`, and other related methods to change the appearance of a form. With those methods, as well as with the methods of the `Graphics` class in Windows Forms, the output disappears the next time the form is painted.

That means that it is typical to do such drawing functions in the form's `Paint` event, and the next example will illustrate this. The next example will also take advantage of the fact that the `System.Drawing` namespace is routinely imported in the module, so that it is not necessary to use the full namespace identifier for the classes that are being used. For example, the `System.Drawing.Graphics` class that is used is declared just as type `Graphics`.

Some of the effects that you can achieve using the `System.Drawing` namespace can be very fancy. Here is the next example, using one of the fancier effects that are available – painting the inside of some text with a bitmap.

As before, start a new Windows Application project. In the automatically-created Form1, get to the code window. Then insert a Paint event by selecting Form1 in the left hand drop-down at the top of the code window, and then selecting the Paint event in the right hand drop-down (just like you would get to a Paint event routine in VB6). Inside the Paint event that was created, insert the code:

```
Public Sub Form1_Paint(ByVal sender As Object, _
        ByVal e As System.WinForms.PaintEventArgs) Handles Form1.Paint

    ' Declare a brush, a font, and a graphics
    ' object to use.
    Dim bshBrush As Brush
    Dim fntFont As Font

    ' We can get the graphic object directly from
    ' the PaintEventArgs parameter of the event.
    Dim grfGraphics As Graphics = e.Graphics

    ' Fix up the brush and the font.
    ' Substitute any bitmap you want in the next line.
    bshBrush = New TextureBrush(New Bitmap("c:\winnt\Prairie Wind.bmp"))
    fntFont = New Font("Impact", 50, Drawing.FontStyle.Strikeout)

    ' Now draw some fancy text.
    grfGraphics.DrawString("VB.NET", fntFont, bshBrush, 10, 60)

End Sub
```

Run the program, and the following form should display:

Note the bitmap inside the text, and the strikethrough effect on the text.

The remaining namespaces in System.Drawing add additional capabilities. We will not look at these in as much detail, but simply note what kind of functionality is in each namespace.

System.Drawing.Drawing2D Namespace

The System.Drawing.Drawing2D namespace adds capability for two-dimensional vector graphics. This is in contrast to the graphics functions we've previously looked at, which were bit-mapped. These vector-based functions include the capability to do such effects as gradient fills.

System.Drawing.Imaging Namespace

The `System.Drawing.Imaging` namespace includes functions to work with various image formats. The formats can be displayed from a file, and saved into a file. Some of the supported formats include:

Format	Description
BMP	Windows bitmap image format
EMF	Enhanced Windows metafile image format
EXIF	Exchangable Image Format
FlashPIX	FlashPIX image format
GIF	Graphic Interchange Format
Icon	Windows icon image format
JPEG	JPEG image format
MemoryBMP	A memory bitmap image format
PhotoCD	Eastman Kodak PhotoCD image format
PNG	W3C PNG (Portable Network Graphics) image format
TIFF	Tag Image File Format (TIFF) image format
WMF	Windows metafile image format

The namespace includes support for reading and writing these formats, and for manipulating the image during rendering.

System.Drawing.Text Namespace

The `System.Drawing.Text` namespace adds additional capability for working with fonts. While the `System.Drawing` namespace includes basic font capability, `System.Drawing.Text` goes beyond this to supply capabilities such as control over line spacing.

Changes from Visual Basic 6 and Earlier

Some of the functionality residing in `System.Drawing` replaces keywords or controls in VB6 and earlier. Here are the relevant keywords that are being retired, and their replacements in the `System.Drawing` namespace:

Retired VB element	Location in VB.NET (namespace)	Member of namespace
`Circle` keyword	`System.Drawing.Graphics` class	`DrawEllipse` method
`Line` keyword Line control	`System.Drawing.Graphics` class	`DrawLine` method

Table continued on following page

Retired VB element	Location in VB.NET (namespace)	Member of namespace
Shape control	`System.Drawing.Graphics` class	`DrawRectangle` method and `DrawPolygon` method
`Pset` keyword	`System.Drawing.Graphics` class, `System.Image` class	No exact equivalent – most functions done by `Pset` in VB6 are done with `Point` structure used in with various methods for VB.NET, or by the `SetPixel` method of the `Image` class.
`Point` method (of forms and picture boxes)	`System.Image` class	No exact equivalent. The `GetPixel` and `SetPixel` methods of the Image class provide similar functionality.

Creating Custom Windows Forms Controls

VB6 has the ability to create custom controls, normally called User Controls. These controls are often assembled from sets of standard controls. A typical example is a set of text boxes that are related. The entire set can be placed in a User Control, with all related logic, and then added as a set to a form by dragging the User Control onto the form.

VB.NET has the same basic capability, but simplifies the process of creating and deploying these custom controls. Access to the GDI+ drawing capabilities of Windows Forms also gives developers an easier way to add complex display functionality to their custom controls. The section above discusses using the GDI+ drawing capabilities.

For an example, we will create a custom control that functions a label, but allows the text to be rendered at any angle.

First, start a new project in VB.NET of type **Windows Control Library**. The created module will have a class in it named `Control1`. Rename the class to `TextRotator` by changing the line that says:

```
Public Class Control1
```

To:

```
Public Class TextRotator
```

Our `TextRotator` control needs to know the angle to rotate the text. So we need a module-level variable and a property procedure to support a `RotationAngle` property. First, place a declaration right under the line that causes the class to inherit the `System.Winforms.UserControl` class:

```
Inherits System.WinForms.UserControl
Private msngRotationAngle As Single = 0
```

Then insert the following property procedure in the class:

```
Public Property RotationAngle() As Single
    Get
        RotationAngle = msngRotationAngle
    End Get
    Set
        msngRotationAngle = Value
        Me.Invalidate()    ' Forces a repaint using the
                           ' Invalidate method of the UserControl class
    End Set
End Property
```

Now, place code to handle the Paint event, that is, to draw the text when the control repaints. We will use some code similar to that in the section on drawing with the GDI+ (above). To provide a place for this code, we override the OnPaint method of the UserControl base class:

```
Protected Overrides Sub OnPaint(ByVal e as _
                                 System.WinForms.PaintEventArgs)

    ' First let the base UserControl take care of painting
    MyBase.OnPaint(e)

    ' Declare a brush, a font, and a graphics
    ' object to use.
    Dim bshBrush As Brush
    Dim fntFont As Font

    ' We can get the graphic object directly from
    ' the PaintEventArgs parameter of the event.
    Dim grfGraphics As Graphics = e.Graphics

    ' Fix up the brush and the font.
    bshBrush = New SolidBrush(Me.ForeColor)
    fntFont = Me.Font

    ' Now draw some rotated text.
    grfGraphics.RotateTransform(RotationAngle)
    grfGraphics.DrawString(Me.Text, fntFont, bshBrush, 0, 0)
    grfGraphics.ResetTransform()

End Sub
```

Now build the control library by selecting Build from the Build menu. This will create a DLL in the /bin directory where the control library solution is saved.

Then start a new Windows Application project. In the Tools | Customize Toolbox dialog, first make sure that the .NET Framework Components tab is selected, and then use the Browse button to point to the deployed DLL for the control library. The toolbox should now contain the TextRotator control.

Drag the TextRotator control on to the form in the Windows Application project. Notice that its property window includes a RotationAngle property. Set that to 20 (for 20 degrees) and set the Text property to anything you like. When you run the project, the TextRotator control will display the string in its Text property at a 20 degree angle.

This control can now be manipulated in code just like any other control.

Inheriting from an Existing Control

The control above inherited directly from `System.Winforms.UserControl`. However, it is just as easy to inherit from a class that implements a standard control such as a list box or a text box. Methods and properties in the base control can be overridden in the new control. That means, for example, that a new text box control could be created that did extensive validation and formatting on the entered text. It would just be necessary to override the `KeyPress` event, validate the keystrokes and format the `Text` property of the control as required.

Going under the Surface

As we've seen in this chapter, Windows Forms has a very rich set of functionality. In fact, this chapter can only skim the surface of all that Windows Forms will do. But there are always situations in which it is necessary to go to a system level to accomplish something. In VB6, this was done using the Windows API.

Using VB.NET, the .NET Framework exposes a way to do almost anything it is possible to do, making the Windows API unnecessary in VB.NET except for very unusual circumstances. Forms and controls expose a `Handle` property, for example, and the .NET Framework exposes many classes that can manipulate the `Handle` of a form or control, such as the `NativeWindow` class.

Just as a sample of what can be done, we will look at a technique for going under the surface of Windows Forms to accomplish something at a deeper level.

Using WndProc Method to Handle Messages

`WndProc` is a method of the `Control` class, which is at the root of the WinForms class hierarchy. It provides the ability to intercept and react to Windows messages. In VB6, this was typically done with third-party controls, though it could be done natively with sophisticated use of `AddressOf`. In VB.NET, `WndProc` exposes the messages, making it as easy to do message handling in VB as in any other .NET language, and much easier than it was in VB6.

As an example just for illustration, here is a program to monitor for the WM_RBUTTONDOWN message, which is sent every time the user clicks the right mouse button. When this message comes in, the program will just display a message box with parameter info from the message. This is not necessarily something a program would really want to do, but it will demonstrate the concept.

Create a new Windows Application in the environment. In the form that is automatically created, get to the code editor and add the following property to the form's code:

```
Overrides Protected Sub WndProc(ByRef m As Message)
    Select Case m.msg
        Case Microsoft.Win32.Interop.win.WM_RBUTTONDOWN
            MsgBox("Right Button  " & m.wParam)
    End Select


    MyBase.WndProc(m)
End Sub
```

The `Overrides` keyword will be discussed in Chapter 5 on object concepts. It basically says that this class is overriding a method that already exists in the base class. That means that, whenever the method would be executed in the base class, execution will pass to this version instead. Note that the last line before the `End Sub` gives the base class a shot at executing its own version of the method in addition to what this class is going to do.

The code that actually does the work of intercepting the message is in the `Select Case`. There is only one case implemented, which checks for the message indicating that the right mouse button has been pressed. We could implement as many other cases as desired, checking for and processing other messages.

Now run and test the program. Press the right mouse button anywhere on the screen, and you should see a message box pop up telling you about it.

By the way, overriding the `WndProc` method means that your routine will see and process every single message that comes through the Window message pump, and there can be hundreds of them a second. So a `WndProc` method override can definitely have an impact on performance.

Summary

With all the functionality available, Windows Forms will take a while to become familiar to Visual Basic developers. This chapter has only looked at some of the most important additions and changes. However, the net effect is an easier way to build more powerful Win32 applications – with less code and far easier deployment and implementation.

In particular we've looked at the `Control`, `RichControl`, `ScrollableControl`, `ContainerControl`, `Form`, and `UserControl` classes, which form the object hierarchy of the Windows Forms. We also compared Windows Forms to the forms we used in VB6 and discussed changes to the controls. After briefly discussing the difference in making and using MDI forms in VB.NET, we moved on to inheritance and its role in creating "template" Windows Forms. We wrapped up this chapter by looking at the use of GDI+ to draw on forms, creating our own custom forms, and working with messages.

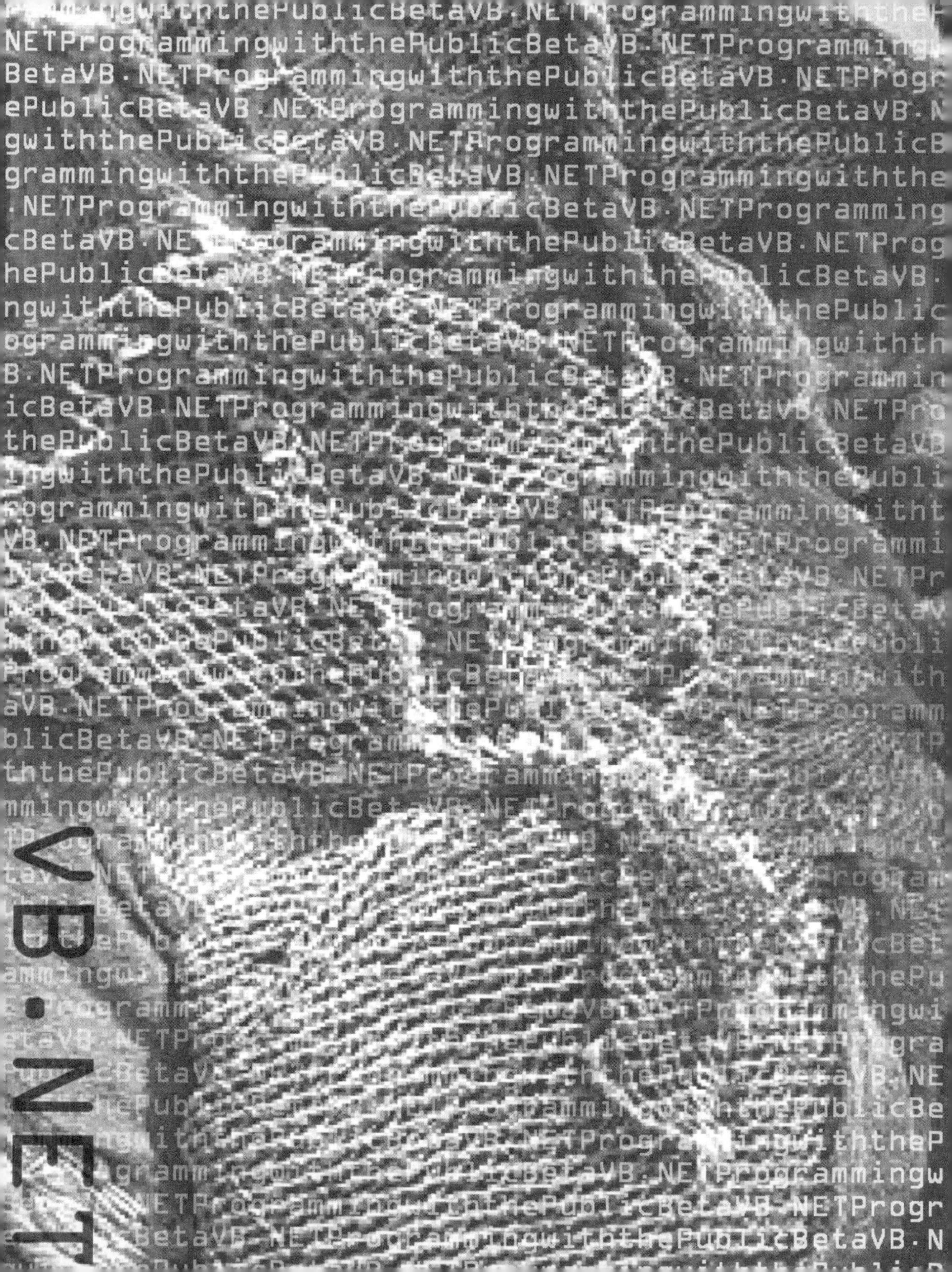
VB.NET
VB.NET Programming with the Public Beta

New Object-Oriented Capabilities of VB.NET

When Visual Basic 4.0 was released, it introduced a whole new era of programming for VB. Object-oriented (OO) programming was finally a possibility. Unfortunately, few OO features were included in the VB language at that point. Most notably lacking were inheritance capabilities, one of the key defining criteria for any OO language. VB was also missing a large number of secondary features such as method overloading and overriding, and constructors.

With VB.NET, the VB language finally completes the transition to a fully OO language. We now have full inheritance, along with all of the associated features we'd expect.

> *While it certainly remains possible to create applications that make no more use of objects than we did in VB3, these new capabilities are quite pervasive and so at least some basic understanding is required to become fully proficient in the use of VB.NET.*

Generally speaking, a language is considered to be OO if it supports four main features:

❑ **Abstraction**. VB has supported abstraction since VB4. Abstraction is merely the ability of a language to create "black box" code – to take a concept and create an abstract representation of that concept within a program. A `Customer` object, for instance, is an abstract representation of a real-world customer. A `Recordset` object is an abstract representation of a set of data.

❑ **Encapsulation**. This has also been with us since version 4.0. It's the concept of a separation between interface and implementation. The idea is that we can create an interface (`Public` methods in a class) and, as long as that *interface* remains consistent, the application can interact with our objects. This remains true even if we entirely rewrite the code *within* a given method – thus the interface is independent of the implementation.

Encapsulation allows us to hide the internal implementation details of a class. For example, the algorithm we use to compute Pi might be proprietary. We can expose a simple API to the end user, but we hide all of the logic used for our algorithm by encapsulating it within our class.

❑ **Polymorphism**. Likewise, polymorphism was introduced with VB4. Polymorphism is reflected in the ability to write one routine that can operate on objects from more than one class – treating different objects from different classes in exactly the same way. For instance, if both `Customer` and `Vendor` objects have a `Name` property, and we can write a routine that calls the `Name` property regardless of whether we're using a `Customer` or `Vendor` object, then we have polymorphism.

VB, in fact, supports polymorphism in two ways – through late binding (much like Smalltalk, a classic example of a true OO language) and through the implementation of multiple interfaces. This flexibility is very powerful and is preserved within VB.NET.

❑ **Inheritance**. VB.NET is the first version of VB that supports inheritance. Inheritance is the idea that a class can gain the pre-existing interface *and behaviors* of an existing class. This is done by *inheriting* these behaviors from the existing class through a process known as subclassing. With the introduction of full inheritance, VB is now a fully OO language by any reasonable definition.

In this chapter we'll discuss all these new features and what they mean to us as VB developers.

Merger of Object- and Component-Oriented Concepts

Since version 4.0, VB has provided us with the ability not only to create objects, but also COM components. In fact, VB's ability to create objects, and the way VB objects worked, was very closely tied to COM and the way objects worked within and between COM components.

In COM, components are pre-compiled binary entities – typically a DLL, EXE or OCX file. Each component contains one or more classes that can be used by client applications. In VB6 we could create ActiveX EXE, ActiveX DLL or user control (OCX) projects – thus creating COM components. Even when we weren't creating these project types, the way VB6 allowed us to create and work with objects was defined by how objects were created within COM components.

It comes as no surprise then that VB.NET is very closely tied to the way .NET handles objects and the way objects work within and between .NET assemblies or components. This represents a pretty substantial change for VB, however, since .NET is substantially more advanced in terms of objects and components as compared to COM.

With COM, objects and components were interrelated, but the marriage of the two was far from seamless. In .NET on the other hand, OO and component-oriented concepts (as defined earlier) are very closely related in ways that we could only dream of in the COM environment.

In .NET we retain the component-oriented features we are used to:

❑ Component-level scoping via the `Friend` keyword

❑ Ability to implement interfaces with the `Implements` keyword

Component-level scoping allows us to create classes or methods that are available to all the other code in our component – but not to code outside our component. We'll discuss this in more detail later, but basically it is a level of scoping that sits between `Private` and `Public` – and is accessed via the `Friend` keyword.

Implementing interfaces via the `Implements` keyword allows each of our classes to have several different "identities" – each with its own interface. This is a powerful technique that is used widely within both COM and .NET, and is something we'll discuss in more detail later.

In addition to these existing features, with .NET we also gain some strong capabilities – most importantly inheritance and the `Inherits` keyword.

VB.NET benefits from this new, closer relationship between objects and components – making both types of concept central to the language and to the way we develop applications.

Let's walk through the OO features in VB.NET.

VB.NET OO Implementation

VB.NET not only provides us with new OO features, but it also changes the way we implement some of the features we are used to from VB6. As we go through these features we'll cover both the new capabilities and also explore the changes to existing features.

Creating Classes

When building classes in previous versions of VB, each class got its own file. While simple, this solution could cause a larger OO project to have many files. VB.NET allows us to put more than one class in a single source file. While we don't have to take this approach, it can be nice since we can reduce the overall number of files in a project – possibly making it more maintainable.

Additionally, VB.NET provides support for the concept of .NET namespaces, as we discussed in Chapters 2 and 3. There are also changes to the syntax used to create `Property` methods, and we can overload methods in our classes. We'll look at all these features shortly. First though, let's look at how we add a class to a project.

Adding a class in VB.NET is similar to adding a class in VB6. In order to do this we need to create a new Windows Application project and choose the **Project | Add Class** menu option to bring up the **Add New Item** dialog:

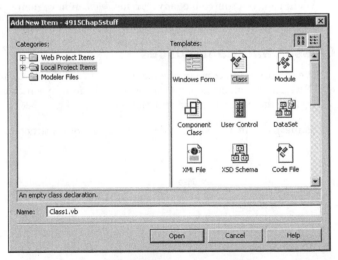

This is the common dialog used for adding any type of item to our project – in this case it defaults to adding a class module. Regardless of which type of VB source file we choose (form, class, module, etc.) we'll end up with a file ending in a `.vb` extension.

> **It is the *content* of the file that determines its type, not the file extension. The IDE creates different starting code within the file based on the type we choose.**

We can name the class `TheClass` in this dialog and, when we click **Open**, a new file will be added to our project, containing very simple code:

```
Public Class TheClass

End Class
```

Though a `.vb` file can contain multiple classes, modules and other code, the normal behavior from the IDE is the same as we've had in VB since its inception – one class, module, or form per file. We can manually add other code to the files created by the IDE with no problems, but when we ask the IDE to create a class for us it will always do so by adding a new file to the project.

At this point we're ready to start adding code.

Class Keyword

As shown in this example, we now have a `Class` keyword along with the corresponding `End Class`. This new keyword is needed in order for a single source file to contain more than one class. Any time we want to create a class in VB.NET, we simply put all the code for the class within the `Class...End Class` block. For instance:

```
Public Class TheClass
    Public Sub DoSomething()
      MsgBox("Hello world", MsgBoxStyle.Information, "TheClass")
    End Sub
End Class
```

Within a given source file (any `.vb` file) we can have many of these `Class...End Class` blocks, one after another.

Classes and Namespaces

We discussed the concept of a namespace thoroughly in Chapters 2 and 3. Namespaces are central to the .NET environment, as they provide a mechanism by which classes can be organized into logical groupings, making them easier to find and manage.

Namespaces in VB.NET are declared using a block structure. For example:

```
Namespace TheNamespace

    Public Class TheClass

    End Class

End Namespace
```

Any classes, structures, or other types declared within the Namespace...End Namespace block will be addressed using that namespace. In this example, our class is referenced using the namespace, so declaring a variable would be done as follows:

```
Private obj As TheNamespace.TheClass
```

Because namespaces are created using a block structure, it is possible for a single source file to contain not only many classes, but also many namespaces.

Also, classes within the same namespace can be created in separate files. In other words, within a VB.NET project we can use the same namespace in more than one source file – and all the classes within those namespace blocks will be part of that same namespace.

For instance, if we have one source file with the following code:

```
Namespace TheNamespace

   Public Class TheClass

   End Class

End Namespace
```

And we have a separate source file in the project with the following code:

```
Namespace TheNamespace

   Public Class TheOtherClass

   End Class

End Namespace
```

Then we'll have a single namespace – TheNamespace – with two classes – TheClass and TheOtherClass.

It is also important to remember that VB.NET projects, by default, have a root namespace that is part of the project's properties. By default this root namespace will have the same name as our project. When we use the Namespace block structure, we are actually adding to that root namespace. So, in our example, if the project is named MyProject, then we could declare a variable as:

```
Private obj As MyProject.TheNamespace.TheClass
```

To change the root namespace, use the Project | Properties menu option. The root namespace can be cleared as well, meaning that all Namespace blocks become the root level for the code they contain.

Creating Methods

Methods in VB.NET are created just like they are in VB6 – using the Sub or Function keywords. A method created with Sub does not return a value, while a Function must return a value as a result.

```
Sub DoSomething()

End Sub
```

```
Function GetValue() As Integer

End Function
```

We retain the three scoping keywords we are used to, and have one more:

- ❑ Private – callable only by code within our class
- ❑ Friend – callable only by code within our project/component
- ❑ Public – callable by code outside our class
- ❑ Protected – new to VB.NET; we'll discuss this later when we cover inheritance
- ❑ Protected Friend – callable only by code within our project/component *and* by code in our subclasses; we'll discuss this later when we cover inheritance

Parameters to methods are now declared ByVal by default, rather than ByRef. We can still override the default behavior through explicit use of the ByRef keyword. We discussed these issues in more detail in Chapter 3.

Creating Properties

In Chapter 3 we discussed the changes to the way Property routines are created. In the past we'd create separate routines for Property Get and Property Let. Now these are combined into a single structure:

```
Private mstrName As String

Public Property Name() As String
  Get
    Return mstrName
  End Get
  Set
    mstrName = Value
  End Set
End Property
```

Refer to Chapter 3 for further discussion, including details on creating read-only and write-only properties.

Default Property

When creating classes in VB6 we could declare a default method, or property, for our class. This was done using the Tools | Procedure Attributes menu option and by setting the Procedure ID to (default). Not an entirely intuitive process, since we couldn't look at the code to see what was going on.

VB.NET changes this behavior in a couple ways. First off, creating a default property is done through the use of a Default keyword – making the declaration much more clear and intuitive. However, VB.NET introduces a new limitation on default properties – to be default, a property must be a property array.

A **property array** is a property that is indexed – much like an array. The Item property on a collection or list object is an example:

```
strText = MyList.Item(5)
```

The `Item` property doesn't have a singular value, but rather is an array of properties accessed via an index.

By requiring default properties to be a property array, we allow the language to avoid ambiguities in the use of default properties. This is a key to the elimination of the `Set` keyword as we knew it in VB6. Consider the following code:

```
MyValue = MyObject
```

Does this refer to the object `MyObject`, or to its default property? In VB6 this was resolved by forcing us to use the `Set` command when dealing with the object, otherwise the default property was used. In VB.NET this statement *always* refers to the object since a default property would be indexed. To get at a default property we'd have code such as:

```
MyValue = MyObject(5)
```

This is not ambiguous, since the index is a clear indicator that we're referring to the default property rather than to `MyObject` itself.

This change means a property array procedure must accept a parameter. For example:

```
Private theData(100) As String

Default Public Property Data(ByVal Index As Integer) As String
   Get
     Data = theData(index)
   End Get
   Set
      theData(index) = Value
   End Set
End Property
```

In the end, this code is much clearer than its VB6 counterpart, but we lose some of the flexibility we enjoyed with default properties in the past. For instance, we'd often use default properties when working with GUI controls, such as the default `Text` property:

```
TextBox1 = "My text"
```

This is no longer valid in VB.NET, since the `Text` property is not a property array. Instead we must now use the property name in these cases.

Overloading Methods

One of the more exciting new polymorphic features in VB.NET is the ability to **overload** a method. Overloading means that we can declare a method of the same name more than once in a class – as long as each declaration has a different parameter list. This can be very powerful.

A different parameter list means different data types in the list. Consider the following method declaration:

```
Public Sub MyMethod(X As Integer, Y As Integer)
```

The parameter list of this method can be viewed as (*integer, integer*). To overload this method, we must come up with a different parameter list – perhaps (*integer, double*). The order of the types also matters, so (*integer, double*) and (*double, integer*) are different and would work for overloading.

Overloading cannot be done merely by changing the *return type* of a function. It is the data types of the actual parameters that must differ for overloading to occur.

As an example, suppose we want to provide a search capability – returning a set of data based on some criteria – so we create a routine such as:

```
Public Function FindData(ByVal Name As String) As ArrayList
  ' find data and return result
End Function
```

In VB6, if we wanted to add a new searching option based on some other criteria, we'd have to add a whole new function with a different name. In VB.NET however, we can simply overload this existing function:

```
Public Overloads Function FindData(ByVal Name As String) As ArrayList
  ' find data and return result
End Function

Public Overloads Function FindData(ByVal Age As Integer) As ArrayList
  ' find data and return result
End Function
```

Notice that both method declarations have the same method name – something that would be prohibited in VB6. Each has different parameters, which allows VB.NET to differentiate between them, and each is declared with the Overloads keyword.

When overloading a method we can have different scopes on each implementation – as long as the parameter lists are different as we discussed earlier. This means we could change our FindData methods to have different scopes:

```
Public Overloads Function FindData(ByVal Name As String) As ArrayList
  ' find data and return result
End Function

Friend Overloads Function FindData(ByVal Age As Integer) As ArrayList
  ' find data and return result
End Function
```

With this change, only other code in our VB.NET project can make use of the FindData that accepts an Integer as its parameter.

Object Lifecycle

In VB6, objects had a clearly defined and well-understood life cycle – a set of events that we always knew would occur over the life of an object. We were guaranteed the following:

Event	Description
Sub Main	Would run as the component was loaded, before an object was created (optional)
Class_Initialize	Would run before any other code in our object; called by the runtime as the object was being created

Event	Description
Class_Terminate	Would run after any other code in our object; called by the runtime as the object was being destroyed

With VB.NET, objects also have a lifecycle, but things are not quite the same as in the past. In particular, we no longer have the same concept of a component-level Sub Main that runs as a DLL is loaded, and the concept of the Class_Terminate event changes rather substantially. However, the concept behind the Class_Initialize event is morphed into a full-blown constructor method that accepts parameters.

Thus, in VB.NET, we are only guaranteed the following:

Event	Description
New	Would run before any other code in our object; called by the runtime as the object was being created

This is quite a change so let's discuss the details further.

Construction

Object construction is triggered any time we create a new instance of a class. This is done using the New keyword – a level of consistency that didn't exist with VB6 where we got to choose between New and CreateObject.

Sub Main

Since VB6 was based on COM, creating an object could trigger a Sub Main procedure to be run. This would happen the first time an object was created from a given component – often a DLL. Before even attempting to create the object, the VB6 runtime would load the DLL and run the Sub Main procedure.

The .NET Common Language Runtime doesn't treat components quite the same way, and so neither does VB.NET. This means that no Sub Main procedure is called as a component is loaded. In fact, Sub Main is only used once – when an application itself is first started. As further components are loaded by the application, only code within the classes we invoke is called.

It wasn't that wise to rely on Sub Main even in VB6, since that code would run prior to all the error handling infrastructure being in place. Bugs in Sub Main were notoriously difficult to debug in VB6. If we do have to use code that relies heavily on the Sub Main concept for initialization, we'll need to implement a workaround in VB.NET.

This can be done easily by calling a central method from the constructor method in each class. For instance, we might create a centrally available method in a module such as:

```
Public Module CentralCode
   Private blnHasRun As Boolean

   Public Sub Initialize()
     If Not blnHasRun Then
       blnHasRun = True
       ' Do initialization here
     End If
   End Sub
End Module
```

This routine is designed to only run one time, no matter how often it is called. We can then use this method from within each constructor of our classes. For example:

```
Public Class TheClass
  Public Sub New()
    CentralCode.Initialize()
    ' regular class code goes here
  End Sub
End Class
```

While this is a bit of extra work on our part, it does accomplish the same effect we're used to with a VB6-style Sub Main routine.

New Method

Like the situation with Sub Main, Class_Initialize is called before any other code in a VB6 class. Again, it is called before the error handling mechanism is fully in place, making debugging very hard; errors show up at the client as a generic failure to instantiate the object. Additionally, Class_Initialize accepts no parameters – meaning there is no way in VB6 to initialize an object with data as it is created.

VB.NET eliminates Class_Initialize in favor of full-blown constructor methods, which have full error handling capabilities and do accept parameters. This means we can initialize our objects as we create them – a very important and powerful feature. The constructor method in VB.NET is Sub New. The simplest constructor method for a class is one that accepts no parameters – quite comparable to Class_Initialize:

```
Public Class TheClass
  Public Sub New()
    ' initialize object here
  End Sub
End Class
```

With this type of constructor, creating an instance of our class is done as follows:

```
Dim obj As New TheClass()
```

This example is directly analogous to creating a VB6 object with code in Class_Initialize.

However, more often than not we'd prefer to actually initialize our object with data as it is created. Perhaps we want to have the object load some data from a database, or perhaps we want to provide it with the data directly. Either way, we want to provide some data to the object *as it is being created.*

This is done by adding a parameter list to the New method:

```
Public Class TheClass
  Public Sub New(ByVal ID As Integer)
    ' use the ID value to initialize the object
  End Sub
End Class
```

Now, when we go to create an instance of the class, we can provide data to the object:

```
Dim obj As New TheClass(42)
```

To increase flexibility we might want to optionally accept the parameter value. This can be done in two ways – through the use of the `Optional` keyword to declare an optional parameter, or by overloading the `New` method. To use the `Optional` keyword, we simply declare the parameter as optional:

```
Public Sub New(Optional ByVal ID As Integer = -1)
    If ID = -1 Then
      ' initialize object here
    Else
      ' use the ID value to initialize the object
    End If
End Sub
```

This approach is far from ideal, however, since we have to check to see if the parameter was or wasn't provided, and then decide how to initialize the object. It would be clearer to just have two separate implementations of the `New` method – one for each type of behavior. This is accomplished through overloading:

```
Public Overloads Sub New()
  ' initialize object here
End Sub
```

```
Public Overloads Sub New(ByVal ID As Integer)
  ' use the ID value to initialize the object
End Sub
```

Not only does this approach avoid the conditional check and simplify our code, but it also makes the use of our object clearer to any client code. The overloaded `New` method is shown by IntelliSense in the VS.NET IDE, making it clear that `New` can be called both with and without a parameter.

In fact, through overloading we can create many different constructors if needed – allowing our object to be initialized in a number of different ways.

Constructor methods are optional in VB.NET. The only exception being when we're using inheritance and the parent class has only constructors that require parameters. We'll discuss inheritance later in the chapter.

Termination

In VB6 an object was destroyed when its last reference was removed. In other words, when no other code had any reference to an object, the object would be automatically destroyed – triggering a call to its `Class_Terminate` event. This approach was implemented through reference counting – keeping a count of how many clients had a reference to each object – and was a direct product of VB's close relationship with COM.

While this behavior was nice – since we always knew an object would be destroyed immediately and we could count on `Class_Terminate` to know when – it had its problems. Most notably, it was quite easy to create circular references between two objects, which could leave them running in memory forever. This was one of the few (but quite common) ways to create a memory leak in VB6.

> To be fair, the problem was worse prior to VB6. In VB6, circular references are only a problem across components. Objects created from classes within the same component would be automatically destroyed in VB6, even if they had a circular reference. Still, the circular reference problem exists any time objects come from different components. The issue is non-trivial and has created a lot of headaches for VB developers over the years.

The clear termination scheme used in VB6 is an example of **deterministic finalization**. It was always very clear *when* an object would be terminated.

Unlike COM, the .NET runtime does not use reference counting to determine when an object should be terminated. Instead it uses a scheme known as garbage collection to terminate objects. This means that in VB.NET we do not have deterministic finalization, so it is not possible to predict exactly when an object will be destroyed. Let's discuss garbage collection and the termination of VB.NET objects in more detail.

Garbage Collection

In .NET, reference counting is not part of the infrastructure. Instead, objects are destroyed through a garbage collection mechanism. At certain times (based on specific rules), a task will run through all of our objects looking for those that no longer have any references. Those objects are then terminated; the garbage collected.

This means that we can't tell exactly when an object will really be finally destroyed. Just because we eliminate all references to an object doesn't mean it will be terminated immediately. It will just hang out in memory until the garbage collection process gets around to locating and destroying it. This is an example of **nondeterministic finalization**.

The major benefit of garbage collection is that it eliminates the circular reference issues found with reference counting. If two objects have references to each other, and no other code has any references to either object, the garbage collector will discover and terminate them, whereas in COM these objects would have sat in memory forever.

There is also a potential performance benefit from garbage collection. Rather than expending the effort to destroy objects as they are dereferenced, with garbage collection this destruction process typically occurs when the application is otherwise idle – often decreasing the impact on the impact on the user. However, garbage collection may also occur with the application is active in the case that the system starts running low on resources.

We can manually trigger the garbage collection process through code:

```
System.GC.Collect()
```

This process takes time however, so it is not the sort of thing that should be done each time we want to terminate an object. It is far better to design our applications in such a way that it is acceptable for our objects to sit in memory for a time before they are finally terminated.

Finalize Method

The garbage collection mechanism does provide some functionality comparable to the VB6 `Class_Terminate` event. As an object is being terminated, the garbage collection code will call its `Finalize` method – allowing us to take care of any final cleanup that might be required:

```
Protected Overrides Sub Finalize()
  ' clean up code goes here
End Sub
```

This code uses both the `Protected` scope and `Overrides` keyword – concepts we'll discuss later as we cover inheritance. For now it is sufficient to know that this method will be called just prior to the object being terminated by the garbage collection mechanism – somewhat like `Class_Terminate`.

However, it is critical to remember that this method may be called long after the object is dereferenced by the last bit of client code (perhaps even minutes later).

Implementing a Dispose Method

In some cases the `Finalize` behavior is not acceptable. If we have an object that is using some expensive or limited resource – such as a database connection, a file handle, or a system lock – we might need to ensure that the resource is freed as soon as the object is no longer in use.

To accomplish this, we can implement a method to be called by the client code to force our object to clean up and release its resources. This is not a perfect solution, but it is workable. By convention, this method is typically named `Dispose`:

```
Public Sub Dispose()
   ' clean up code goes here
End Sub
```

It is up to our client code to call this method at the appropriate time to ensure cleanup occurs. Again, the specific name of this method is up to us, though within the .NET system class libraries the convention is to use the name `Dispose`.

At this point we've largely covered the changes in behavior between VB6 and VB.NET in terms of creating classes and objects. Let's move on and see how the substantial new inheritance feature works.

Inheritance

While the OO features of VB have been very powerful and useful, we have been held back in many cases by the lack of inheritance in the language. Inheritance is the ability of a class to gain the interface and behaviors of an existing class. The process by which this is accomplished is called **subclassing**. When we create a new class that inherits the interface and behaviors from an existing class, we have created a subclass of the original class. This is also known as an "is-a" relationship, where the new class "is-a" type of original class.

There is a lot of terminology surrounding inheritance – much of it redundant. The original class, from which we inherit interface and behavior is known by the following interchangeable terms:

❑ Parent class

❑ Superclass

❑ Base class

The new class that inherits the interface and behaviors is known by the following interchangeable terms:

❑ Child class

❑ Subclass

Inheritance is also sometimes called **generalization**. In fact this is the term used within the Universal Modeling Language (UML) – the most commonly used object diagramming notation.

Inheritance is often viewed through the lens of biology, where, for example, a dog is a canine and a canine is a mammal. Hence, by being a canine, a dog inherits all the attributes and behavior of a mammal. While useful for visualization, these analogies only go so far.

For interested object-oriented aficionados, VB.NET does not allow multiple inheritance – where a subclass is created by inheriting from more than one parent class. This feature is not supported by the .NET runtime and thus is not available from VB.NET. VB.NET does allow deep inheritance hierarchies where a class is subclassed from a class that is subclassed, but it doesn't allow a class to be subclassed from multiple parent classes all at once.

We can contrast inheritance, an "is-a" relationship, with another type of parent-child relationship – the "has-a" relationship. This is also known as aggregation or containment.

In a "has-a" relationship, the parent object owns one or more of the child objects, but the child objects are of different types from the parent. For instance, an `Invoice` has-a `LineItem`. The `LineItem` object isn't subclassed from `Invoice` – it is an entirely different class that just happens to be owned by the `Invoice` parent.

This distinction is important, because the terms *parent* and *child* are used frequently when working with objects – sometimes when referring to inheritance and sometimes when referring to aggregation. It is important to understand which is which or things can get very confusing.

Within this section, we'll use the terms parent, child, and subclass – all in the context of inheritance.

Implementing Basic Inheritance

To explore inheritance, consider a business example with a sales order that has line items. We might have product line items and service line items. Both are examples of line items, but both are somewhat different as well. While we could certainly implement `ProductLine` and `ServiceLine` classes separately, they'd have a lot of common code between them. Redundant code is hard to maintain, so it would be nicer if they could somehow directly share the common code between them.

This is where inheritance comes into play. Using inheritance, we can create a `LineItem` class that contains all the code common to any sort of line item. Then we can create `ProductLine` and `ServiceLine` classes that inherit from `LineItem` – thus automatically gaining all the common code – including interface and implementation in an OO form.

A simple `LineItem` class might appear as:

```
Public Class LineItem
  Private mintID As Integer
  Private mstrItem As String
  Private msngPrice As Single
  Private mintQuantity As Integer

  Public Property ID() As Integer
    Get
      Return mintID
    End Get
    Set
      mintID = value
    End Set
  End Property

  Public Property Item() As String
    Get
      Return mstrItem
```

```
         End Get
         Set
           mstrItem = Value
         End Set
      End Property

      Public Property Price() As Single
         Get
            Return msngPrice
         End Get
         Set
            msngPrice = Value
         End Set
      End Property

      Public Property Quantity() As Integer
         Get
            Return mintQuantity
         End Get
         Set
            mintQuantity = Value
         End Set
      End Property

      Public Function Amount() As Single
         Return mintQuantity * msngPrice
      End Function
   End Class
```

This class has things common to any line item – some basic data fields and a method to calculate the cost of the item.

If a line item is for a product, however, we might have additional requirements. The Item value should probably be validated to make sure it refers to a real product, and perhaps we want to provide a product description as well:

```
   Public Class ProductLine
      Inherits LineItem

      Private mstrDescription As String

      Public ReadOnly Property Description() As String
         Get
            Return mstrDescription
         End Get
      End Property

      Public Sub New(ByVal ProductID As String)
         Item = ProductID
         ' load product data from database
         mstrDescription = "Test product description"
      End Sub
   End Class
```

Note the use of the Inherits statement.

```
Inherits LineItem
```

It is this statement that causes the `ProductLine` class to gain all the interface elements and behaviors from the `LineItem` class. This means that we can have client code like this:

```
Protected Sub Button1_Click(ByVal sender As Object, _
    ByVal e As System.EventArgs)
  Dim pl As ProductLine

  pl = New ProductLine("123abc")
  MessageBox.Show(pl.Item)
  MessageBox.Show(pl.Description)
End Sub
```

This code makes use of both the `Item` property (from the `LineItem` class) and the `Description` property from the `ProductLine` class. Both are equally part of the `ProductLine` class, since it is a subclass of `LineItem`.

Likewise, a line item for a service might have a date for when the service was provided, but otherwise be the same as any other line item:

```
Public Class ServiceLine
  Inherits LineItem

  Private mdtDateProvided As Date

  Public Sub New()
    Quantity = 1
  End Sub

  Public Property DateProvided() As Date
    Get
      Return mdtDateProvided
    End Get
    Set
      mdtDateProvided = Value
    End Set
  End Property
End Class
```

Again, notice the use of the `Inherits` statement that indicates this is a subclass of the `LineItem` class. The `DateProvided` property is simply added to the interface gained from the `LineItem` class.

Preventing Inheritance

By default any class we create can be used as a base class from which other classes can be created. There are times when we might want to create a class that cannot be subclassed. To do this we can use the `NotInheritable` keyword in our class declaration:

```
Public NotInheritable Class ProductLine

End Class
```

When this keyword is used, no other code may use the `Inherits` keyword to create a subclass of our class.

Inheritance and Scoping

When we create a subclass through inheritance, the new class gains all the `Public` and `Friend` methods, properties, and variables from the original class. Anything declared as `Private` in the original class will not be directly available to our code in the new subclass.

The exception to this is the New method. Constructor methods must be re-implemented in each subclass. We'll discuss this in more detail later in the chapter.

For instance, we might rewrite the `Amount` methods from the `LineItem` class slightly:

```
Public Function Amount() As Single
   Return CalcAmount
End Function

Private Function CalcAmount() As Single
   Return fQuantity * fPrice
End Function
```

With this change, we can see that the `Public` method `Amount` makes use of a `Private` method to do its work.

When we subclass `LineItem` to create the `ServiceLine` class, any `ServiceLine` object will have an `Amount` method because it is declared as `Public` in the base class. The `CalcAmount` method, on the other hand, is declared as `Private` and so neither the `ServiceLine` class nor any client code will have any access to it.

Does this mean the `Amount` method will break when called through the `ServiceLine` object? Not at all. Since the `Amount` method's code resides in the `LineItem` class, it has access to the `CalcAmount` method even though the `ServiceLine` class can't see the method.

For instance, in our client code we might have something like this:

```
Protected Sub Button1_Click(ByVal sender As Object, _
     ByVal e As System.EventArgs)
   Dim sl As ServiceLine

   sl = New ServiceLine()
   sl.Item = "delivery"
   sl.Price = 20
   sl.DateProvided = Now

   MsgBox(sl.Amount, MsgBoxStyle.Information, "Amount")
End Sub
```

The result is displayed in a message box, thus illustrating that the `CalcAmount` method was called on our behalf even though neither our client code, nor the `ServiceLine` code directly made the call.

Protected Methods

Sometimes `Public` and `Private` aren't enough. If we declare something as `Private` it is totally restricted to our class, while if we declare something as `Public` (or `Friend`) it is available to both subclasses and client code. There are times when it would be nice to create a method that is available to subclasses, but *not* to client code.

This is where the `Protected` scope comes into play. When something is declared as `Protected`, it is not available to any code outside of the class. However, it *is* available to classes that are derived from our class through inheritance.

For example:

```
Public Class ParentClass
   Protected TheValue As Integer
End Class

Public Class SubClass
  Inherits ParentClass

  Public Function GetValue() As Integer
    Return TheValue
  End Function
End Class
```

Here we have a parent class with a `Protected` member – `TheValue`. This variable is not available to any client code. However, the variable is fully available to any code within `SubClass`, because it inherits from the parent.

In this example, `SubClass` has a `Public` method that actually does return the protected value – but the variable `TheValue` is not directly available to any client code (that is, code outside the class).

Overriding Methods

One key attribute of inheritance is that a subclass not only gains the behaviors of the original class, but it can also override those behaviors. We've already seen how a subclass can *extend* the original class by adding new `Public`, `Protected`, and `Friend` methods. However, by using the concept of overriding, a subclass can *alter* the behaviors of methods that were declared on the parent class.

By default, methods cannot be overridden by a subclass. To allow them to be overridden, the parent class must declare the method using the `Overridable` keyword:

```
Public Class Parent
   Public Overridable Sub DoSomething()
     MessageBox.Show("Hello from Parent")
   End Sub
End Class
```

We can also explicitly disallow overriding through the use of the `NotOverridable` keyword. Of course since this is the default, this keyword is rarely used.

> *However, it may be a good practice to explicitly define whether a method can or cannot be overridden to increase the clarity of code and to protect against the possibility that the default behavior might someday change.*

If we then create a subclass, we can optionally override the behavior of `DoSomething` by using the `Overrides` keyword:

```
Public Class SubClass
   Inherits Parent

   Public Overrides Sub DoSomething()
     MessageBox.Show("Hello from SubClass")
```

```
      End Sub
   End Class
```

Now we can write client code such as:

```
Dim obj As New SubClass()

obj.DoSomething()
```

The result will be a message dialog containing the text Hello from SubClass. This isn't surprising – after all, we overrode the DoSomething method with our new code.

Virtual Methods

However, consider the following client code:

```
Dim obj As Parent

obj = New SubClass()
obj.DoSomething()
```

First off, it seems odd to declare a variable of type Parent, but then create a SubClass object instead. This is perfectly acceptable however – it is yet another way of implementing polymorphism. Since SubClass "is-a" Parent, any Parent or SubClass variable can hold a reference to a SubClass object.

This is true in general. When using inheritance, a variable of the parent type can always hold references to any child type created from the parent.

What may be more surprising is the message that is displayed in our message box when this code is run. The message we see is Hello from SubClass.

How can this be? The variable is declared as type Parent – shouldn't the Parent implementation be called? The reason the DoSomething implementation from the child class is called is that the method is **virtual**. The concept of a virtual method is such that the "bottom-most" implementation of the method is always used in favor of the parent implementation – regardless of the data type of the variable being used in the client code.

> **Unlike many object-oriented languages, all methods in VB.NET are virtual.**

The term "bottom-most" comes from the typical way a chain of inherited objects is diagrammed. Usually the parent class is displayed, with the subclasses underneath. If the subclasses are also subclassed, then those classes are shown even further down. This is illustrated by the following UML diagram:

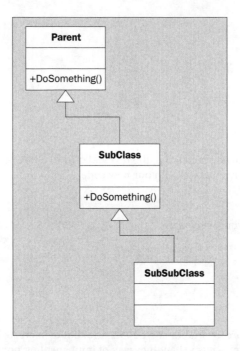

Regardless of the *variable* data type, the implementation of DoSomething will be invoked based on the actual class we use to create the object. In our previous example, we created an object of type SubClass, thus ensuring that the DoSomething implementation in that class would be invoked. This is illustrated by the following diagram, which shows how the method calls are made:

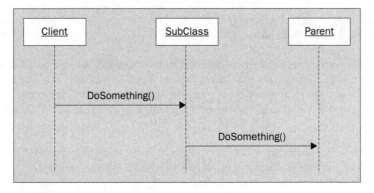

If we create an object from type Parent with the following code:

```
Dim obj As Parent

obj = New Parent()
obj.DoSomething()
```

The DoSomething implementation in the Parent class will be invoked since that is the type of object we created as shown in the following diagram:

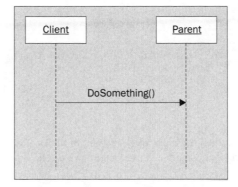

We can also create the object from the SubSubClass class:

```
Dim obj As Parent

obj = New SubSubClass()
obj.DoSomething()
```

In this case, the class doesn't directly implement DoSomething, so we start looking back up the inheritance chain:

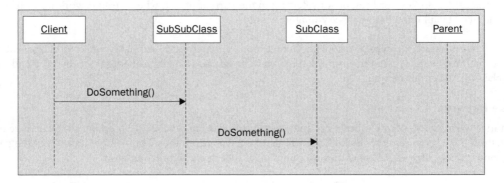

The first class up that chain is SubClass, which *does* have an implementation – so it is that implementation which is invoked. No code from the Parent class is invoked at all.

Me Keyword

The Me keyword is used any time we want our code to refer to methods within the current object. This was used in VB6 – when we might have utilized the Me keyword to refer to the current form, or the current instance of an object – and the same is true in VB.NET.

The Me keyword is analogous to the this *keyword in C++ and C# languages.*

The Me keyword is usually optional, since any method call is assumed to refer to the current object unless explicitly noted otherwise. The exception is when we are working with **shadowed** variables.

A shadowed variable is a procedure-level variable with the same name as a class-level variable. For instance:

```
Public Class TheClass
  Private strName As String

  Public Sub DoSomething()
    Dim strName As String

    strName = "Fred"
  End Sub
End Class
```

The variable `strName` is declared at the class level *and* within the `DoSomething` method. Within that method only the local, or shadowed, variable is used unless we explicitly reference the class-level variable with the `Me` keyword:

```
Public Sub DoSomething()
  Dim strName As String

  strName = "Fred"          ' sets the local variable's value
  Me.strName = "Mary"       ' sets the class level variable's value
End Sub
```

Here we can see that `strName` can be used to reference the local variable, while `Me.strName` can be used to reference the class-level variable.

As useful as the `Me` keyword can be for referring to the current object, when we start working with inheritance, it isn't enough to do everything we want.

There are two issues we need to deal with. Sometimes we may want to explicitly call into our parent class – and sometimes we may want to ensure that the code in *our* class is being called, rather than the code in some subclass that has inherited our code.

MyBase Keyword

At times we might want to explicitly call into methods in our parent class. Remember that when we override a method it is virtual – so the method call will invoke the "bottom-most" implementation – not the parent implementation. However, sometimes we might need that parent implementation.

To invoke the parent class from within our subclass we can use the `MyBase` keyword. For instance:

```
Public Class SubClass
  Inherits Parent

  Public Overrides Sub DoSomething()
    MessageBox.Show("Hello from subclass")
    MyBase.DoSomething()
  End Sub
End Class
```

If we run our client code now, we'll get two message boxes. First we'll get the message from the subclass, followed by the one from the parent class.

The `MyBase` keyword can be used to invoke or use any `Public`, `Friend`, or `Protected` element from the parent class. This includes all of those elements directly on the base class, and also any elements the base class inherited from other classes higher in the inheritance chain.

MyBase *only* refers to the immediate parent of the current class. If we create a SubSubClass that inherits from SubClass, the MyBase keyword would refer to the SubClass code, not the Parent code. There is no direct way to navigate more than one level up the inheritance chain.

MyClass Keyword

A more complex scenario is one where the code in our class might end up invoking code from other classes created *from* our class.

When we create a class, we'll frequently make calls from within our class to other methods within that same class. This occurs in the following code:

```
Public Class Parent
  Public Sub DoSomething()
    OtherStuff()
  End Sub

  Public Overridable Sub OtherStuff()
    MessageBox.Show("Parent other stuff")
  End Sub
End Class
```

In this case, the DoSomething method calls the OtherStuff method to do some work. Notice however, that OtherStuff is marked as Overridable, so a subclass might provide a different implementation for the method. For example:

```
Public Class SubClass
  Inherits Parent

  Public Overrides Sub OtherStuff()
    MessageBox.Show("SubClass other stuff")
  End Sub
End Class
```

As we discussed earlier, VB.NET methods are virtual – which means that an object of type SubClass will always invoke OtherStuff from SubClass rather than from the Parent class. This is true even for code in the Parent class itself – so when the DoSomething method calls the OtherStuff method it will invoke the overridden implementation in SubClass.

This can be illustrated by the following client code:

```
Dim obj As New SubClass()

obj.DoSomething()
```

We will see a dialog displaying **SubClass other stuff**. The DoSomething method in the Parent class invokes the overridden OtherStuff implementation within the SubClass class.

If we don't want this behavior – if we want the code in the Parent class to know for certain that it is calling the OtherStuff implementing from Parent – we need to use the MyClass keyword:

```
Public Class Parent
  Public Sub DoSomething()
    MyClass.OtherStuff()
  End Sub

  Public Overridable Sub OtherStuff()
    MessageBox.Show("Parent other stuff")
  End Sub
End Class
```

We can't use the Me keyword, because that will reference the virtual method. MyClass, on the other hand, forces the call to be handled by the code in the same class as the call – in this case the Parent class.

This example is illustrated by the following diagram, which shows the method calls being made:

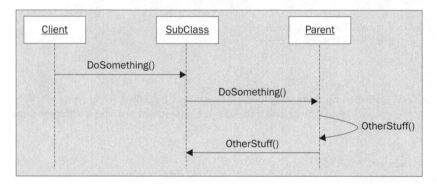

Here we can see that the client calls DoSomething, which is actually invoked from the Parent class. The Parent class then calls OtherStuff, but since it is implemented in SubClass, that is the implementation that is invoked.

Overriding the Constructor Method

We've already seen how we can override methods, and how to use the Me, MyBase, and MyClass keywords to interact with the various overridden methods in our inheritance chain. However, there are special rules that govern the process of overriding the New constructor method.

New methods aren't automatically carried from a parent to a subclass like normal methods. Each subclass must define its own constructors, though those constructors may call into the parent class using the MyBase keyword:

```
Public Class SubClass
  Inherits Parent

  Public Sub New()
    MyBase.New()
     ' other initialization code goes here
  End Sub
End Class
```

When calling the base class constructor, that call *must* be the first line in our constructor code – anything else is an error. This is totally optional, however, since the constructor of the parent class is automatically called on our behalf before our constructor code begins to run, unless we make that call manually.

> **If all constructor methods of the base class require parameters then we must implement at least one constructor in our subclass and we *must* explicitly call `MyBase.New` from within our constructors.**

As we discussed earlier, the `New` method can be overloaded, providing various implementations. If our parent class provides alternate implementations of `New`, we may want to manually make the call in order to cause the correct implementation to be called, based on our requirements.

Creating Base Classes and Abstract Methods

So far, we've seen how to inherit from a class, how to overload and override methods, and how virtual methods work. In all of our examples so far, the parent classes have been useful in their own right. Sometimes however, we want to create a class such that it can only be used as a base class for inheritance.

MustInherit Keyword

Returning to our original sales order line item example, it may make little sense for anyone to create an object based on the generic `LineItem` class. In fact, we may want to ensure that only more specific subclasses derived from `LineItem` can be created. What we want to create is something called a **base class**. This is done using the `MustInherit` keyword in the class declaration:

```
Public MustInherit Class LineItem
```

Typically, no other change is required in our class. The result of this keyword is that it is no longer possible to write client code that creates an instance of the `LineItem` class, so the following would cause a syntax error:

```
Dim obj As New LineItem()
```

Instead, to use the code in the `LineItem` class, we *must* create subclasses and use those throughout our application.

MustOverride Keyword

Another option we have is to create a method that must be overridden by a subclass. We might want to do this when we are creating a base class that provides some behavior, but relies on subclasses to also provide some behavior in order to function properly. This is accomplished by using the `MustOverride` keyword on a method declaration:

```
Public MustOverride Sub CalcPrice()
```

Notice that there is no `End Sub` or any other code associated with the method.

When using `MustOverride`, we *cannot* provide any implementation for the method in our class. Such a method is called an **abstract method** or **pure virtual function**, since it only defines the interface and no implementation.

211

Methods declared in this manner *must* be overridden in any subclass that inherits from our base class. If we don't override one of these methods, we'll generate a syntax error in the subclass and it won't compile.

Abstract Base Classes

We can combine these two concepts – using both `MustInherit` and `MustOverride` – to create something called an **abstract base class**. This is a class that provides no implementation, only the interface definitions from which a subclass can be created. An example might be as follows:

```
Public MustInherit Class Parent
  Public MustOverride Sub DoSomething()
  Public MustOverride Sub DoOtherStuff()
End Class
```

This technique can be very useful when creating frameworks or the high-level conceptual elements of a system. Any class that inherits `Parent` must implement both `DoSomething` and `DoOtherStuff` or a syntax error will result.

In some ways an abstract base class is very comparable to defining an interface using the `Interface` keyword. We'll discuss the `Interface` keyword in detail later in this chapter. For now, be aware that the `Interface` keyword is used to formally declare an interface that can be implemented using the `Implements` keyword as in VB6.

We could define the same interface as shown in this example with the following code:

```
Public Interface IParent
  Sub DoSomething()
  Sub DoOtherStuff()
End Interface
```

Any class that implements the `IParent` interface must implement both `DoSomething` and `DoOtherStuff` or a syntax error will result – and in that regard this technique is similar to an abstract base class.

There are differences however. In particular, when we create a new class by subclassing the `Parent` class, that class can in turn be subclassed. Those classes will automatically have `DoSomething` and `DoOtherStuff` methods due to the nature of inheritance.

Compare this with the interface approach, where each individual class must independently implement the `IParent` interface *and* provide its own implementation of the two methods. If we never intend to reuse the code that implements these methods as we create new classes then the interface approach is fine, but if we want code reuse within subclasses inheritance is the way to go.

Shared or Class Members

While objects are very powerful and useful, there are times when we just want access to variables, functions, or routines that do useful work – without the need for an actual object instance. In the past, we would typically put this type of code into a simple code module even if the routine was technically related to some class.

Shared Methods

In VB.NET we have a better alternative. Not only can a class have all the regular methods and properties we've seen so far – methods and properties only available after creating an instance of the class – but they can also have methods that are available *without* creating an instance of the class. These are known as **shared methods**.

These methods are also known as static methods or class methods in other languages.

A shared method is not accessed via an object instance like a regular method, but rather is accessed directly from the class. The following is a simple example of a shared method:

```
Public Class Math
   Shared Function Add(ByVal a As Integer, ByVal b As Integer) As Integer
      Return a + b
   End Function
End Class
```

We can use this method – without instantiating a `Math` object – as follows:

```
Dim result As Integer

result = Math.Add(5, 10)
```

Notice how, rather than using an object variable, we use the actual class name to reference the method. With a normal method this would result in a syntax error, but with a shared method this is perfectly acceptable.

Shared methods can also be accessed via objects just like regular methods, but their most common use is to provide functionality without the requirement for creating an object. In fact, when a shared method is invoked, no object is created – the method is called directly, much like a procedure in a `Module`.

Shared methods can also be overloaded just like regular methods, so it is quite possible to create a set of variations on the same shared method, each having a different parameter list.

The default scope for a shared method is `Public`. It is possible to restrict the scope of a shared method to `Friend`, `Protected`, or `Private` by prefixing the declaration with the appropriate scope. In fact, when overloading a method we can have different scopes on each implementation – as long as the parameter lists are different as we discussed when covering the `Overloads` keyword earlier.

A good example of how shared methods are used comes from the .NET system class libraries. When we want to open a text file for input we typically make use of a shared method on the `File` class:

```
Dim infile As StreamReader = File.OpenText("words.txt")
Dim strIn As String

str = infile.ReadLine()
```

No object of type `File` is created here. The `OpenText` method is a shared method that opens a file and returns a `StreamReader` object for our use. Another example comes from the `System.Guid` data type. This class represents a globally unique identifier (GUID) value, but creating a new value is handled via a shared method:

```
Dim guidID As Guid()

guidID = Guid.NewGuid()
```

The `NewGuid` method is called directly from the `Guid` class. It creates a new `Guid` object and returns it as a result.

Shared Variables

There is another type of shared member we can create. There are times when it is nice to share a value across all instances of a class – when every object of a given type should share the same variable. This is accomplished through the use of **shared variables**.

A shared variable is declared using the Shared keyword, much like a shared method:

```
Public Class MyCounter
   Private Shared mintCount As Integer
End Class
```

As with shared methods, we can scope the shared variable as required. Where Shared methods are Public by default, Shared variables are Private by default.

> **In general, it is good practice to always explicitly define the scope of methods and variables to avoid confusion.**

The important thing about shared variables is that they are common across all instances of the class. We could enhance our class slightly as follows:

```
Public Class MyCounter
   Private Shared mintCount As Integer

   Public Sub New()
     mintCount += 1
   End Sub

   Public ReadOnly Property Count() As Integer
     Get
        Return mintCount
     End Get
   End Property
End Class
```

As we create each instance of the class the counter is incremented by one.

The += operator is new to VB.NET and is covered in Chapter 3.

At any point, we can retrieve the count value via the Count property. Thus, if we run the following client code we'll get a resulting value of 3:

```
Protected Sub Button4_Click(ByVal sender As Object, _
    ByVal e As System.EventArgs)
  Dim obj As MyCounter

  obj = New MyCounter()
  obj = New MyCounter()
  obj = New MyCounter()
  MsgBox(obj.Count, MsgBoxStyle.Information, "Counter")
End Sub
```

If we run it again we'll get 6, then 9, and so forth. As long as our application is running the counter will remain valid. Once our application terminates the counter also goes away.

This technique can be very useful for server processes that run "forever" since they can keep usage counters or other values over time very easily. The values are only reset when the process is restarted.

Global Values

Another common use for shared variables is to provide a form of global variable. Given a `Public` scoped shared variable:

```
Public Class TheClass
    Public Shared MyGlobal As Integer
End Class
```

We can then use this variable throughout our client code:

```
TheClass.MyGlobal += 5
```

This variable will be available to any code within our application, providing a very nice mechanism for sharing values between components, classes, modules, and so forth.

Events

Events are fully supported within the context of inheritance. If a base class defines a `Public` event, then that event can be raised by both the code in that base class and from any subclasses derived from that base class.

For instance, we may have a simple base class such as:

```
Public Class Parent
  Public Event ParentEvent()

  Public Sub DoEvent()
    RaiseEvent ParentEvent()
  End Sub
End Class
```

It is no surprise that code in this class can raise the `ParentEvent` event. However, we can then create a subclass such as:

```
Public Class SubClass
  Inherits Parent

  Public Sub DoSomething()
    RaiseEvent ParentEvent()
  End Sub
End Class
```

This class is derived from `Parent` through the use of the `Inherits` keyword, gaining not only properties and methods, but also events from the base class.

Events can be declared with any scope. Those `Private` in scope can only be received by the sending object, while those `Public` in scope can be received by any object. `Protected` events can only be received by objects created by the defining class or subclasses, while events declared as `Friend` can be received by any object within the VB.NET project.

Unlike methods, events cannot be overloaded using the `Overloads` keyword. A class can only define one event with any given name. Since any subclass will automatically gain the event from its parent class, the `Overrides` keyword makes no sense and cannot be used with events.

Shared Events

Events may be declared as `Shared`. Shared methods can only raise shared events, not non-shared events. For instance:

```
Public Class EventSource
  Shared Event SharedEvent()

  Public Shared Sub DoShared()
    RaiseEvent SharedEvent()
  End Sub
End Class
```

A shared event can be raised by both shared and non-shared methods:

```
Public Class EventSource
  Public Event TheEvent()
  Shared Event SharedEvent()

  Public Sub DoSomething()
    RaiseEvent TheEvent()
    RaiseEvent SharedEvent()
  End Sub

  Public Shared Sub DoShared()
    RaiseEvent SharedEvent()
  End Sub
End Class
```

Attempting to raise a non-shared event from a shared method will result in a syntax error.

Raising Events across Projects

In Beta 1, events do not appear to be fully implemented. In particular, events cannot be raised from code in one VB project into code in a separate VB project without some extra work on our part.

The `Event` and `RaiseEvent` keywords in VB.NET are actually implemented behind the scenes through the use of delegates. We discussed the `Delegate` keyword and the concept of delegates in Chapter 3. If we want to raise an event from one VB.NET project and have it be received by code in another project, we'll have to use a mix of event and delegate concepts.

Implementing the Remote Event Source

While we'll still use the `RaiseEvent` statement to raise the event, we need to declare the event somewhat differently if it will be received by code in another VB.NET project. In particular, we need to define the event as a delegate using the `Delegate` statement – *outside* the class that will be raising the event.

Create a new Class Library project named `EventSource` and add a simple class to it named `RemoteClass`.

Suppose we want to raise an event that returns a `String` parameter. We'd first declare a delegate with that type of parameter:

```
Public Delegate Sub RemoteEventHandler(ByVal SomeString As String)
```

> *Normally VB.NET automatically creates this delegate for us behind the scenes. However, in Beta 1 this delegate is being created in such a way that it is not available from other projects – thus we must declare it explicitly.*

Then, in the same code file, we can create the class that will raise the event:

```
Public Class RemoteClass

  Public Event RemoteEvent As RemoteEventHandler

  Public Sub DoSomething()
    RaiseEvent RemoteEvent("My event")
  End Sub
End Class
```

The key to success here lies in the declaration of the event itself:

```
Public Event RemoteEvent As RemoteEventHandler
```

The event doesn't declare its parameters explicitly, instead relying on the delegate to make that declaration. Instead, the event is declared as a specific type – that being the delegate that we just defined.

Beyond that, the code to raise the event is as we'd expect – just a simple `RaiseEvent` statement:

```
RaiseEvent RemoteEvent("My event")
```

It provides the parameter value to be returned as the event is raised.

Receiving the Remote Event

In a separate VB.NET project we can write code to receive the event. Add a Windows Application project to the current solution. Right-click on it and choose the **Set As Startup Project** option so it will be run when we press *F5*.

To have access to the class that raises our event, we must add a reference to the `EventSource` project we just created by using the **Project | Add Reference** menu option.

With that done, we can add a button to the form and then open the form's code window. Import the remote namespace:

```
Imports System.ComponentModel
Imports System.Drawing
Imports System.WinForms
Imports EventSource
```

217

In the form's code we need to declare the remote class using the `WithEvents` keyword:

```
Public Class Form1
   Inherits System.WinForms.Form

   Private WithEvents objRemote As RemoteClass
```

We can now see the event listed in the **Method Name** dropdown list in the upper-right of the code window when the `objRemote` entry is selected in the **Class Name** dropdown in the upper-left. When we select this entry the following code is created:

```
Public Sub objRemote_RemoteEvent() Handles objRemote.RemoteEvent

End Sub
```

Unfortunately this code is not correct, as it has no provision for the parameter we're passing. Strangely enough, the IDE knows this is in error (even though it created the code) and flags it as a syntax error. To fix the problem we just need to add the parameter into the declaration:

```
Public Sub objRemote_RemoteEvent(ByVal Data As String) _
    Handles objRemote.RemoteEvent

  Messagebox.Show(Data)

End Sub
```

We've also added code to display the result in a dialog. If we add a button to the form with the following code, we can run the project to see the dialog displayed:

```
Protected Sub Button1_Click(ByVal sender As Object, ByVal e As System.EventArgs)
   objRemote = New RemoteClass()
   objRemote.DoSomething()
End Sub
```

Though a bit of extra work in Beta 1, this technique allows us to raise events from one project and have them received by code in another project.

Interfaces

VB has, for some time, allowed us to create objects with more than one interface. This was done using the `Implements` keyword. Any time our class implemented a new interface we were required to write code to implement each method on the interface. While inheritance provides a preferable alternative to this in many cases, there are still times when we may want to have our objects implement multiple interfaces.

VB.NET preserves the `Implements` keyword, and in fact the entire concept of interfaces is enhanced and made simpler as compared to VB6.

Working with Interfaces

VB.NET introduces a formalized structure for declaring interfaces. It also changes the syntax used in classes that implement an interface, making our code much more intuitive and clear.

Interface Declaration

The most visible enhancement is the introduction of a formal syntax for declaring an interface. This is done by using the `Interface` keyword:

```
Public Interface MyInterface
  Event MyEvent()
  Sub MyMethod()
  Function MyFunction(ByVal Param1 As Integer) As Integer
  Property MyProperty() As String
End Interface
```

This approach is much more formal that the approaches available in VB6. It is also more powerful – notice that not only can we declare `Sub`, `Function`, and `Property` methods, but also declare events as a formal part of an interface.

All the elements described in this interface must be implemented by any class that chooses to implement this interface.

Overloading Methods

Methods (`Sub` and `Function`) can be declared in an interface using the `Overloads` keyword. The rules for overloading are the same as we discussed earlier in the chapter – each overloaded declaration must have a unique parameter list based on data type of the parameters.

Declaring an interface with overloaded methods is done as in the following example:

```
Public Interface MyInterface
  Overloads Sub MyMethod()
  Overloads Sub MyMethod(Data As String)
  Overloads Function MyFunction(ByVal Param1 As Integer) As Integer
  Overloads Function MyFunction(ByVal Param1 As Single) As Integer
End Interface
```

When a class uses the `Implements` keyword to implement an interface with overloaded methods, the class must implement each of the overloaded method declarations.

Implementing an Interface

As with VB6, implementing an interface is done through the use of the `Implements` keyword:

```
Public Class TheClass
  Implements MyInterface
End Class
```

From there, however, things get a bit different. In VB6 we'd implement the various interface elements as a set of specially named `Private` methods. That approach was unintuitive and was the cause for great confusion among many developers new to the language. VB.NET addresses this issue by providing a clear, concise syntax for implementing the interface – again through the application of the `Implements` keyword.

We can simply mark a method in our class as being the implementation of a specific method from the interface:

```
Public Sub MyMethod() Implements MyInterface.MyMethod
```

So, to implement our example interface, we'd have code such as:

```
Public Class TheClass
  Implements MyInterface

  Public Event MyEvent() Implements MyInterface.MyEvent

  Public Function MyFunction(ByVal Param1 As Integer) _
      As System.Integer Implements OOlib.MyInterface.MyFunction

  End Function

  Public Sub MyMethod() Implements OOlib.MyInterface.MyMethod

  End Sub

  Public Property MyProperty() As String _
      Implements OOlib.MyInterface.MyProperty
    Get

    End Get
    Set

    End Set
  End Property
End Class
```

As with VB6, when we implement an interface, we must implement *all* the elements in that interface – including events, methods, and properties.

We can now create client code that interacts with our object via this interface, in addition to the object's normal interface:

```
Dim obj As MyInterface

obj = New Implementer()
obj.MyMethod
```

Contrast this to VB6, where the routine to implement a method from an interface was written as follows:

```
Private Sub MyInterface_MyMethod()
  ' implementation goes here
End Sub
```

The fact that this method implements part of the interface is only shown by its naming – a pretty obscure thing. We could declare this as `Public` and make it available for external use, but the name of the method couldn't change. Now, with VB.NET the name (and scope) of the method is independent of the interface element being implemented.

Implementing Multiple Interfaces

A class can have more than one `Implements` statement – thus implementing more than one interface. Suppose we have the following interfaces:

```
Public Interface MyInterface
  Sub DoSomething()
End Interface

Public Interface OtherInterface
  Sub DoWork()
End Interface
```

We can construct a class that implements both interfaces:

```
Public Class TheClass
  Implements MyInterface
  Implements OtherInterface

End Class
```

Now we have a choice. We can either implement separate methods to handle `DoSomething` and `DoWork`:

```
Private Sub DoSomething() Implements MyInterface.DoSomething
  ' implementation goes here
End Sub

Private Overloads Sub DoWork() Implements OtherInterface.DoWork
  ' implementation goes here
End Sub
```

Or, if they do the same thing, we can have a single method implement both methods:

```
Private Sub DoSomething() _
    Implements MyInterface.DoSomething, OtherInterface.DoWork

  ' implementation goes here
End Sub
```

This is done by combining the list of implemented methods in a comma-separated list following the `Implements` keyword.

Interacting with Objects

With all the changes to the way we declare, construct, and implement classes, it makes sense that there are also some changes in the way we interact with objects. These changes impact on how we instantiate objects, reference and dereference objects, and how we use early and late binding techniques.

Object Declaration and Instantiation

The most obvious change in the way we work with objects comes as we try to create them and work with our object references. VB.NET doesn't use the `CreateObject` statement for object creation. `CreateObject` was an outgrowth of VB's relationship with COM, and since VB.NET doesn't use COM, it has no use for `CreateObject`.

> *Technically VB.NET can use COM objects through an interoperability mechanism. This is discussed in Chapter 9. However, in typical .NET programming, COM doesn't enter the picture.*

New Statement

VB.NET relies on the `New` statement for all object creation. We can use `New` in a number of different locations within our code – all of them perfectly valid.

The most obvious is to declare an object variable and then create an instance of the object in an instance of the class:

```
Dim obj As TheClass

obj = New TheClass()
```

We can shorten this by combining the declaration of the variable with the creation of the instance:

```
Dim obj As New TheClass()
```

In VB6 this was a very poor thing to do, as it had both negative performance and maintainability effects. However, in VB.NET there is no difference between our first example and this one, other than that our code is shorter.

Keep in mind that the scope of our variable comes into play here. If we declare a variable within a block structure, that variable will only be valid within that block structure. In many cases we'll want to declare the variable within the scope of our method, but possibly create instances of the object within a block structure such as a `Try...End Try` or loop structure. In such a case, combining the declaration with the instantiation may be inappropriate.

Another variation on the declaration and instantiation theme is:

```
Dim obj As TheClass = New TheClass()
```

Again, this both declares a variable and creates an instance of the class for our use. This syntax is perhaps more useful when working with inheritance or with multiple interfaces. We might declare the variable to be of one type – say an interface – and instantiate the object based on a class that implements that interface:

```
Dim obj As MyInterface = New TheClass()
```

We can employ more complex syntax at times also. Suppose that we have a method that requires an object reference. We can create an instance of the object right in the call to the method:

```
DoSomething(New TheClass())
```

This calls the `DoSomething` method, passing a new instance of `TheClass` as a parameter. This new object will only exist for the duration of this one method call. When the method completes, the object will be automatically dereferenced by the .NET runtime.

> *Remember that dereferencing an object doesn't mean it is immediately destroyed. As we discussed earlier, objects are only destroyed when the .NET garbage collection process runs through and cleans up orphaned objects.*

This can be even more complex. Perhaps, instead of needing an object reference, our method needs a `String`. We can provide that `String` value from a method on our object – instantiating the object and calling the method all in one shot:

```
DoSomething(New TheClass().GetStringData())
```

Obviously we need to carefully weigh the readability of such code against its compactness – at some point having more compact code can detract from readability rather than enhancing it.

No Set Keyword

Notice that nowhere do we use the `Set` statement when working with objects. In VB6, any time we worked with an object reference we had to use the `Set` command – differentiating objects from any other data type in the language.

In VB.NET, objects are not treated differently from any other data type, and so we can use direct assignment for objects just like we do with `Integer` or `String` data types. The `Set` command is no longer valid in VB.NET. See Chapter 3 for more details.

Dereferencing Objects

In VB6, we'd dereference an object by setting our object reference to `Nothing`. The same is true in VB.NET:

```
Dim obj As TheClass

obj = New TheClass()
obj = Nothing
```

The *effect* of this statement is different in VB.NET, however. As we discussed earlier, VB.NET does not use reference counting to terminate objects, instead relying on a garbage collection mechanism. In VB6, when no more variables held a reference to an object, that object was immediately destroyed. In VB.NET this is not true – the object will be destroyed when the garbage collection process discovers that the object has no references. That is something that may happen seconds or even minutes after the last reference is removed.

This doesn't eliminate the value of dereferencing objects however. If we have a long-running algorithm, it is a good practice to explicitly dereference objects within the process – thus allowing the garbage collector to remove them when possible. As long as our code retains a reference to an object, that object will remain in memory and will not be garbage collected.

Early vs. Late Binding

One of the strengths of VB has long been that we had access to both early and late binding when interacting with objects.

Early binding means that our code directly interacts with the object – knowing its data type ahead of time and thus being able to very efficiently interact with the object. Early binding allows the IDE to use IntelliSense to aid our development efforts and it allows the compiler to ensure that we are referencing methods that do exist and that we are providing the proper parameter values.

Late binding means that our code interacts with an object dynamically at run-time. This provides a great deal of flexibility since our code literally doesn't care what type of object it is interacting with as long as the object supports the methods we want to call. Because the type of the object isn't known by the IDE or compiler, neither IntelliSense nor compile-time syntax checking is possible – but in exchange we get unprecedented flexibility.

VB.NET continues this tradition, providing support for both early and late binding as we work with our objects.

By default, all objects are early bound. The IDE and compiler enforce this as long as `Option Strict On` is set, and this is the default. However, if we set `Option Strict Off` at the top of a source file (as discussed in Chapter 3), we open the door for late binding throughout the code in that file.

Use of the Object Type

Late binding occurs when the compiler can't determine the type of object we'll be calling. This level of ambiguity is achieved through the use of the `Object` data type. A variable of data type `Object` can hold virtually any value – including a reference to any type of object. Thus, code such as the following could be run against any object that implements a `MyMethod` method that accepts no parameters:

```
Option Strict Off

Module LateBind
  Public Sub DoSomething(obj As Object)
    obj.MyMethod()
  End Sub
End Module
```

If the object passed into this routine *doesn't* have a `MyMethod` method that accepts no parameters, then a run-time error will result. Thus, it is recommended that any code that uses late binding should always provide error trapping:

```
Option Strict Off

Module LateBind
  Public Sub DoSomething(obj As Object)
    Try
      obj.MyMethod()
    Catch
      ' do something appropriate given failure to call the method
    End Try
  End Sub
End Module
```

While late binding is flexible, it can be error prone and it is slower than early bound code. To make a late bound method call, the .NET runtime must dynamically determine if the target object actually has a method that matches the one we're calling, and then it must invoke that method on our behalf. This takes more time and effort than an early bound call where the compiler knows ahead of time that the method exists and can compile our code to make the call directly.

Late Binding and Reflection

The .NET Framework supports a concept known as **reflection**. This is the ability to write code that examines other .NET code to determine its composition. Reflection is supported by the System.Reflection namespace.

Reflection allows us to write code that discovers the classes within an assembly and the methods, properties and events exposed by those classes. We can then use reflection to create instances of those classes and call those methods. This entire process can be very dynamic – much like late binding.

In fact, VB.NET uses reflection to implement late binding on our behalf. Rather than forcing us to write the code that uses reflection to find and invoke a method, VB.NET handles this for us when we use late binding coding techniques.

We could implement a limited form of reflection within VB6 by using the typelib DLL. The functions in this DLL allowed us to dynamically discover the classes and methods in a COM DLL, and then invoke them. Of course COM components were described with IDL – a rather inaccurate description of the component. In .NET, assemblies are described by metadata that accurately describes each assembly, making reflection a much more robust solution.

Use of the CType Function

Whether we are using late binding or not, it can be useful to pass object references around using the Object data type – converting them to an appropriate type when we need to interact with them. This is done using the CType function, allowing us to use a variable of type Object to make an *early bound* method call:

```
Module LateBind
   Public Sub DoSomething(obj As Object)
      CType(obj, TheClass).MyMethod()
   End Sub
End Module
```

Even though the variable we're working with is of type Object – and thus any calls to it will be late bound – we are using the CType method to temporarily convert the variable into a specific type, in this case the type TheClass.

> *This technique is often called **casting**. If we think of each interface or class type as a mold, we can cast an object of one type into the mold of another class or interface.*

The CType function can be very useful when working with objects that implement multiple interfaces, since we can reference a single object variable through the appropriate type as needed. For instance, if we have an object of type TheClass that also implements MyInterface, we can use that interface with the following code:

```
Dim obj As TheClass

obj = New TheClass
CType(obj, MyInterface).DoSomething()
```

In this way we can make early bound calls to other interfaces on an object without needing to declare a new variable of the interface type as we had to do in VB6.

Cross-Language Inheritance

VB.NET creates managed code – code that runs within the .NET Framework as discussed in Chapter 2. All managed code can interact with other managed code, regardless of the original language used to create those components. This means that we can create a class in one language and make use of it in another – in any way, including through inheritance.

In fact, we do this all the time. Much of the .NET system class library is written in C#, but we interact with and even inherit from those classes on a regular basis as we program in VB.NET.

Creating the VB.NET Base Class

For instance, we can create a Class Library project in VB.NET named vblib and add a simple class named Parent such as:

```
Public Class Parent
  Public Sub DoSomething()
    MsgBox("Parent DoSomething", MsgBoxStyle.Information, "Parent")
  End Sub
End Class
```

This will act as the base class from which we'll create a subclass in C#.

Creating the C# Subclass

We can then add a new C# Class Library project to the solution (using File | Add Project) and name it cslib. Add a reference to our vblib project by using the Project | Add Reference menu option.

While we are referencing this project directly within the IDE, we wouldn't need the VB.NET source code. Instead, we could have built the vblib project, thus creating an assembly, and then referenced that assembly from within the C# project to gain access to the base class.

In the Class1.cs file change the code to appear as follows:

```
namespace cslib
{
  using System.WinForms;
  using vblib;

  public class csclass : Parent
  {
    public csclass()
    {
      Messagebox.Show("csclass constructor");
    }
  }
}
```

This C# code shares common concepts with the VB.NET code we've seen so far in the book. However, C# is largely derived from C and C++ language syntax so things are a bit different. All lines of code must end with a semicolon to denote the end of the statement. Also, left and right brackets are used to form block structures. In VB.NET we might have a Sub...End Sub block, while in C# we'll have { and }.

Let's walk through it to make everything clear. The first line defines the namespace for the file. In C# all namespaces are explicitly declared in each code module:

```
namespace cslib
```

In C# the using keyword is equivalent to the Imports keyword in VB.NET. Since we're using both the Systems.WinForms namespace and the namespace from our vblib project, we have using statements to make those namespaces easy to use:

```
using System.WinForms;
using vblib;
```

The next line of code declares the class we're creating and indicates that it is a subclass of Parent:

```
public class csclass : Parent
```

In C# a subclass is declared by declaring a class, followed by a colon and then the name of the base class. This is equivalent to the following VB.NET code:

```
Public Class csclass
   Inherits Parent
```

In VB.NET constructor methods are created using the reserved method name New. In C#, constructors are created by using the name of the class itself as the method name:

```
public csclass()
{
   Messagebox.Show("csclass constructor");
}
```

The brackets ({ and }) form a block structure within which we place the code for the method. In this case the method simply displays a dialog box indicating that the constructor method was invoked.

Now we can create client code to work with this new object.

Creating a Client Application

Use File | Add Project to add a new VB.NET Windows Application project to the solution. In this new project add a reference to the cslib project by using the Project | Add Reference menu option. Right-click on the project and choose the Set As Startup Project option so this project will be run when we press F5.

Notice that we have no reference to the vblib project at all. That is fine, since we aren't directly using any code from that assembly. All our client application cares about is the cslib project.

While we are referencing the cslib *project directly within the IDE, we wouldn't need the C# source code. Instead, we could have built the* cslib *project, thus creating an assembly, and then referenced that assembly from within the client project to gain access to our test C# class.*

Now add a button to Form1 and write the following code behind that button:

```
Protected Sub Button1_Click(ByVal sender As Object, _
    ByVal e As System.EventArgs)

  Dim obj As New cslib.csclass()

  obj.DoSomething()
End Sub
```

This is really no different than if we'd created a VB.NET subclass – but in this case our subclass is actually written in a different language.

When we run this application and click the button, we should see a dialog box with a message indicating the constructor from the csclass was called, then another dialog indicating that the DoSomething method from our VB.NET base class was called.

Visual Inheritance

So far we've been discussing the new OO features of the VB.NET language, with a large focus on inheritance.

However, VB.NET also supports **visual inheritance** for Windows Forms. This means that we can create a Windows Forms form, and then inherit from that form to create other forms that have the same layout, controls, and behaviors. This topic was covered in more detail in Chapter 4.

We can also use inheritance to create our own versions of Windows Forms controls. For instance, we may want to create an enhanced TextBox control that performs some specialized validation of the input data. This can be accomplished through inheritance by creating a subclass of the original TextBox control class and enhancing it as needed. This was also covered in Chapter 4.

The same is true of Web Forms controls, where we can take an existing Web Forms control and create a subclass. Our subclass can override existing functionality or add new functionality as required. See Chapter 6 for more on this.

Summary

Of all the features requested for the new version of VB, perhaps the most common was true inheritance. As we've seen in this chapter, not only does VB.NET provide us with inheritance, but we also gain a number of other important new features and enhancements.

VB.NET dramatically enhances the way we create and work with multiple interfaces, making them far easier to use than in the past. Additionally, through the support for events as being a formal part of an interface, we can now express all the elements of an interface through this mechanism – methods, properties, and events.

For most people, the elimination of reference counting in favor of a garbage collection scheme for object termination will be a non issue. However, it is important to be aware of this change, since an object that maintains a reference to expensive system resources will need some mechanism other than its termination to release those valuable resources.

Overall, VB.NET dramatically enhances our ability to create OO applications with VB, while preserving the vast majority of the features we have become used to in previous versions of the language.

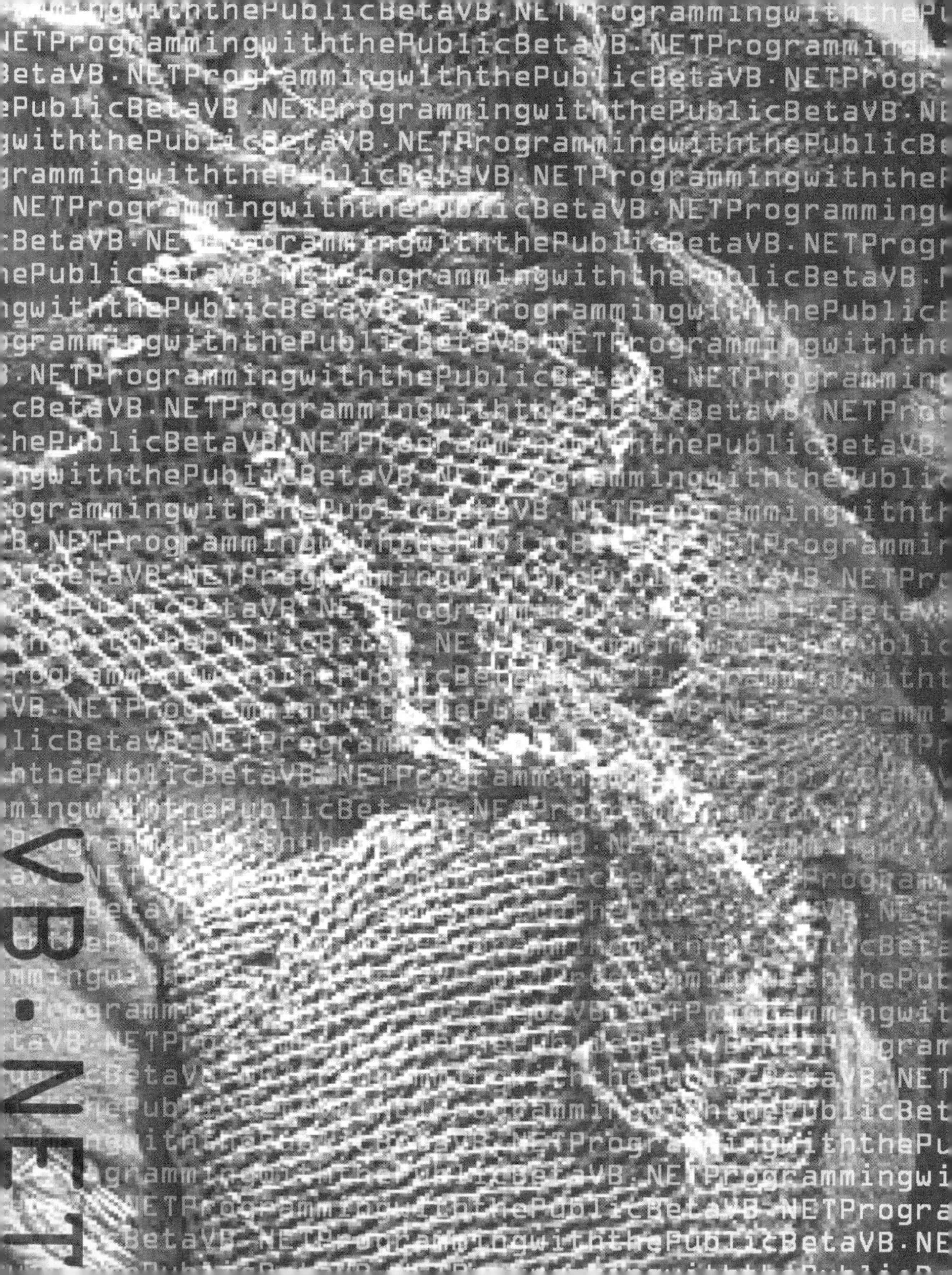
VB.NET
VB.NETProgrammingwiththePublicBeta

6

New Web Capabilities of Visual Basic.NET

The Interface Layer of .NET

As we've previously seen in Chapter 2, the top layer of .NET provides three ways to render and manage user interfaces (Windows Forms, Web Forms, and console applications), and one way to handle interfaces with remote components (Web Services). Two of these, Web Forms and Web Services, are part of the new framework for Internet functionality in .NET, called **ASP.NET**.

It's easy to get a wrong first impression about ASP.NET just from the name. It's far more than just a replacement Active Server Pages (ASP). It encompasses a completely new programming model for Internet user interfaces (Web Forms with server controls), and a new interfacing technology for remote component interaction in Web Services. It replaces existing WebClasses and DHTML Pages in VB6 with a much more consistent and easier to use programming model.

This chapter will look at these technologies from a VB developer's perspective. Web Forms and server controls will be compared to their closest equivalents in today's Visual Basic. Web Services will be discussed as a new mechanism for building applications that are more distributed and Internet-dependent than today's Windows DNA applications to which VB developers are accustomed.

What This Chapter Is Not

Unfortunately, a preview chapter on web technologies in Visual Basic.NET cannot include coverage of general Internet development concepts. There have been many entire books written about Internet development, and it certainly cannot be done justice in a few pages. But we will begin by noting a few of the Internet concepts that VB developers should know before doing Internet development. In particular we will highlight concepts that are helpful in understanding the advantages offered by ASP.NET.

For general coverage on Internet development concepts, the following books from Wrox Press are suggested:

❑   *Beginning Active Server Pages 3.0 (ISBN 1861003382)*

❑   *Beginning ASP Databases (ISBN 1861002726)*

❑   *Beginning Web Development with Visual Interdev 6 (ISBN 1861002947)*

❑   *Instant HTML Programmers Reference (4.0 edition) (ISBN 1861000766)*

❑   *Professional Active Server Pages 3.0 (ISBN 1861002610)*

Pre-Requisites for Web Development

If you are an experienced developer, you already know the areas listed below and can skip down to the section on *What's Wrong With Active Server Pages?* But for the benefit of those who only have experience with forms-based VB programming, here's a quick overview of Internet technologies that are especially important when beginning work in the field of Internet development.

HTML

Everyone knows HTML (HyperText Markup Language) is the markup language format used to render user interfaces on the web. Web servers send pages to browser-based clients as streams of HMTL. It is tag-based, with many tags defined for layout purposes. The tag , for example, makes the text that follows it in an HTML page bold, and the text remains bold in the displayed page until a closing tag of is encountered.

One concept that is helpful in understanding our discussion of Web Forms below is client-side HTML controls. These are just special tags that cause the browser to display something that looks a lot like a control on a VB form.

Before discussing these controls, however, we need to mention an important HTML tag. The <form> tag serves as a container for groups of HTML client-side controls on a page. That is, the <form> and </form> tags delineate the portion of the HTML document used as a form.

Client-side HTML controls must be used inside this region delineated with the <form> tag. Here are the tags that behave as controls when used this way in standard HTML:

HTML tag	Similar VB control (or function if no VB equivalent)
`<input type="button">`	Command button
`<input type="checkbox">`	Checkbox control
`<input type="radio">`	Option button control
`<input type="text">`	Textbox control
`<input type="password">`	Textbox control with `PasswordChar` property set
`<input type="hidden">`	No VB equivalent – used to store state information hidden from the user, fulfilling the same basic purpose as a private variable
`<input type="image">`	Picturebox control
`<input type="file">`	No VB equivalent – allows user to upload files to server

This is a fairly sparse set, which is the reason why many web interfaces are not nearly as sophisticated as VB forms. There is no standard way in HTML to extend these controls either, because the browser must recognize the associated tags. That means there are no packages of "third party" controls in HMTL as there are for Visual Basic. While there are third-party products that can be used in web applications, none of them fill the role of a client-side control. They either render HTML on the server (a component that renders reports in HTML for the web would be an example), or they use ActiveX or Java applets.

An important limitation of HTML controls that is often not understood by those coming from the VB world is that these controls have no ability to maintain their own state between views of a page. Every time an HTML tag-based control is included in a web page, the developer must supply code to tell the control what its state is for that page. If an HTML text box, for example, has a first name in it, and the page has to be refreshed, there must be code in the logic refreshing the page to get the name from somewhere and explicitly place the first name in the control again.

While these HTML controls can be supplemented with Java applets or ActiveX controls, each of those carries its own set of disadvantages. Java applets are difficult to write, require delays to download code and start it up, and are limited in their access to system resources. The drawbacks of ActiveX controls were discussed in Chapter 2 in the section on the presentation tier of the Windows DNA application programming model.

DHTML

One technology added in the last few years to juice up web interfaces is Dynamic HTML, usually abbreviated as DHTML. There are actually two main variants of DHMTL, one implemented in Internet Explorer (version 4.0 and higher), and one implemented in Netscape Navigator (version 4.0 and higher).

DHTML is a client-side scripting technology that offers interaction with the browser, usually in a graphical manner. It is often used for effects such as expanding and collapsing menus. You've probably used web pages with these "tree-view" style menus. Such menus can be done without DHTML, but in that case the page must be completely refreshed every time the user expands or collapses a branch. With DHTML, the expanding and collapsing of such a menu can be done on the fly in the browser, making it unnecessary to refresh the page.

The reason it's important to be aware of what DHTML can do is that server-side controls in ASP.NET (discussed in detail in this chapter) can use DHTML to do their work.

Summary of Browser Features

Besides just displaying HTML to show a web page, browsers also have several other capabilities that are important when developing a web-based user interface. Here are a couple of the most important:

Client-Side Scripting

Except for early, primitive versions, browsers support the ability for a web page to have embedded script. The most widely used language for this script is JavaScript (sometimes called ECMAScript), which uses Java-like syntax, but otherwise is not much like Java. Internet Explorer versions also allow scripting in VBScript. Both of these scripting languages are subsets of their respective "real language" counterparts; that is, JavaScript only offers a subset of the syntax and functionality of Java, and VBScript offers a subset of the syntax and functionality of Visual Basic.

Scripting is used for several purposes, but the most common is validation of user input. Script can be set to run before a page is posted back to the server, and to tell the user if information in an HTML control is missing or invalid.

Client-side scripting is important in the discussion below on how server controls create their user interface.

Client-side scripting should be clearly distinguished from server-side scripting. Server-side script is run as the page is being created for the user. A page that has been rendered for a user does not contain any server-side script, though it may (and usually does) contain HTML that was created by server-side script.

Document Object Model

Because a browser is an application of sorts in its own right, it has capabilities that transcend the web pages sent to it. For example, a browser knows how to print a displayed page. Compare this to a typical VB form, which must have a `Print` function specifically developed.

The capabilities of the HTML Document Object Model (often abbreviated DOM) can be manipulated by Internet developers however. That makes it possible, for example, for a web page to have a button that forces a print.

XML

While HTML is the standard protocol for transmitting visual content to users (people) on the web, XML is the emerging standard for transmitting data. It is also tag-based, but has a few key differences from HTML:

❑   Tags are not pre-defined. Tags describe the structure of the data, and an XML document can contain any tags deemed necessary by the person creating it.

❑   Tags must be closed in XML. Most browsers allow closing HTML tags to be omitted, but an XML document with a closing tag that is missing is considered invalid.

❑   Tags must nest in XML.

Point number three needs a bit more explanation. HTML does not have this limitation of nested tags. That is, tags can overlap one another. Here is a perfectly valid HTML string:

```
This sentence contains <b> some bold text <i> and some bold-italic </b> and
some just italic </i>.
```

This HTML would display like this:

This sentence contains **some bold text** ***and some bold-italic*** *and some just italic.*

In this case, the `<i>` tag begins before the `<b>` tag is closed, but then the bold tag is closed first.

This is invalid in XML. Tags must nest, the way the "name" and "address" tags nest below "person" in the example below:

```
<person>
    <name>
        Sherlock Holmes
    </name>
    <address>
        221B Baker Street
    </address>
</person>
```

It's important to have a basic understanding of XML because it is the glue that holds a lot of .NET together. In particular, XML is the communications format for Web Services, which are covered in this chapter. You don't have to be an XML expert right away, however, because .NET handles a lot of the creation, transmission, and consumption of XML automatically. But you do need to understand that XML is capable of holding complex hierarchical sets of data in a standard way that is self-describing.

Active Server Pages

We cannot cover even the essentials of Active Server Pages. A few concepts, however, are important for doing any kind of Internet development, even with Web Forms. These include items such as:

❑ The concept of a user session and its ability to time out

❑ Native ASP objects such as `Application`, `Session`, `Response`, and `Request`, and what they are used for

❑ General Internet concepts such as how to construct a Uniform Resource Locator (URL), and how to link pages together

If you are unfamiliar with these concepts, you should consult a beginning book on Active Server Pages to gain some minimal understanding. This will make the transition to Web Forms easier and faster. One such book is *Beginning Active Server Pages 3.0* (*Wrox Press, ISBN 1861003382*).

What's Wrong with Active Server Pages?

A lot. Active Server Pages are what I call "dancing-bear" software. That comes from an old quotation – "The amazing thing about a dancing bear is not how well it dances, but that it dances at all." The amazing thing about Active Server Pages is not how well they do Internet interfaces, but that they do them at all.

ASP was Microsoft's first major attempt at a technology to develop web interfaces, and ASP has remained the most widely used way to do web applications on Microsoft platforms. Microsoft did a good job at getting something out fast that at least made it possible to do such development. Certainly many successful applications have been developed with ASP. Alternatives such as developing straight to the ISAPI interface of Internet Information Server (IIS) are relegated to niche roles such as when high performance is absolutely paramount.

But current Internet development with Active Server Pages has some major limitations, some of which stem from the design of ASP and others that are a consequence of limitations in Internet technologies such as HTTP and browsers. From the perspective of someone moving from the forms-based VB world, these major limitations are:

- **Non-structured "spaghetti" code** – Code in Active Server Pages is not created in a structured programming environment. It's all dumped into the ASP page. This makes it more difficult to structure code and encapsulate functionality. "Include" statements can be used to ameliorate this, but it takes discipline and skill.

- **Mixture of presentation and logic** – ASP script code is intermingled with HTML for layout, making construction, debugging, and maintenance of the code all more difficult.

- **Interpreted code** – Code in ASP is interpreted script, which has performance problems in high-volume situations.

- **Weaker user interfaces** – HTML interfaces are very difficult to make as rich as typical VB interfaces. The native set of HTML controls (discussed above) is limited, and there is no programming model to extend them.

- **No state management** – It was previously pointed out that HTML controls have no state management, forcing developers to write reams of code just to maintain state from page to page. The capabilities that are built into ASP that do preserve state, such as the `Application` object and the `Session` object, cause severe problems when scaling to multiple machines. Since ASP has no built-in way to preserve state, most developers rely on a variety of other products and techniques to do this, such as preserving state in a database. All these other techniques have pros and cons of their own, and the variety of techniques used causes inconsistency among ASP applications.

- **Need for multiple browser support in code** – Developers must be aware of browser differences and choose one of two bad options, which are (1) develop to a "lowest-common denominator" standard that seriously limits available interface technologies such as DHTML, or (2) write extra code for whatever classes of browsers need to be supported.

- **Poor support for visual tools** – While Visual Interdev makes a stab at allowing visual layout of web pages, its functionality is so limited that few developers routinely develop pages that way. Interdev's visual design capability was a far cry that which Visual Basic developers are accustomed to.

As we will see in this chapter, ASP.NET and Web Forms address all of these limitations to one extent or another. While Web Forms do not offer the panacea of making web development as easy as forms development in VB, they do make enormous strides in that direction.

Overview of Web Forms

The objective of Web Forms is to bring VB-style drag-and-drop design to the development of Internet interfaces. This programming model is much easier to use than typical existing web development technologies, and has the added advantage of being familiar to the huge existing base of VB developers.

We will start this section with an example of constructing a simple Web Form page. It's a good idea to go through this example step-by-step in Visual Studio.NET. It will set a context for much of the following discussion.

A Web Form in Action

In this example, we will create a Web Form with four controls:

❑   A label that contains some text for us to change

❑   A button to change the text in the label and submit the page

❑   A textbox to enter information

❑   A validation control to check and see if the textbox has anything in it

Begin a new Visual Basic Web Project. This is done by selecting File | New | Project, and then in the New Project dialog box, highlighting the Visual Basic Projects folder on the left and selecting Web Application on the right. The dialog box should then look like this:

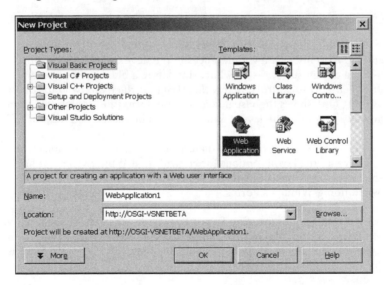

After pressing the OK key, Visual Studio.NET will set up the web project. This includes a lot more files than are created for a typical VB forms project. Also note that the directory to hold these files is, by default, created off the root directory of your web site. If you are running the web server on the same system as Visual Studio.NET, this will typically be `C:\Inetpub\wwwroot`. (The first chapter of this book contains information on setting up Visual Studio.NET, including discussion of running Internet Information Server or Personal Web Server.)

The screen for developing in Web Forms will initially look like this:

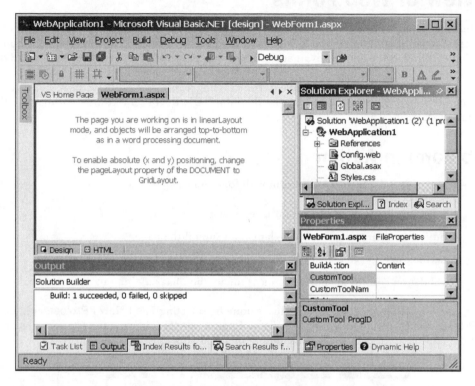

You can see the extra files created for the project, shown in the Solution Explorer in the upper right portion of the screen. Also notice a few differences in the development environment from working with Windows Forms. The design surface is all white, simulating a blank web page, and there is a note about layout options for Web Forms controls. Below that design surface are two tabs that will be familiar to Visual Interdev users. One shows the visual layout of the form (the Design tab), and the other shows the HTML which actually generates the layout and which can be directly edited (the HTML tab).

There are other differences that are not immediately apparent. The tool bars are slightly different, since Web Forms don't have all the layout options for controls that Windows Forms have. And the Toolbox contains a different set of controls. But overall, the environment acts very similarly with Web Forms to the way it acts when doing Windows Forms.

We'll be discussing layout options for Web Forms later in the chapter, but for now you need to know that in the default layout format, the page is conceptually more like a word processing page than a VB form. You can type text directly on it. When a control is dragged onto the form, it is inserted at the current cursor location in the text.

Click on the design surface of the form, and press the *Enter* key a few times. Then position the cursor on the first line of the form. We will use that as the position to insert the first control.

Open up the Toolbox by clicking on it. If it is not already showing Web Form controls, click on the Web Form button in the toolbox to show those controls. Click and drag a Label control onto the design surface and release it. Please note that you cannot just click on the Label control and then "draw" it on the surface the way you can with a control in a VB form or Windows Form. You must drag and drop it.

The label control will appear on the form. Its properties will appear in the Properties window. In the Properties window, change the Text property for the control to Original Text.

Now position the cursor on the second line and drag over a Button control. Then position the cursor on the third line and drag over a Textbox control. Finally, position the cursor on the fourth line and drag over a RequiredFieldValidator control, which will be towards the bottom of the control list. At this point, the screen should look like this:

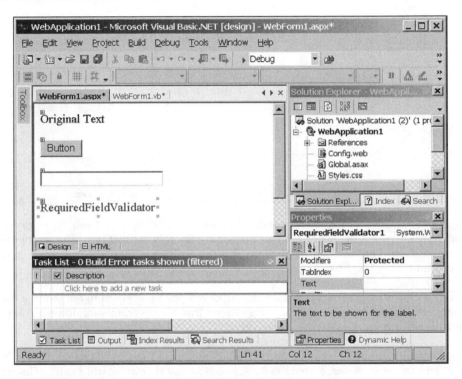

Next, we'll set up the button to change the text in the label control. Double-click on the button, and the button's click event routine (named Button1_Click) will come up, just as with VB forms. In the event routine, type in the following code:

```
Label1.Text = "The text has changed!!"
```

Next, we will associate the RequiredFieldValidator control with the text box. Go back to the form view by clicking on the WebForm1.aspx tab. Then click on the RequiredFieldValidator control. In the Properties window for the RequiredFieldValidator control, find the ControlToValidate property. Click on the right of the property to set it. A drop-down will show the controls that are available to validate, and in this case there is only one (TextBox1). Select it and press Enter. Also change the error message to be displayed by changing the ErrorMessage property of the RequiredFieldValidator to Text box cannot be blank!!

We are now ready to test this Web Form. Press the Start icon in the toolbar. It may take a while to see the resulting screen, especially if this is the first time you have shown a Web Form. The screen that comes up is in Internet Explorer (unless your default browser has been set to something else), and it looks like this:

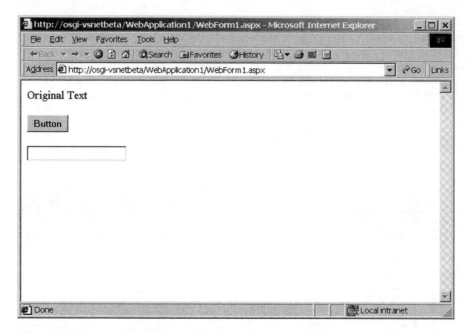

The `RequiredFieldValidator` is not visible because no validation has been done yet. To cause a validation to occur, press the button without placing anything in the text box. The screen then displays a red error message (Text box cannot be blank!!) in the position of the `RequiredFieldValidator` control, just under the text box.

If your web server is on your local machine during development, it's hard to tell that the validation took place completely in the browser, with no server round trip. However, this would be obvious if the page was being accessed on a slow Internet connection.

Now type something into the text box, and press the button. The label will change to say The text has changed!! and the error message from the `RequiredFieldValidator` will vanish. This operation caused a trip back to the server, because the button by default causes a "submit" of the form to the server.

This very short exercise has demonstrated some key ideas about Web Forms:

- ❑ Laying out the form is much like VB forms and Windows Forms, except for the fact that the web page is more like a document.

- ❑ Controls in Web Forms act like VB controls, with properties to set behavior and event code behind them to take actions.

- ❑ Controls on Web Forms maintain their own state. Notice that when the button was pressed, the text box did not lose its information.

- ❑ Validation is easy, and set through properties of a validator control.

ASP.NET as the Run-Time Engine

Execution of a Web Form is more involved than execution of a Windows Form. While a Windows Form is just another class module, which happens to inherit visual form capability, a Web Form actually consists of both code and layout, and the layout part is HTML-based. That HTML page (which is a file with an `.aspx` extension) is executed by the ASP.NET runtime engine. Whereas compiled Windows Forms are executed directly by the Common Language Runtime (CLR), Web Forms use the CLR indirectly. The `.aspx` file controls the page execution and serves as a template for the HTML stream, and then calls the CLR to execute any logic connected to the page. Note, however, that any logic run is compiled, not interpreted, offering a major advantage over the interpreted script of ASP.

We'll go into the structure of a Web Form in more detail below. This section discusses some high level information about the ASP.NET run-time engine.

ASP.NET pages can be edited directly in a text or HTML editor. This development model is similar to today's Active Server Pages. We will not discuss ASP.NET pages done this way, since they only use Visual Basic for scripting inside the page. We will concentrate on Web Forms, since this technique for doing web pages is likely to be most familiar and useful to Visual Basic developers.

If you are interested in the gritty details on ASP.NET, you might want to get *A Preview of ASP+* (*Wrox Press, ISBN 1861004753*). ASP+ was the former name for what we now call ASP.NET. This book covers the technology behind ASP.NET in depth.

There are a few key concepts in ASP.NET that are useful to know, however, even if you are focusing on Web Forms. We will cover those concepts next.

System.Web.UI Namespace

The classes used for ASP.NET user interface constructs, including Web Forms, are in the `System.Web.UI` namespace. This namespace has many classes and a complex hierarchy. Unlike the discussion of Windows Forms, in which the namespace was extensively covered, this chapter will not detail the `System.Web.UI` namespace. We will only discuss some key classes in the namespace later in the chapter.

The Concept of Server Controls

One of the key technologies in ASP.NET that is essential for the operation of Web Forms is server controls. We previously said that HTML has client controls that look a lot like VB controls, but they are limited in interface functionality, and provide no management of their own state. Server controls are the development replacement for these client-side HTML controls, allowing developers to work with controls directly on the server rather than just sending controls out to the client in HTML.

There is a detailed section below on how server controls work, and a listing of server controls available with Visual Studio.NET.

Anatomy of a Web Form

From a development point of view, a Web Form consists of two pieces – an HTML-based template for layout of the web page, and a code module to contain code behind the page.

The Template for Presentation

The HTML template of a Web Form will look generally familiar to an ASP developer. It contains HTML header information, visual HTML elements, and can contain any valid HTML. Here is the template created by our example above (viewable by selecting the **HTML** tab for **WebForm1.aspx**):

```
<%@ Page Language="vb" AutoEventWireup="false" Codebehind="WebForm1.vb"
Inherits="WebApplication1.WebForm1"%>
<html><head>
    <meta name="GENERATOR" content="Microsoft Visual Studio.NET 7.0">
    <meta name="CODE_LANGUAGE" content="Visual Basic 7.0"></head>
  <body>

    <form id="WebForm1" method="post" runat="server">
<p>
<asp:Label id=Label1 runat="server">Original Text</asp:Label></p>
<p>
<asp:Button id=Button1 runat="server" Text="Button"></asp:Button></p>
<p>
<asp:TextBox id=TextBox1 runat="server"></asp:TextBox></p>
<p>
<asp:RequiredFieldValidator id=RequiredFieldValidator1 runat="server"
ErrorMessage="Text box cannot be blank!!"
ControlToValidate="TextBox1"></asp:RequiredFieldValidator></p>
<p> </p>
<p> </p>

    </form>

  </body></html>
```

When just starting out with Web Forms, it's not essential to know what all of this means. You can just create Web Forms with the form designer, and let the designer create this template code and modify it as necessary.

However, to take full advantage of what Web Forms can do, the traditional Visual Basic developer will need to become very familiar with the template (and with HTML), and have the ability to modify the template directly when necessary.

Here are a few things to notice about the template.

❑ The first line has attributes for the page. These include the language used (vb), the location of the module containing the code behind the page (WebForm1.vb), and the web form from which this page is inheriting its layout. The module containing the code behind the page (code connected to various page elements) is discussed later below.

❑ The controls on the Web Form are all defined in the template with a line that begins <asp:. The tags used to identify controls all begin with the asp: prefix to differentiate them from everything else.

❑ Each defined control has an attribute of runat="server". This indicates a server control.

❑ Each defined control has its properties set with attributes inside the definition line. For example, the RequiredFieldValidator control has properties set for ErrorMessage and ControlToValidate.

❏ All of the information about the form is inside the HTML block defined by the `<form>` and `</form>` tags. This allows encapsulation of the form information and the ability to put HTML elements such as page headers and footers in the page easily without disturbing the form.

Layout of Web Forms

There are two quite different ways of laying out Web Forms. Both involve selecting controls in the Toolbox and placing them on the design surface. Where they differ is where the controls end up on the design surface and the way controls are positioned in the underlying HTML. The methods use Linear Layout and Grid Layout. Linear Layout is the default. Which of these is applied to a given Web Form is determined by the `pageLayout` property of the form:

❏ In **Linear Layout**, the design surface is similar to a word processing document. The user can insert text and paragraph marks, and the result is translated into HTML. When a control is dropped onto the design surface, it is placed in the middle of the text that was previously entered, where the cursor is currently positioned.

❏ In **Grid Layout**, the controls are actually placed on a grid on the design surface. They are not interspersed with the underlying text. This allows for a WYSIWYG style display similar to FrontPage and is a big improvement over the original layout editor included with Interdev.

The differences between these layout techniques show up most dramatically in the underlying HTML template. In Web Forms, any control that is placed on the design surface has code generated for it in the underlying HTML template. For example, placing a button on the Web Form in Linear Layout mode will cause the following code to be inserted into the HTML template:

```
<asp:Button id=Button1 runat="server" Text="Button"></asp:Button>
```

This declaration for the control includes no positioning information at all. The control is merely rendered in the Web Form at whatever point it is encountered when running the form.

If a button is dropped in a Grid Layout form, however, the inserted code is more complex. It looks something like this:

```
    <tr valign=top>
        <td width=0 height=44></td>
        <td></td>
        <td colspan=2>
<asp:Button id=Button3 runat="server" Text="Button"></asp:Button></td></tr>
```

Moreover, this code will be in the middle of an HTML table declaration. The table positioning, plus the positioning information in the HTML above, arrange the control in the position in which it was dropped on the form.

A Subclassed Instance of the Page Class

Each Web Forms code page actually inherits from the `System.Web.UI.Page` class. This class contains the properties, methods, and events in the Web Forms page framework. `Page` objects are compiled and automatically cached, which is one of the ways Web Forms differ from earlier Active Server Pages.

Some of the important properties and methods of the Page class include:

Properties	
Application	ASP developers are familiar with the Application object provided by the HTTP runtime, which manages state for an entire ASP-based application and provides global access to the state. The Application property of the Page class provides a reference to this object. Other HTTP objects are also available as properties, as indicated below.
ClientTarget	Indicates the capabilities of the requesting browser. Used during execution to see if the client is running on an uplevel (advanced) browser, or a downlevel (more primitive) browser. Allows code to deliver behavior appropriate to the current browser.
ErrorPage	Gets or sets the error page that will be the target of a redirection in the case of an unhandled exception in the page.
IsValid	Indicates whether page validation succeeded.
Request, Response, Server, Session	Provides a reference to the corresponding HTTP runtime objects. These objects will be familiar to ASP developers. While the objects do not need to be accessed manually as often in Web Forms as in Active Server Pages, there will still be situations where such access is needed.
User	Read-only property indicating the user making a page request.
Validators	The collection of validation controls on the page.

Methods	
LoadControl	Gets a UserControl object from the appropriate file and loads it. User controls are discussed later in the chapter.
Navigate	Redirects the client browser to a different URL, similar to Server.Redirect in ASP.

We will see how a Web Forms page inherits from this class in the next topic.

The Code Behind the Page – Web Forms Code Model

We previously discussed the fact that there are two major parts of a Web Form – the HTML-based template, which handles layout and declares controls, and the code behind the page, which is a code module consisting of various routines. Some of the routines in the code module are directly related to controls on the Web Form, such as control click event routines. Other routines are concerned with page events such as initialization. These routines are called as necessary by the ASP.NET runtime engine, which is responsible for coordinating controls on the Web Form with their related routines. Of course, the code module can also contain standard functions and subroutines.

The code module behind a Web Form is simpler than one for a Windows Form because it does not need to worry about visual layout. But it does take care of all class interfaces and code needed for the Web Form. Here is the code generated by our first example:

```vb
Imports System
Imports System.ComponentModel.Design
Imports System.Data
Imports System.Drawing
Imports System.Web
Imports System.Web.SessionState
Imports System.Web.UI
Imports System.Web.UI.WebControls
Imports System.Web.UI.HtmlControls
Imports Microsoft.VisualBasic

Public Class WebForm1
    Inherits System.Web.UI.Page
    Protected WithEvents RequiredFieldValidator1 As _
        System.Web.UI.WebControls.RequiredFieldValidator
    Protected WithEvents TextBox1 As System.Web.UI.WebControls.TextBox
    Protected WithEvents Button1 As System.Web.UI.WebControls.Button
    Protected WithEvents Label1 As System.Web.UI.WebControls.Label

#Region " Web Forms Designer Generated Code "

    Dim WithEvents WebForm1 As System.Web.UI.Page

    Sub New()
        WebForm1 = Me
    End Sub

    'CODEGEN: This procedure is required by the Web Form Designer
    'Do not modify it using the code editor.
    Private Sub InitializeComponent()


    End Sub

#End Region

    Public Sub Button1_Click(ByVal sender As Object, _
                        ByVal e As System.EventArgs)
        Label1.Text = "The text has changed!!"
    End Sub

    Protected Sub WebForm1_Load(ByVal Sender As System.Object, _
                        ByVal e As System.EventArgs)
        If Not IsPostback Then    ' Evals true first time browser
                                  ' hits the page

        End If
    End Sub

    Protected Sub WebForm1_Init(ByVal Sender As System.Object, _
                        ByVal e As System.EventArgs)
        'CODEGEN: This method call is required by the Web Form Designer
        'Do not modify it using the code editor.
        InitializeComponent()
    End Sub

End Class
```

Let's do a quick walk through of the code.

1. First there are lines to import needed namespaces. Some of these might not be needed in all cases. System.Data, for example, is unnecessary for pages that don't access a database. And, as we shall see later in the discussion on server controls, System.Web.UI.HtmlControls will not be used for all pages.

2. Next come the class declaration and a statement that provides inheritance from the Page class of System.Web.UI.

3. After that come declarations of all the controls used on the Web Form.

4. The next section is Web Form Designer generated code, which is normally collapsed in the code outliner. It will not normally be necessary to look at or modify this code, although examining it can give some insight into how .NET works.

5. After the #End Region statement which terminates the Web Form Designer code, event-handling routines are included. The last two (WebForm1_Init and WebForm1_Load) are inserted by the designer. The Button1_Click event was created as part of our exercise.

Compared to code modules generated for Windows Forms, Web Forms modules like the one above are simpler. The module contains no code to set initialize control properties, for example. That code is in the HTML template.

The designer does insert some code to handle the Load and Init events for the page. The WebForm1_Init routine has similar code to the Sub New constructor in a Windows Form. The WebForm1_Load event includes code that checks to see if a page is being hit for the first time. Code that you would like to execute on the first hit of a page goes inside the If block in the WebForm1_Load event code.

The Button1_Click event looks just like it would in a Windows Form. Most of the coding that a developer would do in this module would be of this type, making it easy for Visual Basic developers to learn how to put code behind a Web Form.

Web Forms Event Model

You may have noticed at this point that there is no direct tie between the layout page and events in the code module. (The PDC Tech Preview of Visual Studio.NET did have such a tie, in the form of an attribute for controls pointing to an event in the code. This has been removed in beta one.) The management of events, and tying them to the web page, is handled behind the scenes by the ASP.NET runtime engine.

The event model for Web Forms must take into account the fact that events are fired on the client, but must be executed on the server. Because of the way the web works, this happens through an HTTP post. The ASP.NET runtime interprets the post, and if it finds an event, it calls the appropriate event-handling routine in the code.

Because the ASP.NET run-time takes care of event management automatically, you don't normally need to worry about how it is happening. You can just write your event routines and expect them to be executed as needed, just as in a VB forms applications.

But there are necessary differences because of the fact that the client is remote, so there are some aspects of event handling in Web Forms of which you should be aware.

Built-In Events are Limited

The biggest difference in event handling for Web Forms is performance. Most Web Form events require a server round-trip. This limits the practicality of some types of events. Many of the mouse moving events that were practical to handle with a VB forms client are not practical in a web model. That means that server controls typically offer a more limited set of events than equivalent Windows Forms controls. The bulk of these server control events are click-type events. (Mouse moving events in a browser can be handled in some cases using JavaScript on the client, but this is distinct from events that must tie into server code, so we will not discuss those techniques in detail.)

Most controls do offer an event to indicate that their contents or state have changed. The name varies with different controls. The CheckBox, for example has such an event, named CheckChanged. However, the TextBox server control does not have a change event that fires every time a character is into it, because handling this event would cause performance issues. Instead, it has a TextChanged event that is only fired when the user leaves the control.

Postback vs. Non-Postback Events

Some controls have events that do not immediately result in a post to the server. These events are captured and then delivered the next time the page is posted. The section on server controls below discusses the details of how these events are handled, and how to override the normal behavior to make such an event force a post.

Application and Session Events

Besides the events generated by the page, there are events that are raised by the ASP.NET Framework. These higher-level events include:

❑ **Application events** – ApplicationStart for initialization of resources used throughout the application, such as file locations, and ApplicationEnd, which provides an opportunity to clean up and dispose of resources when a web application terminates.

❑ **Session events** – Similar to application events, but associated with a user session instead of the whole application. SessionStart fires when a user first starts a session of the application, and SessionEnd fires either when the application closes a session for a user, or the session times out.

In doing Active Server Pages, these events would need to be coded in the Global.asa page. With ASP.NET and Web Forms, the events are coded in the replacement for Global.asa, which is called Global.asax. If this module is selected in the Solution Explorer, it will be displayed in the code window, and the right drop-down list at the top of the window will list the available events.

State Management and the Life Cycle of a Web Forms Page

The life cycle for a Web Forms page is dictated by the necessities of any Web application. Most of the code defining the application runs on the server, but the user interface for the code displays on the remote client. Information must be passed between server and client through HTTP, which is a stateless protocol.

Because HTTP is stateless, Web pages are created from scratch with every round trip. As soon as the server finishes processing a page and sends it to the browser, it is finished with the page and maintains no further connection to the client. The next time the page is posted, the server starts all over in creating and processing it. At their most fundamental level, Web pages are *stateless* – that is, the values of a page's variables and controls are not preserved on the server.

In fact when a web page is recreated, even for the same user, it may not be the same server doing the work as the last time the page was created. In "server farms", each web page request is routed to one of a group of similar servers, and there's no assurance that a user will get the same server that served the last page to the user. That makes it literally impossible for a single server to maintain the state of a user's web page in a multiple web server environment.

The ASP.NET framework manages to get around many of these limitations. Web Forms behave as if the server were maintaining state. In reality, the state information is transmitted with the page, and returned when a page is posted. You can see where the state information is stored on the page by doing a View | Source in the browser. For our earlier example, here are the first few lines in the source HTML that runs in the client browser:

```
<html><head>
<meta content="Microsoft Visual Studio.NET 7.0" name=GENERATOR>
<meta content="Visual Basic 7.0" name=CODE_LANGUAGE></head>
<body>
<form name="WebForm1" method="post" action="WebForm1.aspx" language="javascript"
onsubmit="ValidatorOnSubmit();" id="WebForm1">
<input type="hidden" name="__VIEWSTATE" value="YTB6ODA3NjMwNTk1X19feA==a4a07cc9"
/>
```

The last line contains a hidden field on the page with a Value attribute. The Value attribute contains what looks like a meaningless string of numbers and letters. But that string actually contains the state of all the server controls on the page. The state information is said to be **tokenized**, which means it is translated into a compressed form. The compressed form has to be in text, because the HTTP protocol does not allow a web page to contain binary information.

The above state information was taken from the first loading of the page, so that there is very little state information to transmit. Simply typing something into the text box and posting the page again causes that last line to grow quite a bit. Here is the last line of tokenized state information after typing the name "Sherlock Holmes" in the text box and pressing the button to submit the page:

```
value="YTB6ODA3NjMwNTk1X2Ewel9oejV6MXhfYTB6X2h6NXoxeF9hMHphMHpoelRlXHh0X1RoZSB0ZVx
4dCBoYXMgY2hhbmdlZCEheF9feF9feHhfeHhfeF9feA==173f5fc0" />
```

The tokenized state information can be rather long for a complex Web page. It might be expected that this would result in a performance problem as the information is continually transmitted back and forth, and decoded and re-encoded on the server. However, tests at Microsoft have indicated that this technique for state management yields acceptable performance that is comparable to performance for other state management techniques.

The Web Forms controls' state information stored in the hidden field, plus any information entered by the user, is handled during the posting of the page by the ASP.NET framework. The controls get their state refreshed, and then updated with any new information on the page. All the state information is then automatically available in object properties of the controls on a Web Form, making their programming similar to controls on a VB form. This insulates the developer from needing to manage many of the details in the life cycle of a Web page.

Nevertheless, it is helpful to understand the sequence of events that occurs when a Web Forms page is processed. You can program your Web Forms pages more effectively if you understand some of what is going on behind the scenes. Here is a typical sequence of events that take place during the use of a Web Form:

1. A page based on the Web Form is created on the server and transmitted to the browser. It is in HTML, and any server controls have rendered their interface in HTML as part of the page.

2. The user views the page in the browser and responds to the page.

3. The user performs some action that causes the page to be posted back to the server (this can happen in a variety of ways, the most common being the pressing of a button).

4. The server processes the returned page. Server controls have their state restored from the tokenized state information and then updated with any new information from the user. The events that caused the post of the page are processed.

5. If the page needs to be updated on the client, the server prepares a new version on the page and transmits it to the browser, and the cycle starts over.

This cycle continues until a user is finished with a page, which may happen when a user goes to another page, when the user's session times out, or when the user just shuts down the browser.

It is possible for the page to contain client script for validation of user input or limited user interface programming such as DHTML for sorting a short list of data items in a different order. However, client script does not interact with server components, and so does not affect the above sequence.

Server Controls

The ASP.NET framework depends heavily on server controls to get around the classic limitations of Internet development. Server controls provide a concrete layout element, very similar to the classic VB form control, and they also provide the capability to project a user interface for this UI element via standard HTTP to a browser. Along the way, server controls manage state, provide properties to be manipulated in code, and provide events to hook actions into logic.

Why are Server Controls Needed?

At the beginning of the chapter, we briefly discussed HTML client controls, which are a part of standard HTML. Each client control is created on a page with a standard HTML tag.

HTML client controls are by far the most frequently used interface elements for current web applications. Alternatives such as Java applets and ActiveX controls are far less common.

The reason these controls are used so much is that they work in just about any browser, and they are so lightweight that their performance is acceptable. But, as we previously mentioned, they have some big drawbacks. For the purposes of our current discussion, the two main drawbacks are:

❑ HTML client controls require totally manual state management

❑ It's hard to create rich, sophisticated user interfaces with HTML client controls

Server controls do an excellent job of addressing both of these limitations. In many respects, server controls are the best of both worlds. The developer can program against server controls on the server just as if they were any other component, but the server controls project a user interface in standard HTML, using many of the old-style HTML client controls as necessary to create that client-side user interface.

HTML Server Controls

There are two basic types of server controls. The first type are called HTML server controls. These are basically one-to-one matches for various HTML tags, including the HTML client controls discussed above. Here is a table of the HTML server controls, and their associated HTML tags for HTML client side controls.

Control	Corresponding tag
HtmlAnchor	`<a>`
HtmlButton	`<button>`
HtmlSelect	`<select>`
HtmlTextArea	`<textarea>`
HtmlInputButton	`<input type="button">`
HtmlInputCheckBox	`<input type="check">`
HtmlInputRadioButton	`<input type="radio">`
HtmlInputText	`<input type="text">` and `<input type="password">`
HtmlInputHidden	`<input type="hidden">`
HtmlInputImage	`<input type="image">`
HtmlInputFile	`<input type="file">`
HtmlForm	`<form>`
HtmlImage	`<img>`
HtmlTable	`<table>`
HtmlTableRow	`<tr>`
HtmlTableCell	`<td>`
HtmlGenericControl	Any other unmapped tag, such as `<span>`, `<div>`, etc.

These HTML server controls are not particularly sophisticated compared to ASP.NET controls, which we will discuss below. HTML server controls have an HTML-centric object model, and have no intelligence to target their output to a specific browser. These controls are mostly available to update existing pages to the use of server controls.

Moreover, HTML server controls are not intended as a universal substitute for normal HTML client controls. There is no need to use them if the controls on a page need no server code behind them.

HTML server controls have their own area in the Toolbox, named HTML. To access one of these controls, it is necessary to click the HTML button in the Toolbox, and then drag and drop the HTML control desired. Then right-click the control on the form surface, and select Run as Server Control on the pop-up menu. (If this step is not taken, the control acts like a standard HTML client control, and no server code can be associated with it.)

HTML server controls are expected to play a large role in converting older HTML-based pages to the ASP.NET Framework. However, it is not clear how much these controls will be used in new development, so we will not discuss them in depth. Instead, we'll go on to look at the controls that *will* be used extensively in new Web Forms applications – ASP.NET server controls.

ASP.NET Server Controls

ASP.NET server controls are referred to as "web controls" in some resources. They are far more sophisticated than HTML server controls. Here are some of the ways they differ:

- ❑ ASP.NET server controls have a more flexible object model, and one that is consistent and familiar to VB developers.

- ❑ ASP.NET server controls have no exact equivalents in client-side HTML. ASP.NET controls create appropriate HTML to render their user interface, combining various client-side HTML controls if necessary.

- ❑ ASP.NET server controls do automatic browser detection, and customize their output to the current browser.

- ❑ ASP.NET server controls can use data binding.

Here is a summary of the ASP.NET server controls that come with Visual Studio.NET. Many of them are similar to VB forms or Windows Forms controls.

Some ASP.NET controls are very similar to standard Visual Basic forms controls, all of which have equivalents in Windows Forms. They include:

- ❑ Label
- ❑ TextBox
- ❑ CheckBox
- ❑ ListBox
- ❑ Button (called command button in VB6)
- ❑ Image (similar to Image control or PictureBox in VB6

Here are the additional controls, and descriptions of their functions:

Control name	Function
DropDownList	Acts like a VB combo box with Drop Down style selected
CheckBoxList	Sequence or group of Checkbox controls (similar to VB control array)
RadioButtonList	Set of mutually exclusive option buttons (similar to VB control array)
LinkButton	Works just like Button control, except it displays as a hyperlink
ImageButton	Graphical image used as a button – can provide x and y coordinates of user's click

Table continued on following page

Control name	Function
Table, TableRow, TableCell	Create tables and tabular layouts
Hyperlink	Allows navigation to other URLs
Calendar	Date selections (including date ranges) – resembles calendar controls used in VB
Repeater	Used to generate lists of items, using a snippet of HTML as a template
DataList	Similar to Repeater control, but more control over output
DataGrid	Similar to VB data grid, but works with ADO.NET hierarchical datasets
Image	Similar to Image control or PictureBox in VB6
AdRotator	A control which displays graphic ads, rotating the ads with each page refresh

In addition to the ASP.NET controls packaged with Visual Studio.NET, many third parties are expected in introduce packages of controls. Just as VB's functionality has traditionally been enhanced with third-party OCX controls, now Web Forms web interface functionality can be enhanced with third party ASP.NET controls. In fact, third party server controls for web interface functionality make even more sense, because there is no client install. A server control only needs to exist on the server, lowering the support and deployment costs for third party controls.

How ASP.NET Controls are Referenced in HTML

Each ASP.NET server control has a tag which is used in the HTML template for a Web Form as a reference to the control class. The tag for each control is the control name with the prefix asp:. For example, the tag for a textbox is asp:Textbox.

The tag is used in an HTML reference that defines a control in the HTML template. Here's an example for a simple one-line textbox:

```
<asp:Textbox id=Text1 runat="server" Text="Billy">
</asp:TextBox>
```

A multi-line textbox has a reference like this:

```
<asp:Textbox id=Text1 runat="server" TextMode="Multiline" Rows="3">
Red
Blue
Green
</asp:TextBox>
```

The TextMode property is set to Multiline, and the Rows property tells the definition how many line items to expect. The line items are then listed.

All the controls have similar references in the HTML template. Perhaps the most complex reference is for the controls that create tables. Here is a sample:

```
<asp:Table id=Table1 runat="server" Gridlines="Both">
    <asp:TableRow>
        <asp:TableCell>Top left</asp:TableCell>
        <asp:TableCell>Top right</asp:TableCell>
    </asp:TableRow>
    <asp:TableRow>
        <asp:TableCell>Bottom left</asp:TableCell>
        <asp:TableCell>Bottom right</asp:TableCell>
    </asp:TableRow>
</asp:Table>
```

A reference like this would create a 2x2 table on the web page that looked roughly like this:

Top left	Top right
Bottom left	Bottom right

Note that you don't write this code. The Web Forms designer inserts it into the HTML template (.aspx file) for you.

An example later in the chapter uses several of the server controls on a Web Form.

Validation Controls

Another general class of server controls for Web Forms is **validation controls**. These controls are used specifically to do various kinds of validation of user data in other controls.

For browsers that support client-side scripting, these controls will actually emit the script code to do validation on the client. If the target browser does not support client-side validation, then controls fall back and perform validation on the server.

Validation is normally done when an attempt is made to post a page, but can also be set to run when the user leaves the control.

How to Use Validation Controls

Validation controls must be attached to user input controls. A property called `ControlToValidate` provides the reference to the control that needs validation. You may recall that we used this property in our first Web Forms example to use a `RequiredFieldValidator`, which was attached to the text box that was already on the Web Form.

Summary of Available Validation Controls

The controls that are available to do validation include:

Control	Validation action
RequiredFieldValidator	Ensures that the user fills in an input control, such as a textbox
RangeValidator	Checks that a user's entry falls into a valid range of values. The limits on the range can be declared as preset values, or declared as values in other controls.

Table continued on following page

Control	Validation action
CompareValidator	Checks user's entry in one control against that in another control.
RegularExpressionValidator	Checks user input against a regular expression (there's a short discussion below about regular expressions, in case you are not familiar with them)
CustomValidator	Allows programmer to specify custom logic for validation (client side and/or server side)
ValidationSummary	Provides a text display summary of error messages produced by all validation controls

The example later in the chapter uses a couple of these validation controls, including the ValidationSummary to roll up messages from several other validation controls.

Note that all validation controls consider a blank entry to be valid, except for the RequiredFieldValidator. So a RangeValidator, for example, will accept blank input as valid, even if a zero value is outside the validation range. If blank input is not desired, a RequiredFieldValidator should be used in addition to any other validation controls desired. Notice that more than one validation control can be validating a single user input control.

Regular Expressions

The concept of regular expressions may be unfamiliar to some Visual Basic developers. The RegularExpressionValidator takes a string that expresses how the validation should be done. This string is called a **regular expression**. A string containing a regular expression can be used in a RegularExpressionValidator (and in functions accepting regular expressions) to check for predictable sequences of characters, such as a Social Security number, or a phone number. Here's an example of a regular expression that validates a string as a Social Security number (having 3 digits, then a dash, then 2 digits, then another dash, and finishing with 4 digits):

```
"\d{3}-\d{2}-\d{4}"
```

These expressions have become a commonly used way to express formatting requirements, and they are used in many web applications today. You can consult your MSDN documentation for information on how to construct regular expressions if you are unfamiliar with them.

Laying Out Error Messages on the Page

Each error validation control can have a property set that determines how the error message displays. The property is called Display, and here are the values it can take and the effect of each value:

❑ **Static** – The validation control takes up space on the page even when no error message is displayed. This allows the page to have a fixed layout. Note that two validation controls with Display set to Static cannot occupy the same space on the page, so each control must be given its own location.

❑ **Dynamic** – The validation control takes up no space on the page until an error message is displayed for it. In this case, multiple validation controls can share the same location. The drawback to using dynamic display is that the layout of the page changes when an error is displayed, which may cause controls on the page to jump around.

❑ **None** – For validation controls except for the `ValidationSummary`, this turns off error message display by the individual control, and allows errors to be displayed by the ValidationSummary control only.

If the target browser supports DHTML, there is another option for display of error messages by the `ValidationSummary` control. Such messages can go in a pop-up message box. To enable this behavior, set the `ShowMessageBox` property of the `ValidationSummary` control to `True`.

Disabling Validation

Note that each of the validation controls has an `Enabled` property. Setting this property to `False` causes the control to no longer be rendered into the HTML that the Web Page creates. That means that the control has no client-side presence at all when the `Enabled` property is set to `False`.

Custom Web Form Controls

In addition to the built-in controls that can be placed on Web Forms, you can develop your own controls. There are two basic types of custom controls that can be developed:

❑ A new web form control which extends a single existing Web Form control and gives it new capabilities (by inheriting the existing Web Form control and becoming a subclass of it)

❑ A new Web Form control written from scratch

We will cover the second type in detail, with a step-by-step example, and then comment on differences in creating the other type.

The process of creating a new web form control encompasses these steps:

1. Create a new project of type **Web Control Library**.

2. In the class created for the project, place code in the `Render` method to make the control do anything necessary. This typically involves creating appropriate HTML to render the control's interface.

3. If the control needs any additional properties or methods besides the standard ones inherited from the `System.Web.UI.WebControls` class, then these members should be coded as necessary.

4. Build the project to create a `.DLL` for the control.

5. Create a project to test the control. Reference the control in that project and drag the control onto a page for testing.

The last step has a couple of details that are not currently handled automatically by Visual Studio.NET, and the step-by-step example below will cover those details.

Our simple example will build a control that behaves as a label, but converts its text to upper or lower case before displaying it. We will implement a property that can take on values of upper case or lower case, and the setting of this property will determine whether the control displays in either all upper case or all lower case.

This example has a number of steps that must be performed precisely, so follow the instructions closely:

1. Start a new project from **File | New | Project**. Select the project type of **Web Control Library**. Name the project **NewWebControl**.

2. In the project that comes up, the code window will appear.

3. In the definition line for the class (the line that begins `Public Class`), change the class name to `UpperLowerLabel`. Also change both places in the attribute list that say `WebControl1` to `UpperLowerLabel`. Take care to spell all these changes correctly and exactly the same way.

4. Add the following code directly below the line that says `Dim _text As String`:

```
Public Enum enuCaseType
    caseUpper = 0
    caseLower = 1
End Enum
Dim mCase As enuCaseType
```

5. Create a new property called `Case` with the following code (note that the easiest way to type this is to cut and paste the `Type` property which is already in the code, and then alter that):

```
Property <Bindable(True), Category("Appearance"), DefaultValue("0"), _
           Persistable(PersistableSupport.Declarative)> [Case]() _
           As enuCaseType
    Get
        Return mCase
    End Get

    Set
        mCase = Value
    End Set
End Property
```

6. Place this code in the `Render` method, replacing the single line of code that the designer previously placed in there:

```
Select Case mCase
    Case enuCaseType.caseLower
        output.Write(lcase([Text]))
    Case enuCaseType.caseUpper
        output.Write(ucase([Text]))
    Case Else
        output.Write([Text])
End Select
```

The `output.Write` method sends the text into the HTML stream as HTML. (Another option would be to raise an error in the `Case Else`, but we are going for simplicity in this example.) `Output` is actually a method of the `HTTPResponse` class, which the environment makes available for writing of HTML output.

7. Build the web control by selecting Build from the Build menu.

8. Start a new Web Application project using File | New | Project. (Save the changes from the Web Control Library project when asked.)

9. In this new Web Forms project, select Project | Add Reference. Then, on the Add Reference dialog, click the Browse button.

10. In the Select Component dialog box, choose the icon on the left that says My Projects.

11. Select the NewWebControl directory.

12. Select the bin directory.

13. Select NewWebControl.dll and press the Open button.

14. Back in the Select Component dialog box, press the OK button.

15. Select Tools | Customize Toolbox.

16. Select the .NET Framework Components tab.

17. Click the Browse button.

18. Select the NewWebControl.dll and click Open.

19. Scroll down to the UpperLowerLabel control and ensure the box next to it is checked (it should already be checked). Click the OK button. The UpperLowerLabel control should now be in the Toolbox.

20. Click the HTML tab below the page design surface.

21. Right under the first line of the HTML template, add the following lines:

```
<%@ Register TagPrefix="NewWebControl" Assembly="NewWebControl"
Namespace="NewWebControl"%>
```

> **Until this line is entered, the control cannot be dropped onto the design surface. This is a deficiency in beta one of Visual Basic.NET, and will probably be done automatically in future versions.**

22. Now drag and drop an UpperLowerLabel control on to the Web Form design surface.

23. Set the Text property in the new control to some value.

24. Set the Case property to caseLower. Note that the text in the label goes to all lower case. The Render method is called whenever a property is changed.

25. Set the Case property to caseUpper. Note that the text goes back to upper case on the form.

26. Add other controls onto the Web Form as desired and test. For example, you can add a button to the form, and in the button's Click event add code to change the text in the control, or change the Case property. Then select Build from the Build menu. You are now ready to run and test the project

27. If you get an error when you run the page, go to the Web Form HTML tab, and go to the line that defines the UpperLowerLevel1 control. Take out the part of the line that says Case="caseUpper" or Case="CaseLower". There is a bug in Visual Studio.NET that fails to interpret this line correctly. Then test the Web Form page again.

This exercise demonstrates that constructing a Web Form control is not difficult. The challenge is creating an appropriate Render method. The more you know about HTML, the more sophisticated you can make the Render method. For example, the method can check the browser level, and render different HTML based on what browser is currently being used.

The output.write method used in our example does not add anything to the rendered output. The string that is sent to output.write is sent straight into the HTML stream for the page. If your code inserts HTML tags into the string, those tags are sent into the stream as well.

There is another option to reformat the output string with HTML, and that is to use the System.Web.UI.HtmlTextWriter class. This class has shared properties (fields) for all the common HTML formatting options. Appropriate HTML options can be set on the class, and then the Write method can be used to output a string with all HTML tags automatically added.

Differences for Extending an Existing Web Control

To extend an existing control, start a Web Control Library as before, and make your web control class inherit from the existing control instead of inheriting from the System.Web.UI.WebControls.WebControl class. Then the existing controls, properties, and methods will be inherited, and can be overridden if necessary. Additional properties, methods, and events can also be added to the extended control as necessary.

Data Binding in Web Forms

Displaying data in Web Forms can be done with data binding, and the implementation of data binding in the .NET framework allows more flexibility than data binding in VB6 and earlier. For example, grids can bind to arrays in Web Forms.

Details on data binding in Web Forms, including examples, are in Chapter 7.

A Final Example – A Small Application Using Web Forms

We will conclude our discussion of Web Forms' capabilities by constructing a small application with a Web Form. The application will be a loan calculator. It will take in the amount of the loan, the number of payments, and the interest rate. It will validate each of these to acceptable values using validation controls. If all values are valid, it will calculate and display the payment amount.

All of this will be done without any work in HTML at all. The work will strongly resemble normal VB forms programming.

Step One – Initialize the Project

Start a new web application, and give it an appropriate name. The sample screens have the application name as WebApplication4.

Click on the design surface for the form. In the `Properties` window, change the **pageLayout** property to the value GridLayout. This will allow all controls to be placed on a grid, similarly to the way VB controls are placed on a form.

Step Two – Place the Controls on the Web Form

Drag and drop the following controls onto the form, and set the properties as specified in the property window with the control highlighted. Move the controls so they match the sample screen below.

Control	Location	Properties
Label	At top of screen	Text = "Loan calculator"
Label	To left of screen	Text = "Loan Amount"
Label	To left of screen	Text = "# of Months"
Label	To left of screen	Text = "Interest Rate (%)"
Text box	Beside Loan Amount label	ID = "txtLoanAmount"
Text box	Beside # of Months	ID = "txtMonths"
Text box	Beside Interest Rate (%)	ID = "txtInterestRate"
Button	Below all the above controls	ID = "btnCalculatePayment"
		Text = "Calculate Payment"

The controls should be laid out so that the design surface looks roughly like this:

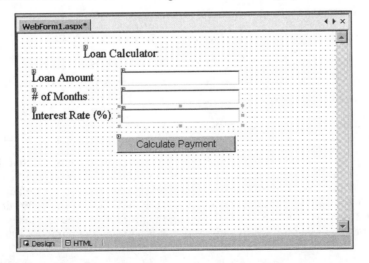

Step Three – Place a Label for the Result on the Form

Now drag and drop a Label control and place it just under the button and to the left. Name the label control lblPaymentAmount. Change its Visible property to False. Change its Text property to "Payment amount goes here".

Step Four – Place the Validator Controls on the Form

Drag and drop the following validator controls onto the form, and set their properties as indicated. Position them below the label inserted in step three.

Control	Properties
RangeValidator	ID = "vldLoanAmount"
	ControlToValidate = txtLoanAmount
	MaximumValue = 500000
	MinimumValue = 100
	ErrorMessage = "Loan amount must be between 100 and 500000"
	Display = Dynamic
	Type = Double
RangeValidator	ID = "vldMonths"
	ControlToValidate = txtMonths
	MaximumValue = 360
	MinimumValue = 3
	ErrorMessage = "# months must be between 3 and 360"
	Display = Dynamic
	Type = Integer
RegularExpression Validator	ID = "vldInterestRate"
	ControlToValidate = txtInterestRate
	ValidationExpression = "\d*[.]{0,1}\d*"
	ErrorMessage = "Interest rate must be numeric"
	Display = Dynamic
ValidationSummary	(no properties need to be set)

Setting the Type property to Double for the RangeValidator controls ensures that the range checking is done numerically instead of with an ASCII compare. If you place a MaximumValue of 1000 and a MinimumValue of 100 in the control, but leave the Type property set to the default (which is String), then an entry of 500 would be considered invalid because the ASCII string "500" does not come between the ASCII strings "100" and "1000". Setting the property to Double takes cares of this, and the number 500 would then be considered valid because it is between the numbers 100 and 1000.

The regular expression used by the RegularExpressionValidator in this example requires the user to enter zero or more digits, then optionally a period, then zero or more digits again.

Actually, in a real application, it would probably be better to validate the interest rate in the same way as the other items, with a RangeValidator, but a RegularExpressionValidator is used in our examples for some variety. Also, a real application would normally use a CompareValidator to check input against a particular data type. The loan amount and interest rate could be validated against a Double, and the number of months against an Integer. This validation would be in addition to the range validation performed by the RangeValidator.

Once all of these are placed on the form, the layout should look roughly like this:

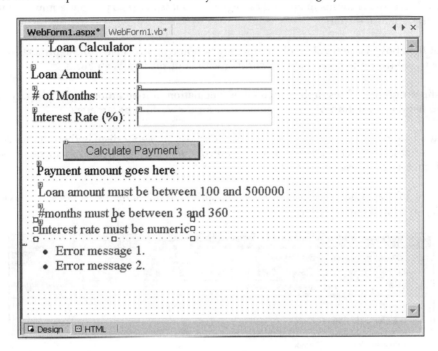

Step Five – Insert Code in the Button's Click Event

Double-click the button to get to its Click event in the code editor, and insert the following code:

```
Public Sub btnCalculatePayment_Click(ByVal sender As Object, _
                                ByVal e As System.EventArgs)

    Dim dblLoanAmount As Double
    Dim intMonths As Integer
    Dim dblInterestRate As Double

    ' Get values from user
    dblLoanAmount = CDbl(txtLoanAmount.Text)
    intMonths = CInt(txtMonths.Text)
    dblInterestRate = CDbl(txtInterestRate.Text) / 1200

    ' Calculate payment using standard function
```

```
    Dim dblPaymentAmount As Double
    dblPaymentAmount = -pmt(dblInterestRate, intMonths, dblLoanAmount)

    ' Make payment amount label visible and display payment
    lblPaymentAmount.Visible = True
    lblPaymentAmount.Text = "Payment is " & _
                            FormatCurrency(dblPaymentAmount)

End Sub
```

The function that calculates the payment amount (pmt) is from a standard library in the .NET Framework. It returns amounts to be paid as negative, so it is necessary to put a minus sign in front to reverse the sign before display.

Notice that the above code would look completely at home in any Visual Basic project. It is literally impossible to tell from the code that it is working with controls in a Web Form.

Now run the program and test it. It should allow calculation of loan amounts and display the result. It should also handle validation of the amounts input for the various parameters.

Notice that all validation controls except the ValidationSummary display their amounts as soon as the user leaves a field. The ValidationSummary control only rolls up the amounts when a post is attempted, such as by pressing the button.

Here is a view of the payment calculator in action (although this screen shot does not have the payment amount displayed in a currency format):

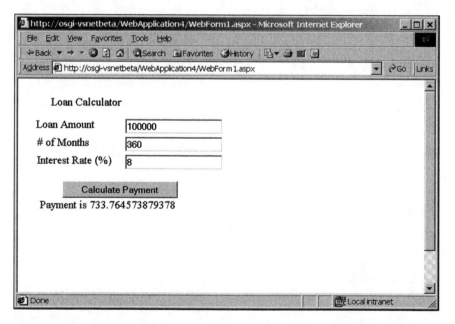

This example is extended in Chapter 10 to add a data grid with a payment schedule in a separate Web Form. It is necessary to cover the ADO.NET syntax in Chapter 7 before we can do that.

Converting Existing VB Applications to Web Forms

Many traditional VB forms-based applications could benefit from being outfitted with a Web interface. In some cases, Web Forms can be the fastest way to do this. This section discusses some of the options available.

There is no automatic option for converting existing VB forms directly into Web Forms. The migration tool that comes with Visual Studio.NET converts VB forms into Windows Forms. However, that conversion takes care of many of the syntax differences in going from VB6 to Visual Basic.NET, so it's probably appropriate to move VB forms into Windows Forms, and then use those modules to cut-and-paste logic into a Web Form. The Web Form will still need to be designed visually, with all the necessary controls dragged onto it and named, before transporting the Windows Form logic.

This section should not be construed to mean that all VB applications should be ported to a web interface. Some applications have no need to be web-enabled. Some applications need the rich, responsive user interface of a Win32 client. And there are applications that do operations such as long database queries that do not fit well with a browser-based UI. Such applications may need to update status information, for example. So it is important to understand whether an application can benefit from being web-enabled before planning how to do it.

Typical Design Cases

VB forms-based applications range from simple user interfaces that rely exclusively on built-in VB controls, such as textboxes, command buttons, and labels, up through very complex user interfaces that rely heavily on advanced controls, often including third party controls. The lower end of this spectrum (the simple interfaces that use typical controls) are reasonably good candidates for converting to Web Forms. The more complex the interface, and the more it relies on advanced or third-party controls, the less likely it is to be a good candidate for such conversion.

Lowering Dependence on Events

Regardless of the controls used, if a user interface depends heavily on continuous processing of events like `MouseOver` or `KeyPress`, then the interface will not move naturally to Web Forms. Many of these events are not available for server controls, because the associated events would cause a server round-trip. There are some options for using DHTML to get this functionality, but that will require a lot of changes, making migration difficult.

Moving Code to the Middle Tier

The best candidates for conversion are those applications that use classes to encapsulate as much business logic as possible, and have "thin" user interfaces, that is, forms without much code in them. So it might be appropriate to refactor the code before conversion by moving any business logic in VB form modules into classes instead.

However, middle tier code that will be used in a web application also needs to manage state appropriately to get a sufficient level of scalability and performance. Books on web development offer many approaches to managing state, and this is far too complex a topic to go into in this book. But you should be aware that middle tier architectures in which components hold a lot of property information (state information) for long periods of time will need extensive changes to work optimally in web applications.

Overview of Web Services

Chapter 2 briefly discussed the concept of **Web Services** as one of the interfaces available in the .NET Framework. That chapter talked about the vision of Web Services, and future possibilities of globally-distributed applications. Web Services is one of the key concepts in .NET, and they are expected to radically change the way applications are designed. The idea of applications being run on discrete, controlled sets of servers is expected to give way to the idea of applications wrapping up, processing, and presenting data from a widely distributed set of resources. These resources could potentially come from a multitude of different servers of different types and operating systems, and the universal interface of Web Services would allow them all to be treated as if there were generated by the same kind of system.

Keep in mind that a Web Service has no user interface. It is for program-to-program communication. We'll see a technique in this section where a developer can "peek" at the results from a Web Service, but this is just for convenience during development. Web Services will normally talk to other programs, not to users.

In this section, we'll look at how to actually program Web Services in Visual Basic.NET. This section will be shorter than you might think, because programming a Web Service is functionally very similar to programming any other kind of component.

What are Web Services used for?

Web Services provides a mechanism for programs to communicate over the Internet, using the SOAP protocol (discussed in more detail below). Conceptually, this is similar to DCOM in that it enables distributed environments, but Web Services works in a much broader context; that is, SOAP (and the client) no longer care what technology is at the target of the call.

Today, almost all data sent across the web is embedded in a web page. With Web Services, data can be sent across the web and then used by the consumer in any way desired. It might be folded into part of a page or screen, consumed by an "agent" program that watches and analyzes the data looking for certain events or trends, or received and stored into a database for future use.

Here are a number of examples of services that might be exposed on the Internet as Web Services:

- ❑ Product status information
- ❑ Shipping and tracking information
- ❑ Current interest rates
- ❑ Stock quotes
- ❑ Current weather
- ❑ Latest items on sale from a retail site
- ❑ Best sellers on a retail site
- ❑ New upcoming items on a retail site available for pre-order
- ❑ Employee benefit information
- ❑ Data sets of real estate properties meeting a certain set of criteria
- ❑ Reminders, tasks, and to-do items

This is just a random sampling of items that are obvious candidates. Web Services could potentially be used for almost any web application that is data-centric.

In this section, we will discuss how Web Services work, starting with an overview of the XML Protocol used for communication with Web Services. Then, after describing how to create a Web Service, and how to consume a Web Service in another application, a step-by-step example will be covered.

Understanding the SOAP Protocol

The Simple Object Access Protocol, usually abbreviated to SOAP, is an XML-based standard for component communication through HTTP. Since it is based on XML, it is text based, and can go through firewalls.

Part of the XML Protocol describes how Web Services initially establish communication with one another. The first phase of communications is called the **discovery phase**. During this phase, the Web Services transmit information about the component interface that is available. That information is transmitted in a sub-protocol called **Service Contract Language** or **SCL**.

Then, once the discovery phase is complete, the stage is set for normal component interface calls. These calls look and act a lot like calls to a local component, except that the information in the calls is being transmitted and received between the components in the XML Protocol.

The final response of a Web Service component is an XML document containing all the information returned by the Web Service. The consumer of the Web Service then interprets this XML document and extracts the information needed.

In Visual Basic.NET, it's not really necessary to know what's going on under the surface. The information sent to a Web Service is translated into the XML Protocol by the .NET Framework automatically. The .NET Framework then manages the process, receives the returning XML document, and places the returned data into component interfaces as necessary.

Creating a Web Service in VB.NET

Web Service components are created by selecting the appropriate option when starting a new project. The dialog for starting a new project looks like this:

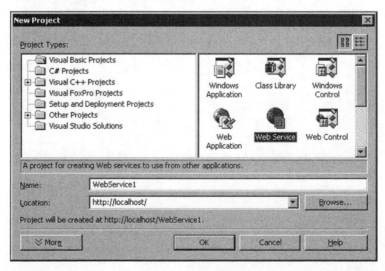

On the right hand side are the types of projects that may be created, and on the bottom row of options is one for **Web Service**. Once selected, it sets up the project parameters for a class library that will be Web Service enabled.

The first view of the Web Service is similar to other component designer interfaces. There is a design surface onto which pre-packaged and system components, such as message queues, can be dragged. However, it is not required to use any such resources to create a web service. It is only necessary to produce a Web-enabled component interface.

Double-clicking on the component design surface will bring up the code editor for the Web Service code module. It will have all the necessary declarations already in it, and also includes a "Hello, world" Web Service-enabled function.

A Web Service component will have some methods that need to be exposed as part of the Web Service, and others that are just for internal use and should not be exposed. Those that are to be a visible part of the Web Service interface are indicated with the WebMethod attribute. Otherwise they look just like other methods. Here is an example of a Web Service-enabled method, which we will implement in our example at the end of this topic:

```
Public Function <WebMethod> Color(iIndex as Integer) As String
    Select Case iIndex
        Case 1
            Color = "Red"
        Case 2
            Color = "Blue"
        Case Else
            Color = "No Color"
    End Select
End Function
```

Note that the only way this differs from a standard function is the <WebMethod> in the declaration line. A declaration done this way adds a .NET attribute to the function. The attribute is stored as part of the metadata for the function, and the Common Language Runtime treats all routines with the WebMethod attribute as appropriate to expose through Web Services.

If you create a Web Service in Visual Basic.NET and then run it, you get a browser-based testing interface for the Web Service. Here is a typical browser screen that comes up when activating a Web Service with the Color function shown above:

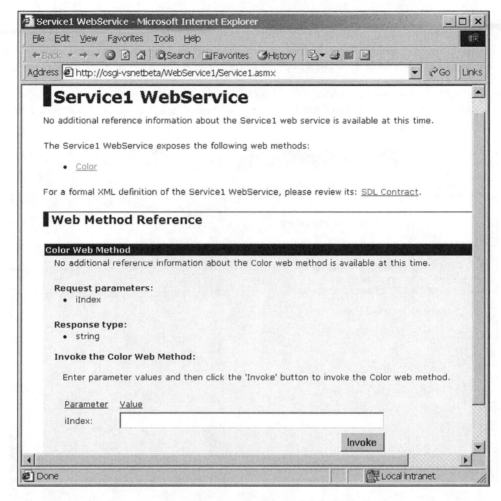

This very useful test bed uses the discovery capabilities of Web Services to query the interface of the Web Service and display information about it. It also provides an input area to feed parameters directly to the Web Service. Once the Invoke button is pressed, the parameters are passed into the Web Service and the browser displays the XML packet that is returned with the output of the Web Service.

If a value for iIndex of 2 were entered, and the Invoke button pressed, the simplest possible version of the returned XML packet would look like this:

```
<?xml version="1.0" ?>
  <string>Blue</string>
```

Depending on the XML Protocol options that are chosen, there may be additional information in the XML packet returned.

Any consumer of this Web Service would get back such an XML packet. If the consumer is integrated into the .NET Framework, the values in the XML will be parsed and placed into a normal component interface. That is, a Web Service component accessed from within a .NET Framework program looks very much like any other component. The next section discusses such Web Service consumers.

Consuming a Web Service in Visual Basic.NET

Any Visual Basic.NET application may need to integrate a Web Service. That could include Windows Forms applications as well as Web Forms applications. It could also include a middle-tier component.

To integrate a Web Service into a Visual Basic.NET project, it is necessary to reference the service. That is done with the Project | Add Web Reference menu option. When that option is chosen, a screen like the following comes up:

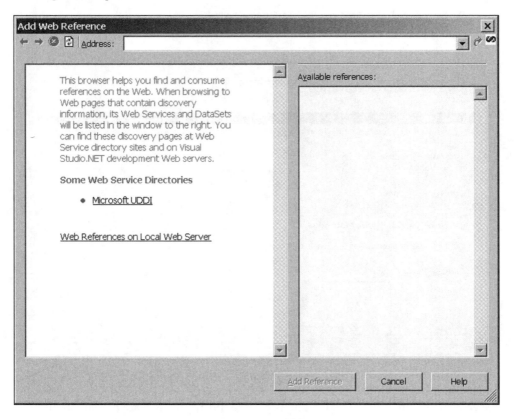

This dialog allows referencing of both local and remote Web Services. It might be appropriate to reference a local Web Service for testing, but in most production situations, the Web Service will be remote.

A remote Web Service can be referenced with its URL. Microsoft includes some Web Service directories on its own servers to provide examples.

Web References on Local Web Server will bring up web-enabled .NET applications that have deployed locally. The option causes such applications to appear in the right-hand list box. If you have created a Web Service, it should show up there, and you can choose it.

Choosing a Web Service displays information about it, including an XML document that details its interface. The Add Reference button becomes enabled, and pressing that button adds the Web Service to the project.

Once a Web Service (local or remote) is referenced, it shows up in the Solution Explorer, and is treated locally just like any other component. The Web Service's interface even shows up in IntelliSense.

To reference a Web Service component, the following syntax is used:

```
Dim objWebService As New servername.servicename
```

The servername may be a complete URL for remote Web Services, but for local Web Services on your own development system, it will typically be "localhost". servicename is the actual name of the Web Service.

Referencing a Web Service this way actually creates a local proxy object with the appropriate interface, and that's what your code is accessing. Behind the scenes, the proxy object is communicating with the actual Web Service using the XML Protocol. The .NET Framework creates and manages the proxy object automatically.

Example – Creating and Consuming a Web Service

We will conclude with a step-by-step example that includes creation of a Web Service in Visual Basic.NET and integration of the Web Service into a Windows Form.

1. Start a new project in Visual Studio.NET by selecting the menu option File | New | Project. In the New Project dialog, select the Web Service project type. Note that the system creates a blank Web Service named Service1.

2. Double-click on the design surface for Service1 to bring up the code editor.

3. Enter the following routine into the code for Service1.vb:

```
Public Function <WebMethod> Color(iIndex as Integer) As String
    Select Case iIndex
        Case 1
            Color = "Red"
        Case 2
            Color = "Blue"
        Case Else
            Color = "No Color"
    End Select
End Function
```

4. Run the project. On the Internet Explorer screen that comes up, test the Web Service by putting some values into the input box for iIndex, and examining the XML that is returned. Here is typical returned HMTL:

```
<?xml version="1.0" ?>
  <string xmlns="http://tempuri.org/">Blue</string>
```

5. Start another new project using File | New | Project. Select a Windows Application project.

6. Add a reference to the Web Service (Service1) created earlier. Select the menu option **Project | Add Web Reference**, and on the dialog, click the **Web References on Local Server** hyperlink on the left side of the dialog.

7. After a while (a long while, usually), the box on the right side will show available local web references. Choose http://localhost/Service1. After another delay, XML information associated with Service1 will display, and you can click the **Add Reference** button.

8. Go to the blank form that is created for the Windows Application (Form1), and place a label, a textbox, and a button side by side, and another label under all three of them. Change the text in the first label to read **Color Index**. Change the text in the button to read **Get Color**. The form should now look like this:

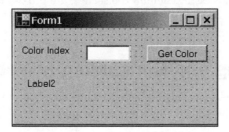

9. Double click the button to get to its event handling routine. In that Button1_Click routine, place the following code:

```
Protected Sub Button1_Click(ByVal sender As Object, _
                            ByVal e As System.EventArgs)

    Dim objColor As New localhost.Service1()
    Dim sColor As String
    Dim iIndex As Integer
    iIndex = Cint(TextBox1.Text)
    sColor = objColor.Color(iIndex)
    Label2.Text = "Color is " & sColor

End Sub
```

In the first line of this code, localhost refers to the fact that the Web Service is on the local web server. Service1 refers to the name of the service when it was compiled. Recall that the Web Service project created earlier included a service with the default name Service1.

Note that, after the declaration of objColor as a Web Service, there is no further indication in the code that a Web Service is being used. objColor looks just like a locally created object, as far as the rest of the code is concerned.

10. Run the project. Place the number 2 in the textbox and press the button. The second label will change to say **Color is Blue**.

Notice that after the Web Service object was declared in the first line of code in Step 7, the Web Service object is treated no differently from any other object in code. For example, you may have noticed that IntelliSense was available when typing the fifth line. This is just as true of remote Web Services as local Web Services. Once they are referenced into a project, they are used in code just like any other component. The work behind the scenes (doing discovery of the interface, transmitting information to and from the Web Service in XML) is handled transparently by the .NET Framework.

Summary

In Internet projects, Visual Basic has long been relegated to the middle tier. No longer. With Visual Basic.NET, Web-based user interfaces can be designed quickly and easily with high-productivity visual tools. Services can be exposed to the web as easily as writing a function.

That does not mean, however, that VB developers who have only done forms-based applications can become instant web developers. The learning curve has been shortened, but not eliminated. It is still necessary to become proficient at the basics of HTML, DHTML, and XML, and to have a general understanding of Web technologies and concepts such as state management. It is also helpful to know such client technologies as JavaScript.

But, with Visual Basic.NET, the days of needing to know all the vagaries of Active Server Pages just to do a simple Web application are gone. Web-enabling business applications has just become dramatically easier.

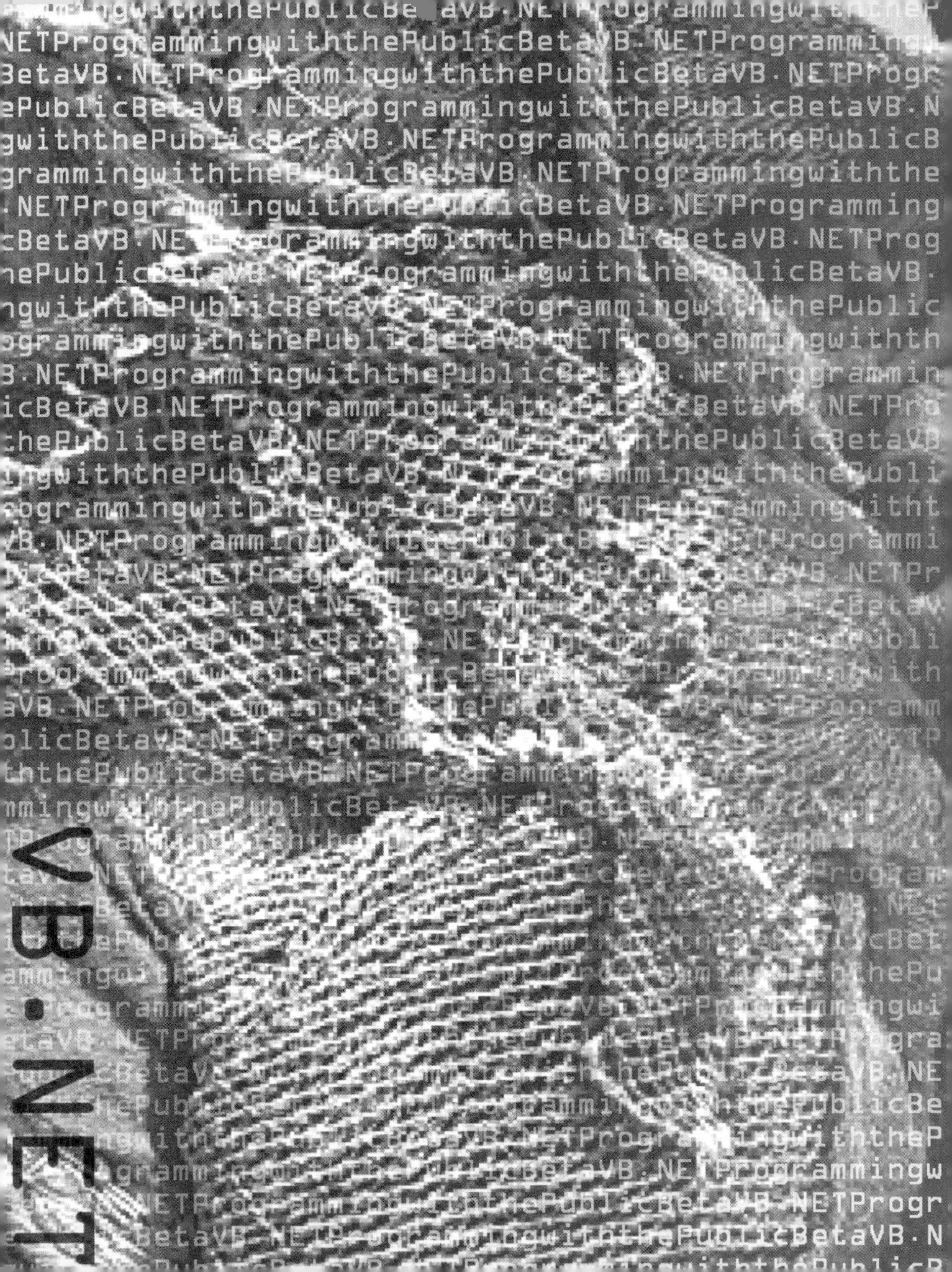
VB·NET
VB·NETProgrammingwiththePublicBeta

Data Access in Visual Basic.NET

Visual Basic was around for a couple of years before it started to become popular for serious corporate development projects. It is easy to pinpoint the reason that VB started being successful in the corporate world – version 3.0 added built-in capabilities to extract data from relational databases. Today, most systems written in VB access relational data stores of some kind, the most common being SQL Server and Oracle.

Data access techniques in VB have evolved quickly in the last few years. This has caused some consternation among developers, but many of the changes have been necessary to adapt to evolving application architectures. We have gone from local access to client-server access to Internet access, all in about seven years.

The first data access model specifically for VB was called Data Access Objects, abbreviated to DAO. It was created for access to *local databases* in the Access Jet format. It could also be extended to use databases on a server, but was less than ideal for this function because its performance was optimized for local databases. This was the first object model that made getting to data easy, offering an alternative to lower level access methods like ODBC.

The successors to DAO were Remote Data Objects (RDO) and ActiveX Data Objects (ADO). Both were designed primarily for *client-server* use. RDO didn't hang around too long, but ADO is still with us today. It has been extended to the Internet world, with capabilities such as Remote Data Services (RDS). ADO is still the easiest to use for client-server projects, but is more cumbersome for the highly distributed environment of the Internet.

For the .NET Framework, ADO has been redesigned and extended for *distributed Internet* use. Called **ADO.NET** (previously **ADO+**), it uses the same access methods for local, client-server, or Internet access. While ADO.NET has some significant similarities to ADO, it also has some major differences.

ADO.NET can be used for accessing many kinds of data stores. This is a continuation of a trend begun by ADO. In ADO, data is accessed through an OLE DB provider, and such a provider can be written for all kinds of data sources, such as file systems and flat files, in addition to traditional relational stores. ADO.NET goes even further by converting just about any data fed into it into XML, and then accessing that. This makes it even easier to write a provider for ADO.NET because it simply has to translate data into XML format.

Most data access involves traditional relational databases, and the examples in this chapter emphasize that type of data access. However, with XML as its internal data format, ADO.NET can naturally be used to access native XML, with no relational database engine involved at all. The last section of this chapter covers reading and writing directly to and from XML files with ADO.NET.

This chapter covers ADO.NET from the point of view of a VB developer. Of course, as part of the .NET Framework, ADO.NET is accessible to any .NET-enabled language.

Important Note Regarding Changes in Beta Two

It is known at the time this book goes to press that there will changes in the syntax of ADO.NET from beta one to beta two. All the examples in this chapter were constructed with beta one, and it is expected that many of them will not work in beta two. The Wrox web site (www.wrox.com) will contain updated examples for this chapter after beta two comes out. If you are working on beta two while using this chapter, please be sure to get those changed examples.

ADO.NET – An Evolution from ADO

ADO.NET is designed for loosely coupled, highly distributed applications. Such applications will normally use HTTP for communication among logical application tiers. This makes XML an excellent choice to communicate data among tiers because the text-based XML format works very well on HTTP, as opposed to various binary data formats that do not. Binary formats may be preferred for performance reasons when tiers are known to be on the same network, but XML communication offers far more flexibility.

Comparison to ADO

Traditional ADO was designed for tightly coupled, connected architectures, and, by default, passes data around in a binary, proprietary format through COM interfaces. It has therefore needed to evolve quickly to be usable in Internet applications. The history of ADO has led to several issues for today's Internet-based development:

❑ Maintaining a connection to a database, as done in "vanilla" ADO, is resource intensive and limits scalability of applications. Such architecture is unsuitable for most Internet applications.

❑ The main alternative for disconnected access is Remote Data Services (RDS). This exposes new Internet functionality, but introduces additional complexity. Developers have a tough learning curve before being able to use the right features of ADO for a given application architecture.

❑ XML support is not built-in, so accessing XML means going through the MSXML libraries and accessing the XML DOM.

❑ Multiple versions of ADO exist, and are mutually incompatible. All applications running on a given system must use the same version of the Microsoft Data Access Components (the infamous MDAC) and, if an update to MDAC is necessary, all applications have to be adjusted and recompiled as necessary.

ADO.NET and the .NET Framework together solve all of these limitations:

❑ A set of data in ADO.NET can be passed to any appropriate application tier in XML, so no continuous connection to the database is necessary.

❑ The same access techniques in ADO.NET can work for local, network, or Internet access.

❑ XML support is built in. This makes ADO.NET a flexible alternative, suitable for many different kinds of data access in VB.NET.

❑ The .NET Framework allows side-by-side access to multiple versions of the same components. Applications in .NET will always use the correct ADO.NET installation.

For upward compatibility, the .NET Framework also includes support for traditional ADO. In most cases, it will not be necessary to change the data access logic in old code to use it. This chapter will not discuss data access in VB.NET using ADO, since it is quite similar to ADO usage in VB6.

Similarities between ADO and ADO.NET

The programming model for ADO.NET will not look too alien to developers accustomed to ADO, once a couple of key new concepts are understood. The logic for getting a connection is similar, for example. Both models manipulate collections of rows and fields. Both models have support for transactions through the connection object. And both models can be bound to controls for automatic data handling.

One of the biggest differences that developers will notice is ADO.NET's simplicity. The programming model has been unified for all typical data access scenarios – local, network, and Internet.

ADO.NET – Important Concepts

This section will introduce some of the most important concepts in ADO.NET in a way that should be fairly easy to digest. Then the rest of the chapter will get into more details about these concepts.

Location of the ADO.NET Classes

The classes for ADO.NET are all in the `System.Data`, `System.Data.ADO`, and `System.Data.SQL` namespaces. Almost all the examples in this chapter presume that these namespaces have been referenced in a code module with these lines:

```
Imports System.Data
Imports System.Data.ADO
```

None of the examples in this chapter use the `System.Data.SQL` namespace, and the reason for this is discussed later in the chapter.

Replacing Recordsets

A major difference between ADO and ADO.NET is that the new functionality in ADO.NET does not support a `Recordset` class. Note that existing ADO capabilities, including recordsets, are available for compatibility and for a few server-side uses where traditional ADO is still superior.

For many data access purposes, the more flexible `DataSet` has replaced the `Recordset` concept in the new ADO.NET syntax. Especially those functions related to changing, manipulating, and randomly accessing data, `DataSets` are a nice new innovation, and much of the chapter discusses how to use them.

In addition to `DataSets`, there is another data class available in ADO.NET for read-only access to data. It is called a `DataReader`, and it is similar to a read-only `Recordset` with a forward-only cursor. It has the advantage of much higher performance for such sequential, read-only situations. This chapter also includes an example of creating and using a `DataReader`.

`DataSets` are a bit more difficult to understand than `DataReaders`, so we begin by getting a better idea of what a `DataSet` is.

What is a DataSet?

A `DataSet` is a collection of mini-tables or recordsets, and the relationships between them. Perhaps the best way to picture a `DataSet` is a miniature relational database, in which the data is kept in memory.

This "virtual" local relational database is totally disconnected from the original source of the data, yet it has very flexible relational capabilities. This contrasts strongly with disconnected `Recordsets` in ADO, which only support the minimal cursor operations of `MoveNext`, `MovePrevious`, `MoveFirst`, and `MoveLast`.

This relational `DataSet` is thus a local copy of relational data and is used for local processing, whether on a client workstation, a web server, or a remote Internet client. All operations that need to be carried out on the data are done on this local copy, with no connection to the original data store. This has the major advantage of avoiding the need for a continuous connection to the database.

When all processing operations have been completed on the local `DataSet`, it is submitted as a whole to be resolved with the original store. Any changed records can be updated in the source database, records can be added, and so forth.

> We'll examine the `DataSet` – its object model, the process of getting data into it, operating on the data, and returning it back to the original data store – later in the chapter. We will also discuss issues relating to data concurrency – that is, what to do if data in the original store was changed while the local `DataSet` was being manipulated.

While `DataSets` are typically manipulated in memory, they are passed between application tiers as XML. The XML document for a `DataSet` contains both the schema and the data. As befits an XML-based technology, once the data has been placed in a `DataSet`, the original source does not matter. The data is operated on identically regardless of how it came to be in the `DataSet`.

This design for `DataSets` fixes a lot of the drawbacks of using `Recordsets` in VB6. Let's briefly recap these ADO limitations now.

Using Recordsets for Handling Related Data in VB6

`Recordsets` are an object abstraction of a table or view in a relational database. A `Recordset` consists of a number of rows, each with an identical structure. Each row contains a collection of data fields. Individual fields usually correspond to fields in the database.

The limitation of `Recordsets` is that they do not handle hierarchical data structures very well. A typical hierarchical example is a table of customers with a related table of orders. Each customer can have any number of orders. There are basically two ways (with several variations) to handle such data constructs using ADO `Recordsets` in VB6.

In the first technique, all information about both customers and orders is contained in a single `Recordset`. Using the relationship between the `Customers` table and the `Orders` table, you can construct a `Recordset` that contains rows with both customer information and order information. A typical SQL statement to do so would look like this:

```
SELECT
   Customers.CustomerID,
   Customers.CompanyName,
   Customers.Phone,
   Orders.OrderID,
   Orders.OrderDate
FROM
   Customers INNER JOIN Orders ON Customers.CustomerID = Orders.CustomerID
WHERE ...
```

In this `Recordset`, there may be several rows containing order information for a given customer. Each row will repeat the customer information, but different rows will have different order information.

Processing such a `Recordset` – to print a report from it, for example – requires logic to loop through the `Recordset` and look for "breaks" in the data. That is, the logic has to detect when the customer information has changed and take appropriate action to wrap up one customer before processing the first record for the next.

In the second technique, separate `Recordsets` can be constructed for customer and order information. The customer `Recordset` contains one row for each customer. The order `Recordset` has one row for each order. There is no redundant, repeated customer information. The SQL statements to construct the `Recordsets` might look like this:

```
SELECT CustomerID, CompanyName, Phone FROM Customers WHERE ...
```

And this:

```
SELECT OrderID, CustomerID, OrderDate FROM Orders WHERE ...
```

While this solves the redundancy problem, another big problem with getting the data this way is that the relationship between customers and orders must be completely managed in code, creating a much more complex job for the programmer.

How DataSets Provide More Flexibility

Since a DataSet can contain multiple tables or Recordsets, the situation above for handling information on both customers and orders can be accommodated. The customers needed for the current operation can be in one of these tables in the DataSet, and the orders for those customers can be in another. Because the DataSet contains relational capability, it includes the ability to specify the relationship between customers and orders. It is then possible to access customers and orders with the following pseudo-code logic:

```
' This is pseudo-code, not real code!!
For Each Customer In Customers
    Print Header Information for Customer
    For Each Order In Orders
        Print Information on the Order
    Next Order
Next Customer
```

We will see actual code in an example below that implements this operation. We will need to cover the syntax of ADO.NET before we get to it, however.

This technique is far better than either of the VB6/ADO possibilities presented previously. Once the data is in a properly constructed DataSet, the code to work with the data is significantly simpler in ADO.NET.

DataSets are also more flexible than Recordsets because their structure can be changed on the fly. For example, new columns in a table can be created that are derived from other columns, and dynamically inserted into the DataSet schema.

It's worthwhile to note that a DataSet with just one table in it fills the same conceptual role as a Recordset. Such a DataSet needs no relationships set up within it and might not use any of the other advanced features of DataSets. However, it's not a good idea to simply port old designs to ADO.NET by substituting one-table DataSets for Recordsets. DataSets open up new design possibilities that will work better in most typical data processing applications.

Data Flow Overview for ADO.NET

Data used in ADO.NET usually starts in a traditional relational data store such as SQL Server or Oracle. From there, it is extracted for use by a part of ADO.NET called a **managed provider**. This is conceptually similar to the role played in ADO by an OLE DB provider. A managed provider is the interface technology that knows how to connect to a database and get data into and out of it. We discuss managed providers in more detail below.

Once the data has been extracted by a managed provider and placed in a DataSet, there is no longer a need to continue a connection to the database. The data can then be operated on in a variety of ways.

One of the most common operations is to specify relationships in the DataSet so that the data can be treated relationally. Then code and/or bound controls can change the data in the DataSet, adding in new rows, changing or deleting old ones, etc. When those changes are finished, the managed provider then resolves the changes. It looks through the DataSet, finds the changed or added data, and attempts to place the changes or additions into the original data store. If there are concurrency problems, or other problems such as having the database go off-line, then the managed provider can raise appropriate errors.

Here is a diagrammatic representation of the steps described above. The process starts in the upper left with data being extracted from the original data store:

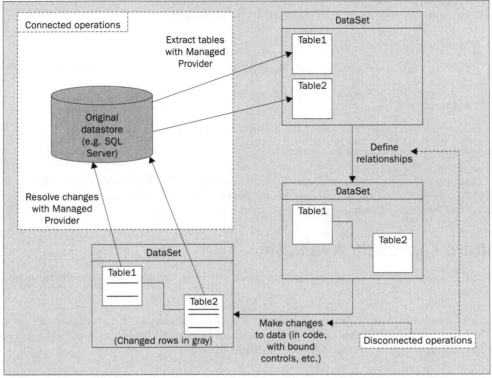

The diagram illustrates the parts of the cycle that take place in a connected fashion, all of which involve the managed provider. Other operations take place disconnected from the main data store.

This diagram does not explicitly state where the DataSet resides. That's because the cycle is the same no matter where the DataSet gets manipulated. It could be on the same system as the data store, or on a client workstation on the same network, or in a browser on an Internet client. Even if the DataSet is on the local machine with the database, manipulation of the DataSet takes place without a connection to the database being necessary.

There are additional operations that are not included in the above example. Some of the possibilities include:

❑   Adding constraints to the relational structure in the DataSet

❑   Attaching a schema to the DataSet to help with operations such as data validation

❑   Defining and adding new columns to the tables in the DataSet, such as derived columns that are calculated from other columns for reporting purposes

These operations will be discussed below in the section describing the DataSet in more detail. That section will cover DataSet-related elements in the ADO.NET namespace and classes.

However, before going into some more details on DataSets, it's helpful to understand how the data gets into them, via managed providers.

Managed Providers

Managed providers were mentioned above as the ADO.NET constructs that provide an interface to the original data store. Managed providers take care of the functions like the following:

❑ Making a connection to a database

❑ Getting a stream of data from the database to place into a read-only set of query results

❑ Getting a stream of data from the database to place into a table in a DataSet for manipulation

❑ Examining changed DataSets for differences that need to be recorded in the source database

❑ Raising errors during data resolution

As the diagram shown previously indicated, operations carried out by the managed providers are done while connected to the original data store. Managed providers carry out all of the database interaction that needs to be done in a connected fashion.

Providers Currently Available

The .NET Framework currently includes two managed providers, and more are expected from Microsoft or third parties.

One of the included providers is a generic provider that talks to a variety of OLE DB providers. It takes care of the interface to the COM-based OLE DB provider, and exposes the functionality of the OLE DB provider in the .NET Framework. It is called the **ADO Managed Provider**.

The other included provider is specifically for SQL Server. It is called the **SQL Managed Provider**.

All of the classes in the ADO Managed Provider are prefixed with ADO and all of the classes in the SQL Managed Provider are prefixed with SQL.

The ADO Managed Provider

The ADO Managed Provider is a generic provider that should work with most OLE DB providers. It has been tested with the following:

❑ SQLOLEDB – SQL OLE DB provider

❑ MSDAORA – Oracle OLE DB provider

❑ JOLT – Jet OLE DB provider

❑ MSDASQL/SQL Server ODBC – SQL Server ODBC driver via OLE DB

❑ MSDASQL/Jet – Jet ODBC driver via OLE DB

The SQL Managed Provider

The SQL Managed Provider provides access only to Microsoft SQL Server. It is implemented totally in the .NET Framework and does not go through a COM-based OLE DB provider. Because of this design, the SQL Managed Provider is expected to yield better performance than the ADO Managed Provider going through SQLOLEDB.

For consistency, all the examples in this chapter use the ADO Managed Provider. The interface of both managed providers is the same except for the different prefixes in the class names (as mentioned previously, and covered in more detail below), so there should be no problem in translating examples for use with the SQL Managed Provider if you wish.

Classes Implemented by Managed Providers

The classes are:

Type of Class	Name in ADO Managed Provider	Name in SQL Managed Provider	Function
Connection	ADOConnection	SQLConnection	Establishes a connection to the database. Very similar to the Connection object in ADO.
Command	ADOCommand	SQLCommand	Carries out an operation while connected to the database. Conceptually similar to the Command object in ADO, but contains new functions.
DataReader	ADODataReader	SQLDataReader	Holds a stream of data from the database for a query operation. Loosely corresponds to a forward-only, read-only Recordset.
DataSet Command	ADODataSetCommand	SQLDataSetCommand	Transfers data back and forth between the database and a DataSet.

The easiest way to see how these classes work is to examine code that uses them. Here are two brief code examples, one for constructing a DataReader and another for creating a DataSet and placing a table in it.

Creating a DataReader

The following code uses the Northwind database in SQL Server, creating a Connection object and a Command object, and then using them to initialize a DataReader. The DataReader is then put in a loop to display some of the information placed into it.

This code will work fine in just about any circumstances, as long as the server (MYSERVER) is changed to the correct name, and any other necessary login information is entered into the connection string. For example, the code could be place in a button event on a Windows Form (which is actually where I tested it):

```
' Code to create and use a DataReader
' Module must also have the following lines
' in the declarations section:
'     Imports System.Data
```

```
'         Imports System.Data.ADO

' Create ADO connection and command objects
Dim sConnectionString As String = _
    "Provider=SQLOLEDB.1; User ID=sa; " & _
    "Initial Catalog=Northwind;Data Source=MYSERVER"
Dim myConnection As New ADOConnection(sConnectionString)
Dim myCommand As New ADOCommand("SELECT * FROM Customers", myConnection)

' Declare the DataReader
Dim myReader As ADODataReader

' Open the connection and stream data into the reader
Try
    MyConnection.Open()
    MyCommand.Execute(myReader)

    ' Check the data in the reader
    While (myReader.Read)
        Console.WriteLine("customer name: {0}", myReader("CompanyName"))
    End While

Catch myException As Exception
    MsgBox(myException.ToString())

Finally
    ' Close the connection and flush the reader
    If myConnection.State = Data.DBObjectState.Open Then
        MyConnection.Close()
    End If
    If Not myReader Is Nothing Then
        MyReader = Nothing
    End If
End Try
```

> If you have trouble making the code above work with a SQL Server 2000 installation, and the exception indicates an invalid login, you should check to make sure your SQL Server is configured to accept SQL Server logins such as the **sa** login above. It may be set to accept Windows logins only, because that is the default setting at installation. So, if you are on a freshly installed test machine (highly recommended, since VB.NET is beta one software), go to SQL Server's Enterprise Manager, right-click on the server name and select **Properties.** On the dialog that appears, click the **Security tab.** If the **Windows only** option is selected under **Authentication,** you will have to either: (1) change the option to **SQL Server and Windows;** or (2) change your connection string to use a Windows login.

Let's do a short walk-through on the code. First, the ADOConnection and ADOCommand objects are declared and initialized. Notice that the code uses the new ability in VB.NET to pass parameters to a class at instantiation. The equivalent code to declare a Connection object in VB6, for example, would require separate lines to declare the object and then pass in an initialization string.

While it is useful to understand how this code for creating `Connection` and `Command` objects works, you actually won't have to write much of it if you use the new component designer in VS.NET. An example later in the chapter covers the same operations using the component designer. In that example, there is no code typed in to create or manage the `Connection` or `Command` objects – it's all handled by the designer.

After the `Connection` and `Command` objects are created and initialized, the `DataReader` is declared. Then the connection is opened and data is streamed into the reader. This code also shows how exceptions generated during database operations are typically coded. More extensive discussion on handling exceptions is included later in the chapter.

Then a `While` loop is used to display the data in the `DataReader` to the console (which is accessed in Visual Studio.NET as the Output window):

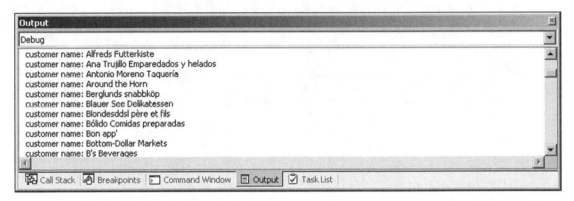

Note that, since the `DataReader` is forward-only, once the data is read in a loop like this, the `DataReader` has no more data in it to access. It must be reinitialized before being used again.

A new `DataReader` is positioned to a `Null` record until the `Read` method is executed for the first time. This contrasts with typical ADO logic in VB6, in which a new set of records is positioned at the first record by default. The main difference that this causes in code is that the `Read` method for the `DataReader` is accessed at the top of the `While` loop, where typical ADO logic would use a `MoveNext` just prior to the end of the loop.

After looping through all the records with the `DataReader`, the `Catch` structure takes care of exceptions, in this case by just displaying the error message in a message box. Then the `Finally` structure closes the database, if it is still open, and makes sure the `DataReader` object is set to `Nothing`.

Creating a DataSet

The code for creating a `DataSet` is similar in some respects to the `DataReader` code above, particularly in the section that creates the `ADOConnection` and `ADOCommand` objects. Here's the code:

```
' Code to create and use a DataSet
' Module must also have the following lines
' in the declarations section:
'     Imports System.Data
'     Imports System.Data.ADO

' Create ADO connection and command objects
```

```
Dim sConnectionString As String = _
    "Provider=SQLOLEDB.1; User ID=sa; " & _
    "Initial Catalog=Northwind;Data Source=MYSERVER"
Dim myConnection As New ADOConnection(sConnectionString)
Dim myCommand As New ADOCommand("SELECT * FROM Customers", myConnection)

' Here's where the code is different from the previous example. . .
Dim myDataSetCommand As New ADODataSetCommand(myCommand)

' Declare the DataSet named Example1
Dim myDataSet As New DataSet("Example1")

' Open the connection and put customer data
' into the DataSet as a table named Customers
Try
    MyConnection.Open()
    MyDataSetCommand.FillDataSet(myDataSet, "Customers")

    ' Check the data in the DataSet
    Dim rowCustomer As System.Data.DataRow
    For Each rowCustomer In MyDataSet.Tables("Customers").Rows
        Console.WriteLine("customer name: {0}", _
                        rowCustomer("CompanyName"))
    Next

Catch myException As Exception
    MessageBox.Show(myException.ToString())

Finally
    ' Close the connection and destroy the DataSet
    If myConnection.State = Data.DBObjectState.Open Then
        MyConnection.Close()
    End If
    If Not myDataSet Is Nothing Then
        myDataSet = Nothing
    End If
End Try
```

The code doesn't really show any differences until after the Connection and Command objects are created. To build a DataSet, there's a new step at this point. It is necessary to create a DataSetCommand object. This object is attached to the ADOCommand object created earlier. The DataSetCommand object has a FillDataSet method, which is used a few lines later.

After the DataSet is instantiated, the connection is opened and the DataSet is filled with a table. The name of the table is specified in the FillDataSet method as "Customers", but that designation is for the use of the programmer, and does not indicate the source of the data. The actual source of the data was established when the ADOCommand object was initialized (with a SQL statement selecting all the customers). The DataSetCommand object is associated with that ADOCommand object, so any operation done by the DataSetCommand object takes place on that customer data.

The section below contains more details on manipulating DataSets and also includes coverage of the process of using the DataSetCommand object to place data back in the original database.

Structure of a DataSet

The relational capabilities of a `DataSet` are implemented in the following object model:

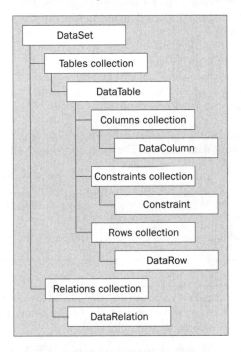

For a `DataSet` to be functional, it must contain at least one `DataTable` object in its `Tables` collection, and, to contain any data, the `Rows` collection of the `DataTable` must have some rows whose layout is described by the `Columns` collection. All the other elements of the object model are optional.

The relational structure and capabilities of the `DataSet` are described in the `Tables`, `Columns`, `Constraints`, and `Relations` collections. The layout of the tables, including information such as data types, is in `Tables` and `Columns`, the constraints for a particular table are in `Constraints`, and the relationships between tables are in `Relations`.

It's worth mentioning a potential point of confusion in comparison to previous data access models, such as DAO and ADO. With these models, no explicit `Rows` collection existed. Instead, a `Recordset` was positioned to a row (sometimes referred to as a record) using various methods of the `Recordset` (`MoveNext`, `MoveFirst`, `Seek`, etc.). Then the `Fields` collection (in DAO or ADO) or the `Columns` collection (in RDO) of the `Recordset` could be used to access data in that row.

In ADO.NET, each `DataTable` contains both a `Columns` collection and a `Rows` collection. The `Columns` collection is accessed to get or set schema information about the fields in each row. The `Rows` collection contains individual `DataRow` objects representing a row or data record in the table. Each `DataRow` has an `Item` property, indexed with column names from the `Columns` collection, to get to individual fields in the row. The syntax for getting information out of tables and rows is discussed in the section below called *Working with a DataSet*.

Let's go through the classes in the object model and gain a better understanding of what each one does.

DataTables

A DataTable object contains one table of in-memory data. It has a collection of columns that contain the schema for the table; the DataColumn class for columns is described in the next section. A DataTable also contains a Rows collection of DataRow objects. Each DataRow represents an individual data record. DataRows are also discussed below.

As we saw in the first code example on creating a DataSet, the ADOCommand object can create a DataTable's schema from a database automatically, and then add in the appropriate data into the table. Alternatively, a schema for the DataSet can be created in code, and then data added manually. To create the schema in code, the Columns collection is created (described below).

To add new rows to a DataTable, the NewRow method returns an object reference to a new row. Then each field (column) in the row can have data inserted. The NewRow method automatically adds the row to the Rows collection.

A DataTable can also contain a Constraints collection. The capabilities of constraints are discussed below.

DataTables have several useful properties and methods. Here are some examples:

Properties	
HasErrors	Indicates if there are errors in any of the rows in any of the tables in the DataSet to which the DataTable belongs (because of violation of constraints, for example).
PrimaryKey	Gets or sets an array of columns that make up a primary key for the DataTable.
Methods	
AcceptChanges	Accepts all changes made to the table since the last call of AcceptChanges (or since the table was loaded if this is the first call to AcceptChanges).
Clear	Clears the table of all data.
GetErrors	Returns a collection of DataRow objects that contain errors.
NewRow	Creates a new, empty DataRow with an appropriate structure for holding data from this DataTable, and returns a reference to it.
RejectChanges	Throws away all changes made to the table since it was loaded, or since the last time AcceptChanges was called.
Events	
ColumnChanging	Occurs when a data value in the DataTable is being changed. The event arguments specify the row being changed, the column within the row, and the new value being proposed.
RowChanging	Occurs when a DataRow is being changed in any way. Event arguments specify the action that is taking place and the row affected. The change can be cancelled by throwing an exception in this event.

Events	
RowChanged	Occurs after a DataRow has been changed. Same event arguments as RowChanging.
RowDeleting	Occurs when a DataRow is being about to be deleted. The deletion can be cancelled by throwing an exception in this event.
RowDeleted	Occurs after a DataRow has been deleted.

Remember that a DataTable must be declared using the WithEvents keywords to make events accessible.

DataColumns

The DataColumn represents a schema element for a field in a DataTable. A DataColumn object has a DataType property to hold the data type for the column. Behavior of the column can be set with properties such as AllowNull, Unique, and ReadOnly.

A DataColumn can be set to automatically insert an incremented value for the column in new rows, similar to an Identity column in SQL Server or a Counter field in Access. The AutoIncrement property turns this feature on, and the AutoIncrementSeed and AutoIncrementStep properties control where the value starts and how it is incremented.

Most columns will hold simple data values, but a column can also be set to hold an expression that calculates a value based on other columns. For example, a column could be created in a Recordset to hold WholeSalePrice, which is calculated from a SuggestedRetailPrice column and a WholesaleDiscount column. The code would look like this:

```
MyTable.Columns("WholeSalePrice").Expression = _
        "SuggestedRetailPrice * (WholeSaleDiscount / 100)"
```

DataRows

As previously discussed, the DataRow contains actual data values (in contrast to the DataColumn which contains only schema information). The Item property of the DataRow class is indexed on the column name (which is taken from the DataColumn object for a column). So, if we have a DataColumn object named FirstName, then, for a particular DataRow, the value in the FirstName column can be fetched with code like this:

```
sFirstName = MyDataRow.Item("FirstName")
```

However, the Item property is the default property for a DataRow, and it is an indexed property, so the following syntax is also permitted:

```
sFirstName = MyDataRow("FirstName")
```

The columns can also be accessed by their numerical index. If the DataColumn for FirstName had a numerical index of 4 in the DataTable, then the following code would also work:

```
sFirstName = MyDataRow(4)
```

Changing Data in a Row

`DataRows` can be changed by simply accessing the columns and setting values. For small, routine changes, this is the simplest way to get changes into a `DataTable`. The code is just the reverse of the example above:

```
MyDataRow("FirstName") = sFirstName
```

However, each such change generates an event and this may be undesirable. Besides the performance problems, if the event performs some validation that depends on other columns, and the other columns have not been set yet, the validation will fail.

To take care of this, the row can be placed in an editing mode. While in the editing mode, no events or validation will be performed. Events and validation will only take place when the editing mode is exited. Here are the methods that control the editing mode:

Method	Description
BeginEdit	Starts editing the row. (Not present in ADO – a row is available for edit when it becomes the current row in an ADO `Recordset`.)
CancelEdit	Cancels editing the row and throws away any changes made. Similar to `CancelUpdate` in ADO.
EndEdit	Commits the changes to the row and ends editing on it. Similar to the `Update` method in ADO.

There is a big difference in the way these changes work compared to a `Recordset` in ADO. In a `Recordset`, the comparable methods are executed for the current row in that `Recordset`. This means that, in traditional ADO, only one row at a time can be in an edit state. In an ADO.NET `DataTable`, each row is a separate entity and can be treated separately from any other rows. That means it is possible to have several rows in an editing state at once.

In addition to the option to set the edit state for rows individually, the `AcceptChanges` method of a `DataTable` does an implicit `EndEdit` on each row.

Examining Different Versions of Data in a Row

One of the most important capabilities of the `DataRow` class is to expose various versions for the data in a row. This allows considerable latitude in the logic that edits or commits changes for rows. Versions of data in a `DataRow` can include:

Method	Description
Current	The current data in the row, as of the last time changes to the row were accepted or rejected.
Default	The original default values in the row. These are the values that would be in a row when it had just been created by a `NewRow` method on the `DataTable`.
Original	The data in the row when the table was first added to the `DataSet`, or the data in the row after the last time an `AcceptChanges` was done on the `DataTable`. (Note that an `AcceptChanges` on the `DataRow` does not affect the `Original` version of the data – it just puts the `Proposed` value into the `Current` value.)

Method	Description
Proposed	The row has some new data that has not been committed with an AcceptChanges method on the DataTable or the individual DataRow. Such data can be rolled back with a RejectChanges method on the DataTable or DataRow and returned to its previous value.

At any given time, a particular row may have data in more than one of these versions. That is, a given row may simultaneously have an Original version of its data, a Current version, and a Proposed version.

For a column in the row, the value for each version is obtained using an optional parameter of the Item property. To get the proposed value in a FirstName column for example, the line of code would look like this:

```
sFirstName = MyDataRow("FirstName", DataRowVersion.Proposed)
```

However, this will generate an error, as the data version requested does not exist in the row. To check the versions that are available for the row, the DataRow's HasVersion method is used. There are various circumstances under which a data version may not exist. For example, the Proposed version of data only exists in a row after changes to the row have been made but not accepted with an AcceptChanges method.

Here is code to look at a row and check for new, proposed data within it. If the row has proposed data that is different from the original data in the row in the FirstName field, then the changes will be accepted. But if the proposed data in FirstName is the same as the original data in FirstName, the editing will be cancelled.

```
If MyRow.HasVersion(DataRowVersion.Proposed)
  Then
    If MyRow("FirstName", DataRowVersion.Current) = _
          MyRow("FirstName", DataRowVersion.Proposed)
      Then
        MsgBox("FirstName is unchanged - edit cancelled")
        MyRow.CancelEdit
      Else
        MyRow.AcceptChanges
    End If
Else
  MsgBox("Row has no proposed data")
End If
```

Constraints

The Constraints collection of a DataTable contains a set of objects that describe constraints for working with data in the DataTable. There are two constraint classes, ForeignKeyConstraint and UniqueConstraint.

A ForeignKeyConstraint object must be set with:

❏ The related DataTable that the foreign key points to

❏ The column(s) containing the foreign keys in the DataTable that contains this constraint

❏ What action is to be taken if the constraint is violated

289

The other type of constraint class is UniqueContstraint. It is much simpler. It is only necessary to set the columns in the `DataTable` that must contain unique values by associating them to a `UniqueContraint` constraint.

DataRelations

Relations are associated with the `DataSet` as a whole. Each `DataRelation` object in the `Relations` collection contains information linking two `DataTables` in the `DataSet`'s `Tables` collection. The `DataTables` are linked by specifying a column in each table for the linkage, very much like associated a primary and foreign key when specifying a relationship in a relational database.

The relationship is a parent-child relationship. A typical example would be a parent `Customers` table related to a child `Orders` table. That is, for each row in the `Customers` table, there would be zero, one, or many related records in the `Orders` table for that particular customer. In this case, the `Customers` table might have a primary key named `CustomerID`, and the `Orders` table might have a foreign key with the same name. Here is a code example to specify such a relationship for a `DataSet`:

```
Dim ParentColumn As DataColumn
Dim ChildColumn As DataColumn
ParentColumn = MyDataSet.Tables("Customers").Columns("CustomerID")
ChildColumn = MyDataSet.Tables("Orders").Columns("CustomerID")

' Ready to create the DataRelation object
' and add it to the Relations collection
Dim relCustomerToOrders As New DataRelation("CustomersToOrders", _
        ParentColumn, ChildColumn)
MyDataSet.Relations.Add(relCustomerToOrders)
```

Notice that the parameters used to create the relation are the name of the relation (which can be anything desired by the programmer), the correct column reference in the parent table, and the correct column reference in the child table. Both columns must have the same data type.

Once such a relationship is specified, it is possible to get individual orders associated with a particular customer record. We covered pseudo-code to do that very early in this chapter. Now that we have covered some actual syntax for ADO.NET, we are ready to translate that pseudo-code into actual VB.NET code:

```
Dim rowCustomer As System.Data.DataRow
Dim rowOrder As System.Data.DataRow

For Each rowCustomer In DataSet.Tables("Customers").Rows
    ' Work with header information for customer, like this
    Console.WriteLine(rowCustomer("CompanyName"))

    ' Now get orders associated with the customer
    For Each rowOrder In rowCustomer.GetChildRows("CustomersToOrders")
        Console.WriteLine(rowOrder("OrderDate"))
    Next

Next
```

This kind of logic is significantly cleaner than any equivalent functionality in traditional ADO. The sections for dealing with customer header information and for dealing with individual order information are cleanly separated, and easy to manage.

Note that the `DataSet` could have another relationship defined to connect a parent `Orders` table to a child `OrderDetails` table. Then a `For Each` loop for order details could be nested inside the `For Each` loop for orders.

Working with a DataSet

We've discussed the fact that accessing data with a `DataSet` is simpler and more consistent than accessing `Recordsets` in ADO. In this section we will look at how to work with `DataSets` to accomplish common programming tasks.

It's important to understand that the simpler model of ADO.NET removes a lot of the concepts experienced ADO developers might expect. The idea of different types of cursor (forward-only vs. client vs. server) is missing in `DataSets`, eliminating confusion over which cursor to choose for a given situation. And regardless of the location of the `DataSet` (local, remote, in a client browser, etc.), the full object model of the `DataSet` is available.

However, it's worthwhile noting that ADO.NET does not contain equivalent functionality to a server-side cursor. For design situations that require such functionality, the traditional ADO library syntax (accessed through a .NET wrapper) must be used.

Creating a DataSet Manually

Since the entire object model of ADO.NET is exposed, it is possible to create and work with a `DataSet` manually, totally divorced from any database server. Here is a code example that creates a simple `DataSet`, adds a single table to it, and adds a couple of columns for the table:

```
' Create DataSet
Dim MyDataSet As New DataSet("ManualDataSet")

' Create a new DataTable and add it to the DataSet
Dim tblDataTable As New DataTable("SampleTable")
MyDataSet.Tables.Add(tblDataTable)

' Create two columns for the table, set their properties
' and add them to the Columns collection for the table
Dim colDataColumn As New DataColumn("FirstColumn")
colDataColumn.DataType = System.Type.GetType("System.String")
colDataColumn.DefaultValue = "Default"
tblDataTable.Columns.Add(colDataColumn)

Dim colDataColumn2 As New DataColumn("SecondColumn")
colDataColumn2.DataType = System.Type.GetType("System.Int32")
tblDataTable.Columns.Add(colDataColumn2)

' Create a DataRow, add it to the table, and set its values
Dim rowMyDataRow As DataRow
rowMyDataRow = MyDataSet.Tables("SampleTable").NewRow
MyDataSet.Tables("SampleTable").Rows.Add(rowMyDataRow)
rowMyDataRow("FirstColumn") = "New text"
rowMyDataRow("SecondColumn") = 10000
MyDataSet.AcceptChanges()
```

```
' Loop through the rows and display values
Dim rowDataRow As DataRow
For Each rowDataRow In MyDataSet.Tables("SampleTable").Rows
    MsgBox(rowDataRow.Item("FirstColumn").ToString & " - " & _
           CStr(rowDataRow("SecondColumn"))),,"Show data")
Next
```

Walking through the code, we begin by creating a new `DataSet` with the name `ManualDataSet`. Then a new `DataTable` named `SampleTable` is created and added to the `DataSet`. At this point the table has no columns.

The next section creates two columns for the `DataTable` and sets their properties. Setting the `Default` property for the first column is actually optional, but is included as an example of the possibilities. Actually, the only property that must be set for a column is `DataType`. After each column is created and initialized, it is added to the `Columns` collection of the `DataTable` named `SampleTable`.

Then a single `DataRow` is created. Notice that it is necessary to create the `DataRow` with the `NewRow` method of the `DataTable` to get the proper structure (schema) of the row. However, the `NewRow` method *does not* add the row automatically to the `Rows` collection. This must be done explicitly.

Finally, code is included to loop through the `Rows` collection (in which there is only one row at this point) and display the value of the two columns in each row. If this code is run, the result should be a message box that displays the string **New text – 10000**.

At this point, any manipulation of the `DataSet` can be carried out. For example, one of the columns in the table could be set to be a primary key, or a constraint could be added to make a column only accept unique values.

Creating a DataSet from a Database

While it may occasionally be useful to construct a `DataSet` manually, as in the above example, the typical way is to extract the data from a database with a managed provider. We covered a brief example of this operation early in the chapter. That example included code to manually create a connection to the database, create an `ADOCommand` object, and use it to copy a table from the database into a `DataSet`.

Windows Form Example

As an alternative to doing all of this manually, VS.NET offers a visual component designer that can handle a lot of the routine coding. Let's step through an exercise that uses the designer to create a component that creates and exposes a `DataSet`. Our `DataSet` will be taken from the `Northwind` sample database in SQL Server, with its `Customers` and `Orders` tables. The `DataSet` will contain a set of customers and their related orders.

For simplicity, the exercise will use a bound DataGrid in a Windows Form to allow access to the `DataSet` for viewing and changing data.

Begin by creating a new Windows Application project in VS.NET and then select **Project | Add Component** to add a new **Component Class** to the project. Name it **CustomerOrders**.

In the Toolbox, select the Data tab. Drag an ADODataSetCommand on to the design surface of the component.

A wizard to configure the ADODataSetCommand control will begin. Press the Next button. You will be asked to select a connection. The connection you need probably does not exist yet, so press the New Connection button:

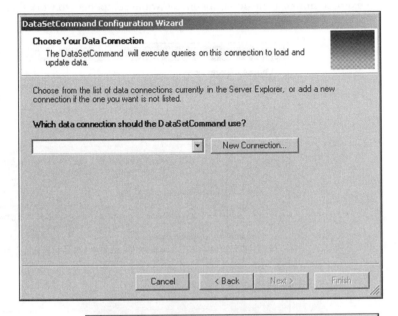

A dialog to configure a connection will appear. Enter information as appropriate on the Connection tab. A finished form will look something like this, though your server name will have to be substituted and you may use different login information:

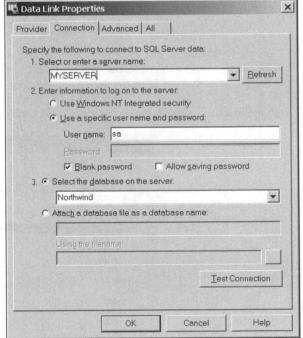

Press the Test Connection button to see if you have correctly configured the connection. If you are having trouble getting a connection to work, take care of that before proceeding with the exercise. Once the connection has been configured correctly, press the OK button to create the connection.

Press the Next button on the wizard to proceed to the next window, which is to Choose a Query Type. There are three options. The default is to Use SQL statement and we will take this option to keep the exercise simple. (The other options allow the component to work through stored procedures, either by specifying ones that already exist or by having the wizard create new ones.)

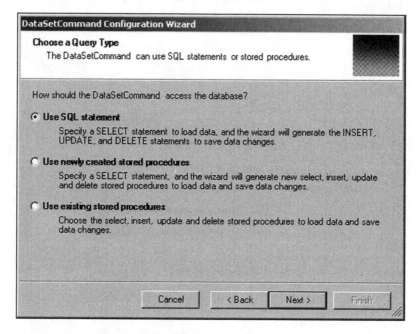

Press the Next button. The following screen allows you to choose the SQL that will be used to specify the data to be fetched by the ADODataSetCommand control. The SQL can be typed in manually, but it's easier to use the SQL Builder. Press the SQL Builder button.

On the first dialog that appears, select the Customers table, press the Add button, and then press Close:

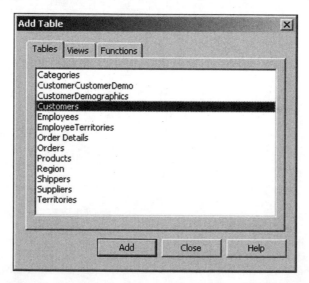

The resulting screen looks like this:

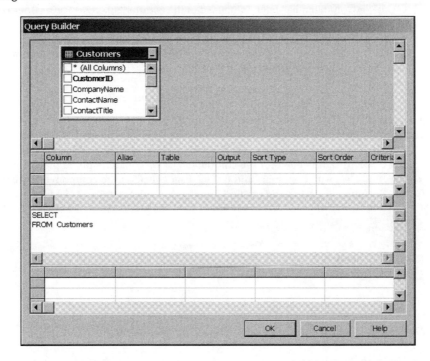

You have almost certainly worked with query construction screens like this before, probably in Access. In the box at the top, containing the listing of columns in the Customers table, check the following: CustomerID, CompanyName, and Phone. Notice that the SQL to get these fields is automatically generated. After checking off the columns, press the OK button.

The following screen displays a summary of the generated SQL:

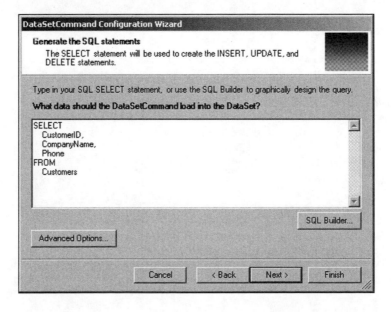

Confirm this by pressing **Next** and then the **Finish** button. Looking at VS.NET's design surface now, you can see that the ADODataSetCommand has been initialized in the component as ADODataSetCommand1, and the connection has been initialized as ADOConnection1.

Drag another ADODataSetCommand onto the component design surface. Go through the wizard again for this ADODataSetCommand, with the following differences:

❏ There is no need to define the connection – just select the existing Northwind connection.

❏ In the **SQL Builder**, select the following columns from the Orders table: OrderID, CustomerID, and OrderDate.

Now ADODataSetCommand2 is defined for the component class. We are ready to place a method in the component to fill a DataSet with customers and orders. Right-click on the component design surface and select **View Code**. Then type the following method into the CustomerOrders class:

```
Public Function FillPurchaseOrdersDataSet() As DataSet

    ' declare a new DataSet
    Dim myDataSet As New DataSet()

    ' Open a connection and use the DataSetCommand
    ' objects to put two tables in the DataSet.
    ' Close the connection when done.
    Try
        ADOConnection1.Open()
        ADODataSetCommand1.FillDataSet(myDataSet, "Customers")
        ADODataSetCommand2.FillDataSet(myDataSet, "Orders")
    Catch eFillException As System.Exception
        MsgBox(eFillException.ToString)
        'TODO: Handle errors here
    Finally
        ADOConnection1.Close()
    End Try

    ' Add a relation between the tables
    Try
        myDataSet.Relations.Add("CustomerOrders", _
        myDataSet.Tables("Customers").Columns("CustomerID"), _
        myDataSet.Tables("Orders").Columns("CustomerID"))
    Catch eException As System.Exception
        MsgBox(eException.ToString)
        'TODO: Handle errors here
    End Try

    ' We're done - return the DataSet
    Return (myDataSet)
End Function
```

Go to the design surface for Form1. Select the **Win Forms** tab in the **Toolbox**. Drag a Button and a DataGrid onto the form.

Set the Text property of the Button to **Get Data**. Position the DataGrid at the bottom of the form and set its Anchor property to BottomLeftRight (Chapter 4 on Windows Forms discusses the Anchor property and how to set it). The layout of the form should now look something like this:

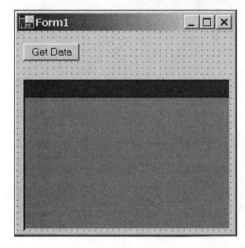

Right click on the form and select **View Code**. Add the following two Imports statements:

```
Imports System.Data
Imports System.Data.ADO
```

Go back to the form's design surface. Double-click the button to get to its Click event code. Insert the following:

```
Protected Sub Button1_Click(ByVal sender As Object, _
                            ByVal e As System.EventArgs)

    Dim objCustomerOrders As New CustomerOrders()

    Dim MyDataSet As DataSet

    MyDataSet = objCustomerOrders.FillPurchaseOrdersDataSet()

    DataGrid1.DataSource = MyDataSet

End Sub
```

Now run the project. The form will appear. Press the button. After a delay to access the data, a box with a plus sign should appear in the DataGrid. At this point, the DataGrid is loaded. If this did not work, you should have received a message box with information on the error, which probably is due to a typo in the code.

Press the plus sign in the DataGrid. Then choose **Customers**. From that point, you can play around with the DataGrid, trying different displays of customers and their orders.

By now, the DataSet is created and placed in the grid and, since the DataGrid is bound to the DataSet, any changes typed into the grid are placed into the DataSet.

However, at this stage, there is no code to move the changes from the `DataSet` back into the database. Let's do that next.

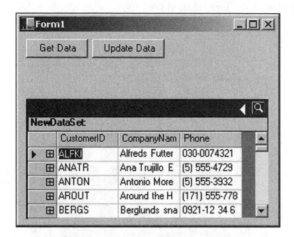

Close the running project by closing the form. Go to the code window for the `CustomerOrders` component and add the following method to the class:

```
Public Sub UpdateDataSet(ByVal updatedDataSet As DataSet)

    Try
        ' This updates the customers table
        ADODataSetCommand1.Update(updatedDataSet)

        ' This updates the orders table
        ADODataSetCommand2.Update(updatedDataSet)

    Catch eException As System.Exception
        Throw eException
    End Try
End Sub
```

We don't really expect any errors, either here or in the calling routine, but it's good practice to "catch" errors in a component like this and "throw" them to the calling application if an error does occur. Place another button on the form beside the existing one. Set its `Text` property to **Update Data**. Double-click the new button to get to its `Click` event. Place the following code inside:

```
Dim objCustomerOrders As New CustomerOrders()
Dim MyDataSet As DataSet

MyDataSet = CType(DataGrid1.DataSource, DataSet)

objCustomerOrders.UpdateDataSet(MyDataSet)
```

> *The* `CType` *function in the third line of code is only necessary if you have* `Option Strict` *turned on for the project.* `Option Strict` *is on by default when VS.NET beta one is installed. It can be turned off by right-clicking on the project in the* **Solution Explorer,** *and going to the* **Common Properties | Build** *category on the property page.*

Run the program. As before, press the **Get Data** button. When the data is loaded into the DataGrid, go to **Orders** and change the first **OrderDate**. Then press the **Update Data** button. The changed data will be saved to the database. (You can test to see that the changes in the grid are only saved if the **Update Data** button is pressed.)

There is an important item to note about the code used in this example. The component is completely stateless. It is created when needed, and can be destroyed as soon as it has carried out its operation. This makes the component completely suitable for use in a web application as well as with a Windows Form. Creating such stateless components is easy with ADO.NET because the `DataSet` contains all the data information needed, rendering it unnecessary for a data component to hold any state or maintain any connections.

Web Forms Example

Creating a Web Forms version of this example is straight forward, although there are differences because the Web Forms DataGrid is not as flexible as the Windows Form DataGrid. The Web Forms DataGrid does not support in-place editing so this example is read-only. Also, the Web Forms DataGrid can only be bound to one table at a time by using a DataView, and cannot be hierarchical. Some of these limitations may change in beta two.

To make a Web Forms version, follow the exact steps above except for the following differences:

❑   Open a new Web Application project instead of a Windows Application this time.

❑   Place one Button (instead of two) and a DataGrid control on the designer, dragging them off the **Web Forms** tab in the Toolbox.

❑   In the `Click` event for the button, the code needs to change a little. It should look like this:

```
Dim objCustomerOrders As New CustomerOrders()

Dim MyDataSet As DataSet
Dim rowCustomer As System.Data.DataRow
Dim rowOrder As System.Data.DataRow

MyDataSet = objCustomerOrders.FillPurchaseOrdersDataSet()
```

```
' Server controls cannot bind to a DataSet or DataTable in beta one.
' Must bind to a DataView instead. DataViews are explained below.
' This code creates a DataView from the Customers table and binds it
' to the data grid.
DataGrid1.DataSource = New DataView(MyDataSet.Tables("Customers"))
DataGrid1.DataBind()
```

Rather than rebuilding the component from scratch, you can copy and paste it from the Windows Form example above.

The running application will look like this in Internet Explorer:

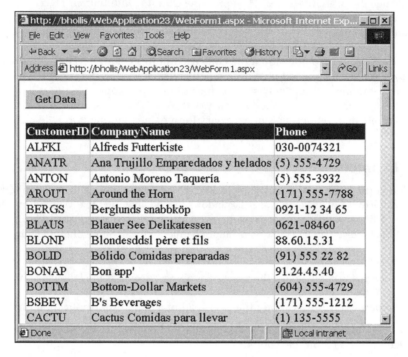

Chapter 10 contains some more advanced examples that use many of these same techniques, but add such capabilities as specifying select criteria for the `DataSet`.

Using DataViews

We've already seen that `DataSets` are very flexible. The concept of `DataViews` adds another layer of flexibility in ADO.NET.

A `DataView` is a `DataTable` with filtering and/or sorting applied. The `DataView` can be set to return subsets of the rows in the original `DataTable` and to specify the sorting order for the rows.

One common use of `DataViews` is to provide for databinding to controls, particularly in Web Forms. We used a `DataView` in our previous example to bind data to a DataGrid in a Web Form. (A Web Form DataGrid cannot bind directly to a `DataSet` because it cannot hold hierarchical data.)

Another use of `DataViews` is to provide multiple, simultaneous views of the same data in different controls. For example, one grid on a form could hold all rows in a table, while another grid simultaneously displays only deleted rows or only changed rows. Editing the rows in either control would cause the underlying data in the `DataTable` to be changed, and would then affect the data in the other control when it was refreshed.

Creating a new `DataView` for a given `DataTable` is done by declaring the `DataView` and passing a reference to the desired `DataTable` into the `DataView` constructor – like this:

```
Dim MyNewDataView As New DataView(MyDataSet.Tables("Customers"))
```

When first created like this, the `DataView` defaults to all the rows in the `DataSet`. Properties are available for getting a subset of the rows into the `DataView`, or for sorting it, and these are covered below. These properties can be changed on the fly to dynamically alter the output of a `DataSet`.

Getting a Subset of Data into a DataView

Getting a subset of data is done with the `RowFilter` property and/or the `RowStateFilter` property of the `DataView` class. The `RowFilter` property is used by supplying an expression to filter with. For example, for our `DataView` defined just above for the `Customers` table, we could set the `DataView` to only return customers with company names beginning with the letter "A" by using this code:

```
MyNewDataView.RowFilter = "CompanyName Like 'A*'"
```

`RowFilter` expressions can be quite complex, and may include arithmetic computations and comparisons involving various columns in the data and constants.

The `RowStateFilter` works differently. It has defined values that fetch specific subsets of the data in the `DataTable`. Here are the available settings for `RowStateFilter`:

Settings	Description
CurrentRows	Shows current rows including unchanged, new, and modified rows, but leaving out deleted rows.
Deleted	Shows deleted rows. Note that a row is only considered deleted if the `Delete` method of the `DataTable` or `DataView` was used to delete it. Removing rows from the `Rows` collection will not mark them as deleted.
ModifiedCurrent	Shows rows with a current version of data that is different from the original data in the row.
ModifiedOriginal	Shows modified rows, but displays them with the original version of the data (even if the rows have been changed and have another current version of the data in them). Note that the current version of data in these same rows is available with the `ModifiedCurrent` setting.
New	Shows new rows. These are rows added with the `AddNew` method of the `DataView`.
None	Shows no rows at all. Could be used initially on a `DataView` for a control before the user has chosen viewing options.
OriginalRows	Shows all rows with their original data version, including unchanged and deleted rows.
Unchanged	Shows rows that have not been changed.

These settings can be combined in various combinations by adding them together when setting the `RowStateFilter` property. For example, this line of code causes the `DataView` to expose only new rows and deleted rows:

```
MyNewDataView.RowStateFilter = DataViewRowState.New + _
                      DataViewRowState.Deleted
```

Sorting a DataView

The `Sort` property of a `DataView` takes a string that describes the desired sorting. Sorting can be done on one or more columns, and each column can be sorted in ascending or descending order. The string to specify the sorting should contain a column name, optionally followed by the letters `ASC` for ascending or `DESC` for descending. The default is ascending.

For multiple column sorting, the string should have a comma after the first column, and then another column name followed by `ASC` or `DESC`. This can be repeated for as many columns as needed. Here is an example:

```
MyNewDataView.Sort = "PostalCode DESC, CompanyName ASC"
```

This would sort the rows in the `DataView` first by `PostalCode` (called zip code in the US) in descending order. Then, within a given `PostalCode`, the rows would be sorted in ascending order of `CompanyName`.

Typed DataSets

Data is normally accessed in traditional ADO using indexes on collections in the object model. All the examples in ADO.NET we've covered up to now also use this syntax. Here's an example from earlier in the chapter illustrating the syntax, with some lines removed to simplify the example:

```
Dim rowCustomer As System.Data.DataRow

For Each rowCustomer In DataSet.Tables("Customers").Rows
    Console.WriteLine(rowCustomer("CompanyName"))
Next
```

This syntax works well but it has a couple of drawbacks. It's a bit difficult to read, and it does not check the index values used in the collections for misspellings at compile time. If the second line of code here has "Customers" misspelled as "Cutsomers", that generates a run time error, not a compile time error.

A more intuitive syntax for the above access might look like the following:

```
Dim rowCustomer As System.Data.DataRow

For Each rowCustomer In DataSet.Customers.Rows
    Console.WriteLine(rowCustomer.CompanyName)
Next
```

With ADO.NET, it is possible to create a variation on a `DataSet` that does support such syntax. Such a `DataSet` is called a **typed DataSet**. These are specially subclassed `DataSets` generated by the data designer tool in VS.NET, and they have a schema attached to provide the information to do the typing. The schema can be automatically generated from the source database, or can be attached from an existing XML schema document.

Typed `DataSets` support the easier, more intuitive syntax above (called strongly-typed syntax). Errors in the syntax caused by misspellings are detected at compile time rather than run time. The syntax support includes IntelliSense and auto-completion on the syntax elements. This means that when you access a collection of tables in a `DataSet`, you get a pop up list of all the available tables, rather than struggling to remember the table name you created a few days ago.

Let's step through an example creating such a `DataSet`, and then go through some code that uses strongly-typed syntax.

In VS.NET, bring up the project that you created for the *Windows Form Example* in the *Creating a DataSet from a Database* section above.

Bring up the design surface for the component (`CustomerOrders.vb`). Right-click on the design surface and select the menu option **Generate DataSet**. A dialog box will appear that requests the name of the `DataSet` class, and a check box that says **Add an instance of this class to the designer**. Enter the name **TypedCustomerOrders** in the text box and place a check mark in the check box. The typed `DataSet` will automatically use the `DataSetCommand` objects already on the form to construct a schema that relates customers and orders.

> **Beta one bug warning: Several dialog boxes, including the one used to add TypedCustomerOrders to the designer, have cosmetic problems on systems with a desktop set to "Large Fonts". If you are using large fonts in your desktop, you will only be able to see the top edge of the OK button. In that case, after entering the name and checking the checkbox, press the *Enter* key on the keyboard to activate the OK button.**

The design surface will have a new element named `TypedCustomerOrders1`. The project will also now have a `TypedCustomerOrders.xsd` file in the Solution Explorer. The `.xsd` file is the XML template file (sometimes called an XSD template). You can open it up if you wish and examine the XML created to define the template.

Right-click on the design surface for the component, and select **View Code**. Enter the following code into the component's code module:

```
Public Sub TestTypedDataSet()

    Try
        ADOConnection1.Open()
        ADODataSetCommand1.FillDataSet(TypedCustomerOrders1, "Customers")
        ADODataSetCommand2.FillDataSet(TypedCustomerOrders1, "Orders")
    Catch eFillException As System.Exception
        MsgBox(eFillException.ToString)
        'TODO: Handle errors here
    Finally
        ADOConnection1.Close()
    End Try

    Dim rowDataRow As TypedCustomerOrders.CustomersRow
    For Each rowDataRow In TypedCustomerOrders1.Customers.Rows
        Console.WriteLine("customer name: {0}", rowDataRow.CompanyName)
    Next

End Sub
```

On the Windows Form, place a new button and change its `Text` property to **Test Typed DataSet**. Double-click the button and enter the following code in the button's `Click` event:

```
Dim objCustomerOrders As New CustomerOrders()
objCustomerOrders.TestTypedDataSet()
```

Run the project and press the **Test Typed DataSet** button. You will see the customer names listed in the Output window, just as in some previous examples.

The important thing to note about this example is the last four lines of code in the `TestTypedDataSet` subroutine. These lines used strongly-typed syntax instead of indexed collections in the object model. All of the tables and columns of the `DataSet` are similarly available using strongly-typed object syntax.

Exception Classes for ADO.NET

The .NET Framework includes a base class for exceptions – the `System.Exception` class. It has some general features for containing error information. The .NET Framework also includes a number of classes derived from `System.Exception` that have additional capabilities for special circumstances.

ADO.NET includes two of these exception classes. The `ADOException` class contains exceptions resulting from use of the ADO Managed Provider, and the `SQLException` class contains exceptions resulting from use of the SQL Managed Provider. In addition to the capabilities supported by the generic `Exception` class, these classes also have an `Errors` collection to hold multiple errors (whereas the generic `Exception` class only holds one error).

You can use the capabilities of these classes to gain more precise control over errors in a `Try ... Catch ... Finally` construct, and to print out error information. For example, instead of using the generic `Exception` class in the `Catch` statement (as we have done in examples throughout this chapter), you can use code with multiple `Catch` clauses instead. Each `Catch` clause checks for a different type of exception. The general structure of such a `Try ... Catch ... Finally` code block would look like this:

```
Try
    ' Some ADO.NET data handling logic goes here
Catch MyADOException As ADOException
    ' do error handling on ADO exceptions here
Catch MyGeneralException As Exception
    ' do error handling on any other exceptions here
Finally
    ' wrap up code goes here
End Try
```

You can also have special routines to log or print information from the ADO.NET exception classes. Here is a routine to print errors out of an `ADOException` instance:

```
Public Sub DisplayADOErrors(ByVal myADOException As ADOException)
    Dim iIndex As Integer
    Dim sErrorSummary As String
    Dim sCrLf As String = CStr(Chr(13)) & CStr(Chr(10))

    sErrorSummary = "Error generated by object " & _
                    myADOException.Source.ToString
```

```
        For iIndex = 0 To myADOException.Errors.Count - 1
            sErrorSummary = sErrorSummary & sCrLf & "Index #" & iIndex & _
                " - Error: " + myADOException.Errors(iIndex).ToString()
        Next iIndex

        MsgBox(sErrorSummary)
    End Sub
```

It is recommend practice to use these exception classes in your code whenever doing database access through the ADO.NET managed providers.

Accessing XML through ADO.NET

Since DataSets are based internally on XML, it is relatively straightforward to create a DataSet from a valid XML document. The DataSet method to do this is ReadXML. Here is an exercise that uses an XML document to create a DataSet. It is similar to a part of the previous exercise that created a DataSet from a database, emphasizing the commonality of these situations.

Open your favorite text editor or XML editor, and enter the following XML document. If you have a small, valid XML document with hierarchical data in it, you can use that instead. Save the document as xmltest.xml.

```
<root>
<Customer>
    <CompanyName>Northern Access, Ltd</CompanyName>
    <Order>
        <OrderDate>12-19-2000</OrderDate>
        <ShipVia>UPS</ShipVia>
    </Order>
    <Order>
        <OrderDate>01-07-2001</OrderDate>
        <ShipVia>FedEx</ShipVia>
    </Order>
</Customer>
<Customer>
    <CompanyName>Southern Access, Inc.</CompanyName>
    <Order>
        <OrderDate>12-22-2000</OrderDate>
        <ShipVia>UPS</ShipVia>
    </Order>
</Customer>
</root>
```

Start a new Windows Application in Visual Studio.NET.

Go to the design surface for Form1. Select the Win Forms tab in the Toolbox. Drag a button and a DataGrid onto the form.

Set the `Text` property of the button to **Get Data**. Position the DataGrid at the bottom of the form, and set its `Anchor` property to `BottomLeftRight` (Chapter 4 on Windows Forms discusses the `Anchor` property and how to set it). The layout of the form should now look something like this:

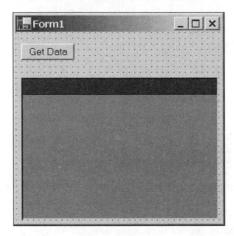

Right click on the form, and select **View Code**. Place the following two lines at the top of the code for the form, just under the other `Imports` statements:

```
Imports System.Data
Imports System.Data.ADO
```

Go back to the form's design surface. Double-click the button to get to its `Click` event code. Insert the following logic in the `Click` event, substituting your own location for your XML file created earlier:

```
Dim MyXMLDataSet As New DataSet("XMLDataSet")
MyXMLDataSet.ReadXml("C:\TEMP\xmltest.xml") ' substitute your path here

DataGrid1.DataSource = MyXMLDataSet
```

Now run the project. The form will come up. Press the button. A box with a plus sign should appear in the DataGrid. At this point the DataGrid is loaded. As before, you can now navigate the hierarchical `DataSet` in the DataGrid.

At this point, the `DataSet` is created and placed in the grid, and since the DataGrid is bound to the `DataSet`, any changes typed into the grid are placed into the `DataSet`. As with the earlier example, those changes are not automatically placed back in the XML file. However, you can create another button with the following code in it to save the data:

```
Dim MyXmlDataSet As DataSet
MyXMLDataSet = CType(DataGrid1.DataSource, DataSet)
MyXMLDataSet.WriteXml("C:\TEMP\xmltest.xml")
```

Of course, you can save the XML data to any file, not just the one you originally got it from.

Note that while the data is in the `DataSet`, you can manipulate it with any of the `DataSet` syntax covered earlier in the chapter. You can add rows, add columns, change data items, etc. The saved XML will then contain all of these changes.

Accessing XML through the DOM

Manipulating XML data through ADO.NET (as in the example above) is quite a bit simpler than many of the alternatives, such as using the XML Document Object Model (DOM). The ADO.NET syntax is consistent with other data manipulation code, making it unnecessary to learn a different, more complex object model for routine manipulation of XML data.

However, XML is used for a lot of different purposes other than simple ADO-like data manipulation, and not all XML data is easily accessed through the relational model used in a `DataSet`. So the .NET Framework also includes the ability to work with XML through the DOM.

The System.XML Namespace

All of the classes to work with XML outside ADO.NET are in the `System.XML` namespace. The technology in `System.XML` is the replacement for (and descended from) the MSXML libraries that are distributed with recent versions of Internet Explorer.

Manipulating XML through the DOM is beyond the scope of this book. Complete books have been written on how to do it in VB6. If you already understand such programming, you can tackle doing it through `System.XML`. The object models in the `System.XML` namespace have a fair amount of similarity to the object models in MSXML.

Summary

This chapter has covered the basics of doing data access using ADO.NET. The central idea of a `DataSet` has been extensively discussed. If you understand what a `DataSet` is, how to create one, how to manipulate one, and how to save the results, you are well on your way to being proficient at data access in VB.NET.

In particular, in this chapter we have looked at:

- ❑ The role of a managed provider in connecting to a database, streaming data from a database, examining `DataSets` for changes that should be recorded in the database, and raising errors during data resolution.

- ❑ The `DataReader` object and its similarity to the `Recordset` object in ADO.

- ❑ Working with `DataSets` and the `DataTable`, `DataColumn`, `DataRow`, `DataRelation`, and `DataView` objects.

- ❑ Working with typed `DataSets` to create easier and more intuitive syntax in your code.

- ❑ Querying the exception classes to catch errors and print out error information.

- ❑ Accessing XML data with ADO.NET.

In the next chapter we will discuss advanced topics such as deployment and building middle-tier components in VB.NET.

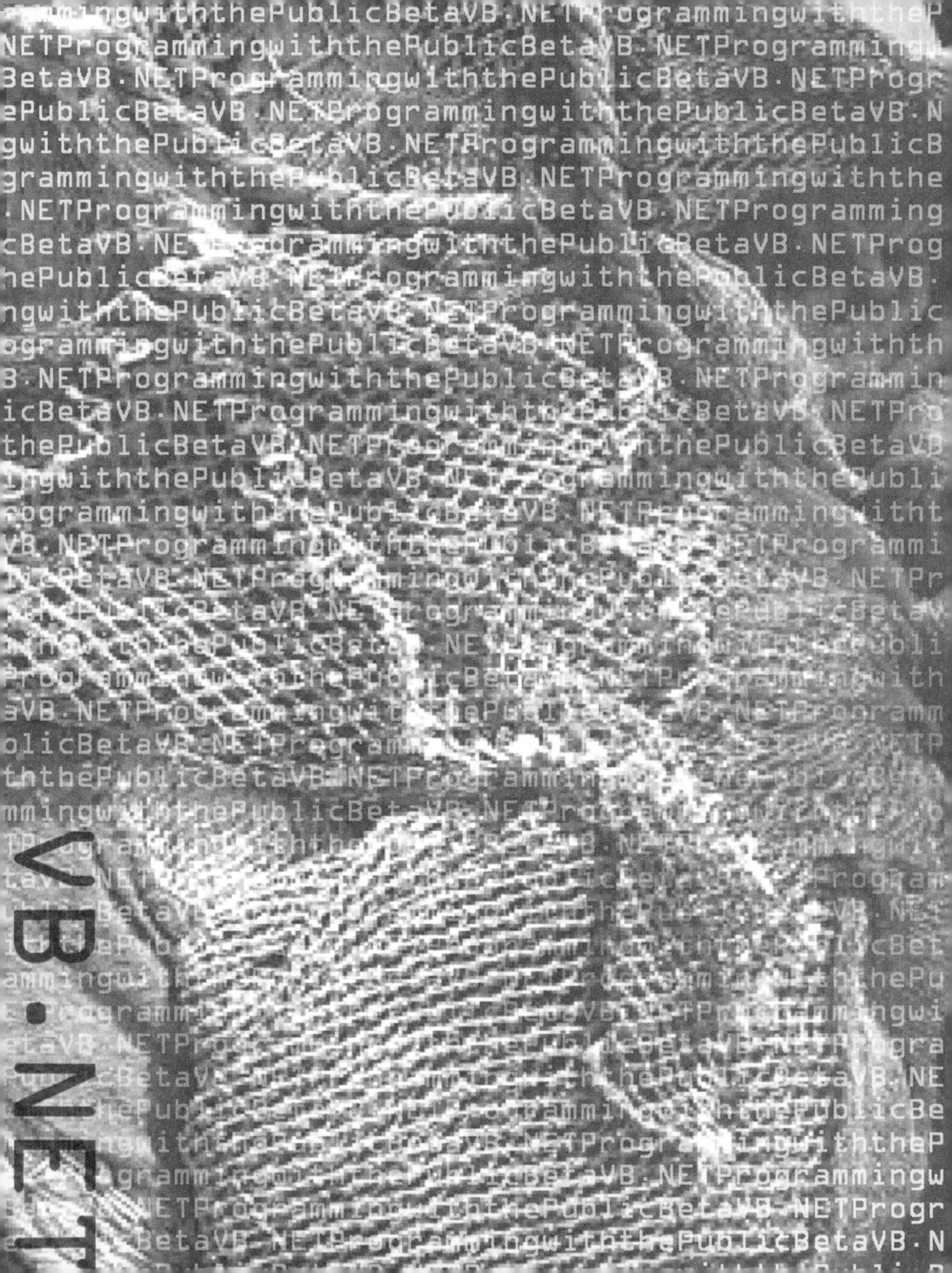
VB.NET
VB.NETProgrammingwiththePublicBeta

8

Advanced Topics

So far in this book we've been covering fairly mainstream features and capabilities of VB.NET – Windows Forms, Web Forms, language changes and enhancements, and data access. However, there are several more advanced features and capabilities that are important to consider as well. These are either provided directly by VB.NET, or flow from the .NET system class libraries but are of interest to VB developers.

The .NET Framework and VB.NET are tightly integrated. The Framework was discussed in Chapter 2, it provides us with extensive capabilities – many of which were difficult to access in the past since they required calling Win32 APIs, or were impossible to access due to limitations of VB. Now, however, VB can make use of any of the capabilities provided by the .NET Framework, opening up a great many possibilities.

We won't try to cover all of them here, but there are some major features, or changes to existing functionality, available now that are worth quick exploration, including:

❑ Creating middle-tier components

❑ Free threading

❑ Creating console applications

❑ Printing with VB.NET

❑ Deployment of VB.NET applications

❑ Calling Win32 APIs more easily

❑ Creating Windows NT/Windows 2000 services

❑ Monitoring the file system for changes

❑ Cross language development

❑ Command line options and tools

Obviously, these topics are largely unrelated, so we've lumped them together in this chapter devoted to covering various advanced topics. As we mentioned way back in Chapter 1, the .NET Framework and VB.NET have so many features that there's no way to do them all justice in a single book. This is certainly made clear in this chapter, where we'll touch on the basics of a number of capabilities and features – each of which is very extensive.

Middle-Tier Components

Over the past few years VB has become used increasingly for the development of middle-tier components. These components include those running on a web server for use by ASP pages and those running in MTS packages or COM+ applications. There are also times when these middle-tier components are accessed directly via DCOM (Distributed COM), without using either MTS or COM+. In environments where queued messaging is employed, they also are typically the components that interact with MSMQ.

VB.NET supports these scenarios as well, though not always quite in the same manner.

We've already seen how ASP.NET and VB.NET work together to create applications that run on the web server itself. This is directly analogous to using COM components behind ASP, but with much tighter integration, better performance, and the elimination of the deployment issues presented by COM components in that environment.

What we'll explore in this section is the creation of .NET assemblies that can be used in a middle-tier scenario, much like COM components accessed via DCOM or running in a COM+ application. Included in this discussion will be the creation of transactional methods – methods of .NET objects that run within the context of COM+ and thus gain the transactional benefits of that environment. We'll wrap up this section by taking a brief look at the `System.Messaging` namespace, which allows us to make use of MSMQ for queued messaging.

Class Libraries and DLLs

VB.NET allows us to easily create DLL files containing our application code. These are not the COM DLLs created by VB6, but rather are .NET assemblies designed to run within the context of a .NET application.

In Chapter 9 we'll see that these .NET DLLs can be used from COM clients just like a regular COM component – giving us the best of both worlds.

There are two options available for creating middle-tier DLLs in VB.NET:

❑ Create a Class Library type project with classes designed so they are accessible from other applications

❑ Create a Web Service type project

No DLL can run without some type of host application. We can either create our own host application, or allow IIS to act in that capacity. Web Service projects are automatically hosted within IIS, but if we're creating a Class Library project we have the choice of either hosting it in a custom host application or accessing it via IIS.

Finally, we need to use the `System.Remoting` namespace to configure both the host and client applications so they can communicate over the network. We'll walk through these stages now.

Passing Objects by Reference

A VB.NET class library is much like a conventional ActiveX DLL from VB6, in that it is a DLL that contains a set of classes for use by our applications. In the case of both .NET and COM DLLs, a host application (EXE) is required for the code in the DLL to be run – but there the similarity largely stops.

Default of No Remote Access

By default, a .NET class is set up for direct use by an application – not for use remotely across the network or even from another application on the same machine. To make a regular class work properly in a networked environment, we need to take some extra steps.

.NET objects are, by default, available only by other code running in the same process or host application. Within the host application, all the objects are passed by reference – just as objects are in VB6.

In VB6 we could make an object available to code running in other processes or host applications by creating an ActiveX EXE or running our ActiveX DLL in MTS or COM+. Client applications were able to get a reference to the object – communicating with it between processes or even across the network.

Outside of a single process or host application .NET objects are, by default, unavailable. They are not passed by reference like COM objects in VB6 – at least not without us making some code changes. In particular, we need to specifically indicate that our object can be passed by reference by inheriting from the correct base class – something we'll discuss in detail shortly.

Passing Objects by Value

.NET objects can also do something that VB6 COM objects could not do – be passed by value. In this case, the client application doesn't get a reference to our object, but rather gets a *copy* of the object that runs in the client application's process rather than in the original process. By default .NET objects cannot be passed by value – we need to specifically mark the class with an attribute to indicate that it should be passed by value.

Serialization is the process of converting an object into a simple stream of bytes, which can be easily moved from one process to another or from one machine to another. This stream of bytes can then be *deserialized* to create a copy of the original object within the new process or on the new machine. It is this technique that allows objects to be passed *by value* between processes or across the network.

By default, .NET objects are not serializable – meaning that they can't be passed by value. To make an object serializable, we need to mark the class with the Serializable attribute.

> *In Beta 1, all VB.NET objects are serializable by default. This is not the way things will be in the end however, so it is important to explicitly mark objects as* Serializable.

If we mark a class as serializable, using the <Serializable()> attribute, and access it from across the network or from another process on the same machine, it will be passed *by value* rather than by reference. In COM, objects are always passed by reference – there isn't even a built-in provision to allow for passing objects by value. In .NET, by contrast, objects can be passed by value.

> **To achieve a type of behavior comparable to that which we get with DCOM, MTS, or COM+, we need to pass our objects by reference.**

The Object class from which all other classes are ultimately derived (even without an explicit Inherits statement) is designed for passing by value. So, for us to pass an object by reference we need to derive our class from some other base class that is designed to be passed by reference.

Using Inheritance for By Reference Access

It is the MarshalByRefObject base class that is used to create objects for use across the network or across process boundaries. For our objects to be available across the network by reference, we must inherit from MarshalByRefObject or another subclass of this class.

In reality we have two main options for creating objects that will be passed by reference. We can create a simple class that inherits from MarshalByRefObject, or we can create a component class that inherits from System.ComponentModel.MarshalByRefComponent. Both approaches allow us to easily create objects that can be invoked by clients from across the network.

Either way, we can continue to use inheritance within our application designs as normal. By default, all classes inherit from the System.Object class and we work from there. All we're doing here is making our top-level class so it now inherits from one of the by reference bases rather than the by value System.Object base class.

Directly inheriting from MarshalByRefObject allows us to create a class with the least amount of code. However, the VS.NET IDE provides extra features to component classes that are derived from System.ComponentModel.Component – most notably drag-and-drop capabilities within the component designer. By simply changing the component class to inherit from MarshalByRefComponent, we retain those IDE benefits and are still able to create a middle-tier object.

Create a new **Class Library** project in VS.NET, and name it **Chapter8Library**. The default class created by the IDE is a component class. This means it inherits from the Component class:

```
Public Class Class1
   Inherits System.ComponentModel.Component
```

To make this class available by reference, while retaining the functionality of the VS.NET IDE, we can simply change the Inherits statement:

```
Public Class Class1
   Inherits System.ComponentModel.MarshalByRefComponent
```

Then add a method to be called remotely:

```
Public Function GetValue() As Integer
   Return AppDomain.GetCurrentThreadId.ToInt32
End Function
```

This method returns the current thread ID – a number uniquely identifying the thread of execution that is running our code. This is a useful debugging technique, since we'll be able to prove that our remote object is running on a different thread from the client because the thread ID values will be different for the server from the client.

With that change, our class is now ready for use by remote clients.

In order to make use of the class remotely, however, we need to explore the concept of **remoting** – including creation of a host application, a client application, and a couple of configuration files.

Remoting

In VB6, any time we wanted to interact with an object across the network we typically relied on DCOM. We might have also used MSMQ, Remote Data Services (RDS), or more recently, the SOAP Toolkit. However, most people have relied on DCOM. This is true whether the remote object was hosted in an ActiveX EXE, in MTS, or in COM+.

DCOM has its strengths and weaknesses. It is very simple to use, it provides location transparency in conjunction with COM, and it is integrated with the Windows security system. However, DCOM is very difficult to implement across a firewall since it makes use of many ports. It is also often considered a 'heavy' protocol, especially when compared to lightweight counterparts such as pure IP socket-based communication or HTTP.

We could also use Remote Data Services (RDS) to access COM objects through port 80. This technology solved some of the problems, but used a proprietary communication scheme as opposed to .NET, which defaults to using the emerging SOAP standard.

The .NET Framework does not use DCOM for cross-process or cross-network communication, preferring instead to make use of either Web Services (as discussed in Chapter 6 and later in this chapter) or the remoting technology built into .NET.

The built-in remoting technology offers some flexibility when compared to DCOM, but does require some effort to implement.

Remoting separates the concept of calling an object from the underlying transport mechanism for the call. COM automatically invoked DCOM as a transport, but remoting allows us to specify the transport or connection mechanism via configuration files, outside of our program code. This means we can switch from one type of connection to another without recoding – at least in theory.

These transports or connections are called **channels** in remoting parlance. The currently supported channels include:

❑   HTTP

❑   Direct TCP sockets

❑   HTTP via IIS

Both the HTTP and direct TCP socket technologies create direct connections from the client application to the server over a specified port of our choice.

In the case of the HTTP channel, our host application acts as an HTTP listener, accepting requests and sending the response via HTTP. With this channel the data is transferred back and forth using SOAP formatting – which is XML-based.

Similarly, a host using the direct TCP technology provides a socket listener, accepting and responding over that socket in a binary format – basically a binary derivative of SOAP.

The IIS option relies on the IIS web server to broker the request, requiring our server assembly to be located in a `bin` directory below a virtual directory accessible to the web server. This is quite comparable to the HTTP channel, but we're relying on IIS to act as the HTTP listener instead of having the listener provided directly by our host application. When the .NET Framework is installed on a web server it registers the `.soap` file extension with IIS. It is this extension that is used to indicate a request for a remote object as opposed to an ASP.NET page (`.aspx`) or a regular web service (`.asmx`).

Setting up remoting involves a number of pieces. These are illustrated in the following diagram:

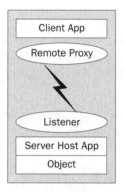

The remoting infrastructure sets up a proxy on the client that represents the object to the client, but actually makes any calls to the object's methods across the network to the real object. On the server side, our host application invokes the remoting infrastructure to set up a listener to receive those method calls. The host application also provides the process in which our server-side object will run.

For those familiar with DCOM, or any other type of object remoting technology, this diagram should seem familiar. Most major remoting technologies involve the same basic concepts of a client talking through a proxy object to a server where the object is hosted.

Creating a Host Application

Any code that is run in Windows must run within a process. A `DLL` relies on some other executable program to create the process and then load the `DLL` into that process. This is true in COM and VB6, and it remains true in .NET. We've seen how to create a .NET assembly in the form of a `DLL`, and how to subclass from `MarshalByRefObject` or `MarshalByRefComponent` such that our object will be passed by reference rather than by value. Now we need to create a process to house that `DLL` so it can be used by other applications.

> **Instead of creating our own host application, we can use IIS to load our `DLL` on our behalf. In such a case we wouldn't need to create a host application or host configuration file as described here.**

The host application can be virtually any type of executable program, including the Windows Forms applications we discussed in Chapter 4 or a console application or Windows service like those we'll discuss later in this chapter.

> *.NET assemblies can also be hosted within COM+ and be accessed via DCOM – a topic we'll touch on in Chapter 9.*

For this example, we'll create a simple Windows Forms application since that style of program is quite familiar to most VB developers.

Simply create a new Windows Application project in the IDE, and call it Chapter8Host. It is also easiest to add our Chapter8Library class library project to this solution, which can be done using the File | Add Project | Existing Project menu option. By including the class library as part of our overall solution we can more easily leverage the capabilities of the IDE. Setting up this program to act as a remoting host involves just a few more steps from this point.

Use the Project | Add Reference menu option to add a reference to the class library from our host application. The dialog has three tabs, including a Projects tab that will allow us to reference other projects in our solution – including Chapter8Library:

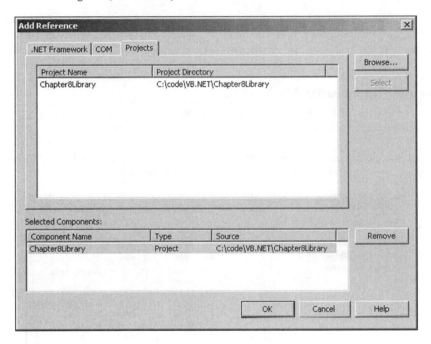

Next, open the code window for the Form1 file. We need to add an Imports statement at the top of this file to make it easier to work with the remoting namespace:

```
Imports System.Runtime.Remoting
```

The System.Runtime.Remoting namespace contains the basic classes needed for remoting to work. Importing this namespace makes the namespace available to our code. However, we also need to add a reference to the actual System.Runtime.Remoting assembly by using the Project | Add Reference dialog.

Finally, we need to simply add a line of code to invoke the remoting functionality. This is added in the constructor for the form, thus ensuring it is run as the application is loaded:

```
Public Sub New()
  MyBase.New()
```

```
Form1 = Me

'This call is required by the Win Form Designer.
InitializeComponent()

'TODO: Add any initialization after the InitializeComponent() call
RemotingServices.ConfigureRemoting("..\remhost.cfg")
End Sub
```

Notice that we're simply invoking the ConfigureRemoting procedure contained within the remoting namespace, passing it a path to a configuration file. It is this configuration file that defines how our host will receive requests from clients. We'll discuss the configuration file shortly.

Now build the solution. This will build both the library containing our class and the host application. It will also cause the DLL containing our server-side object to be automatically copied by the IDE into the same directory as the host application's EXE. At this point all we need is the configuration file and we're ready to host.

Setting Up the Host Configuration File

A nice feature of the VS.NET IDE is that it allows us to attach arbitrary files to our project, including simple text files such as the configuration file required to set up a remoting host.

In our host application project, Chapter8Host, choose the Project | Add New Item menu option. In the resulting dialog, choose the Text File option and name the file remhost.cfg:

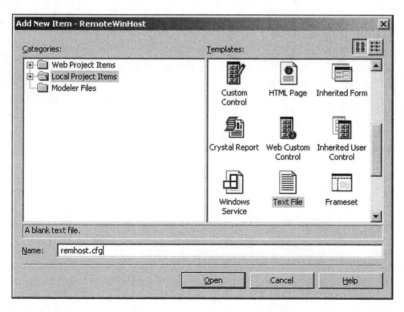

This file can contain a number of different entries. Unfortunately they are relatively arcane, but they are not terribly complex. Throughout the configuration file, the hash symbol (#) is used as a delimiter.

This cryptic file structure is used in Beta 1. The plan is for Beta 2 to make use of an XML file to contain this configuration data. For details on the current file structure beyond what is covered here, refer to the remoting sample provided with the .NET Framework SDK.

First off, we need to add a line indicating the name of our host application. Note that this is an arbitrary name we are using to identify the host application – it is not the name of the class library, nor does it necessarily have to even match the name of the host application's EXE – it is just a name that identifies our host:

```
Name#Chapter8Host
```

This is a simple name-value pair indicating that the `Name` field's value is `Chapter8Host`. Next, we need to define the object that is to be made available via remoting. This is done by using the `WellKnownObject` tag:

```
WellKnownObject#Chapter8Library.Class1#Chapter8Library#Class1.soap#SingleCall
```

This needs to be all on one line within the config file. There are several parts to this line, so let's break them down. Each # symbol delimits a different piece of important data.

Data	Description
`WellKnownObject`	The name for this tag.
`Chapter8Library.Class1`	The full type name for the class we want to expose for remote use. In this example, the class library's namespace is `Chapter8Library` and the class name itself is `Class1`.
`Chapter8Library`	The assembly name for the assembly that contains the class. This can be different from the namespace used to reference the class, since this is actually referring to the DLL name itself.
`Class1.soap`	The URI for the object. Unlike a URL, a URI can refer to things that are entirely virtual – and that is the case here. While this looks like a path, it is actually just a unique identifier used to locate the appropriate service for a client call.

The URI defined here will be used by the client to locate the specific object that is to be used. |
| `SingleCall` | This is the object mode indicator. This must be one of two keywords that indicate how the object will be referenced. The keywords are:

❑ `SingleCall`: An object is created for each method call

❑ `Singleton`: All calls to methods are sent to the same instance of the object |

Finally, we need to specify the channel over which the communication will take place:

```
Channel#System.Runtime.Remoting#System.Runtime.Remoting.Channels.HTTP.HTTPChannel#
ports=50000
```

This needs to be all on one line in the config file too. As with the previous line, this one has several component parts:

Data	Description
`Channel`	The name for this tag.
`System.Runtime.Remoting`	The assembly name for the channel to be used. Typically all channels come from the `Remoting` namespace.
`System.Runtime.Remoting.Channels.HTTP.HTTPChannel`	The full type name for the channel class. Other channel options are listed later in this section.
`ports=50000`	The ports on which the host should listen for incoming requests. Be careful not to use a value of a port already in use by another application on the host machine.

There are different channels available for our use, each of them referenced by changing the full type name referenced in the `Channel` line. These include:

❑ HTTP channel: `System.Runtime.Remoting.Channels.HTTP.HTTPChannel`

❑ Direct TCP socket channel: `System.Runtime.Remoting.Channels.TCP.TCPChannel`

In either case, we need to specify the ports on which the host will listen for requests. When choosing a port, keep the following port ranges in mind:

❑ 0-1023 are well-known ports reserved for specific applications such as web servers, mail servers, etc.

❑ 1024-49151 are registered ports that are reserved for various widely-used protocols such as DirectPlay

❑ 49152-65535 are intended for dynamic or private use – such as for applications that might be performing remoting with .NET

With the host created and the configuration file set up, we are ready to create a client application that will use our object – either from the same machine or from another application on the same machine.

Programmatically Configuring the Host

Configuration of the host application can be done programmatically as well – thus avoiding the process of creating a config file. The advantage to this is that we avoid creating the configuration file, but the drawback is that the configuration is hard-coded into our application instead of being defined externally.

To configure our host application through code we would change the `New` method in `Form1` as follows:

```
                  'TODO: Add any initialization after the InitializeComponent() call
             Dim c As New Channels.HTTP.HTTPChannel(50000)
             ChannelServices.RegisterChannel(c)

             RemotingServices.RegisterWellKnownType( _
               "Chapter8Library", "Chapter8Library.Class1", _
               "Class1.soap", WellKnownObjectMode.SingleCall)
         End Sub
```

Instead of calling the `ConfigureRemoting` method, we're now creating our own `HTTPChannel` object on port 50000 and registering it with the `RegisterChannel` method.

We then call the `RegisterWellKnownType` method, providing basically the same information as we put on the `WellKnownObject` line in the config file.

This code accomplishes the same end result as the config file – making our server-side class available for use by remote client applications.

Testing the Host via Browser

We can now quickly test the host by using the browser. To do this, run the host application and then using Internet Explorer, navigate to the URI specified in the config file:

```
http://localhost:50000/Class1.soap
```

The result should be a display of XML within the browser. This is the definition of our component from a SOAP perspective. If nothing is displayed or the browser returns an error then we know immediately that something is not configured correctly in our host application or its config file.

Creating a Client Application

Client applications also use the `System.Runtime.Remoting` namespace and a configuration file. These are used in concert to allow the client application to locate and invoke the remote object. A client application can be easily created by creating a new **Windows Application** project in VB.NET. Call it **Chapter8Client**.

As with the host application we created earlier, we need to add a reference to the class library project that contains the object we want to call. This can be done using the **Project | Add Reference** menu option, then browsing to the `Chapter8Library.dll` file in the `Chapter8Library` project directory.

Once the class library is referenced, we need to add a couple of `Imports` statements to the top of the `Form1` module:

```
    Imports System.Runtime.Remoting
    Imports Chapter8Library
```

Also make sure to use **Project | Add Reference** to add a reference to the `System.Runtime.Remoting` assembly or it won't be available to our application.

At this point our **Chapter8Client** application is ready to make use of our object, which is nice since we'll get full Intellisense and type checking capabilities as we code. We still need to initialize the remoting system, which is done in the same way as we initialized it in the host application.

Within the constructor method of `Form1` we can simply make a call to initialize remoting:

```
Public Sub New()
    MyBase.New()

    Form1 = Me

    'This call is required by the Win Form Designer.
    InitializeComponent()

    'TODO: Add any initialization after the InitializeComponent() call
    RemotingServices.ConfigureRemoting("..\remclient.cfg")
End Sub
```

As with the host application, our client application will require a simple text configuration file which is referenced in this code and which we'll discuss shortly. The configuration can also be done programmatically – which we'll also cover.

We can now write code within our application to make use of the remote object, just as though it were local to our program. Remember that our server-side class returns its thread ID as a value. In our client application we'll display both the client's thread ID and the value returned from the server. They should be different – thus proving that the object was run in a separate process on a separate thread.

Add a button to the form and the following code:

```
Protected Sub Button1_Click(ByVal sender As Object, _
            ByVal e As System.EventArgs)

    Dim obj As Class1

    MsgBox(AppDomain.GetCurrentThreadId.ToString, _
      Microsoft.VisualBasic.MsgBoxStyle.Information, "My thread")

    obj = New Class1()

    MsgBox(CStr(obj.GetValue), _
      Microsoft.VisualBasic.MsgBoxStyle.Information, "Remote thread")
End Sub
```

After we build the client application, all that remains is to create the configuration file so the remoting system can locate the server-side object.

Setting Up the Client Config File

As before, the client configuration file is a simple text file that contains some simple data, delimited with the hash (#) symbol. Add the file to our project as before, naming it `remclient.cfg`. Now let's walk through the lines needed in the file.

The first line is used to designate the name of our client application:

```
Name#Chapter8Client
```

Here we've denoted that our client application's name is `Chapter8Client`. The next line indicates the details of the assembly that we're going to be using remotely:

```
Assembly#Chapter8Library#Chapter8Host#Chapter8Library.Class1=http://localhost:5000
0/Class1.soap
```

Again, this needs to be all on one line in the configuration file. The elements of this line are detailed as follows:

Data	Description
`Assembly`	The name for this tag.
`Chapter8Library`	The assembly name for the remote object.
`Chapter8Host`	The application name for the remote host. This is the name we designated in the `Name` tag of the host config file.
`Chapter8Library.Class1=`	This is the class name of the remote class we are going to invoke.
`HTTP://localhost:50000/Class1.soap`	This is the URI that is used to address the remote object. It includes the remote server name and port number to use, followed by the URI we specified in our host config file.
	This last portion of the URI *must* match the URI specified in the host config file for this to work.

Finally we define the channel to be used when connecting to the remote host:

```
Channel#System.Runtime.Remoting#System.Runtime.Remoting.Channels.HTTP.HTTPChannel
```

This line is identical to the channel line used in the host config file as discussed earlier. In fact, it is important that both host and client agree on a common channel otherwise they'll be unable to communicate.

With the config file set up, we should be able to run the client application and have it call our server-side object, whether in a separate process on the same machine or across the network to another machine that is hosting the object.

Setting Up the Client Programmatically

As with the remote host, we can also skip the config file for the client and configure the client programmatically. This has the advantage of avoiding the creation and maintenance of the config file, but it also means we can't use the `New` keyword to create the remote object. Instead, the remote object is created using the `Activator.GetObject` method. `Activator` is a class from the `System.Runtime.Remoting` namespace.

In the `New` method of `Form1`, remove the call to `ConfigureRemoting`:

```
'TODO: Add any initialization after the InitializeComponent() call
'RemotingServices.ConfigureRemoting("..\remclient.cfg")
End Sub
```

Then we need to change how we invoke the remote object within our button's `Click` event:

```
Protected Sub Button1_Click(ByVal sender As Object, _
                            ByVal e As System.EventArgs)

    Dim obj As Class1

    MsgBox(AppDomain.GetCurrentThreadId.ToString, _
      Microsoft.VisualBasic.MsgBoxStyle.Information, "My thread")

    Dim c As New Channels.HTTP.HTTPChannel()
    ChannelServices.RegisterChannel(c)

    obj = _
      CType(Activator.GetObject(GetType(Chapter8Library.Class1), _
      "http://localhost:50000/Class1.soap"), Class1)

    MsgBox(CStr(obj.GetValue), _
      Microsoft.VisualBasic.MsgBoxStyle.Information, "Remote thread")
End Sub
```

First we create an `HTTPChannel` object with which to communicate to the server. This must be the same type of channel as is used by the server or the communication will fail:

```
Dim c As New Channels.HTTP.HTTPChannel()
ChannelServices.RegisterChannel(c)
```

We can then create an instance of the remote object by using the `Activator` class:

```
obj = _
  CType(Activator.GetObject(GetType(Chapter8Library.Class1), _
  "http://localhost:50000/Class1.soap"), Class1)
```

The `GetObject` method returns an object of type `System.Object`, so we use the `CType` function to convert it to the `Class1` type we need. The `GetObject` method accepts parameters indicating the type of the object to be created and the URI where the remote object is to be found. This is the same URI as used in both the host and client config files.

Web Services

Another, and generally easier, way to invoke methods on remote objects is to host those objects within web services. However, since web services were discussed in Chapter 6, we won't revisit the topic of creating them in this chapter. We will, however, make use of them as we discuss how to build and interact with transactional components using COM+ and VB.NET.

Transactional Components

One of the strengths of the Microsoft Windows DNA platform has long been its strong and highly integrated support for transactional processing. This was first accomplished through the Distributed Transaction Coordinator (DTC), but the DTC was rather hard to work with. Microsoft then created Microsoft Transaction Server (MTS) which automatically invoked the DTC on our behalf, making transactional processing a practical reality for most developers. More recently, Windows 2000 introduced COM+, which further refines the MTS environment by making it easier, more powerful, and faster.

Microsoft continues to support transactional processing in the .NET environment, relying on COM+ to take care of the details behind the scenes.

The transactions we're talking about here are distributed 2-phase commit transactions. Simpler transactions that can be handled directly through ADO.NET were discussed in Chapter 7.

Because the underlying transactional support for .NET is provided by COM+, the overall process should be quite familiar to those who have created MTS or COM+ components in VB6.

While it is possible to create a regular .NET DLL that is transactional, doing so involves the use of COM interoperability – a topic we'll cover in Chapter 9. In this chapter, we'll work instead with web service components. A web service can more easily be made transactional, since it runs within the context of ASP.NET and that environment provides some basic underlying support for transactions – simplifying our task immensely.

Creating a Transacted Web Service

Making a web service class transactional is very straightforward. Start by creating a new Web Service project in the VS.NET IDE named Chapter8Service. This will start us with a project that has a web service code module named Service1.asmx. Creating a web service was covered in Chapter 6, so we'll assume we can set up a basic web service project.

Upon opening the code window for the Service1.asmx file, we'll see the code for the underlying web service class. To this code we can easily add some methods that update data elements in the pubs database on a couple different database servers.

As we discussed in Chapter 7, when working with data we need to reference and import the ADO.NET assemblies. The VS.NET IDE automatically adds a reference to the System.Data.dll assembly for the Web Service type project. However, since this code will use SQL Server we'll want to add another Imports statement to the top of the Service1.asmx file:

```
Imports System.Data.SQL
```

We can then add a couple of methods within the Service1 class:

```
Public Sub <WebMethod()> UpdateLName(ByVal au_id As String, _
                         ByVal au_lname As String)
    UpdateDB1(au_id, au_lname)
    UpdateDB2(au_id, au_lname)
End Sub
```

This method updates the last name of an author in the pubs database in two different databases. We provide it with the au_id value and the new last name and it updates the databases by calling the UpdateDB1 and UpdateDB2 methods.

For this to work, we'll need two SQL Server database servers. If we don't have two servers available this example could be altered to update two different tables in two different databases on the same server. Either way, the point is to prove that we have 2-phase transactional support as we do updates across multiple databases. If any update fails, the updates to all the databases should be rolled back.

These two methods are essentially identical – each one opening a specific database and updating the indicated record:

```
Private Sub UpdateDB1(ByVal au_id As String, ByVal au_lname As String)
    Const dbConn As String = "server=server1;uid=sa;pwd=;database=pubs"
    Dim cn As SQLConnection
    Dim cm As SQLCommand
    Dim SQL As String

    SQL = "update authors set au_lname='" & au_lname & _
          "' where au_id='" & au_id & "'"
    cn = New SQLConnection(dbConn)
    cn.Open()
    cm = New SQLCommand(SQL, cn)
    cm.Execute()
End Sub

Private Sub UpdateDB2(ByVal au_id As String, ByVal au_lname As String)
    Const dbConn As String = "server=server2;uid=sa;pwd=;database=pubs"
    Dim cn As SQLConnection
    Dim cm As SQLCommand
    Dim SQL As String

    SQL = "update authors set au_lname='" & au_lname & _
          "' where au_id='" & au_id & "'"
    cn = New SQLConnection(dbConn)
    cn.Open()
    cm = New SQLCommand(SQL, cn)
    cm.Execute()
End Sub
```

This simple code accepts a record ID and new last name value and updates that row on two different database servers. Nothing complex, but enough to illustrate how we might use the transactional capabilities of .NET and COM+ to transactionally protect the operation.

Were we using VB6, we'd just mark the class module with a `RequiresTransaction` property. Then when we put the DLL into COM+ it would pick up that attribute and automatically set up the component to require a transaction. The concept in .NET is comparable, but the process is actually easier.

To make our code transactionally protected we simply alter the `WebMethod` attribute for our method:

```
Public Sub <WebMethod(TransactionMode:=TransactionMode.Required)> _
    UpdateLName(ByVal au_id As String, ByVal au_lname As String)
```

Rebuild the web service project and we're all done. At this point, if an error occurs anywhere during the update process, neither database will be updated – we have full 2-phase commit transactional protection.

To prove this, change the `UpdateDB2` method so it intentionally causes an error by adding the following:

```
Private Sub UpdateDB2(ByVal au_id As String, ByVal au_lname As String)
    Const dbConn As String = "server=server2;uid=sa;pwd=;database=pubs"
```

```
Dim cn As SQLConnection
Dim cm As SQLCommand
Dim SQL As String

' force an error to prove the rollback occurs
Err.Raise(1, , "Our forced error")
SQL = "update authors set au_lname='" & au_lname & _
      "' where au_id='" & au_id & "'"
cn = New SQLConnection(dbConn)
cn.Open()
cm = New SQLCommand(SQL, cn)
cm.Execute()
End Sub
```

Now when we invoke the web service it will fail – *after* updating the first database. That update should be automatically rolled back due to the error, thus proving that we have the desired transactional protection.

This functionality uses the automatic complete feature of COM+ by default, so if our code doesn't raise an error, the transaction will be committed.

Interaction between .NET and COM+ for Transactions

We can opt to take more explicit control if we like – just as we could with COM+ and VB6. We do this by explicitly calling SetComplete or SetAbort depending on whether our code completes. Here too, our task is a bit easier than it was in VB6 with COM+ or MTS.

Simply use **Project | Add Reference** to add a reference to the **Microsoft.ComServices** assembly. Then add an Imports statement to the top of the Service1 code module:

```
Imports Microsoft.ComServices
```

With this done, our code now has access to quite a few new objects, including the ContextUtil object. This object provides access to the COM+ object context. To use this in VB6 we needed to call the GetObjectContext function, but in VB.NET we can just use the ContextUtil object as is.

To indicate our code completed successfully we can call the SetComplete method:

```
ContextUtil.SetComplete()
```

Alternately, if our code didn't succeed we can cause a rollback by calling SetAbort:

```
ContextUtil.SetAbort()
```

This gives us the same level of control available to us in VB6, with a bit less coding on our part. We'll explore transactions some more in Chapter 9 as we discuss COM interoperability.

Using Microsoft Message Queue (MSMQ)

Another key middle-tier technology is the ability to use asynchronous queued messaging. MSMQ provides us with a powerful set of services to fill this need, and the .NET system class library includes the System.Messaging namespace to give us access to MSMQ.

> To make use of the **System.Messaging** functionality you'll need to have MSMQ installed on your machine.

In addition, the Server Explorer window in the VS.NET IDE can be used to further simplify our use of MSMQ by providing queue management options, including the ability to add or remove queues from within the development environment. Better still, we can actually drag-and-drop a queue from the Server Explorer directly onto a form or component designer.

Another way to drag-and-drop a queue is from the Toolbox under the Components tab, where we find a MessageQueue entry. If we take this approach however, we need to manually set the properties on the object such that it references the queue that we want to use.

Either way, we'll need to do some coding to make use of the queue, requiring us to gain some familiarity with the System.Messaging namespace.

The System.Messaging Namespace

The System.Messaging namespace provides us with access to the messaging assembly. If we used the Server Explorer or Toolbox to drag-and-drop a queue onto our form or component, this assembly is automatically referenced. Otherwise, before using the System.Messaging namespace we need to use Project | Add Reference to add a reference to System.Messaging.dll.

With this done, we can add an Imports statement to the top of our code module:

```
Imports System.Messaging
```

At which point we are all ready to make use of the MSMQ subsystem.

In this book we'll keep things relatively simple, so we'll see how to send and receive a basic String containing some text.

> *Of course "simple" is relative. The MSMQ support in .NET is largely geared toward the transmission and reception of objects that are passed by value. Sending and receiving a simple text value is deceptively difficult. The Quickstart example provided with the Beta 1 SDK refuses to read from the queue as shown.*

Referencing the Queue

We can reference a queue by either using the drag-and-drop functionality mentioned earlier, or through code by instantiating our own MessageQueue object. Prior to this step, make sure to reference and import the System.Messaging assembly.

We can declare a MessageQueue object variable as:

```
Dim q As MessageQueue
```

At this point we can either open an existing queue or create a new one. To open an existing queue we can provide the queue's path to the constructor:

```
q = New MessageQueue(".\private$\test")
```

In this case we're opening a private local queue named `test`. We'd use this same syntax to open any queue – public or private – as long as we know the queue's path. If the queue doesn't exist this will result in a trappable error.

To create a new queue we can use the shared `Create` method:

```
q = MessageQueue.Create(".\private$\test")
```

Again, this code demonstrates the creation of a private queue named `test`. If the queue already exists this will result in a trappable error. However, we may want to use the shared `Exists` method to see if the queue exists as follows:

```
Dim q As MessageQueue

If MessageQueue.Exists(".\private$\test") Then
  q = New MessageQueue(".\private$\test")

Else
  q = MessageQueue.Create(".\private$\test")

End If
```

In the end, assuming no errors, our code will have a reference to a queue.

Sending a Text Message

Sending a text message with VB6 and MSMQ was quite simple – we could simply set a `Message` object's `Body` property to a `String` value. If we do this in VB.NET, the data will be wrapped in XML using SOAP encoding automatically on our behalf. This makes it consistent with other messaging within .NET, but may not be ideal for communicating with non-.NET code that isn't as well versed in SOAP.

To avoid this behavior, we can use the `Message` object's `BodyStream` property instead. This property accepts a raw data stream and does no extra formatting on the data. This implies some understanding of streams and how they work.

In the .NET Framework we have access to an object of type `Stream` from the `System.IO` namespace. A stream is merely a holder for data, with services for writing data into the stream and reading data from the stream. Streams can be associated with files (which is how we read and write from files in .NET), IP sockets (so we can read and write from sockets) and memory. A memory stream is a section of memory to which we can read and write data. Memory streams can be used for a lot of things, including formatting chunks of data that we may want to send through a queue.

After importing the `System.IO` namespace, we can read and write from a stream using a `StreamReader` or `StreamWriter` as appropriate. There are different types of readers and writers, but we'll use a `BinaryRead` and a `BinaryWriter` here, since they provide the ability to read and write most native data types, such as the `String` type.

To write a `String` value into an MSMQ `Message` object, we must first put the value into a `MemoryStream`. This can be done using the following code:

```
Dim bw As New BinaryWriter(New MemoryStream())
bw.Write("Test message")
```

The code creates a new `MemoryStream` and associates it with a new `BinaryWriter`. We then place our text into the stream by calling the `BinaryWriter` object's `Write` method.

With this done, we can place the value into an MSMQ `Message` object with the following code:

```
Dim m As New Messaging.Message()
m.BodyStream = bw.BaseStream
```

Notice that we reference `Messaging.Message` rather than just `Message`. This is because the class `Message` is ambiguous in some cases – in particular if the `System.WinForms` namespace has been imported. This syntax avoids the ambiguity that we'd otherwise see both in the IDE and as a build error when we tried to compile.

Given a `Message` object, we just set its `BodyStream` property to the stream referenced by our `BinaryWriter` object. This is the `MemoryStream` object we created in the last step, and is the stream into which we wrote our text value.

Finally, we can send the message using the `MessageQueue` object's `Send` method:

```
q.Send(m)
```

The following code shows all this pulled together – opening or creating the queue, putting the text data into a stream and then into the `Message` object, and finally sending the message to a queue:

```
Dim q As MessageQueue
Dim m As New Messaging.Message()
Dim bw As New BinaryWriter(New MemoryStream())

If MessageQueue.Exists(".\private$\test") Then
  q = New MessageQueue(".\private$\test")
Else
  q = MessageQueue.Create(".\private$\test")
End If

bw.Write("Test message")
m.BodyStream = bw.BaseStream
m.Label = "a test"

q.Send(m)
```

Once this code is run our queue will hold a message containing some text, with a simple label. We're ready to move on and see how to read messages from the queue.

Receiving a Text Message

Receiving a message involves opening the queue and calling its `Receive` method to retrieve a `Message` object. Given that `Message` object, we can retrieve the data either from the `Body` or `BodyStream` property. In our case, since we're bypassing the `Messaging` namespace's automatic formatting behaviors, we'll use the `BodyStream` property.

When receiving a message, we get a `Message` object as a result of the `Receive` method call. The following code assumes we've already opened the queue:

```
Dim m As Messaging.Message
Try
  m = q.Receive(New TimeSpan(0, 0, 3))
Catch
  ' no message was in the queue
End Try
```

First we declare a `Message` variable, and then use the `Receive` method to instantiate an object from the queue. We also create a new `TimeSpan` object from the `System` namespace, which is used to tell the `Receive` method how long to wait for a message before timing out – hours, minutes, seconds. In this case we're indicating it should wait 3 seconds before timing out.

If no message is in the queue by the time the timeout expires we'll get a trappable error and can take appropriate action.

Now that we've retrieved a message from the queue, we need to pull our data out of the `Message` object. This is done using a `BinaryReader` object with the following code:

```
Dim br As BinaryReader
Dim txt As String

br = New BinaryReader(m.BodyStream)
txt = New String(br.Readchars(CInt(m.BodyStream.Length)))
```

The first step is to create a new `BinaryReader` object and associate it with the `BodyStream` property of the `Message` object. Then we're ready to read the data from the stream into a `String`.

The `BinaryReader` object's `ReadChars` method returns an array of type `Char`, which we need to convert into a `String`. The easiest way to do this is to create an instance of a `String`, since one of the constructors available on the `String` class accepts an array of `Char` – automatically converting it into a `String`.

> *This really highlights how we can treat regular data types such as `String` or `Integer` like classes or objects. This is quite a departure from VB6, where there is a differentiation between native data types and data types that come from classes.*

The result is that our `txt` variable holds the text contained within the message from the queue. The following code pulls this together to retrieve a message from a queue:

```
Dim q As MessageQueue
Dim m As Messaging.Message
Dim br As BinaryReader
Dim txt As String

If MessageQueue.Exists(".\private$\test") Then
  q = New MessageQueue(".\private$\test")
Else
  q = MessageQueue.Create(".\private$\test")
End If

Try
  m = q.Receive(New TimeSpan(0, 0, 3))
```

```
    br = New BinaryReader(m.BodyStream)
    txt = New String(br.Readchars(CInt(m.BodyStream.Length)))
Catch
    ' no message was in the queue
    txt = "(no message)"
End Try
```

Support for MSMQ in the .NET Framework is much more capable and sophisticated than that which we've seen here, but these examples demonstrate how to use MSMQ in a fashion similar to how we typically used it in VB6.

.NET Threading

One of the most anticipated features of VB.NET is the ability to create full multi-threaded or free-threaded applications. VB6 had some serious limitations in its design that prevented the use of free-threading, unless you were willing to jump through some tricky hoops.

With free-threading, we can now create applications that do their work in the background while still allowing the user to interact with the user interface. In VB6, for instance, it was difficult to create a dialog box with a Cancel button to stop a long-running task since the long-running task consumed the application's thread. In VB.NET we can have the task run on a separate thread, leaving the UI fully responsive and able to accept user input.

In VB.NET, using threads is quite easy due to the threading support built into the .NET system class library. In fact, we can not only create multi-threaded applications in VB, but the `System.Threading` namespace also provides facilities for thread pooling and other advanced features. In this section we'll focus on basic multi-threading within VB.NET applications.

> **Before we get too far into this discussion, it is important to realize the dangers and difficulties involved in writing free-threaded applications. When we create more than one thread in a single process, all the threads share the same memory, the same variables, and the same environment. It is *very* easy to create complex bugs in free-threaded code.**

We can easily tell which thread our code is using by calling the `AppDomain.GetCurrentThreadID()` method. This method returns an `Integer` value indicating the ID for the current thread. We'll use this method in our examples to prove to ourselves that our code is, in fact, running on various threads.

Starting a Thread

Every process has at least one thread. Typically, our applications run in processes that have just one. Unless some code explicitly creates another, our code will always run on this thread. New threads can be created directly by our code. Threads can also be created by other classes, including those in the .NET system class library. Often these threads are started because we requested an asynchronous operation – something we'll discuss briefly after we get through basic thread creation.

To simplify our use of threads we can use the `Imports` statement:

```
Imports System.Threading
```

If we add this line to the top of a code module, then the code in that module can make easy use of the threading objects.

Before we create a thread, we'll need some code for the thread to execute. In VB.NET, we use the `AddressOf` operator to find the address of any routine or method that is to be called in such a manner. So, as we create a thread, we'll pass it the address of a method that is to be run.

Starting with a **Windows Application** project, add a ListBox control to `Form1` and use the `Dock` property to make it fill the entire form. We'll display output from our threads in this control.

In the code window, add the following method to the form:

```
Private Sub Worker()
  SyncLock(ListBox1)
    ListBox1.Items.Add("Running on thread " & _
      CStr(AppDomain.GetCurrentThreadId()))
  End SyncLock
End Sub
```

This routine simply adds a line to the `ListBox1` control indicating the thread on which the code is running. However, it is also making use of a new VB.NET keyword – `SyncLock`.

SyncLock

When working with multiple threads, any code we call must be written so as to be **threadsafe**, otherwise we risk introducing unforeseen bugs, very likely causing our application to crash entirely. Threadsafe code is code that will operate properly when more than one thread is running within that same code. Without extra effort, most code is not threadsafe.

If we are working with code that is *not* threadsafe (or code that we don't *know* is threadsafe) we can use various synchronization methods to ensure that only one thread uses that code at any one time.

To make this easier, VB.NET includes the `SyncLock` keyword – a block structure that protects all the code in that block. `SyncLock` accepts an object as a parameter, and that object is used as the lock key. Any object can be used to synchronize our code, but keep in mind that each instance of the same *class* is a different *object*. It is a singular instance of an object that is used here – not the class. Any time we are within a `SyncLock` block based on a given object, we know that no other code in our application can also be in a `SyncLock` block using that *same object*. `SyncLock` blocks based on other objects are a whole other matter.

In this code sample, the ListBox control is not threadsafe. Two threads attempting to interact with the ListBox control at the same time will cause our application to crash. By wrapping our code in a `SyncLock` block based on the `ListBox1` control, we can know that only one thread at a time will ever attempt to run this code.

> **In general, the Windows Forms classes in the .NET system class library are *not* threadsafe, so care is needed when working with them in a multi-threaded application.**

Any other code in our application that interacts with the `ListBox1` control would need to be similarly placed in a `SyncLock` block structure.

We can call this routine 10 times from within a regular program, for instance:

```
Dim Index As Integer
For Index = 1 To 10
  Worker()
Next
```

The `ListBox1` control will display the exact same text over and over, since there's only one thread involved here.

Creating Threads

However, we can create another method in `Form1` that creates threads:

```
Private Sub SpinThreads()
  Dim Index As Integer
  Dim t As Thread

  For index = 1 To 10
    t = New Thread(AddressOf Me.Worker)
    t.Start()
  Next
End Sub
```

This code declares a `Thread` variable, then creates 10 threads in a loop – each one calling `Form1`'s `Worker` method. We can call this method from `Form1`'s constructor, so when the form loads this code will run:

```
'TODO: Add any initialization after the InitializeComponent() call
SpinThreads()
End Sub
```

The result will be a display with a different thread ID for each line, something like this:

As we can see, each time the `Worker` method was invoked, it ran on a different thread.

Thread Lifetimes

We have code to start our threads – but how do they stop? A thread will continue running until one of the following occurs:

❑   The method it is running completes

❑   The process containing the thread terminates

❑   We call the `Stop` method on the thread object itself

In our example, as is typically the case, each thread stops when its method is complete. As soon as the code in the `Worker` method is done, the thread running that code will automatically terminate. However, if we had a method that went into an infinite loop then that thread would not terminate, but would continue running within that loop until either that thread's `Stop` method was called or the process was terminated – typically due to the user closing our application.

Interacting with the Current Thread

Throughout our code we can use the `Thread.CurrentThread` object to interact with the currently active thread. This object has a number of methods that allow us to retrieve information about the thread and manipulate the thread in various ways, including altering the thread's priority and putting the thread to sleep for a time.

Using the `Sleep` method is very nice, since it stops the thread from processing without consuming any CPU time like a busy wait in a loop would. For instance, the following line of code will cause the current thread to sleep for 42 milliseconds:

```
Thread.CurrentThread.Sleep(42)
```

This method can be used even on the main thread created in a process – so we can use it in any application, even if we aren't creating our own threads.

> *There is also a shortcut for the `Sleep` method, since it is exposed as a shared method of the `Thread` class itself – we can call `Thread.Sleep()` instead of referring explicitly to the `CurrentThread` property.*

Passing Data to a Thread

In our `Worker` method example we didn't pass any data to the method as it was started. In fact, it is not possible to directly pass parameters to a method that is being invoked in this manner. If we need our new thread to have specific data we'll have to take a different approach.

The easiest technique is to create a class that has properties for the data we'll need, and then place the worker method into that class. For each thread we want to create, we can create a new instance of the class and start the thread within that instance. In this way, each thread has its own object – each object containing the data specific to that thread.

To illustrate this we'll need to change `Form1` and also create a new class. Let's create the class first. Add a class with the following code:

```
Imports System.WinForms

Public Class ThreadObj
  Private theForm As Form1
  Private Count As Integer

  Public Sub New (ByVal Frm As Form1, ByVal ID As Integer)
    theForm = Frm
    Count = ID
  End Sub

  Public Sub Worker()
    SyncLock (theForm)
      theForm.Display(CStr(Count) & " starting on thread " & _
        CStr(AppDomain.GetCurrentThreadId()))
    End SyncLock
  End Sub
End Class
```

So we can continue to display the output in Form1, we're passing a reference to the form into this object. Additionally, this object will contain a numeric ID value – provided by the calling code via the object's constructor method. We've also moved the Worker method here from Form1, though it is slightly altered so it now calls a Display method on Form1 rather than interacting directly with the ListBox1 control.

Also notice that the SyncLock statement is now synchronizing against the form variable – ensuring that no two threads are ever talking to the form at the same time.

In VB.NET only code within a form can interact with that form's controls. For outside code to make use of a control, the form class must expose methods to do that work.

We can now alter the Form1 code by removing the Worker method and adding a Display method as follows:

```
Public Sub Display(ByVal Data As String)
  ListBox1.Items.Add(Data)
End Sub
```

We'll also need to alter the SpinThreads method to make use of the new object. The new version of the method will create an instance of the ThreadObj class, providing it with the values to be used on the thread and then starting the method using that object's Worker method:

```
Private Sub SpinThreads()
  Dim Index As Integer
  Dim t As Thread
  Dim obj As ThreadObj

  For Index = 1 To 10
    obj = New ThreadObj(Me, Index)
    t = New Thread(AddressOf obj.Worker)
    t.Start()
  Next
End Sub
```

For an `ID` value, the loop index is passed as a parameter. Now when we run the code, we'll get a similar result to before, but the index value of the thread will also be displayed:

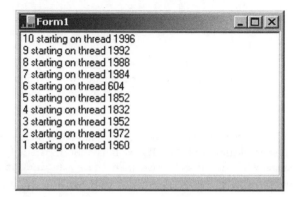

Notice that the threads don't necessarily display in straight numeric order. This directly illustrates how the threads are running concurrently – each being blocked and run according to the operating system thread scheduler.

While using individual objects to provide data to each thread is the easiest approach, it is also possible to use global variables to provide such data. Keep in mind however, that all the threads have equal access to those global variables and if more than one thread interacts with the variables at the same time the results can be very unpredictable. Make sure to use some synchronization technique, such as `SyncLock`, to ensure that only one thread interacts with the global variables at any one time.

Asynchronous Processing

Now that we've seen how to explicitly start threads through the use of the `Thread` object, let's take a look at asynchronous processing – a concept frequently used within the .NET system class libraries that can also cause threads to be started.

Asynchronous processing is used in a number of places within the system class libraries. These include:

❑ File I/O

❑ IP sockets

❑ Sending and receiving MSMQ messages

❑ HTTP processing

❑ Data access

The .NET system class libraries follow a general pattern for each of these by providing us with a `BeginXXX` method to start the process, and an `EndXXX` method that can be called when the process is complete. We know when a process is complete because the class library will call back into our application using a delegate that we provide.

For instance, to start an asynchronous process we might have code something along this line:

```
Public Sub Start()
  Dim obj As New SomeLibraryObject ()
```

```
    AddHandler obj.XXXCompleted, _
      New XXXCompletedEventHandler(AddressOf OnXXXCompleted)

    obj.BeginXXX()
  End Sub
```

The code creates an instance of the class (such as a `FileStream`, `MessageQueue`, or `Socket`), then uses the `AddHandler` statement to add an event handler (or delegate) to that object so it knows how to call back into our code. This statement accepts the address of a method within our code that will receive the completed event when the operating is done.

The specific `BeginXXX` and `EndXXX` method names vary depending on the specific operation being performed. For instance, if we're dealing with MSMQ, we'll have `BeginReceive` and `EndReceive` methods to receive a message, while the IP sockets classes have `BeginConnect` and `EndConnect` to handle making a connection to another machine.

> **In some cases the `BeginXXX` method accepts the address of the callback delegate as a parameter. Consult the documentation for each individual function to see how it works.**

Finally, this code calls the `BeginXXX` method to start the process. The code in our application will continue to run normally, with the newly started operation running on another thread in the background. Our application can continue to do other processing, interact with the user, or whatever is required.

When the background task is complete, it will call back into our code by calling the method we indicated with the `AddHandler` statement. That method may look like this:

```
  Private Sub OnXXXCompleted(ByVal sender As Object, _
                             ByVal e As AsyncEventArgs)
    Dim obj As LibraryObject = CType(sender, LibraryObject)

    obj.EndXXX()

    ' process the results here

    obj.BeginXXX()
  End Sub
```

> **The callback will typically occur on a different thread than our main application is using – so multi-threading and synchronization issues are important when using this type of technique.**

Our example event handler does its processing *before* calling the next `BeginXXX` method. This ensures that only one event will occur at a time. If we want to allow multiple events to be processed simultaneously – on different threads – we can change the code to do its processing *after* calling `BeginXXX`:

```
Private Sub OnXXXCompleted(ByVal sender As Object, _
                          ByVal e As AsyncEventArgs)
   Dim obj As LibraryObject = CType(sender, LibraryObject)

   obj.EndXXX()

   obj.BeginXXX()

   ' process the results here
End Sub
```

As soon as we call BeginXXX we indicate that we're ready to receive another event, so if any are pending we'll get it right away – even if our current thread isn't done processing the first event.

The parameters passed to this method are the same as for any standard event – a reference to the sending object and the event arguments. Typically, the event arguments are of a specific type for the operation we're performing, but they are always derived from AsyncEventArgs.

> **Of course, as with any good rule, there are always exceptions. Some events will not follow this pattern, so we need to consult with the documentation appropriate to the operation we're trying to perform.**

Since we often want to interact with the calling object, it can be beneficial to declare an object of the appropriate type and cast the sender parameter into the appropriate data type using the CType method.

Typically there will be an EndXXX method that we can call to tell the sending object that we're processing the result. Often this method is a function that will return some value. For instance, when reading from an IP socket the return value is the number of bytes read from the socket.

Next we'd have code to do any work we need to do as a result of the task being complete.

Finally we'll want to call the BeginXXX method to restart the asynchronous processing. If we don't make this call, no further asynchronous processing will occur.

The location where we place the code to process the event is important. As shown in this example, the processing will occur before the next asynchronous task is started. This design ensures that we'll only ever be processing the results from one task at a time.

We can put our processing code *after* the call to BeginXXX, thus allowing the asynchronous task to run in the background as we process the current result. This design will allow multiple completed tasks to occur at once, since this event could be called again before we're done with the first call. In such a case, we need to be very sensitive to the fact that multiple threads may be running through the same routine at the same time.

IP Socket Example

As a quick example of asynchronous coding, let's take a look at some simple code to read data from an IP socket.

> *When looking to do a lot of work with sockets, make sure to look at the other classes available in the* System.Net.Sockets *namespace, as there are often simpler ways to interact with sockets than the one shown here.*

Create a new Windows Application named `Chapter8IP`. To use sockets we need to add a reference to the `System.Net.dll` assembly.

Next we need to add a new class module named `IPRead`. Here's the code; we'll walk through the key parts next:

```
Imports System.IO
Imports System.Net
Imports System.Net.Sockets

Public Class IPRead
  Private s As Socket
  Private b(4096) As Byte      ' bytes just received

  Public Sub New(ByVal Host As String, ByVal Port As Integer)
    Connect(Host, Port)

    s.BeginReceive(b, 0, b.length, AddressOf Me.ReceiveData, Nothing)
  End Sub

  Private Sub ReceiveData(ByVal ar As System.IAsyncResult)
    Dim cnt As Integer
    Dim idx As Integer
    Dim d() As Char
    Dim txt As String

    cnt = s.EndReceive(ar)

    ReDim d(cnt)
    For idx = 0 To cnt - 1
      d(idx) = CChar(b(idx))
    Next
    txt = New String(d)

    ' do something with the data in txt
    MsgBox(txt, MsgBoxStyle.OKOnly, "Text")     ' for example

    s.BeginReceive(b, 0, b.length, AddressOf Me.ReceiveData, Nothing)
  End Sub

  Private Sub Connect(ByVal Host As String, ByVal Port As Integer)
    s = New Socket(AddressFamily.AfINet, SocketType.SockStream, _
                ProtocolType.ProtTCP)
    Dim host_addr As IPAddress = DNS.Resolve(Host)
    Dim ep As New IPEndPoint(host_addr, Port)
    If (s.Connect(ep) <> 0) Then
      Err.Raise(1, , "Client connection failed")
    End If
  End Sub
End Class
```

The constructor method accepts the host and port indicating the server to which we want to connect. The `Connect` method creates a `Socket` object and binds it to the host and port we provided. We won't get into detail here, since our focus is on the asynchronous reads.

The call to `BeginReceive` starts the read process. This method accepts the address of the callback delegate method as a parameter, so we provide it with the address of our `ReceiveData` method:

```
s.BeginReceive(b, 0, b.length, AddressOf Me.ReceiveData, Nothing)
```

The method also accepts a `Byte` array (b) into which to put the data, the position within the array to start writing the data, and the maximum number of bytes to be read and a state object – which we pass as `Nothing`.

Our application will continue to run, allowing the user to interact with our form or anything else. In the meantime, in the background we have a task waiting for input from the socket. As soon as the socket has data, our `ReceiveData` method will be called to process that data.

The first thing the `ReceiveData` method does is call the socket's `EndReceive` method. This method returns the actual number of bytes read from the socket:

```
cnt = s.EndReceive(ar)
```

The next section of code converts the `Byte` array into a `String` so we can more easily work with the data:

```
ReDim d(cnt)
For idx = 0 To cnt - 1
  d(idx) = b(idx)
Next
txt = New String(d)
```

At this point we can work with the data as required. Finally, the `BeginReceive` method is called again – restarting the background task to listen for further incoming data via the socket:

```
s.BeginReceive(b, 0, b.length, AddressOf Me.ReceiveData, Nothing)
```

This illustrates the basic flow of an asynchronous process. By using this process, we're implicitly creating a multi-threaded application, since the .NET system class libraries can and will create threads for us in the background in order to service the asynchronous tasks we request.

To finish our test application, open up the designer for `Form1`. We'll create a quick IP listener that will send some text when a client such as `IPRead` connects. Add a button to the form and add the following code:

```
Protected Sub Button1_Click(ByVal sender As Object, _
                          ByVal e As System.EventArgs)

    Dim objRead As New IPRead("localhost", 5000)
End Sub
```

This will instantiate an `IPRead` object – having it connect to the local machine on port 5000. Our code to process the result is a `MsgBox`, so we'll see any returned text displayed in a dialog.

Now let's build the listener part of the app. Add a couple `Imports` statements to `Form1`:

```
Imports System.Net
Imports System.Net.Sockets
```

Now add a method to listen for incoming IP socket requests:

```
Private Sub DoListen()
   Dim myListener As TCPListener = New TCPListener(5000)

   myListener.Start()

   ' Program blocks on Accept() until a client connects
   Send(myListener.Accept())

   myListener.Stop()
End Sub
```

This code makes use of a helper class in the `System.Net` namespace – the `TCPListener`. This class listens on the specified port and returns a new socket as the result of the `Accept` method. This socket is connected to the new client. In our code, we're passing this new socket to a `Send` method – so let's write that next:

```
Private Sub Send(ByVal s As Socket)
   Dim txt As String = "Hello world"
   Dim c() As Char
   Dim b(Len(txt)) As Byte
   Dim idx As Integer

   ' convert the string to an array of char
   c = txt.ToCharArray

   ' convert the char array to a byte array
   For idx = 0 To c.Length - 1
     b(idx) = CByte(c(idx))
   Next

   ' send the byte array to the socket
   s.Send(b, b.Length, 0)
End Sub
```

The `Socket` object also has a `Send` method – which accepts an array of bytes that it sends across the socket. In order to pass a `String` value through a socket, we need to convert it to a byte array. Unfortunately there's no direct way to convert a `String` to an array of type `Byte`.

We have to convert the `String` to an array of type `Char` first – which is easy. We can then convert each `Char` in the array into a `Byte` in the target array. This obviously only works for ASCII text – if our text was in some other Unicode character set we'd also have to put the second byte in each `Char` into the `Byte` array.

Finally, update `Form1`'s constructor so the listener is running on a separate thread:

```
'TODO: Add any initialization after the InitializeComponent() call
Dim t As New System.Threading.Thread(AddressOf DoListen)
t.Start()
```

Now when the app starts it will start listening for incoming socket requests on a background thread, leaving the main thread available so the UI will be responsive to the user. If the user clicks our button, it will run the code to create an `IPRead` object – which will connect to our listener via a socket and get our text.

Console Applications

VB has always been about creating Windows GUI applications. More recently it has become a commonly used tool for the development of middle-tier objects – typically allowing ASP code to generate the user interface. Another type of user interface that can be very useful, but has always been off-limits to VB developers, is the console application.

Console applications accept input and display output via a Windows text console, often called a DOS window. VB.NET allows us to easily create applications for this environment, including directly reading and writing from the standard input and output streams.

In fact, in the VS.NET IDE, Console Application is one of the standard project types available to VB.NET developers. When we create a new Console Application project, we are presented with a `Module` that contains an empty `Sub Main` routine:

```
Module Module1

    Sub Main()

    End Sub

End Module
```

The first code run in such an application is always a `Sub Main` routine. From there we can either directly write our code as a set of procedures, or invoke objects as needed.

Use of the System.Console Namespace

Console applications get their input from the console and write their output back to the console window. The objects that support these, and other useful operations for console applications, come from the `System.Console` namespace. When creating console applications it is often useful, though not always necessary, to import that namespace:

```
Imports System.Console
```

Writing Text to the Console

To write a line of text to the standard output stream, we can use the `WriteLine` method:

```
Sub Main()
    WriteLine("This is a test")
End Sub
```

Without importing the namespace, we can write this code as:

```
    Sub Main()
        Console.WriteLine("This is a test")
    End Sub
```

The `WriteLine` method can take different forms, including various control characters and replaceable parameters. For instance, we can print out a couple of values in the text as follows:

```
    WriteLine("The number {0} is {1}", 5, "five")
```

This will print out the following:

```
    The number 5 is five
```

The `WriteLine` method always sends a carriage return and line feed at the end – causing the cursor to move to a new line. If we want to continue to append to the same line we can use the `Write` method:

```
        Write("Hello ")
        Write("World")
        WriteLine("!")
```

This will result in the following single line of output:

```
    Hello World!
```

The `Write` method also supports control characters and replaceable parameters.

Reading from the Console

Likewise, we can read from the console by using the `ReadLine` method. This method accepts input from the console, returning it to our application when the user presses *Enter*.

```
    Dim txt As String

    txt = ReadLine()
```

If we want to read character-by-character, we can use the `Read` method:

```
    Dim txt As Char

    txt = CType(Read(), Char)
            ' type conversion because Read is Integer and txt is Char
```

Asynchronous Support

We can also perform asynchronous reading and writing in a console application. This is accomplished through the `OpenStandardInput`, `OpenStandardOutput`, and `OpenStandardError` methods – each of which provide access to the corresponding underlying `Stream` object. These stream objects have methods that enable asynchronous reading and writing, as discussed earlier in the section on threading in VB.NET. For instance, the `OpenStandardInput` object has a `BeginRead` method that starts an asynchronous read operation:

```
    OpenStandardInput.BeginRead(b, 0, b.length, AddressOf OnRead, Nothing)
```

Of course, this assumes we implement an `OnRead` method to accept the callback:

```
Sub OnRead(ByVal e As IAsyncResult)
  Dim cnt As Integer

  cnt = OpenStandardInput.EndRead(e)

  ' process input

  OpenStandardInput.BeginRead(b, 0, b.length, AddressOf OnRead, Nothing)
End Sub
```

We can implement similar code against the other stream objects.

New Printing Model

VB.NET relies on a set of objects from the .NET system class library to provide printing support. VS.NET also includes a new version of the Crystal Reports system for report generation, but our focus here will be on the more native printing functionality available to us as developers.

PrintDocument and Related Objects

In VB6 we had a `Printer` object that we could use to create output that would be sent to the printer. The .NET system class libraries include a `PrintDocument` class that provides relatively comparable functionality. This class is found in the `System.Drawing.Printing` namespace, and provides more comprehensive support than the venerable `Printer` object available in the past.

There are some other key objects we'll probably use when printing, since we may want to control the layout of the page, the printer we're printing to, and other aspects of the process. These objects include:

Object	Description
PrinterSettings	Object containing the printing settings, including the printer on which the document will be printed.
PageSettings	Object containing the printing settings for a particular page.
PrintDialog	Object providing access to the Windows printer selection dialog.
PageSetupDialog	Object providing access to the Windows page properties dialog.
PrintPreviewDialog	Object providing access to a standard print preview dialog.
PrintPreviewControl	The control that displays a print preview.
PrintPageEventArgs	This object is the parameter to the delegate method we must create to print a page. It contains information about the current page, including margins and the very surface on which we'll print.

Implementing Printing

Printing in .NET is done using asynchronous callbacks, one for each page to be generated. This is quite different from the approach taken in previous versions of VB, where printing was a relatively linear process. Instead, in VB.NET, we set up the details of the printing process, tell the printing engine the address of our delegate method that will render each page, and then call the `Print` method to start the process.

This means that our "real" printing code will be contained in a method that is called by the print engine when it is ready for more information.

Basic Code Structure

This provides us with a lot of flexibility. The basic structure of code to handle printing to a printer is as follows:

```
Private WithEvents MyDoc As PrintDocument

Public Sub StartPrint()
  MyDoc = New PrintDocument()
  MyDoc.Print()
End Sub

Private Sub PrintPage (ByVal sender As Object, _
    ByVal ev As System.Drawing.Printing.PrintPageEventArgs) _
    Handles MyDoc.PrintPage

End Sub
```

To start the printing process, we simply call the `Print` method on the document. This will cause the document to automatically fire the `PrintPage` event for each page that is to be printed. Notice the use of the `Handles` keyword to link our `PrintPage` method to the appropriate event from the document.

Implementing Print Preview

The code we've just seen would cause the printing to occur on the default printer. If we want to do a print preview instead of printing to the printer, we'd merely change the code that invokes the print process:

```
Public Sub StartPrint()
  Dim PPdlg As PrintPreviewDialog = New PrintPreviewDialog()

  PPdlg.Document = MyDoc
  PPdlg.ShowDialog()
End Sub
```

Again, the `PrintPage` event will fire for each page that is to be printed, but this time the output will be displayed in a print preview window instead of being printed to the printer. This requires no change to the `PrintPage` code that actually renders the output.

Creating an Example

Let's create a simple test application. Open a new Windows Application named `PrintTest`. Add an `Imports` statement to the top of `Form1`:

```
Imports System.Drawing.Printing
```

This namespace includes some important classes that we'll be using. We also need to add some class-level variables:

```
Public Class Form1
   Inherits System.WinForms.Form

   Private Data() As String
   Private CurrentLine As Integer
```

The array will contain the text we're printing, while the CurrentLine variable will act as a line counter as we index through the array of text.

Using Form1's designer, add a PrintDocument control from the Toolbox. This control is an instance of the System.Drawing.Printing.PrintDocument class.

We could also create this class by hand – declaring it using the WithEvents keyword – and get the same effect.

Then add a button to the form, along with the following code:

```
Protected Sub Button1_Click(ByVal sender As Object, _
                            ByVal e As System.EventArgs)

   ReDim Data(5)
   Data(0) = "This is line 1"
   Data(1) = "This is line 2"
   Data(2) = "This is line 3"
   Data(3) = "This is line 4"
   Data(4) = "This is line 5"

   PrintDocument1.Print()
End Sub
```

This simple code just populates the array from which we'll get our data and then uses the PrintDocument1 control's Print method to start the printing process.

Rendering the Output

To actually render our text to the printer we need to implement a method to handle the PrintDocument1.PrintPage event. This code can draw virtually anything onto the 'surface' of the current page – including text or graphics. Such flexibility is powerful, but has its drawbacks. It also means that we need to keep track of our own X and Y coordinates so we can draw our text where we want it to be.

This implementation will vary depending on the source of the data to be printed. The data could come from virtually anywhere – an ADO.NET DataSet, and ADO Recordset, a String variable, a text file or, as in our simple example, from an array.

Add the PrintPage method to Form1:

```
      Private Sub PrintPage(ByVal sender As Object, _
            ByVal ev As System.Drawing.Printing.PrintPageEventArgs) _
         Handles PrintDocument1.PrintPage

         Dim yMax As Single
         Dim LineHeight As Single
         Dim yPos As Single
         Dim LeftMargin As Single = ev.MarginBounds.Left
         Dim PrintFont As Font

         PrintFont = New Font("Arial", 10)

         LineHeight = PrintFont.GetHeight(ev.Graphics)

         yPos = ev.MarginBounds.Top

         Do

            yPos += LineHeight

            ev.Graphics.DrawString(Data(CurrentLine), PrintFont, _
              Brushes.Black, LeftMargin, yPos, New StringFormat())

            CurrentLine += 1

         Loop Until ypos >= ev.MarginBounds.Bottom Or _
            CurrentLine = UBound(Data) + 1

         If CurrentLine < UBound(Data) + 1 Then
            ev.HasMorePages = True
         Else
            ev.HasMorePages = False
         End If
      End Sub
```

Let's take a closer look at this code. It makes heavy use of the PrintPageEventArgs object that we receive as a parameter. This object provides us with some key information about the print margins, as well as providing the surface on which we'll render the output.

The operative line of code in this routine is the one that draws our text onto the print surface:

```
         ev.Graphics.DrawString(Data(CurrentLine), PrintFont, _
            Brushes.Black, LeftMargin, yPos, New StringFormat())
```

The DrawString method renders text onto the drawing surface. The first parameter is the text to be rendered, which in our case is coming from the array. If the data were coming from some other source then this would vary.

The other two key parameters worth noting are the LeftMargin and yPos values. These specify the X and Y coordinates on the print surface where the text will start. Earlier in the method we retrieved the left margin value from the PrintPageEventArgs object:

```
         Dim LeftMargin As Single = ev.MarginBounds.Left
```

The yPos variable is a bit more complex, since it will change as we continue to print lines on the page. As each line is printed we recalculate the Y position, in pixels, by adding the height of the font being used – in this case a 10 point Arial. First we calculated the line height:

```
LineHeight = PrintFont.GetHeight(ev.Graphics)
```

Then, as each line is printed, we increment the yPos variable:

```
yPos += LineHeight
```

This causes the print to move down the page as appropriate. There are two conditions where we need to stop printing on this page. We could run out of space or data for the particular page. These conditions are checked in the Loop statement:

```
Loop Until ypos >= ev.MarginBounds.Bottom Or _
    CurrentLine = UBound(Data) + 1
```

Once we fall out of the loop, we need to determine if there's more data to be printed. This is important, since we need to tell the print engine whether it should raise the PrintPage event again to render another page. The final code in the routine does this check, setting the HasMorePages property as appropriate:

```
If CurrentLine < UBound(Data) + 1 Then
    ev.HasMorePages = True
Else
    ev.HasMorePages = False
End If
```

This simple routine illustrates the basis for printing to a printer or to a print preview window. However, we can provide more options to the user by displaying the print and page dialogs and utilizing the choices made by the user.

We should now be able to run our application and have the text print out on the printer. Alternately, we could generate a print preview of the text by changing the code behind our button to:

```
Protected Sub Button1_Click(ByVal sender As Object, _
        ByVal e As System.EventArgs)

    ReDim Data(5)
    Data(0) = "This is line 1"
    Data(1) = "This is line 2"
    Data(2) = "This is line 3"
    Data(3) = "This is line 4"
    Data(4) = "This is line 5"

    Dim PPdlg As PrintPreviewDialog = New PrintPreviewDialog()

    PPdlg.Document = PrintDocument1
    PPdlg.ShowDialog()
End Sub
```

No change is required to the code that renders our page – just to the routine that invokes the print process.

Invoking the Print Dialog

The Print dialog allows the user to select the printer and set any properties of the printer that they require. This dialog is easily invoked through the use of the `PrintDialog` class. In our sample application we could alter the code behind our button:

```
Protected Sub Button1_Click(ByVal sender As Object, _
        ByVal e As System.EventArgs)

    ReDim Data(5)
    Data(0) = "This is line 1"
    Data(1) = "This is line 2"
    Data(2) = "This is line 3"
    Data(3) = "This is line 4"
    Data(4) = "This is line 5"

    Dim Pdlg As New PrintDialog()
    Pdlg.Document = PrintDocument1

    Dim result As DialogResult = Pdlg.ShowDialog()

    If result = WinForms.DialogResult.OK Then
      PrintDocument1.Print()
    End If
End Sub
```

The first couple of lines in this routine create the `PrintDialog` object and associate it with the `PrintDocument` object we're using, `PrintDocument1`. These objects take care of working together by themselves, so we don't have to worry about those details.

Next, we call the `ShowDialog` method, capturing the result in a `DialogResult` object. The result will indicate which button was clicked by the user to exit the dialog, and we only want to invoke the print process if the user clicked the **OK** button. Finally, if the user did click OK, we call the `Print` method of the document.

The printer selected by the user will be automatically provided to the document by the dialog, so the printing will go to the selected location.

Invoking the Page Dialog

The other major print dialog users often expect to see is the page dialog, allowing them to specify details such as portrait vs. landscape and other print settings. This dialog basically acts as an editor for a `PageSettings` object. We need to maintain this object within our application and supply it to the `PrintDocument` before calling the final `Print` method.

In `Form1` declare a module-level `PageSettings` object as:

```
Private MyPageSettings As PageSettings
```

Then we can use this object when we invoke the page setup dialog. In our button code do the following:

```
Protected Sub Button1_Click(ByVal sender As Object, _
          ByVal e As System.EventArgs)
```

```
      ReDim Data(5)
      Data(0) = "This is line 1"
      Data(1) = "This is line 2"
      Data(2) = "This is line 3"
      Data(3) = "This is line 4"
      Data(4) = "This is line 5"

      Dim Pdlg As New PageSetupDialog()

      If MyPageSettings Is Nothing Then
        MyPageSettings = New PageSettings()
      End If

      Pdlg.PageSettings = MyPageSettings

      Pdlg.ShowDialog()

      If Not MyPageSettings Is Nothing Then
        PrintDocument1.DefaultPageSettings = MyPageSettings
      End If

      PrintDocument1.Print()
    End Sub
```

This code creates a new `PageSetupDialog` object. We then check to see if we already have a `PageSettings` object – which would indicate that the user has already used this dialog once before. If there is such an object we'll use it so that the user sees their previous selections – otherwise we create a new object to use.

Either way, the `PageSettings` object is provided to the page setup dialog so it can store its data in our object, and the `ShowDialog` method is called to display the dialog for the user.

Deployment in .NET

Perhaps the biggest single issue we had to deal with in the world of COM and VB6 was deployment. Deploying VB client applications, especially those that used COM, ActiveX, or DCOM components could be very complex – leading us deep into the realm of "DLL Hell".

At first glance it appeared that web technologies would solve this problem, and they do in terms of client deployment. Unfortunately, due to the way IIS and COM components interact, deployment of a COM-based solution on a web server was not easy either. Not only might we run into DLL Hell issues on the web server, but IIS locks any COM components it uses – requiring that we restart the IIS process any time we want to update a DLL.

Even if we put our COM DLLs in an MTS Server Package or COM+ Server Application things weren't perfect. While we could stop the package to update a DLL, it still meant stopping all users from making use of our application during the update process.

The .NET Framework takes DLL Hell head on, making it much easier to deploy and update applications to our client workstations and to our web servers. In fact, one of the stated goals for .NET is to enable "XCOPY deployment" – meaning that deploying an application should be as easy as using the venerable DOS XCOPY command to copy the application's files to the target machine.

> **It really is possible, though often not preferable, to deploy many .NET applications with the XCOPY command.**

Obviously, while this illustrates a high level of simplicity, actually using XCOPY isn't desirable for most end-user scenarios. We still want to provide our users with simple, graphical install and uninstall options much like we have today with products such as InstallShield, Wise Installer, and the VB Package and Deployment Wizard.

In today's world, a good installer interacts closely with the Windows Installer, helping to avoid file conflicts and to ensure that uninstalls of an application are complete and don't accidentally remove files shared with other applications.

VB.NET provides us with a range of deployment options, relying on the underlying .NET Framework to ensure our components don't conflict with other components during the installation or update process.

Installation Options

The Visual Studio.NET tool provides us with powerful installation options, including:

- ❏ Self-installing Cab file
- ❏ Setup via an `msi` file (Windows System Installer)
- ❏ Deployment to a web server

VS.NET will also create a merge module, which is a pre-built installation component that can be used by another install option at a later time.

We also have two wizards at our disposal to help simplify the whole process:

- ❏ Deploy Wizard – assists us in deploying our application to a remote client machine or to a remote web server
- ❏ Setup Wizard – assists us in creating setup applications that will install our application when run on the target machine

The installation options available in VB.NET are displayed in the Visual Studio Setup and Deployment Projects menu choice, which is available via the File | New | Project or File | Add Project | New Project menu options. Upon selecting this project category, we are presented with a dialog similar to the following:

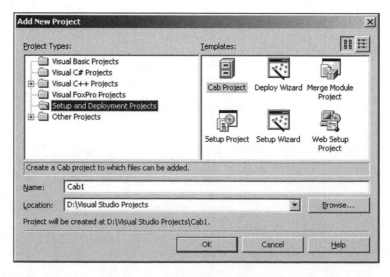

Typically, this type of project is added to an existing solution using the File | Add Project menu option, thus allowing the wizards to automatically run against the other project or projects in the solution.

In Beta 1 the .NET runtime itself isn't installed by these installation options. Any machine where we want to install .NET applications will need the .NET Framework SDK installed first. Obviously this doesn't apply to client machines that are accessing ASP.NET applications via the browser unless those applications download .NET components to the client workstation.

We won't cover all the options in detail in this book, focusing instead on the high-level steps needed to create installations for a rich client and web server.

Windows Install

To create an installation package for a Windows installation on a rich client we have a number of options. We can use the Setup Wizard option, which will walk us through the process of creating the appropriate type of install for our needs. Otherwise, if we know the type of installation we want to create, we can simply create it directly. Our primary options are:

- ❑ Cab Project – create a self-installing Cab-based installation that can be run from a network share or downloaded over the web
- ❑ Setup Project – create a self-contained msi file that will install using the Windows System Installer

We can also use the Deploy Wizard to not only create a setup package for a client machine, but also to directly deploy our application to that machine. This process requires the target machine to have the VS.NET extensions installed and that we have administrative security privileges on the target machine to copy the files and update the system.

Web Server Install

To deploy an application to a web server we have two primary options. We can use the Setup Wizard to create a Windows System Installer package (msi file) that can be installed on the web server machine. Alternately, we can use the Deploy Wizard. This wizard will directly deploy the required files to the web server machine. As with the Windows Install, this process requires that the VS.NET extensions are installed on the target machine and that we have administrative security privileges.

A third option is to create a Web Setup Project directly – which is the equivalent of using the Setup Wizard – either way we end up with a self-contained msi file that handles the installation on the web server through the use of the Windows System Installer.

Creating a Windows NT/Win2K Service with VB

When developing complex systems it is often desirable to have some of our code always running on a server, even when no one is logged onto the server machine. In the Windows environment, this typically translates to the use of a Windows NT or Windows 2000 service. A service is a program that can be automatically started as the operating system boots up – having nothing to do with whether a user is logged into the machine or not.

Creating a Windows Service

Services typically also provide other administrative functionality, including the ability to start, stop, and pause the service while it is running. In addition, services have no guarantee of an actual user interface, since they start as the system is booted – when no user may be logged into the system at all. Because of this, they typically utilize the system's Application Log if they need to output any informational data or error messages.

Historically, VB has had no native support for the creation of a Windows service. Various "hacks" have been created over the years, including programs that host another program as a service, an ActiveX control that makes a VB program into a service, and frameworks that load an ActiveX DLL as a service.

The Windows Service Project

With VB.NET however, we have full native support within VB for the creation of Windows services. In fact, Windows Service is a project type available to us within the IDE:

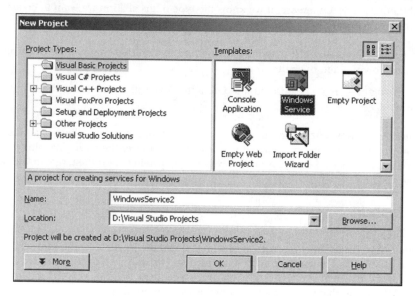

Name the project WindowsService and click OK. This project type starts us out with a UserService1 code module which contains a class.

This class is derived from the ServiceBase class:

```
Inherits System.ServiceProcess.ServiceBase
```

The base class also provides us with the general capabilities needed when creating a Windows service application, including overridable methods in which we can place our code to start and stop the service's process as appropriate:

```
Protected Overrides Sub OnStart(ByVal args() As String)
    ' TODO: Add code here to start your service. This method should set things
    ' in motion so your service can do its work.
End Sub
```

```
Protected Overrides Sub OnStop()
    ' TODO: Add code here to perform any tear-down
    ' necessary to stop your service.
End Sub
```

Similarly, we can implement `OnPause` and `OnContinue` methods, if appropriate, for our service. If we choose to implement these methods, we'll want to set the `CanPauseAndContinue` property to `True` as the service is initialized.

Writing to the Application Log

At a minimum, we'll probably want to log the fact that our service has started. We can do this by using the `System.Diagnostics.EventLog` class:

```
Protected Overrides Sub OnStart(ByVal args() As String)
    ' TODO: Add code here to start your service. This method should set things
    ' in motion so your service can do its work.
    System.Diagnostics.EventLog.WriteEntry("TestService", "Starting", _
        Diagnostics.EventLogEntryType.Information)
End Sub
```

This will write a message to the system's Application Log, which we can view using the **Event Viewer** tool available in Windows.

Creating Worker Threads

When creating a service, it is strongly recommended that all actual work be done on threads other than the main application thread. The main application thread should be free to accept start, stop, and pause requests from the user or operating system. We discussed threads and the multi-threaded capabilities of .NET earlier in this chapter.

It is also very important that our worker thread uses as few system resources as possible when it is not actively working, since a service is always running, from the time when the system boots up until the time it shuts down. If the service has busy wait loops or allocates huge amounts of memory, those resources will never be available to other applications on the machine. Instead, we need to use blocking waits and minimize the amount of memory or other resources we're consuming.

Services, by their very nature, are often designed to perform asynchronous tasks. Earlier in this chapter we discussed asynchronous processing and how it relates to multi-threading. It is quite common for a service to start an asynchronous process in the `OnStart` method, allowing each completed request to be processed on a separate thread automatically.

Another easy way to cause processing to occur on another thread is to use the `System.Timers.Timer` class. This timer fires its `Tick` event on another thread automatically. Better still, we can make use of the `Timer` control under the **Components** tab in the **Toolbox** to work with this timer. Simply drag-and-drop this timer control onto the designer surface for `UserService1` and we're ready to go.

Make sure to set the control's `Interval` property as appropriate (perhaps try `500`), and set its `Enabled` property to `False`. As our service is loaded we don't want the timer to fire. It shouldn't be enabled until the `OnStart` event occurs within the service.

Now we can change the `OnStart` and `OnStop` methods to start and stop the processing:

```
Protected Overrides Sub OnStart(ByVal args() As String)
    ' TODO: Add code here to start your service. This method should set things
    ' in motion so your service can do its work.
    System.Diagnostics.EventLog.WriteEntry("TestService", "Starting", _
        Diagnostics.EventLogEntryType.Information)
    Timer1.Enabled = True
End Sub

Protected Overrides Sub OnStop()
    ' TODO: Add code here to perform any tear-down
    '  necessary to stop your service.
    Timer1.Enabled = False
End Sub
```

The code to do any work will go in the `Tick` event handler for the timer control:

```
Protected Sub Timer1_Tick(ByVal sender As Object, _
        ByVal e As System.EventArgs)

    System.Diagnostics.EventLog.WriteEntry("TestService", _
        "Working on thread " & AppDomain.GetCurrentThreadID(), _
        Diagnostics.EventLogEntryType.Information)
End Sub
```

In this case we're simply writing an entry to the event log, but this routine could do any other work required by our application.

Installing the Service

Service applications can't be run from the VS.NET IDE or from the command line – they must be installed into the Windows environment so we can control them from the **Service Management Console**. To install the service we can use the installation options described earlier in the chapter, or we can use the `installutil.exe` command line utility.

Either way, however, we need to do some extra coding so the install process can properly install the service. In particular, we need to add a special class to our project that will interact with the installer during the install process. This class sets up the behaviors for our service, including what user account the service will run under, and its default startup mode (`Manual` or `Automatic`).

Add a new class module to the project and name it `ProjectInstaller.vb`:

```
Imports System
Imports System.Collections
Imports System.Configuration.Install
Imports System.ServiceProcess
Imports System.ComponentModel

Public Class <RunInstaller(True)> ProjectInstaller
    Inherits Installer

    Private serviceInstaller As ServiceInstaller
    Private processInstaller As ServiceProcessInstaller
```

```
    Public Sub New()
      MyBase.New()

      processInstaller = New ServiceProcessInstaller()
      serviceInstaller = New ServiceInstaller()

      ' Service will run under system account
      processInstaller.RunUnderSystemAccount = True

      ' Service will have Start Type of Manual
      serviceInstaller.StartType = ServiceStart.Manual

      serviceInstaller.ServiceName = "Test.Service"

      Installers.Add(serviceInstaller)
      Installers.Add(processInstaller)
    End Sub
  End Class
```

We'll also need to add a reference to the `System.Configuration.Install.dll` for this to work.

This class is derived from the `Installer` class, and only has a constructor method with no parameters. In the constructor we need to do any setup required by our service. In particular, we need to specify the account under which it will run, the startup mode for the service, and the name it will be referenced by in the Service Management Console.

In this example we're setting the `RunUnderSystemAccount` property to `True` – indicating that the service should run under the `System` account on the machine. This account has no password and is used primarily to run services – but it may have security access greater than the typical user.

We can also set this value to `False` and instead set the `Username` and `Password` properties to a valid account. This will still allow the server to start as the system boots up (when no user is logged in interactively), but also allows us to control the security privileges of the user account that will be running the service.

If we set this value to `False` and do not set the `Username` and `Password` properties, we will be prompted for account information as the service is installed and can provide the information at that time.

At this point we can build the project and use the `installutil.exe` utility to install the service. This utility is run from a console window, when in the project's `bin` directory, as follows:

```
installutil windowsservice.exe
```

To uninstall the service use the `/u` switch:

```
installutil windowsservice.exe /u
```

Note that the uninstall won't actually complete while the Service Management Console is open. If the console is open, it must be closed and reopened to allow the uninstall to complete.

At this point we can use the Service Management Console to start and stop the service:

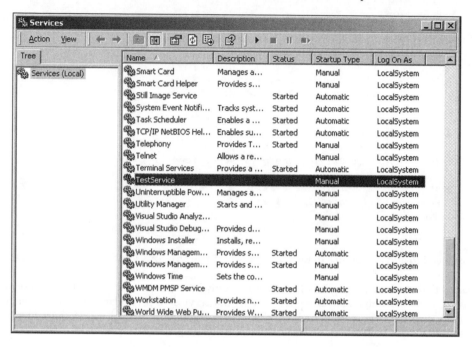

Upon starting and then stopping the service, we can go to the Event Viewer utility and view the Application Log:

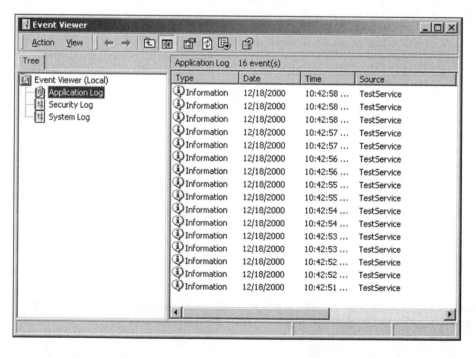

Each of the entries here was created by the service as it ran. They look something like this:

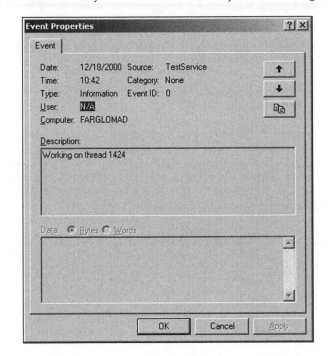

We can see the text written to the event log from our code, along with various other useful pieces of information.

The `ServiceBase` base class also automatically writes some entries on our behalf, noting when the service has started and stopped successfully. These entries are worded The service has started successfully and The service has stopped successfully.

At this point we have a functioning service, ready for use.

Monitoring the File System

The Windows file system allows applications to be notified when a directory is changed. This capability can be easily illustrated by opening two explorer windows to display the same directory. Add or delete a file, and both windows automatically update to show the new status. Sometimes it is nice to have this capability within our applications as well – perhaps when writing an application that acts on files as they are copied to our server via FTP.

The .NET Framework provides hooks that allow us to easily write an application that monitors the file system for changes. When a change occurs, we can react appropriately based on the requirements for our application. This capability can be combined with the ability to create a Windows service as discussed earlier in this chapter, to create many interesting types of application.

This functionality is encapsulated within the `FileSystemWatcher` class, which is located in the `System.IO` namespace. We can create an instance through code or drag-and-drop the component from the **Components** tab of the Toolbox onto a form or component designer window.

The `FileSystemWatcher` allows us to easily watch a file, directory, or subdirectory for changes. It can also be used to watch network drives and remote directories.

> *There are some limitations when watching remote directories. Refer to the on-line help on the `FileSystemWatcher` class for further details.*

We can watch for various events, including writes to the file or directory, file size changes, attribute changes, security changes, and file access.

Creating a Windows application to log when new files are added or removed from a directory is quite straightforward. Create a new Windows Application project and add a ListBox control to the form, setting its `Dock` property to `Fill`. Also add a FileSystemWatcher control (name it `FSW`) from the **Components** tab of the Toolbox. Set the `Path` property to the directory to be watched; in this example we'll use `c:\`.

Open the code window and add the following to the `Form1` class:

```
Public Sub FSW_Created(ByVal sender As Object, _
        ByVal e As System.IO.FileSystemEventArgs) Handles FSW.Created
    ListBox1.Items.Add("File: " & e.FullPath & " created")
End Sub

Public Sub FSW_Changed(ByVal sender As Object, _
        ByVal e As System.IO.FileSystemEventArgs) Handles FSW.Changed
    ListBox1.Items.Add("File: " & e.FullPath & " changed")
End Sub

Public Sub FSW_Deleted(ByVal sender As Object, _
        ByVal e As System.IO.FileSystemEventArgs) Handles FSW.Deleted
    ListBox1.Items.Add("File: " & e.FullPath & " deleted")
End Sub

Public Sub FSW_Renamed(ByVal sender As Object, _
        ByVal e As System.IO.RenamedEventArgs) Handles FSW.Renamed
    ListBox1.Items.Add("File: " & e.OldFullPath & " renamed to " & e.FullPath)
End Sub
```

These methods handle the `Created`, `Changed`, `Deleted`, and `Renamed` events generated by the `FileSystemWatcher` component, and log the resulting changes to the `ListBox1` control on the form. When we run this program, any changes to the directory or its files will be logged to our form.

Command Line Options

VB has always been primarily a graphical development tool. While VS.NET continues to provide us with a powerful graphical IDE for development, there are times when we may want to do some operations from a console window, command line, or batch file.

VB.NET has a compiler that can be invoked from the command line, and the .NET Framework SDK provides us with a number of command line tools and utilities that we may find useful in some circumstances.

> **In fact, using a text editor, the command line compiler for VB.NET, and the .NET utilities, it is technically possible to create any VB.NET application without using the VS.NET IDE.**

Obviously this would require us to write all the code that is automatically generated by the IDE, and so this approach is rarely ideal, but the fact that it is possible illustrates the power at our disposal through the command line compiler and the various other tools.

vbc Command Line Parameters

The VB.NET compiler is named `vbc.exe` and can be invoked from within a console window. Try typing `vbc` with no parameters at the prompt and you will see help information on how to use the command.

Using the command line compiler is a bit trickier than allowing the VS.NET IDE to do the work for us. In particular, all the references we add to a project need to be explicitly added to the command line. For instance, even the simplest console application is compiled using the following command:

```
vbc /t:exe /r:system.dll mysource.vb
```

We don't always need to explicitly reference `System.dll`. *In fact we wouldn't need to in this example. However, there are times when not referencing the* `system.dll` *will cause applications to fail, so it is best to always reference this DLL.*

The `/t:exe` flag indicates that the target type for the application is a console application. An application that makes use of Windows Forms functionality would also reference that assembly, and might look like this:

```
vbc /t:winexe /r:system.dll /r:system.winforms.dll mysource.vb
```

Basically, any references to assemblies that we would have added within the VS.NET IDE need to be added to the command line using `/r` flags.

The flag `/t:winexe` indicates that the application is a windows application, but we also need to explicitly add the reference to the `system.winforms.dll` for the application to compile.

A key to success in deployment and management of .NET applications is the proper use of versioning. When doing command line compilation we must handle versioning on the command line by using the `/version` switch:

```
vbc /t:exe /r:system.dll /version:1.0.0.1 mysource.vb
```

The four parts of `/version`'s value refer to major version, minor version, revision, and build.

Obviously, there are many other options available for our use, but these are the most common ones used when building applications by hand.

Compiling is only half the story though. For instance, Windows services must be installed on the machine and web services must be advertised for discovery by clients. These operations are provided either by the VS.NET IDE, or by using various other command line tools and utilities included in the .NET Framework SDK.

Description of Tools in the \bin Directory

When the .NET Framework SDK is installed, it includes a set of important tools and utilities for our use. These are located in the `bin` directory where the SDK is installed, often in a path similar to `C:\Program Files\Microsoft.NET\FrameworkSDK\bin`.

The majority of these tools are run from the command line, though some are graphical Windows applications. The VS.NET IDE has most of the functionality provided by these tools built in, so most applications can be created without any need to use them.

Configuration and Deployment Tools and Utilities

The first group of tools is used to configure and deploy .NET applications of all sorts:

Tool	Description
Assembly Generation Utility `al.exe`	Accepts as input one or more files that are either MSIL format or resource files, and outputs a file with an assembly manifest.
Global Assembly Cache Utility `gacutil.exe`	Used to view and manipulate the contents of the global assembly cache. This utility can be used from build scripts, make files, and batch files.
Installer Utility `InstallUtil.exe`	This tool works in conjunction with the Installer Framework. It allows you to install and uninstall server resources with an assembly, by executing the installer components of that assembly.
Assembly Registration Tool `RegAsm.exe`	Enables classic COM clients to call managed classes. `RegAsm` reads the metadata within an assembly, then adds the necessary entries to the registry so classic COM clients can create the managed classes transparently.
Services Registration Tool `RegSvcs.exe`	Adds managed classes to Windows 2000 Component Services by performing several tasks within a single utility. These tasks include loading and registering the assembly, and generating, registering, and installing the type library into an existing COM+ 1.0 application.
Assembly Cache Viewer `shfusion.dll`	Windows shell extension for viewing and manipulating the contents of the global assembly cache using the Windows Explorer. This cache is in an `ASSEMBLY` directory under the system root directory – often something like `C:\WINNT\ASSEMBLY`.
Isolated Storage Utility `storeadm.exe`	Used to manage isolated storage for the currently logged in user. Isolated storage is a mechanism within .NET that allows our applications to store user files without possibility of naming collisions with other users or viewing other user's files.
Type Library Exporter `TlbExp.exe`	Using a managed assembly as input, generates a type library containing COM definitions of the public types defined in that assembly.

Tool	Description
Type Library Importer `Tlbimp.exe`	Converts the type definitions found within a COM type library into equivalent definition in managed metadata format.
Web Service Utility `WebServiceUtil.exe`	Installs and uninstalls managed code Web Services.
Common Language Runtime XML Schema Definition Tool `xsd.exe`	Used for working with XML Schemas that follow the XML Schema Definition (XSD) language proposed by the W3C.

Windows Forms Design Tools and Utilities

These tools are primarily used when building and designing Windows Applications:

Tool	Description
Windows Forms ActiveX Control Importer `aximp.exe`	Using an ActiveX control's type library as input, generates a wrapper control that allows the ActiveX control to be hosted by a Windows Forms form.
License Compiler `lc.exe`	Using text files containing licensing information as input, produces a binary `.licenses` file that can be embedded in a managed binary executable.
Resource File Generator Utility `ResGen.exe`	Reads text files containing name/value pairs and produces a managed binary `.resources` file. The utility can also be used to decompile the binary `.resources` file.
Windows Forms Designer Test Container `windes.exe`	Used for testing the design time behaviour of Windows Forms controls.

Security Tools and Utilities

These utilities are used to configure and alter security settings, create security certificates and to sign our code:

Tool	Description
Code Access Security Policy Utility `caspol.exe`	Used to examine and modify machine and user code access security policies.
Software Publisher Certificate Test Utility `cert2spc.exe`	Creates, for test purposes only, a Software Publisher's Certificate (SPC) from one or more X.509 certificates.
Certificate Manager Utility `certmgr.exe`	Used to manage certificates, certificate trust lists (CTLs), and certificate revocation lists (CRLs).
Certificate Verification Utility `chktrust.exe`	Checks the validity of an Authenticode signed file.

Tool	Description
Certificate Creation Utility `makecert.exe`	Creates, for test purposes only, X.509 certificates. These may be used as input to the `cert2spc.exe` utility.
Permissions View Utility `permview.exe`	Used to view the permission sets requested by an assembly.
Secutil Utility `SecUtil.exe`	Extracts Strong Name public key information or Authenticode™ publisher certificates from an assembly, in a format that can be incorporated directly into code.
Set Registry Utility `setreg.exe`	Changes registry settings related to test certificates.
File Signing Utility `signcode.exe`	Signs a PE file with requested permissions to give developers more detailed control over the security restrictions placed on their component.
Strong Name Utility `Sn.exe`	Creates and verifies assemblies with strong names.

General Tools and Utilities

The following are a set of assorted tools and utilities that are useful in various situations:

Tool	Description
Common Language Runtime Debugger `cordbg.exe`	A command-line utility that can help tools vendors and application developers find and fix bugs in programs that target the Common Language Runtime.
Common Language Runtime Visual Debugger `DbgUrt.exe`	This is a basic debugger with a graphical interface, and is located in the SDK's GuiDebug sub-directory. Documentation for this debugger can be found in the SDK documentation under ".NET Framework Tools and Debugger". Note: The Common Language Runtime Visual Debugger is not installed on Windows 9X platforms by the .NET Framework SDK installation.
Common Language Runtime IL Assembler `ilasm.exe`	Using IL as input, generates a PE file containing the IL and the required metadata. The resulting executable can be run to determine whether the IL performs as expected.
Microsoft .NET Framework IL Disassembler `ildasm.exe`	Used to disassemble and inspect the IL code in a PE file.
PEVerify Utility `peverify.exe`	Assists in validating the type safety of code prior to release. Also assists in generating IL, and in determining if IL code and associated metadata meets type safety verification requirements.

Tool	Description
Soapsuds `soapsuds.exe`	Converts CLR MetaData to and from an XML Schema. Fully represents the full CLR type system needed for CLR Remoting.
Windows Forms Class Viewer `wincv.exe`	Finds the managed classes matching a specified search pattern, then uses the reflection API to display information about those classes.

The tools and utilities provided with the .NET Framework SDK provide a powerful set of capabilities for our use. While particularly useful when developing applications outside of the VS.NET IDE, some of these tools may be useful when configuring, deploying, securing, and debugging any application.

Summary

Along with all the exciting advances in the VB language and the VS.NET IDE, we also gain a lot of powerful capabilities from the .NET Framework and the .NET system class libraries. As we've seen in this chapter, many things that were impossible or very difficult in the past have now become quite easy.

Obviously, this chapter merely scratches the surface of the capabilities available to VB developers within the .NET environment. The system class libraries contain many more features and capabilities that go far beyond what we could show here, and also provide capabilities in areas we haven't even discussed.

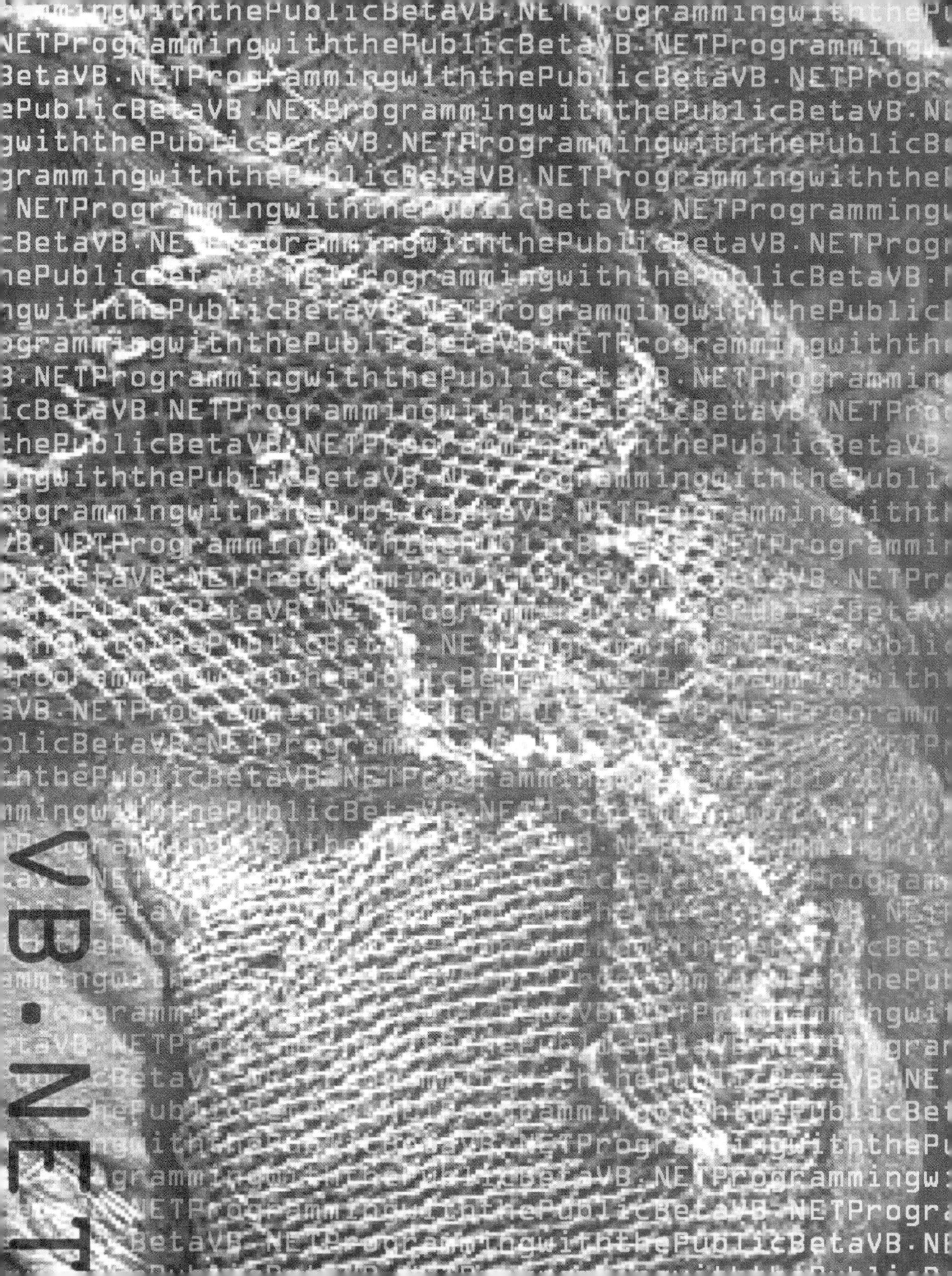
VB.NET
VB.NET Programming with the Public Beta

Interoperability and Migration

By this point in the book it has become apparent that .NET and VB.NET are quite different from COM and VB6 in many ways. Yet most people have substantial investments in the COM and VB6 technologies, and it is unrealistic to expect that our .NET applications will exist independently in most cases. To meet this need, the .NET Framework has a mechanism for interoperating with COM and ActiveX components. This mechanism provides bi-directional capabilities – allowing .NET applications to call COM components, and also allowing COM components or applications to call .NET assemblies.

While .NET provides the new ADO.NET data access technology, there are times when we may want to use the original ADO for data access. This can be particularly useful in cases where pessimistic locking or persistent database connections are required, since ADO.NET doesn't support these concepts. Fortunately, ADO is represented as a set of COM components and so we can use the COM interoperability support to access ADO when needed.

Additionally, though the .NET system class libraries are extensive, there are times, such as when calling specialized functionality like DirectX, when applications may need more direct access to the underlying operating system. VB.NET supports this concept, allowing us to call Win32 API functions when necessary.

There are occasions when interoperability may not be sufficient and we'll need to migrate existing VB6 code into VB.NET. Microsoft has stated that they are working on a migration tool to assist in this effort, and we'll take a quick look at this tool in its current, very early, state.

COM/DCOM/COM+ Interoperability

Since the release of version 4.0, VB developers have been developing applications based on ActiveX and COM. Many applications are designed to use ActiveX DLLs. Others are designed as ActiveX EXE projects, and many make use of user-created ActiveX controls. All of these are examples of COM components that are likely to be used within our existing applications.

The same is true for web applications. While some ASP applications are written entirely in scripting code within the ASP pages, a great many sites are designed to have the ASP script code call into COM components. These components are often written in VB as ActiveX DLL projects.

Given the tremendous use of COM for development, it comes as no surprise that Microsoft has included COM interoperability support in the .NET platform. It will be a rare .NET application that makes no use of COM components, since most of us will want to make use of our existing code when building new applications – regardless of whether they are COM or .NET.

The interoperability support is fairly extensive, though there are limitations. .NET applications can make calls into COM components – including ActiveX DLLs (both local and though DCOM) and ActiveX controls. It is also possible to design .NET assemblies so they are accessible from applications based on COM, so the support is bi-directional. Since there are substantial differences between the COM platform and the .NET platform however, it is very important to test each individual component or control to ensure it works appropriately through interop.

Invoking COM Components from .NET

The .NET Framework provides extensive support to allow managed code in .NET to call out to COM components. The VS.NET environment uses this support to make accessing a COM component as simple as adding a reference to the component from within the IDE.

Designing COM Components for .NET

There are some rules that must be followed by the designer of the COM component for this mechanism to work properly. Fortunately, these rules are automatically followed by virtually all COM components created with VB6, with no extra effort on our part.

However, for those developing COM components in other languages, the following is a summary of the rules and best practices for success:

- ❑ Create a type library
- ❑ Provide version and locale information in the type library
- ❑ Use only data types supported by COM automation
- ❑ Use types common to both COM and .NET (isomorphic types)
- ❑ Avoid chatty interfaces
- ❑ Name enums and structures clearly – these names carry through
- ❑ Explicitly free resources
- ❑ Do not use methods with the same method names as the System.Object class in .NET
- ❑ Use the Binary Compatibility setting in VB6

Let's look at some of these points in more detail now.

Providing a Type Library

It is mandatory that we provide a type library or .NET won't be able to determine how to call into the component. COM components created using VB6 automatically incorporate the type library directly into the component (DLL, EXE, or OCX), so we typically don't need to worry about this issue.

Ideally the type library would include versioning and locale information, as that information is carried through into the .NET environment.

When a COM DLL is imported into .NET, a "wrapper" object is created within .NET by which we can reference the component. This wrapper object is derived from the base `System.Object` type in .NET, meaning that it will automatically have methods named `Equals`, `Finalize`, `GetHashCode`, `GetType`, `MemberwiseClone`, and `ToString`. To avoid conflicts, the COM component should not use any of these names as members of its interface.

Marshaling Between .NET and COM

Data is marshaled between the .NET and COM environments every time we make a method or property call. There are a couple of implications here.

First off, for the marshaling to work the data types must be convertible between the two environments. The marshaling mechanism understands the COM automation types and the Common Language Interface (CLI) types from .NET. The best thing to do is to stick with types that are common in both environments (such as integer and floating point numbers) as they marshal most easily. Other types (such as strings or dates) require conversion during the marshaling process which can have a negative performance impact.

> **Remember that the integer data type sizes are different in VB.NET from those in VB6 as was discussed in Chapter 3.**

Strings are one of the most commonly passed data types. .NET strings are always Unicode, and can be efficiently marshaled to code that expects Unicode string data, while ANSI string data must be converted to and from Unicode. Fortunately the native VB6 `String` data type is Unicode, so, again, we typically have little to worry about here.

Arrays are also of concern because all VB.NET arrays are now zero-based. If we are using anything other than zero-based arrays in our applications, the wizard will be unable to fix all our array index values and we'll have to go through and upgrade that code by hand.

Because data must be marshaled between the two environments, we should always strive to minimize the number of methods called from .NET into a COM component. Each call from one environment into the other will take time – so the more calls we make the poorer our application will perform. Ideally, the COM components we call would have very few methods, each of which does quite a lot of work. We should avoid interacting with COM components that have a lot of small methods or properties, as this leads to "chatty" interaction between the .NET code and the COM component.

> *If we must interact with a fine-grained COM component (one with many properties and methods), it may be beneficial to create a second COM component with just a few methods that can "automate" or wrap our calls into the original component. This technique is described by the well-known design pattern named Facade. Refer to "Design Patterns" by Erich Gamma, et al. (ISBN 0201633612) for further details.*

Component Termination and Garbage Collection

.NET makes the COM component available to our code via a .NET wrapper object. It is this wrapper that holds the actual reference to the COM object behind the scenes. Because this wrapper is a .NET object, it will be destroyed by the .NET garbage collection mechanism as opposed to being destroyed when we de-reference the object. The COM component itself won't be released until the .NET wrapper object is terminated.

> **This means that the COM component may be retained in memory for an indeterminate period of time before it is released.**

To avoid resource reclamation problems, COM components that use expensive resources such as database connections or file locks should have a method to explicitly release those resources. The .NET code can then call this method when it is done with the component, so the component can release the resources without waiting, until it is eventually released by the garbage collection mechanism. See Chapter 5 for more information about this.

VB6 and Binary Compatibility

While most of the major rules for making a .NET-friendly COM component are automatic when building the components with VB6, there is one key step that is unique to the VB environment – the use of **binary compatibility**.

When a COM component is referenced by .NET, the reference is against the component's unique CLSID value. In VB6, by default, each time a component is recompiled it gets a new ID value – meaning that all .NET code will lose access to the component. .NET will see the newly compiled version as an entirely different DLL.

By using Binary Compatibility within the VB6 IDE (on the Component tab of the Properties window, reached via the Project | Properties menu) two things happen. First, any time the component's interface is changed, we'll be warned that it will be incompatible with the existing component. Second, as long as we *don't* change the interface such that it becomes incompatible with the existing component, the CLSID value will be preserved as we compile. This means that .NET won't lose access to the component each time we recompile.

Calling a COM Component

Now that we have some background, let's take a look at how we can call a COM component from within VB.NET. First we'll create a simple ActiveX DLL using VB6, reference it from within VB.NET, and then write some code to interact with the object.

Creating the COM Component

We can easily create a simple COM component in VB6 by creating an ActiveX DLL project. Name the project COMserver and rename Class1 to be COMclass. Then add the following code:

```
Option Explicit

Public Function GetValue(Data As String) As String
  GetValue = "The data is " & Data
End Function

Public Function GetNumber() As Long
  GetNumber = 42
End Function

Public Function GetArray() As Integer()
  Dim a(5) As Integer

  a(1) = 1
```

```
      a(2) = 2
      a(3) = 3
      a(4) = 4
      a(5) = 5
    GetArray = a
  End Function

  Public Function GetVar() As Variant
    GetVar = Now
  End Function

  Public Function GetDate() As Date
    GetDate = Now
  End Function
```

With this code, our object will return a variety of data types, including text, numeric, date, Variant, and an array.

It is not possible, at least in Beta 1 of VB.NET, to return a user-defined type (UDT) as a result. Interestingly enough, however, a Public Type declared in our VB6 class *will* be a valid data type within the .NET environment, just like a Structure declared in VB.NET itself.

We can also make use of Public Enum declarations, since they will be made available within our VB.NET project. An Enum data type can be passed to and from a COM component as a parameter or return value without difficulty – after all, an Enum is just a numeric data type in disguise.

Once we compile this code to create the COMserver.DLL file, we are ready to switch into VS.NET and build a program that makes use of these methods.

Referencing the Component

In a VS.NET project we can gain access to the COM component by just adding a reference to the component. Choose the Project | Add References menu option and then select the COM tab within the dialog. After a short wait while all the COM components on the machine are cataloged, we'll be presented with a list of available components. Scroll down to the COMserver entry and double-click:

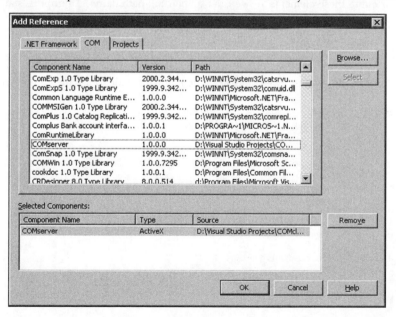

When we click the **OK** button, the VS.NET IDE will add a reference to this component to our project. This reference is more complex than it might appear at first. The IDE will examine the component's type library – the information describing the component's interface – and will use that information to generate a .NET wrapper that makes the component look and feel like a .NET assembly. We don't actually see any of this, including the wrapper. Instead, it appears to us that we've just added a new assembly to our project.

The new reference is visible in the **Solution Explorer** window just like any other reference:

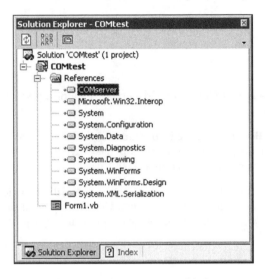

At this point we can write code to make use of the new "assembly".

Using the Object

Once referenced, a COM component appears to our code just like any other .NET assembly. This includes having a namespace by which the component's elements are referenced. We can use the `Imports` statement to provide a shortcut to these elements, or we can use their full path name. An imports statement for our example component would appear as:

```
Imports COMserver
```

In a VB.NET **Console Application** we could write the following code to use the component:

```
Imports System.Console
Imports COMserver

Module Module1

  Sub Main()
    Dim com As New COMclass()

    WriteLine(com.GetValue("sample data"))

    WriteLine(com.GetNumber())

    WriteLine("It is now {0}", com.GetDate)

    WriteLine("The array contains:")
```

```
      Dim num As Short
      Dim a() As Short = com.GetArray()
      For Each num In a
        WriteLine(num)
      Next

      WriteLine("It is now {0}", CDate(com.GetVar()))

      Read()
    End Sub

  End Module
```

The `GetValue` method accepts a `String` and returns a value as a `String`. It is pretty straightforward.

The `GetNumber` method returns an `Integer` value. Remember that we declared it as type `Long` in VB6, which corresponds to the `Integer` data type in VB.NET as we discussed in Chapter 3.

The `GetDate` method returns a `Date` data type. While the name of the data type is the same from VB6 to VB.NET, the underlying structure is not identical, but the marshaling process takes care of those details for us.

The `GetArray` method returns an array of type `Short` rather than `Integer`. The VB6 `Integer` data type corresponds to the VB.NET `Short` type. This array can be treated like any other array, including looping through all the elements as shown. Remember that all VB.NET arrays are zero-based, so even the array we created in VB6 (with indices from 1 to 5) will give us values from 0 to 5.

> *This is generally true of arrays as we move them back and forth. They will always be zero-based in VB.NET and will be based however we've declared them in VB6.*

The `GetVar` method returns a value of type `Object`. In VB6 this method returned a `Variant`, which roughly corresponds to `Object` in VB.NET. Because `Option Strict On` is the default, there's very little we can do with this return value unless we convert it to a meaningful type. Since we know that it is returning a `Date` we can use `CDate` to make that conversion.

When we run this application we should get output similar to the following:

Accessing a COM component is virtually as easy and painless as using a native .NET assembly.

Using ADO from VB.NET

Given that we can easily access COM components from within .NET, and given that ADO is exposed as a set of COM components, it naturally follows that our .NET applications can make use of ADO for data access if needed.

Of course .NET provides us with the new ADO.NET data access technology, and that is the preferred mechanism for data access. However, there may be times when ADO is required – for instance, pessimistic locking is not supported by ADO.NET, so if we need that feature we'll need to use ADO.

Gaining access to ADO is as simple as adding a reference to the appropriate ADO library by using the COM tab after choosing the Project | Add References menu option:

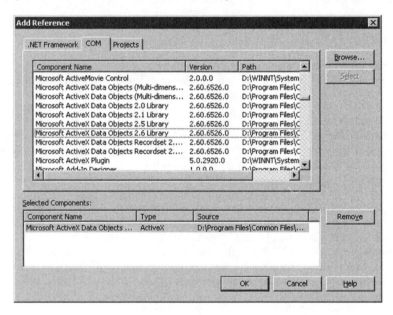

With that reference in place, we'll have access to ADO via the ADODB namespace.

For instance, in a Windows Application with a ListBox control on the form, we could write the following method:

```
Private Sub LoadData()
  Dim rs As New ADODB.Recordset()
  Const dbConn As String = "PROVIDER=SQLOLEDB;Data Source=myserver;" & _
    "Initial Catalog=pubs;User id=sa;Password=;"

  rs.Open("select au_lname, au_fname from authors", dbConn, _
    ADODB.CursorTypeEnum.adOpenForwardOnly, _
    ADODB.LockTypeEnum.adLockReadOnly)

  Do While Not rs.EOF
    ListBox1.Items.Add(CStr(rs.Fields("au_lname").Value) & _
      ", " & _
      CStr(rs.Fields("au_fname").Value))
```

```
        rs.MoveNext()
    Loop

    rs.Close ()
End Sub
```

When this code is run it will populate the ListBox control with a list of the names of authors from the pubs database. For the most part, this code should look quite familiar to anyone used to working with ADO.

Gaining access to the data in each row is a bit different however, since we're explicitly using the Value property from each Field object. This is required, since VB.NET doesn't work with default properties in the same way as VB6, and so the Value property is not treated as a default property. Instead, we must explicitly reference the Value property to gain access to the data in each field.

The only other change is that each method call must have parentheses, just like any other method in VB.NET.

Using ActiveX Controls from Windows Forms

The Windows Forms technology used by VB.NET to create Windows applications provides its own mechanism for creating and managing controls – different from the ActiveX controls we're used to in VB6. This is discussed in more detail in Chapter 4.

It is possible to use ActiveX controls on a form created using Windows Forms in a manner very similar to how we can use COM components directly from code. The VS.NET IDE allows us to add an ActiveX control to the Toolbox so we can use it on our forms.

When an OCX file is added to the Toolbox, VS.NET automatically creates .NET wrapper classes for each control in the file. These wrapper classes are based on the AxHost class, which provides the ActiveX control with the illusion that it is running in an ActiveX container, and provides the actual Windows Forms host with the illusion that the ActiveX control is a Windows Forms control.

Of course VB.NET uses COM interoperability to interact with ActiveX controls, since those controls are just specialized COM components. This means that we have the same performance issues with ActiveX controls as we do with COM components in general, in that all property and method calls to a control are marshaled from the .NET environment into the COM environment.

Adding a Tab to the Toolbox

While not strictly necessary, it is nice to put any imported ActiveX controls on their own tab within the Toolbox to keep things organized.

Adding a tab to the Toolbox is straightforward. Just right-click on the Toolbox and choose the Add Tab menu option. A new tab will be added, with the cursor placed in the name field. Enter a name for the tab – such as ActiveX – and click on the new tab to open it.

Adding an ActiveX Control to the Toolbox

Adding a control to the Toolbox is equally simple. Just right-click on the Toolbox and choose the Customize Toolbox menu option. Click the checkbox next to the control to be imported, as shown in the following diagram:

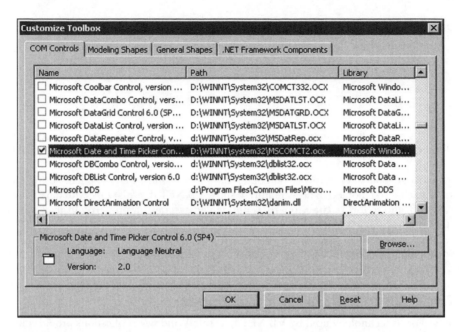

When we click **OK**, the IDE will import the OCX and create wrapper classes for each control within it, placing the controls on the open tab in the **Toolbox**. In this example we're adding the **Date and Time Picker** control.

If the ActiveX control's interface (properties, methods and events) is changed later we'll need to re-import the control so VS.NET can create an updated wrapper class. This is particularly important to keep in mind when importing VB6 UserControls that we may be altering later.

Using the ActiveX Control

Once the control has been added to the **Toolbox** we can use it like any other control, either using a double-click or drag-and-drop approach to adding instances of the control to a form.

Once the control is on a form, we can write code to interact with the control, and the user can interact with the control when the program is running. For instance, we might have code in our form similar to the following:

```
Public Sub AxDTPicker1_Change(ByVal sender As Object, _
    ByVal e As System.EventArgs) Handles AxDTPicker1.Change

  MsgBox(AxDTPicker1.Value)
End Sub
```

This code responds to the Change event from the control, displaying the value selected by the user.

Notice that the default name for any ActiveX control will start with Ax to differentiate them from native Windows Forms controls.

Using ActiveX Controls from Web Forms

We can also use ActiveX controls when creating Web Form applications using ASP.NET. Creation of web applications was discussed in Chapter 6, so here we'll assume familiarity with the basic concepts.

.NET web controls are intelligent server-side controls that enhance web developer productivity. When the user accesses the web page, the controls are not downloaded to the client – rather they run on the server and render appropriate HTML that is sent to the browser for display.

ActiveX controls are different. ActiveX controls are not designed to emit HTML for display in a browser – they are designed to provide display in a Windows environment. When an ActiveX control is placed on a web page and the user navigates to that page, the ActiveX control will run on the user's machine in the user's browser.

If the user does not have the ActiveX control installed on their computer, either the user will receive an error or the ActiveX control may be downloaded and installed. The control can only be downloaded and installed if we have set the codebase property to point to a CAB file. This CAB file must contain all the required files to install and configure the ActiveX control.

> **Since the ActiveX control will be running on the client workstation, this approach will only work if we know the client workstation is running a Win32 operating system with Internet Explorer as the browser (or Netscape with the relevant plug-in).**

There are serious security considerations involved when working with ActiveX controls on web pages. Typically IE only allows download of signed controls, and then only when approved by the user. Once installed and running on the client's computer, an ActiveX control can do anything any other Windows application could do on that machine.

Because ActiveX controls are not designed for the Web Forms environment, they do not raise events like Web Form controls. In fact, ASP.NET treats an ActiveX control merely as an <OBJECT> tag on the page – a client-side artifact that will be rendered along with any other static HTML on the page.

> **We cannot write ASP.NET server-side code to interact with ActiveX controls.**

Any code that is to interact with the ActiveX control will need to be written as client-side script code using JScript or VBScript by using the HTML view of the page in the VS.NET IDE.

Adding the Control to the Toolbox

Adding an ActiveX control to the Toolbox for use on a Web Form is exactly the same as adding one to the Toolbox for use with a Windows Form. Please refer to the previous discussion on *Adding an ActiveX Control to the Toolbox* for details.

Using the Control

Once the ActiveX control is available on the Toolbox, adding it to a web page is as easy as adding any other control. Just double-click or drag-and-drop to place the control on the page designer.

With the control on the designer, we can move ahead to write code that interacts with the control. Remember that this will be client-side script code running in the browser, not on the server along with the rest of the code in the page. To author client-side code, we need to use the page designer's HTML tab (at the bottom of the Design pane) or View | HTML Source.

For instance, open a new **Web Application** project. Add a **Button** control from the **HTML** tab of the **ToolBox** and a **TextBox** control from the **Web Forms** tab. Now add the **Date and Time Picker** control – which we stored previously in the **Toolbox**'s **ActiveX** tab – to the page. The control appears visually in the designer window and as a collapsed region of code in the **HTML** view. Collapsing code regions are discussed in Chapter 3.

By default, the control has no `id` property, and so there's no way to write code against it. If we click on the collapsed code block, or the control itself in the design window, we can set its properties using the standard VS.NET `Properties` window. At the very least, we need to set the `(id)` property to a meaningful name against which we can program. In this example, set the `id` to `DTPicker`.

Then we can write script code directly in the HTML displayed in the **HTML** tab of the designer. The code may appear something like this:

```
<html><head>
<script language=vbs>
    Sub Button1_OnClick()
        WebForm1.TextBox1.value = WebForm1.DTPicker.Value
    End Sub
</script>
<meta content="Microsoft Visual Studio.NET 7.0" name=GENERATOR>
<meta content="Visual Basic 7.0" name=CODE_LANGUAGE></head>
```

We will get an error in the task list – **Element 'object' may not be nested within element 'form'**. This appears to be a Beta 1 bug in the IDE, since we can still save and run the page and it will work fine.

When the HTML `Button` control is clicked, it will fire a client-side `OnClick` event, which is caught by this VBScript code. The code then sets the `value` property of `TextBox1` to the value selected by the user in the `DTPicker` control. This will occur entirely on the client without requiring a round-trip to the server for any processing.

There are serious limitations to the use of ActiveX controls in the web environment – especially in the areas of deployment and security. Nonetheless, the VS.NET IDE makes it relatively easy to incorporate them into ASP.NET web pages, allowing us to simply drag-and-drop from the **Toolbox** and write client-side script code to interact with them as needed.

DCOM

Many existing Visual Basic applications make use of COM components that are actually running on other machines across the network. They interact with these components using Distributed COM (DCOM). As we discussed in Chapter 8, the .NET platform uses either web services or the .NET remoting technology to interact with assemblies running on other machines – not DCOM.

However, DCOM is still available for our use when we are writing .NET applications that require access to COM components running on other machines. This is due less to .NET than to COM itself. One of the major strengths of COM and DCOM is that they provide us with **location transparency**. This is the concept that our code can't tell the difference between interacting with a component running on our machine or running on another machine. Either way, the client code is identical.

In VB6 we might write the following code to interact with a COM component:

```
Dim obj As Aclass

Set obj = New Aclass
obj.DoSomething
```

Looking at this code there's no way to tell if `Aclass` is included in our application, is loaded into our application from a `DLL`, is running in MTS or COM+ on our machine, or is running on another machine somewhere on the network. In fact, with no changes to this client code at all, we can reconfigure the application into any of those scenarios and the code will still work. This is location transparency.

We've already seen how VB.NET allows us to interact with COM components by simply adding a reference to the component from within our project. This same location transparency benefit extends to us in .NET as it did in VB6. Since the .NET runtime relies on COM itself to handle the COM component, we can communicate with a remote COM component as easily as one running on our local machine.

To invoke a DCOM component from .NET, the component must be installed on the remote machine and registered on the local workstation as a remote component. This process is no different from what we'd do with VB6 to make a remote component available.

Beyond this configuration process, interacting with a DCOM component is identical to interacting with any other COM component as we discussed earlier in the chapter. The VS.NET IDE provides the component with a .NET wrapper class, and our code interacts with this class just as if the component were native to the .NET platform.

One key thing to remember is that .NET doesn't have deterministic finalization, so the remote component may not be released immediately upon our .NET application de-referencing the wrapper object. The remote component will be released when the .NET garbage collection process terminates the wrapper object. Because of this, it is very important to make sure that the remote object doesn't retain any expensive resources such as database connections or file locks any longer than necessary.

Also keep in mind that when .NET interacts with a component through DCOM, it must marshal all method and property calls from the .NET environment to the COM environment – incurring the performance penalties that we discussed earlier. However, this technique is powerful, in that it can allow our .NET applications to make use of COM components running on other machines on the network in MTS or COM+.

Invoking .NET Components from COM

We've seen how easy it is to invoke a COM component from within .NET. We can also do the reverse – invoking a .NET assembly from within the COM environment. This process is nearly as easy, though we can't do everything from within the VS.NET IDE.

A .NET assembly can be made available for use from COM-based applications by running a command line utility (`Regasm.exe`). This utility is used to create a COM type library for the assembly and to register that type library in the system registry. At this point, the assembly will appear as a COM component on the machine – meaning we can add a reference to it from within the VB6 IDE.

One key thing to keep in mind is how .NET finds assemblies for an application. By default, .NET assemblies are local to each application and the runtime locates them by searching in the same directory or the directory tree. For an assembly to be available to all applications it must be loaded into the global assembly cache – a process requiring several extra steps during the creation of the assembly.

This affects how COM-based applications interact with .NET assemblies. For COM to interact with an assembly, the assembly must be physically installed in the same directory as the COM application, or the assembly must be loaded into the global assembly cache. For our example here we'll put the client application and the assembly in the same directory.

It is important to keep in mind, however, that while a .NET DLL can be installed in several directories on a machine – thus being available to several .NET applications – it can only be registered in *one directory* for use by COM. This is because there is only one registry entry for a given component under COM. Thus, if our assembly is to be used by multiple COM applications, then it will most likely need to be loaded into the global assembly cache.

Earlier in the chapter we discussed how data is marshaled between COM and .NET when a COM component is called from .NET. This marshaling process also occurs when a .NET assembly is called from COM, and so many of the rules and best practices we discussed earlier apply equally in this case:

- ❏ Provide version and locale information in the assembly
- ❏ Use only data types supported by COM automation
- ❏ Use types common to both COM and .NET (isomorphic types)
- ❏ Avoid chatty interfaces
- ❏ Name enums and structures clearly – these names carry through
- ❏ Explicitly free resources
- ❏ Do not use methods with the same method names as the System.Object class in .NET

Creating a .NET Assembly for COM

For the sake of symmetry, let's create a .NET class that acts as a mirror image to the COMclass we created earlier in this chapter to demonstrate calling into COM from .NET. Create a **Class Library** package in VB.NET. Name the project COM2NETtest, and rename Class1 to NETclass.

Add the following methods to NETclass:

```
Imports System.ComponentModel

Public Class NETclass
    Inherits System.ComponentModel.Component

    Public Sub New()
        MyBase.New()

        'This call is required by the Component Designer.
        InitializeComponent()

        ' TODO: Add any initialization after the InitializeComponent() call

    End Sub

    Public Function GetValue(ByVal Data As String) As String
        Return "The data is " & Data
    End Function
```

```
Public Function GetNumber() As Integer
    Return 42
End Function

Public Function GetArray() As Short()
    Dim a() As Short = {0, 1, 2, 3, 4, 5}

    Return a
End Function

Public Function GetDate() As Date
    Return Now
End Function

Public Function GetVar() As Object
    Return Now
End Function

#Region " Component Designer generated code "
#End Region

End Class
```

This code is equivalent to the code we wrote earlier in COMclass, returning a variety of data types for use by our COM client application. Notice for instance, that the integer data types are the .NET equivalents of their COM counterparts as we discussed in Chapter 3.

Once this is done, build the assembly and close the VS.NET IDE. The next step must be done at the command line.

Registering the Assembly

Open a console window and navigate to the bin directory containing the COM2NETtest.dll file. Alternately, we can copy the COM2NETtest.dll file to the directory where we want to build the COM client application first. Then navigate to that directory instead.

Before the assembly can be used from COM, it must be registered as a COM component. For this to happen, it will need a COM type library. The Regasm.exe utility (discussed briefly in Chapter 8) is used to perform these functions. This utility is invoked with the following command line:

```
regasm /tlb:com2nettest.tlb com2nettest.dll
```

The utility will examine the .NET assembly and will use its information to generate a type library file named com2nettest.tlb. Once that step is complete it will automatically register the assembly in the system registry.

At this point we are ready to build a client application.

Creating a COM Client

The COM client application can be written in any language that can invoke COM components. In this example we'll use VB6 to create the client.

The client application must be physically located in the same directory as the .NET assembly, or the assembly must be installed in the global assembly cache. For this example, we'll compile the application into the same directory as the assembly.

For a client application, just create a standard Windows project in VB6. Add a **ListBox** control to the form. Add the following code to manage the size of the `ListBox` control:

```
Private Sub Form_Resize()
   List1.Move 0, 0, ScaleWidth, ScaleHeight
End Sub
```

Now we can move on to the real work.

Adding a Reference to the Assembly

We can make use of the assembly via late binding or early binding. Obviously, performance will be better through early binding. Let's now add a reference to the assembly to our project, using the **Project | References** menu option and selecting the **COM2NETtest** entry:

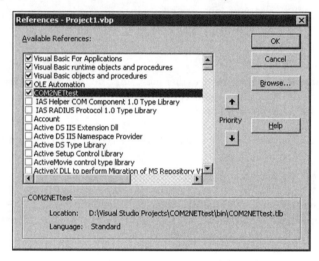

With this reference added, our application is ready to use the assembly.

Using the Object

To use the `NETclass` object, add the following code:

```
Private Sub Form_Load()
   Dim obj As COM2NETtest.NetClass
   Dim a() As Integer
   Dim val As Variant

   Set obj = New COM2NETtest.NetClass

   List1.AddItem obj.GetValue("sample data")
   List1.AddItem obj.GetNumber
   List1.AddItem "The date is " & obj.GetDate

   List1.AddItem "The array contains"
   a = obj.GetArray
   For Each val In a
```

```
    List1.AddItem val
  Next

  List1.AddItem "The date is " & obj.GetVar
End Sub
```

This code is functionally equivalent to the client code we created in .NET earlier when working with the COMclass object. It just calls each of the methods we created, displaying the results into the ListBox control on the form.

This application can't be run from the VB6 IDE because the application is technically run out of the directory where the VB IDE program is located, not where our project is located. This means that the .NET assembly won't be found and the object creation will fail. We have two options at this point.

We can place the .NET assembly into the directory where VB6.EXE resides and register it in that location using regasm. This will allow us to run the VB6 application within the IDE, using the debugger.

Alternately, we can compile the program into the same bin directory as the .NET assembly and run it from there (by double clicking on the exe). Obviously for deployment purposes it is important to ensure that any setup program places the .NET assembly in the same directory as the VB6 application on the target machine.

The result should be a display similar to the following:

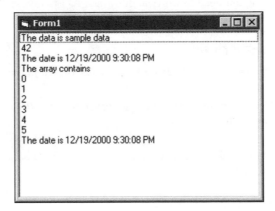

Calling a .NET assembly from COM is nearly as simple as doing the reverse. We can easily pass most common data types between the two environments – providing solid interoperability between the new .NET platform and the COM platform.

Calling Windows APIs

Though the .NET system class libraries are quite comprehensive, there may be times when we need to directly call Win32 API functions from our application. It is preferable to make use of any .NET functionality whenever possible, but the .NET Framework does include provisions for calling native operating system API functions when needed.

API functions are stored in static DLL files and may have been written by Microsoft, third-party vendors, or others. Because, at its core, much of the .NET system class library interacts with the Win32 API, there is obviously a very good mechanism built into the .NET Framework for interacting with these DLL functions.

Using the Platform Invocation Services

The technologies used to access APIs are called the Platform Invocation Services, or **PInvoke** for short. PInvoke takes care of locating the appropriate DLL, loading it into our process memory, locating the function address, and making the call. This typically also includes marshaling data from the .NET environment to the unmanaged API and back again.

This may sound familiar, since it is the same basic process followed when we interact with an existing COM component. In fact, the general process for invoking an API function is the same as for a COM method, though the actual code within our VB.NET application is somewhat different when calling an API since VS.NET doesn't automatically wrap API calls the way it does with COM components.

PInvoke is very powerful. It not only handles the marshaling, but it has a great deal of intelligence in terms of locating the API function we want to invoke. It uses fuzzy name matching to find the right API. This is particularly important when we look at all the APIs that support both ANSI and Unicode text. In these cases there is an API ending in the letter A that handles the ANSI call, and one ending in W for the Unicode call. PInvoke can automatically use the right one based on whether we indicate we're passing an ANSI or Unicode data type – entirely eliminating our need to worry about which API to invoke. We'll discuss this later, but first let's look at a simple example.

Calling a Simple API Function

For our first example, we'll call the MessageBox API, which is located in the user32.dll.

> *Normally of course, we'd simply use the VB MsgBox function or call the .NET MessageBox class rather than directly calling the API.*

To use PInvoke we must reference the Microsoft.Win32.Interop assembly. To keep our code shorter it is also a good idea to import the namespace:

```
Imports System.Runtime.InteropServices
```

This will save a lot of typing and make our code more readable.

Declaring an API in VB.NET

Before we can use an API function within our application we need to declare it. Basically, what we're doing is creating a function wrapper in VB.NET that describes the function within the .NET environment. Using attributes, we also provide metadata that PInvoke can use to locate the actual function on the system. When an application invokes our wrapper function, PInvoke automatically delegates the function call to the appropriate function in the appropriate DLL.

Conceptually, this wrapper is comparable to the one VS.NET creates for a COM component. However, static DLLs have no type library or other self-description mechanism and so it is not possible to automatically generate the wrapper. Thus we end up creating the wrapper ourselves.

To be fair, the most useful and commonly used APIs are already wrapped – via the .NET system class library. Only when we want to interact with a less common API or with a DLL created by a third party will this issue come into play.

An API function is declared in VB.NET just like any other function – with the addition of the `DllImport` attribute. Start a new **Windows Application** project and add a class to it, calling it **API**. Then declare the `MessageBox` API by adding the following code to the class:

```
Imports System.Runtime.InteropServices

Public Class API

    Public Shared Function <DllImport("user32.dll")> _
        MessageBox(ByVal Hwnd As Integer, ByVal [Text] As String, _
        ByVal Caption As String, ByVal Type As Integer) As Integer
    End Function

End Class
```

On the surface, this is just a function with no implementation.

Note the square brackets around the `Text` parameter. As we discussed in Chapter 3, the square brackets allow us to make use of reserved words as parameter or method names.

Notice that we have both `Function` and `End Function` statements to form a complete block – but no code inside. Instead, the declaration uses the `DllImport` attribute:

```
<DllImport("user32.dll")>
```

`DllImport` can accept a number of parameters, but typically, we just need to specify the actual static DLL where the function is located. PInvoke will take care of locating that DLL and calling the specified function inside.

For this to work properly, our declaration of the `MessageBox` function must have exactly the same parameters as the actual API function – matching in order, data type, and quantity. Also note that VB.NET doesn't support the `As Any` syntax of previous versions of VB, so we must provide matching data types for all parameters.

Calling the API Function

We can now write code behind a button on the form to call the function. Add a **Button** and the following code to `Form1`:

```
    Protected Sub Button1_Click(ByVal sender As Object, _
        ByVal e As System.EventArgs)

      API.MessageBox(0, "Hello world", "Hi", 0)

    End Sub
```

This is no different to calling any other `Shared` method on a class – we've entirely hidden the fact that the function is actually using a Win32 API.

Aliasing a Function

Sometimes we don't want to use the actual name of the API function within our application. This may be to avoid a naming conflict or to increase the readability of our application.

We can alias an API function by adding an extra parameter to the DllImport attribute. For example, we could rename the MessageBox function to PopUp with the following declaration:

```
Public Shared Function <DllImport("user32.dll", EntryPoint:="MessageBox")> _
    PopUp(ByVal Hwnd As Integer, ByVal [Text] As String, _
        ByVal Caption As String, ByVal Type As Integer) As Integer
    End Function
```

We just renamed the function name to PopUp and added the EntryPoint parameter to the DllImport attribute:

```
<DllImport("user32.dll", EntryPoint:="MessageBox")>
```

Now throughout our application we can refer to this function as PopUp instead of MessageBox.

Hiding an API Interface

At times we may not like the parameter list required by an API. For instance, perhaps in our newly renamed PopUp method we don't want to require the user to provide the Hwnd or Type parameters. While we can't change the signature of the API method declaration itself, we can provide a surrogate implementation, which just calls the actual API method.

To do this, we can change the code in the API class as follows:

```
Private Shared Function <DllImport("user32.dll")> _
    MessageBox(ByVal Hwnd As Integer, ByVal [Text] As String, _
        ByVal Caption As String, ByVal Type As Integer) As Integer
    End Function

Public Shared Function PopUp(ByVal [Text] As String, _
    ByVal Caption As String) As Integer

    Return MessageBox(0, [Text], Caption, 0)
End Function
```

We've change the API declaration back to its original form and, more importantly, declared it as Private in scope. This means the API function can't be directly called by code outside our class.

The PopUp function has been changed to be a regular VB.NET function that accepts only the parameters we want the user to provide. The call is then delegated to the Private API function to do the actual work.

In this way we can change the external interface for an API function into whatever form makes sense for our application.

Using Automatic ANSI/Unicode Location

As we mentioned earlier, PInvoke can automatically invoke the appropriate API function when faced with a choice between the ANSI version (ending in A) and the Unicode version (ending in W). For instance, to retrieve the system directory path, we can call the `GetSystemDirectory` API. However, in reality, there is no `GetSystemDirectory` API – instead there are the two flavors; `GetSystemDirectoryA` and `GetSystemDirectoryW`.

Because of the way PInvoke uses fuzzy name matching, however, we can declare the `GetSystemDirectory` API in VB.NET as follows:

```
Public Shared Function _
   <DllImport("kernel32")> _
   GetSystemDirectory(ByVal Buffer As StringBuilder, _
   ByVal Size As Integer) As Integer
End Function
```

Here, we are specifying neither the A nor W version of the API. Rather, we are allowing PInvoke to determine which version to call as appropriate, based on the underlying operating system and whether it supports ANSI or Unicode strings in the API.

Note that we are using the `StringBuilder` class to provide the buffer. This class comes from the `System.Text` namespace, so we should import it at the top of our code module.

We can then call this method from the form (again importing the `System.Text` namespace) using the following code:

```
Protected Sub Button1_Click(ByVal sender As Object, _
    ByVal e As System.EventArgs)

  Const MAX_PATH As Integer = 256
  Dim str As New StringBuilder(MAX_PATH)

  API.GetSystemDirectory(str, MAX_PATH)

  MsgBox(str.ToString, , "System Dir")
End Sub
```

The appropriate API will automatically be called by PInvoke, without our having to worry about which version is appropriate.

Passing Structures as Parameters

Some API functions require complex structures as parameters. In Chapter 3, we discussed how to declare a `Structure` in VB.NET. The trick with these structures is that we don't know exactly how they are stored in memory, so, when passing them to an API function, they must be laid out in memory in such a way that the API can write into them.

To ensure a structure is stored in memory appropriately, we need to use attributes when declaring the structure. As an example, consider the API that generates a GUID value – `CoCreateGuid`. This API fills in a structure composed of a set of numeric values, which we can then use to create an object of type `System.Guid`.

Again, it is preferable and easier to use the built-in Guid.NewGuid() *method to generate a* Guid, *but this API is a good example of using a structure as a parameter.*

The structure we'll pass as a parameter can be declared in our API class as:

```
Private Structure <StructLayout(LayoutKind.Sequential)> GUIDstruc
   Public Guid1 As Int32
   Public Guid2 As Int16
   Public Guid3 As Int16
   Public Guid4a As Byte
   Public Guid4b As Byte
   Public Guid4c As Byte
   Public Guid4d As Byte
   Public Guid4e As Byte
   Public Guid4f As Byte
   Public Guid4g As Byte
   Public Guid4h As Byte
End Structure
```

The key here is the StructLayout attribute:

```
<StructLayout(LayoutKind.Sequential)>
```

This attribute indicates that the structure should be stored sequentially in memory, preventing the .NET runtime from storing the various parts of the structure in different locations in memory. This is critical since the API doesn't write the data field by field, but rather writes a stream of bytes into a contiguous section of memory. If our structure wasn't all stored in the same spot, who knows what the API might overwrite?

Given this structure declaration, we can declare the CoCreateGuid API as follows:

```
Private Shared Function _
   <dllimport("OLE32.DLL")> _
   CoCreateGuid(ByRef Buffer As GUIDstruc) As Integer
End Function
```

The parameter we provide to this function is of type GUIDstruc, allowing the API to populate the structure appropriately. Notice that this function is declared as Private. For ease of use, we can create a Public function that returns a variable of type Guid:

```
Public Shared Function NewGuid() As Guid
   Dim Buffer As GUIDstruc
   Dim result As Long
   Dim g As Guid
   Const S_OK As Integer = 0

   result = CoCreateGuid(Buffer)

   If result = S_OK Then
     g = New Guid(Buffer.Guid1, Buffer.Guid2, _
       Buffer.Guid3, Buffer.Guid4a, Buffer.Guid4b, _
       Buffer.Guid4c, Buffer.Guid4d, Buffer.Guid4e, _
       Buffer.Guid4f, Buffer.Guid4g, Buffer.Guid4h)

     Return g
   Else
     err.Raise(1, "GUIDgen", "Unable to create GUID value")
   End If
End Function
```

This function calls the CoCreateGuid method, passing in a GUIDstruc parameter. If the API completes successfully, the elements of the structure are provided to the constructor of the Guid class to create a new object.

This illustrates how we can attribute a structure to make it safe for passing as a parameter to an API function.

Using the Migration Tool

Given all the differences between VB.NET and VB6, it is obviously not trivial to migrate an existing application from VB6 into the VB.NET environment. Fortunately, Microsoft is working on a Migration Wizard to assist with this process. It will be a rare project that can be automatically migrated without any intervention on our part, but the wizard should help a great deal.

The Migration Wizard in Beta 1 is a very early version of the tool and, as such, is presumably only a hint of what the tool will eventually do for us. At this time, the tool is of relatively limited use, though it does save a lot of effort around repetitive code changes. For almost any project however, there is quite a lot of work to do by hand once the wizard is finished.

The Migration Process

The Migration Wizard is automatically invoked when we attempt to open a VB6 project in the VB.NET IDE. It will run through the code in the original project, generating a new VB.NET project. The new project will be partially upgraded and will have comments where the wizard was unable to upgrade the code. The wizard will also generate an upgrade report listing any problems that it was unable to address.

When run against a VB6 project group, only the first project in the group is migrated.

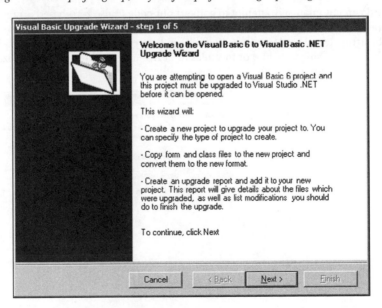

Running the Wizard

The wizard automatically detects
the type of project being upgraded
– whether it is an ActiveX EXE or
ActiveX DLL, for instance. Based
on this information, it creates the
appropriate target project type.
We are allowed to specify a
couple of additional actions that
the wizard can perform:

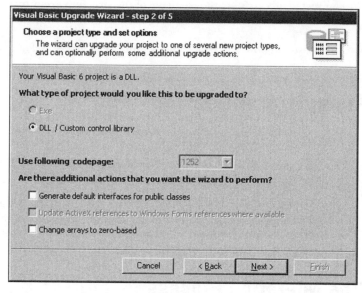

We can have the wizard generate default interfaces for any public classes in our project. At this point in time, selecting this option appears to have no impact on the migration process.

We can also have the wizard convert ActiveX controls to Windows Forms controls where possible. Otherwise, the wizard will include the ActiveX control itself into the VB.NET project using COM interoperability, as discussed earlier in this chapter. Currently, this option is disabled, but is obviously intended to exist in the final release of the wizard.

Lastly, the wizard can automatically attempt to convert our code to use zero-based arrays. Some VB6 code is written using one-based arrays, but in VB.NET all arrays are zero-based. Depending on how our code interacts with the array, the wizard may or may not be able to completely convert the code to be zero-based. In particular, we may be using variables or formulas to derive index values – and the wizard would be unable to convert our math code appropriately in all cases.

Next, we are asked where the new
VB.NET project should be created.

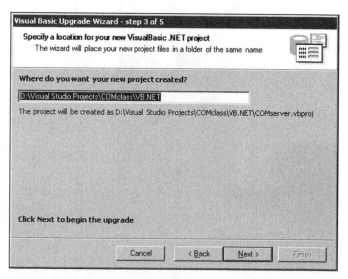

By default the new project will be created in a subdirectory beneath the existing project directory.

> **Remember that .NET applications cannot be run from a network drive, so ensure that the target directory is located on a drive local to the development workstation.**

If the target directory doesn't exist, we'll be prompted to create it.

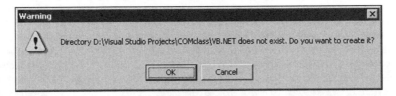

Once the target directory is specified and created, the wizard will run through the VB6 project, converting it into a VB.NET project. The wizard displays progress information as the conversion occurs, before showing a final screen:

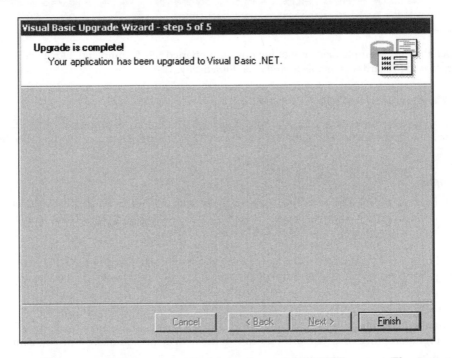

At this point, we'll be in a position to work with the newly created VB.NET project. The project should contain files corresponding to each of the original code files in the VB6 project, along with an upgrade report.

The Upgrade Report

The upgrade report is presented as a DHTML page included as a file in the project. This page includes information about the upgrade process, including the date and time of the upgrade, the upgrade wizard settings, and a list of the files upgraded along with the status of each.

For those files that could not be entirely upgraded, the report will include a list of issues that need to be addressed manually. In general, this list should correspond to the list of upgrade issues in the Task List window. For instance, the following diagram shows the results of an upgrade attempt on a relatively complex VB6 ActiveX DLL project in the Task List.

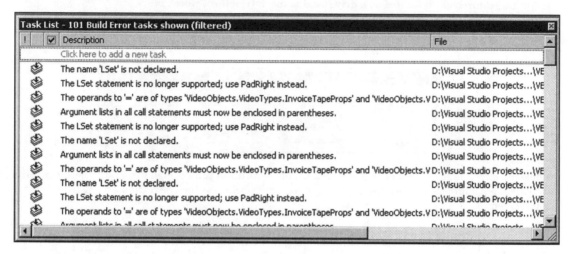

We can see that this example made use of the now unsupported LSet command, along with various other behaviors that the wizard was unable to update automatically.

General Wizard Activities

There are some activities performed by the wizard that are common to all project types. We'll take a quick look at these, and then take a look at the steps performed by the wizard when converting specific types of project.

Syntax Changes

Some of the changes from VB6 to VB.NET are relatively straightforward. Most of the syntax changes – such as how a Property routine is built, or the change from Long to Integer data types – can be easily accommodated by the upgrade wizard and will occur automatically.

The wizard converts UDT declarations to Structure declarations and removes the Set statements where object assignments occur. Most other simple syntax or code structure changes are handled automatically.

Option Strict Off

The wizard automatically adds Option Strict Off statements to the top of each code module. This helps the migration process, since most VB6 code relies heavily on automatic type coercion rather than explicit casting.

Microsoft.VisualBasic.Compatibility.VB6 Library

When upgrading applications from VB6, there are a number of keywords and functions that are no longer directly accessible in VB.NET. Many of these are available via the Microsoft.VisualBasic.Compatibility.VB6 namespace. We discussed this in more detail in Chapter 3.

The wizard automatically references this library in any upgraded projects, and often makes use of keywords or functions contained in this namespace to perform the upgrade.

Data Access

Data access is another area of concern. Most existing VB6 applications make use of ADO for data access. The Migration Wizard uses COM interoperability to allow the upgraded code to continue to use ADO. If we want to upgrade our code to use ADO.NET, we'll have to make those changes manually.

VB6 ActiveX DLL projects often migrate with relatively little difficulty. They are typically primarily composed of code and make little use of ActiveX controls or other concepts that are difficult to migrate. Applications that act as clients to such DLLs are a different matter however.

Forms-based Applications

VB6 graphical forms are a bit trickier. While some of the standard VB controls can be migrated to Windows Forms counterparts, there are many controls that can't be automatically migrated. While this includes most especially third-party controls, it also includes a number of standard controls that don't have counterparts in VB.NET, such as the Shape control.

With others, such as the DriveList control, it appears that the wizard is intended to upgrade them but that support is incomplete at this time and so the upgrade fails. In any case, there are also many properties of controls that are no longer supported. For instance, code that sets the FillColor or FillStyle properties will need manual intervention when upgrading.

ActiveX DLL Projects

In general, upgrading an ActiveX DLL project is easier than upgrading a forms-based application. Most DLL projects are composed of a set of class modules that perform business processing or data access. This type of code can generally be upgraded to VB.NET with minimal effort on our part. We can, however, run into issues with arrays, or VB6 keywords that are no longer supported in VB.NET, if those features are used in the ActiveX DLL code.

This beta version of the Migration Wizard gives us a glimpse into the future. While the wizard will almost certainly improve from where it is in Beta 1, there's also no doubt that the migration of any significant VB6 application will still require a fair number of manual changes even when the wizard is fully functional.

Summary

As we move into the world of .NET, we'll need to continue to support and interact with existing COM applications. VB.NET makes it very easy to write .NET applications that call into COM components, whether they are DLLs on the local machine or running in MTS or COM+ on a remote machine. The same is true with ActiveX controls, which can be directly hosted within a Windows Forms application or even used within a Web Forms application.

Likewise, .NET assemblies can be made available for use by COM applications, allowing existing applications to be enhanced to interact with new .NET applications as they are created.

The .NET Framework includes the PInvoke services, which provide very strong support for calling into Win32 API functions or other functions exported from static DLLs. While most common API functionality is already built into the .NET system class library, when we need to we can easily call into the API functions directly.

Obviously, there will also be a need to upgrade some existing VB6 applications into VB.NET. This process will never be painless, but Microsoft is working on a Migration Wizard to ease the process. The wizard provided in Beta 1 is somewhat useful, but is obviously an early release of the tool.

With the strong interoperability support built into .NET, upgrading applications may not be terribly critical, since we can instead choose to build new .NET applications that make use of existing code. This is a powerful and cost effective overall strategy.

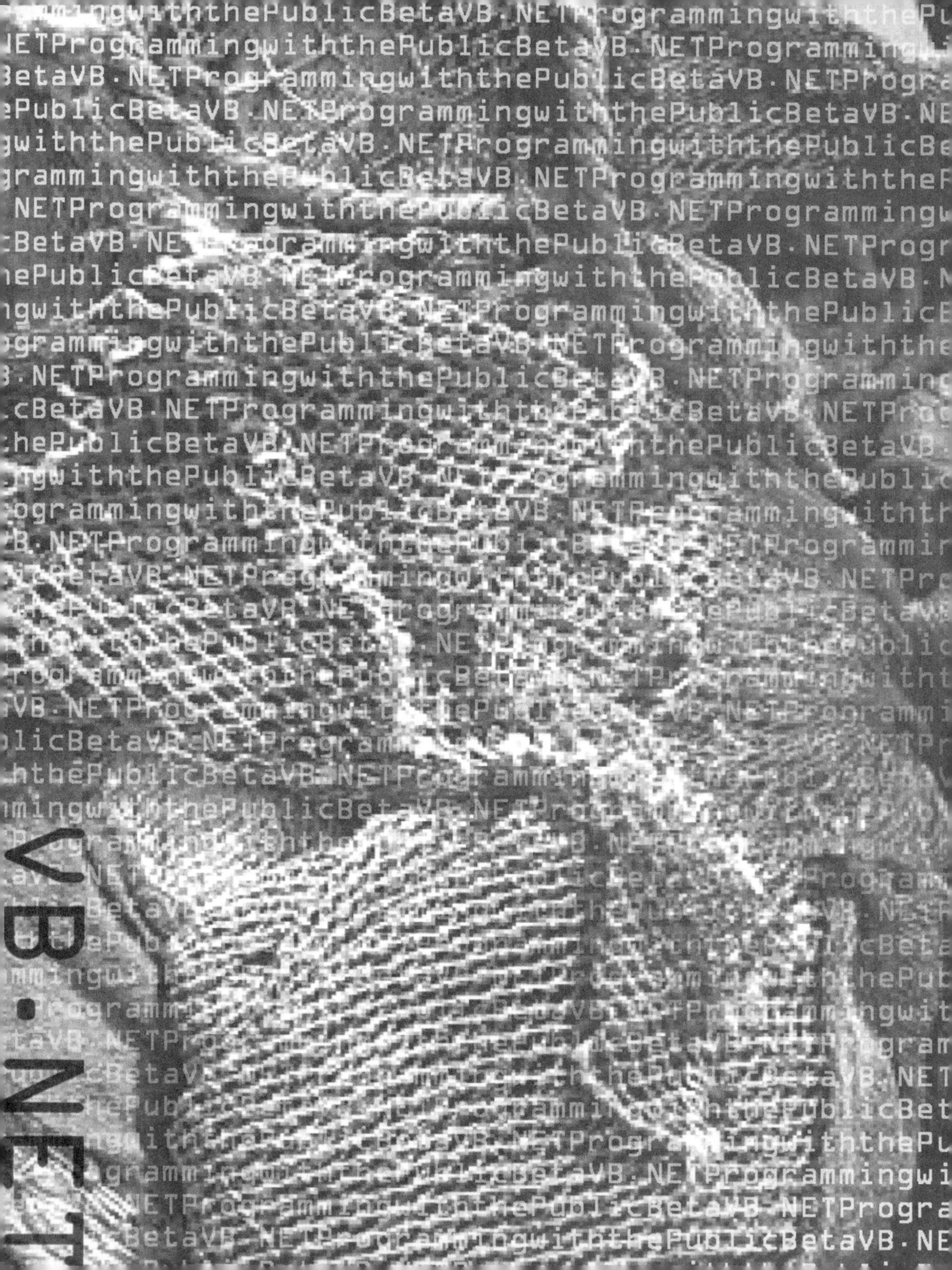
VB.NET
VB.NETProgrammingwiththePublicBeta

10

More Development Examples in Visual Basic.NET

To round out many of the concepts in this book, this chapter concludes with some functional examples of VB.NET programs. Each example was selected to have the following characteristics:

❑   Fulfills typical programming purpose in real-world applications

❑   Uses or illustrates new capabilities in VB.NET

The examples have been kept as simple as possible, so they should not be considered anything close to production ready. They are for illustrative purposes, but the ideas behind them should be practical enough to evolve to real-world usage.

Extending the Web-Based Payment Calculator

In Chapter 6, a Web Forms example was discussed that implemented a simple payment calculator. It allowed the user to put in a loan amount, the number of months in the loan, and an interest rate, and then calculated the payment amount. This example covered the basics of Web Forms, concentrating on validation controls.

A common feature of a payment calculator is the ability to display a payment schedule, that is, a list of the payments. Each payment is broken down into the amount applied to the principle, the amount applied to interest, and the remaining principle on the loan. In this example, we will add this capability to our payment calculator.

The starting point here will be the completed Web Forms payment calculator done in Chapter 6.

Bring up the project for the Web Forms payment calculator in Visual Studio.NET. On the existing Web Form, add a new button next to the **Calculate Payment** button, which is named btnPaymentSchedule. Change the Text property for the new button to **Payment Schedule**.

Double-click the **Payment Schedule** button. In the Click event for the button, insert the following code:

```
Public Sub btnPaymentSchedule_Click(ByVal sender As Object, _
                                    ByVal e As System.EventArgs)

    Dim webSession As System.Web.SessionState.HttpSessionState
    webSession = Me.Session
    webSession("LoanAmount") = txtLoanAmount.Text
    webSession("Months") = txtMonths.Text
    webSession("InterestRate") = txtInterestRate.Text

    Me.Navigate("WebForm2.aspx")

End Sub
```

This code places the values entered on WebForm1 into the Session object managed by the ASP.NET Framework. This allows those values to be accessible to other Web Forms in this same user session.

> *See the section below called* Notes on this Example *for discussion of the advisability of using the* Session *object for this purpose.*

Create a new Web Form. It will automatically be named WebForm2. On this Web Form, do not use the grid layout, as was used for WebForm1, but rather the default linear layout. To make some space for insertion of controls on the web page, position the cursor in WebForm2 and press the *Enter* key five or six times.

Put a button on the first line of the web form (name it btnNewLoan) and change its Text property to **New Loan**.

Drag and drop four labels onto each of the next four lines of the Web Form. Name the first label control lblLoanAmount, name the second label lblMonths, name the third label lblInterestRate, and name the last label lblPaymentAmount.

Place the cursor in front of the lblLoanAmount label (the label on the second line). Type in the following text right on the page: **Loan amount:**

Place the cursor in front of the lblMonths label (the label on the third line). Type in the following text right on the page: **Number of payments:**

Place the cursor in front of the lblInterestRate label (the label on the fourth line). Type in the following text right on the page: **Interest rate:**

Place the cursor in front of the lblPaymentAmount label (the label on the fifth line). Type in the following text right on the page: **Payment amount:**

Place a DataGrid control on the line directly under the lblPaymentAmount label. At this point, WebForm2 should look about like this:

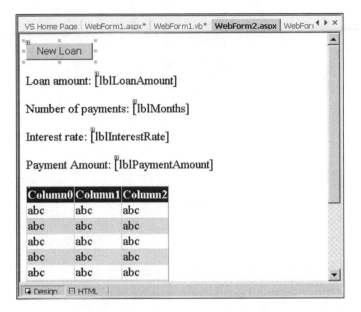

Double-click the New Loan button and place the following text into its Click event routine:

```
Me.Navigate("WebForm1.aspx")
```

In the code window for WebForm2, go to the WebForm2_Load event routine. Under the existing code in that routine (just above the End Sub), insert the following code:

```
' Calculate payments, based on session variables
Dim dblLoanAmount As Double
Dim intMonths As Integer
Dim dblInterestRate As Double

dblLoanAmount = CDbl(Me.Session("LoanAmount"))
intMonths = CInt(Me.Session("Months"))
dblInterestRate = CDbl(Me.Session("InterestRate")) / 1200

Dim dblPaymentAmount As Double
dblPaymentAmount = -pmt(dblInterestRate, intMonths, dblLoanAmount)

' Fill all labels with payment/loan data
lblLoanAmount.Text = CStr(Me.Session("LoanAmount"))
lblMonths.Text = CStr(Me.Session("Months"))
lblInterestRate.Text = CStr(Me.Session("InterestRate"))
lblPaymentAmount.Text = "Payment is " & CStr(dblPaymentAmount)

' Now ready to populate the grid
' First create a dataset and set its schema
Dim MyDataSet As New DataSet("PaymentSchedule")
Dim tblDataTable As New DataTable("Payments")
MyDataSet.Tables.Add(tblDataTable)

Dim colDataColumn As New DataColumn("PaymentNumber")
```

```
colDataColumn.DataType = System.Type.GetType("System.Int32")
tblDataTable.Columns.Add(colDataColumn)

Dim colDataColumn2 As New DataColumn("ApplyToPrinciple")
colDataColumn2.DataType = System.Type.GetType("System.Decimal")
tblDataTable.Columns.Add(colDataColumn2)

Dim colDataColumn3 As New DataColumn("InterestPaid")
colDataColumn3.DataType = System.Type.GetType("System.Decimal")
tblDataTable.Columns.Add(colDataColumn3)

Dim colDataColumn4 As New DataColumn("RemainingPrinciple")
colDataColumn4.DataType = System.Type.GetType("System.Decimal")
tblDataTable.Columns.Add(colDataColumn4)

' Now ready to calculate payment schedule and place in the dataset
Dim iPaymentIndex As Integer
Dim rowMyDataRow As DataRow
Dim dblPrinciple As Double
Dim dblInterest As Double
Dim dblPrincipleRemaining As Double = dblLoanAmount
For iPaymentIndex = 1 To intMonths

    dblPrinciple = -ppmt(dblInterestRate, iPaymentIndex, _
                    intMonths, dblLoanAmount)
    dblInterest = -ipmt(dblInterestRate, iPaymentIndex, _
                    intMonths, dblLoanAmount)
    dblPrincipleRemaining = dblPrincipleRemaining - dblPrinciple

    rowMyDataRow = MyDataSet.Tables("Payments").NewRow
    MyDataSet.Tables("Payments").Rows.Add(rowMyDataRow)
    rowMyDataRow("PaymentNumber") = iPaymentIndex
    rowMyDataRow("ApplyToPrinciple") = Round2Digit(CDec(dblPrinciple))
    rowMyDataRow("InterestPaid") = Round2Digit(CDec(dblInterest))
    rowMyDataRow("RemainingPrinciple") = _
                Round2Digit(CDec(dblPrincipleRemaining))
    MyDataSet.AcceptChanges()

Next iPaymentIndex

' Dataset is complete - bind it to the grid
DataGrid1.DataSource = New DataView(MyDataSet.Tables("Payments"))
DataGrid1.DataBind()

' Ready to show the page...
```

This code fetches the loan parameters from the `Session` object, recalculates the loan, and then builds a `DataSet` containing the entire payment schedule. First the `DataSet` is created, a single table is added to it, and the table has four columns defined: `PaymentNumber`, `ApplyToPrinciple`, `InterestPaid`, and `RemainingPrinciple`. Then a loop builds rows in the table and adds each row to the `DataSet`. Finally the `DataSet`'s default `DataView` is bound to the DataGrid.

Add in the following routine to the code in `WebForm2`:

```
Private Function Round2Digit(ByVal decInput As Decimal) As Decimal
    decInput = Decimal.Round(decInput, 2)
    Return decInput
End Function
```

This function just rounds the payment information down to two digits.

Now run the application. Fill in some information on the initial calculation screen, and press the Calculate Payment button. When the payment amount appears, press the Payment Schedule button. A screen something like this one should appear:

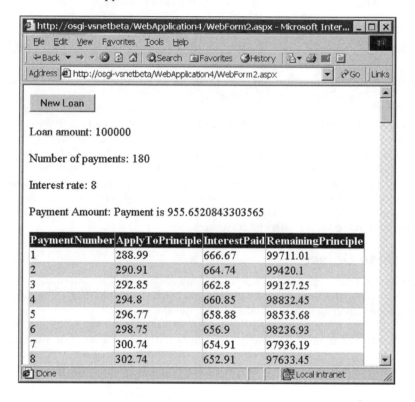

Notes on this Example

There are three key points I would like you to take away from this exercise, and I have outlined them below.

Value of Dynamically Created DataSets

A key concept demonstrated by this example is the ability to construct DataSets on the fly, in this case from calculated data.

In VB6, this example would most likely have been done with a complicated loop that first calculated the amounts for a payment, and then implemented the HTML to display the amounts in a table row. The drawback to this coding technique is that there is no separation between calculation and display – both are mashed in together.

In VB.NET, by contrast, the calculation of the payment schedule is a completely separate step from displaying the information. Uncoupling these functions makes it easier to change either one without affecting the other. The code calculating the payment schedule could easily be placed in a function that returned a `DataSet`, and then it could be used wherever needed.

Transferring Control among Web Forms

Note that Web Forms do not have a `Show` method as Windows Forms do. Each Web Form is considered to be a separate web page, even for those in a single application like `WebForm1` and `WebForm2` above.

The following line redirects to `WebForm1`, but each time such a redirection to `WebForm1` happens, all the state information from any previous page is lost:

```
Me.Navigate("WebForm1.aspx")
```

Note in the above application that when the **New Loan** button is pressed on `WebForm2`, the new `WebForm1` page that appears has no information in its controls.

There are a number of ways to deal with this. For example, `WebForm1` could check the `Session` object to see if values existed already for the loan amount, number of payments, and interest rate. If those parameters were present in the `Session` object, the information could be loaded in the controls. That code should be placed in the `WebForm1_Load` event routine. Alternatively, the information could be passed between the forms using the QueryString in the URL, and the information would then be fetched using the `QueryString` property of the `Request` object. These are all typical web development techniques, and there are others such as using cookies or hidden fields. The correct choice varies with circumstances.

Using the Session Object

The example uses the `Session` object as a repository to hold transfer state information between Web Forms. As mentioned just above, this is by no means the only technique available. This technique was chosen for its simplicity and ease of understanding for traditional VB developers.

However, developers with significant web development experience are aware that using the `Session` object in today's Active Server Page applications can cause serious scalability problems. The scalability of the `Session` object in ASP.NET will need to be looked at as the .NET Framework gets closer to release.

Generating SQL with Inherited Classes

In the next example, we confront a common programming situation. We want to create a simple query screen for the `Titles` table of `pubs` database, which is a sample database included with SQL Server. The `Titles` table contains information about books, such as title, the year published and the price. Our simplified query screen will allow the user to enter search information for the title and the price. It will be straightforward to extend the concept presented to other searching criteria if desired.

We will use Windows Forms in this example. Our end result will be a screen that looks much like this one:

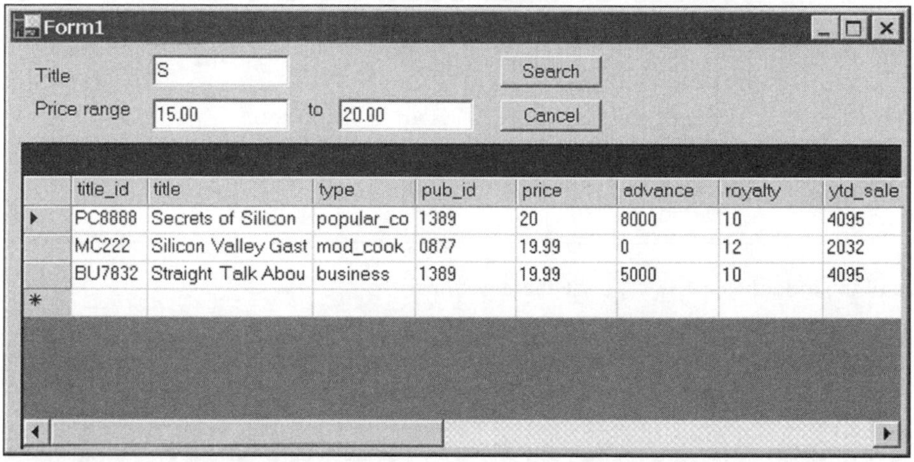

The information for the `title` field is used on a "partial match" basis. For example, if the user entered "CO" in the Title textbox, the program would find all the books with a title beginning with the letters "CO".

The desired price is entered as a range. If a high value for the range is specified, but a low value is not, then the low range is assumed to be zero.

The user can use either or both fields. If both title and price have information entered, then there is a logical AND used to make sure that the displayed titles satisfy both criteria.

For simplicity, a data bound grid is used to display the titles.

Constructing the Program

We will go through the construction of this program step-by-step. First, we'll construct a form that just shows all the records in the `Titles` table. Then we will add enhancements for selection.

Creating the Form

There's no need to go into too much detail for this step, since the work will be familiar to an experienced VB developer. Start a new Windows Application project, and work with the default Windows Form that it automatically creates. Construct the form with the following controls, with a layout like that shown above:

Control Type	Name	Special Properties
Textbox	txtTitle	Text = " "
Textbox	txtLowestPrice	Text = " "
Textbox	txtHighestPrice	Text = " "
Label	lblTitle	Text = "Title"

Table continued on following page

Control Type	Name	Special Properties
Label	lblPrice	Text = "Price range"
Label	lblTo	Text = "to"
Button	btnSearch	Text = "Search"
Button	btnCancel	Text = "Cancel"
DataGrid	DataGrid1	Anchor = All

At the top of the module for Form1, place these two lines:

```
Imports System.Data
Imports System.Data.ADO
```

If you like, you can set the AcceptButton property of Form1 to the btnSearch button, and the CancelButton property of Form1 to btnCancel. This will cause btnSearch to be activated when the Enter key is pressed in a text box, and btnCancel to be activated when the Esc key is pressed.

In the Click event for btnSearch, place the following code, with your own server name in the connection string in place of MYSERVER, and other login information changed as necessary:

```
Dim sSQL As String
sSQL = "SELECT * FROM Titles "

' Code to create and use a DataSet for Titles
' Create ADO connection and command objects
Dim sConnectionString As String = _
    "Provider=SQLOLEDB.1; User ID=sa; " & _
    "Initial Catalog=pubs;Data Source=MYSERVER"
Dim myConnection As New ADOConnection(sConnectionString)
Dim myCommand As New ADOCommand(sSQL, myConnection)

Dim myDataSetCommand As New ADODataSetCommand(myCommand)

' Declare the dataset named SelectedTitles
Dim myDataSet As New DataSet("SelectedTitles")

' Open the connection and get data
' from the Titles table
Try
    MyConnection.Open()
    MyDataSetCommand.FillDataSet(myDataSet, "SelectedTitles")
    DataGrid1.DataSource = MyDataSet.Tables("SelectedTitles")

Catch myException As Exception
    MessageBox.Show(myException.ToString())

Finally
    ' Close the connection and flush the reader
    If myConnection.State = Data.DBObjectState.Open Then
```

```
            MyConnection.Close()
        End If
        If Not myDataSet Is Nothing Then
            myDataSet = Nothing
        End If
    End Try
```

The form will now display data in the grid when the Search button is pressed, but it ignores anything in the text boxes, and just displays all data in the `Titles` table. Start the project and press the Search button to make sure there's nothing wrong up to this point. You should see data displayed in the grid after a brief pause to get the data from the server.

The most likely thing to go wrong is that the connection fails. If you have problems, check that first.

To finish up the form control logic, put a line in the `btnCancel_Click` event to end the program:

```
    End
```

Remove Option Strict from the Project

To simplify the coding of this example, we need to remove the default `Option Strict` property of the project. Right-click on the project in the Solution Explorer and select Properties. Select Build in the left-hand window. In the middle of the form, change the Option Strict parameter to Off and close the project properties dialog.

Creating a Set of Selection Criteria Classes

Next we want to place some logic behind the Search button to construct a SQL statement to get the appropriate records. You have probably written a lot of such code. Usually, it contains a lot of string manipulation to tie the parameters entered in the text boxes into the SQL statements. You probably write such code more-or-less from scratch every time you need to construct some SQL on the fly.

Such code is messy. It is easy for bugs to creep into it. It's tough to maintain. And it's not reusable for other projects.

We will handle the construction of the SQL statement with a set of specially designed classes, using the power of inheritance in VB.NET. This approach will yield code that is far clearer and more maintainable. It will also be reusable for other projects.

How the Approach Works

The foundation for our approach is to create a set of classes that can hold selection criteria. An instantiation of a class can hold the selection criteria from one parameter.

Those individual selection criteria objects are then placed in a collection. Each object in the collection will be able to generate a piece of a WHERE clause and make it available in a property.

The collection will have the capability to assemble the entire WHERE clause by getting the individual pieces from the objects in the collection, and putting them together in the right way.

For example, suppose the Title textbox has "CO" entered in it, and the text boxes for the price range have "15.00" and "20.00" entered into them. The collection would hold two objects. The first object would generate a piece of the WHERE clause that said:

```
" [title] LIKE 'CO%' "
```

The second object would generate a piece of the WHERE clause that said:

```
" [price] BETWEEN 15.00 AND 20.00 "
```

Then the collection would combine these pieces to get:

```
" WHERE [title] LIKE 'CO%' AND [price] BETWEEN 15.00 AND 20.00 "
```

Here are the steps that will need to be done to construct these objects.

Creating the Base Class for Selection Criteria Objects

We will first create a base class from which all selection criteria classes will be derived. This base class will not even be able to be instantiated by itself – it is only used by being inherited by another selection criteria class.

Take the Project | Add Class menu option. Name the new class SQLCriteriaBase. In the class module that appears, type in the following code:

```
Public MustInherit Class SQLCriteriaBase
    Dim msColumnName As String
    Public Property ColumnName() As String
        Get
            ColumnName = msColumnName
        End Get
        Set
            msColumnName = Value
        End Set
    End Property

    Public MustOverride ReadOnly Property WhereClause() As String

End Class
```

Notice that the first line declares the class as MustInherit. This prevents the class from being instantiated.

This base class has one property implemented that will be used by all classes, named ColumnName. This holds the name of a column in the database that is being used for selection criteria.

This class also declares another property called WhereClause. However, the WhereClause property is declared with the MustOverride keyword, so it contains no logic at all. Any class that inherits from this class will be required to implement a string property named WhereClause.

Next we will create two subclasses of SQLCriteriaBase – one to do partial matches and one to handle ranges.

Creating the Partial Match Class

The partial match class will hold selection criteria from a single text box, and it will be able to do partial matches on the information entered in the text box.

First create a new class module and name it `PartialStringMatch`. It should inherit from `SQLCriteriaBase`, and will have two string properties called `PartialMatch` and `WhereClause`. Here is the code to implement these properties:

```
Public Class PartialStringMatch
    Inherits SQLCriteriaBase
    Dim msPartialMatch As String

    Public Overrides ReadOnly Property WhereClause() As String
        Get
            WhereClause = "[" & MyBase.ColumnName & "] LIKE '" & _
                          msPartialMatch & "%'"
        End Get
    End Property

    Public Property PartialMatch() As String
        Get
            PartialMatch = msPartialMatch
        End Get
        Set
            msPartialMatch = Value
        End Set
    End Property
End Class
```

The `PartialMatch` property holds the value that a partial match will be selected on, and it is a very typical property, using a member variable to hold the value.

The `WhereClause` property is more interesting. It overrides the declared `WhereClause` property in the base class. Notice that `WhereClause` is a read-only property. That is, it doesn't make sense for some external module to tell the object what its WHERE clause is. The object must construct the WHERE clause from information fed to it.

This property needs to construct a piece of a WHERE clause using the information from the `ColumnName` property (implemented in the base class, but not shown in this class at all) and the `PartialMatch` property.

We need the brackets around the field name in the `WhereClause` logic because some field names have embedded spaces.

Creating the Numeric Range Class

The numeric range class is very similar in concept to the partial match class just above, but is intended to generate WHERE clause pieces for a range between two numeric values.

Add a new class and call it `NumericRange`. Here is the code for it:

```
Public Class NumericRange
    Inherits SQLCriteriaBase

    Dim msLowerRange As String
    Dim msUpperRange As String
    Public Overrides ReadOnly Property WhereClause() As String
        Get
            WhereClause = "[" & MyBase.ColumnName & "] BETWEEN " & _
```

```
                            msLowerRange & " AND " & msUpperRange
        End Get
    End Property

    Public Property LowerRange() As String
        Get
            LowerRange = msLowerRange
        End Get
        Set
            msLowerRange = Value
        End Set
    End Property

    Public Property UpperRange() As String
        Get
            UpperRange = msUpperRange
        End Get
        Set
            msUpperRange = Value
        End Set

    End Property

End Class
```

Now we need two properties besides `WhereClause`. One holds the lower limit of the range and the other holds the upper limit. The `WhereClause` property uses both of them with the BETWEEN keyword to establish the range in SQL.

Creating the Collection of Selection Criteria Objects

Now we will create a collection class to hold the individual instantiations of various selection criteria objects. Add a new class to the project and name it `SearchCriteriaCollection`.

We will use a `Queue` collection class. As explained in Chapter 3, VB.NET does not have an exact analog of the `Collection` object type except in a compatibility library. For our purposes, the `Queue` type of collection will work fine.

The collection class gets almost all of its functionality by inheriting from the `Queue` class. It only needs to implement a string property called `WhereClause`, which will combine the values of the WHERE clause pieces generated by members of the collection.

Here is the code for the `SearchCriteriaCollection` class:

```
Public Class SearchCriteriaCollection
    Inherits System.Collections.Queue
    Public ReadOnly Property WhereClause() As String
        Get
            Dim objCriterion As SQLCriteriaBase
            Dim iIndex As Integer
            Dim sTempWhereClause As String

            sTempWhereClause = ""
            While Me.Count > 0
```

```
                    objCriterion = Me.Dequeue

                    If sTempWhereClause <> "" Then
                        sTempWhereClause = sTempWhereClause & " AND "
                    End If
                    sTempWhereClause = sTempWhereClause & _
                                    objCriterion.WhereClause

                End While
                If sTempWhereClause <> "" Then
                    sTempWhereClause = " WHERE " & sTempWhereClause
                End If

                WhereClause = sTempWhereClause

            End Get
        End Property
    End Class
```

The class first inherits from System.Collections.Queue. This provides the methods needed to place objects in the collection. In the case of the Queue type collection, the main methods are Enqueue to place an object on the queue, and Dequeue to remove it from the queue. The Queue class removes objects with a first-in-first-out sequence.

Then the class implements the read-only WhereClause property. Please note that this WhereClause property is for the whole collection, and should not be confused with the WhereClause property of the individual selection criteria classes. If you find it difficult to keep these separated in your mind, you may wish to name the WhereClause properties in the selection criteria classes something different, like WhereClauseSegment.

Let's go over the logic in the WhereClause property briefly. We declare an object named objCriterion and make it of type SQLCriteriaBase. That allows the object to hold all of the subtypes of selection criteria objects that inherit from SQLCriteriaBase. (It is possible to declare an object to be type SQLCriteriaBase for this purpose, but note that such an object cannot be instantiated as a SQLCriteriaBase type because SQLCriteriaBase is marked MustInherit). We also declare a loop index and a string to hold the SQL WHERE clause as it is being generated.

We use the objCriterion object in a loop through the queue. This While loop watches to see when there are no more objects left in the queue. Note that as each object is used from the queue during an iteration of the loop, it is removed and the queue's count drops by one. When the last object is removed, the count drops to zero, and the loop will stop executing.

Each iteration of the loop gets a piece of a WHERE clause from an individual element of the collection and appends it to sTempWhereClause. There is some straightforward logic to handle the AND connectors between the pieces.

For example, if we had two elements in the collection, and they generated individual WHERE clause pieces of:

```
" [title] LIKE 'CO%' "
```

And:

```
" [price] BETWEEN 15.00 AND 20.00 "
```

Then at the end of the loop, sTempWhereClause would have the value

```
" [title] LIKE 'CO%' AND [price] BETWEEN 15.00 AND 20.00 "
```

Then all we need to do is put the WHERE keyword on the front. However, we do need to check and make sure that we have some pieces. If the collection is empty, at the end of the loop sTempWhereClause is empty, too. In that case, we don't want to pass back a WHERE clause that just says "WHERE ", because that would generate a SQL syntax error. So we only put a WHERE keyword on the front if we have a non-empty WHERE clause.

Then we send the value of the temporary variable sTempWhereClause back as the property value, and we're done.

Finish the Inquiry Form

Now go back to Form1. We need to enhance the logic in the **Search** button's Click event to create the collection and extract the WHERE clause from it. Here is what that logic should look like, with the changed parts highlighted:

```
Protected Sub btnSearch_Click(ByVal sender As Object, _
                              ByVal e As System.EventArgs)

        ' Create selection criteria collection
    Dim colSelectionCriteria As New SearchCriteriaCollection()

    Dim objTitleCriterion As PartialStringMatch
    Dim objPriceCriterion As NumericRange

    If txtTitle.Text <> "" Then
        objTitleCriterion = New PartialStringMatch()
        With objTitleCriterion
            .ColumnName = "Title"
            .PartialMatch = ucase(txtTitle.Text)
        End With
        colSelectionCriteria.Enqueue(objTitleCriterion)

    End If

    If txtHighestPrice.Text <> "" And txtLowestPrice.Text <> "" Then
        If txtHighestPrice.Text = "" Then
            txtHighestPrice.Text = "999999"
        End If
        If txtLowestPrice.Text = "" Then
            txtLowestPrice.Text = "0"
        End If
        objPriceCriterion = New NumericRange()
        With objPriceCriterion
            .ColumnName = "Price"
            .LowerRange = txtLowestPrice.Text
            .UpperRange = txtHighestPrice.Text
        End With
        colSelectionCriteria.Enqueue(objPriceCriterion)
```

```
    End If
    Dim sSQL As String
    sSQL = "SELECT * FROM Titles " & colSelectionCriteria.WhereClause

    ' Create ADO connection and command objects
    Dim sConnectionString As String = _
        "Provider=SQLOLEDB.1; User ID=sa; " & _
        "Initial Catalog=pubs;Data Source=MYSERVER"
    Dim myConnection As New ADOConnection(sConnectionString)
    Dim myCommand As New ADOCommand(sSQL, myConnection)
    ' Code from here on is unchanged. . .
```

This logic checks information in the text boxes and builds selection criteria objects accordingly. It declares a collection at the top, and then looks first at the text box for title, and then the text boxes for price range.

Once the collection is built, the collection's WhereClause property is appended to the SQL statement used to fetch the titles. The program should now allow you to enter either title information, or a price range, or both, and fill the data grid accordingly.

Note that this logic is very easy to extend to other criteria. If you wanted to do a partial match on type, or a range on ytd_sales, the controls and code could easily be added. Let's discuss some other possible extensions to this example.

Extending this Example

There are several obvious extensions to this project. We would ideally like our selection criteria to handle things like exact match, range between two string variables, and other types of criteria.

Using inheritance, it's easy to add such capabilities to this foundation. Right now, we just have two selection criteria classes. But we could create variations of it with names like ExactMatch, StringRange, and so forth. The collection of criteria (SearchCriteriaCollection) would accept any combination of these. Each such class only needs to know how to produce its own little piece of a WHERE clause, and then it can be plugged in to the overall scheme.

Ideally, the SearchCriteriaCollection class could override the Enqueue method of the Queue base class to check the type of classes being added to the queue. It could do that by declaring the object being added to the collection as type SQLCriteriaBase. This is similar in concept to declaring a parameter of type Control in VB6. Such a parameter can then be any object that is a control. In our case, a parameter declared as SQLCriteriaBase could be any of the subclasses.

In our example above, the grid can be used to edit the data, but we have not yet included code to place the changes back in the database. Chapter 7 on data access in VB.NET shows an example of restoring data from a grid back to the database.

Another extension of this project would be to use the data grid to select a record for editing, and then to pass control to another form with the record loaded for editing.

Summary

In the first example we saw how to create DataSets on the fly, and that in VB.NET we have gained the ability to keep calculation code for a web page completely separate from display code – something that wasn't possible before. We also saw that each Web Form is considered to be a separate web page, and hence all state information is lost when we redirect from one Web Form to another. In our example, we used the Session object to hold state information, but you should be aware that Session object might be subject to changes in ASP.NET as it is scales badly in ASP.

The second example was chosen to show the power of inheritance in a class hierarchy that could have use in real world programming, even in a web environment. Since the classes in this example are instantiated as needed, used, and quickly thrown away, they are entirely suitable for use in stateless web architectures. This puts to rest the mistaken concept that object capabilities such as inheritance have no place in a stateless web environment.

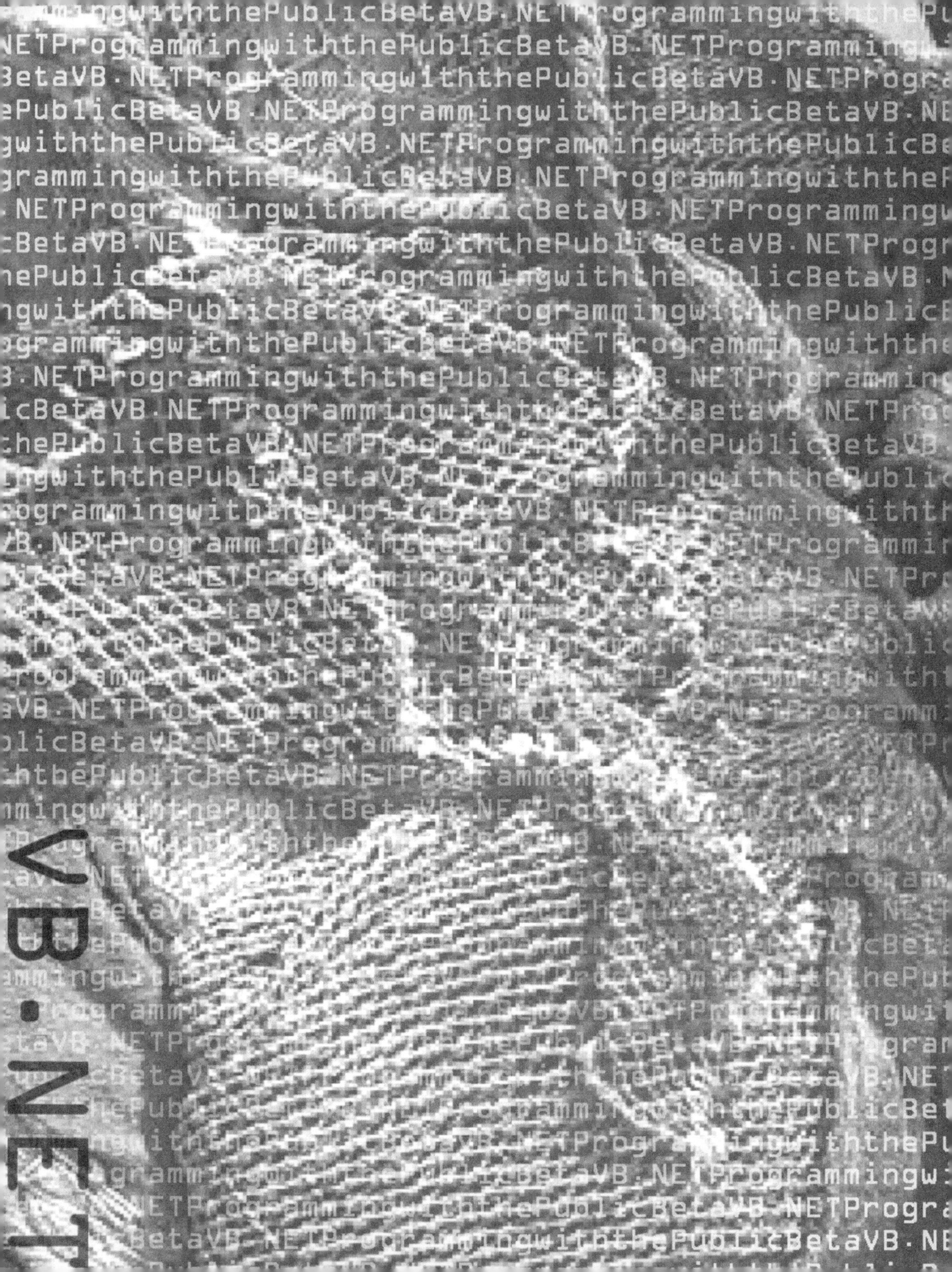
VB.NET
VB.NET Programming with the Public Beta

11

Wrap-Up

VB.NET is the biggest thing to hit Visual Basic since Visual Basic 4.0. Some have said it is the biggest change ever. Regardless, VB.NET is very exciting and offers Visual Basic developers great opportunities to utilize their existing development skills in a new and more powerful environment.

In this chapter we'd like to conclude by reviewing a few of the key points presented in the book in the context of what the changes mean for current VB6 projects, and list some key web sites and other resources to use when working with and learning about VB.NET and the .NET Framework.

Recommendations

This book has discussed Visual Basic.NET mostly in the context of new development. But in this section we're going to concern ourselves with changes you should be making to current VB6 projects to make the transition to VB.NET easier.

Syntax Conventions for Current Visual Basic Projects

At times it looks as though Visual Basic.NET was specifically designed to punish sloppy coders. There are a number of coding techniques that are undesirable in VB6, but are still supported. Many of these bad techniques are no longer supported in VB.NET.

There are also techniques commonly used today that are not perceived by most developers to be bad, but are nevertheless no longer supported in VB.NET because of syntax changes. Most of these techniques have alternatives in VB6 that are similar or identical in VB.NET.

That leads to several areas where coding conventions for present VB6 projects can relieve some of the problems likely with later migration to Visual Studio.NET. Here is a quick summary, based on differences in Visual Basic.NET that have been discussed in various places throughout the book, mostly in Chapters 3 and 5:

- ❑ Don't use default properties or methods

- ❑ Declare each variable on a separate line

- ❑ Make arrays zero-based and do not use the nth element in an array declared to be size "n"

- ❑ Make all parameters explicitly ByRef or ByVal

- ❑ Place default values on all optional parameters

- ❑ Consider controls private to the form they are on – do not refer to them from outside the form (use property procedures instead)

- ❑ Don't use obsolete keywords such as Gosub and DefInt

- ❑ Avoid late binding

- ❑ Don't use the default instance of a form – instead declare and instantiate forms using the same syntax for declaring and instantiating a class (discussed in Chapter 4)

- ❑ Do not depend on deterministic finalization (discussed in Chapter 2)

- ❑ Use the Date type to store dates rather that putting a date in a Double

Most of these are already in use by many development shops, because they lead to more maintainable and understandable code.

There are also a couple of additional recommendations that need a little more explanation.

Remove Processing Actions from Conditionals

Suppose you have this code in VB6:

```
If len(sID) = 0 And (InitializeRecord(sNewID)) Then ...
```

In VB6, both parts of the conditional expression are always evaluated. That is, it doesn't matter whether the value of len(sID) = 0 is True or False – VB6 runs the function InitializeRecord in either case.

Most other languages don't work this way because of the implications of Boolean logic. If you have the conditional, and you know A is False, then you also know that the combined conditional A And B is also False, no matter what B is.

A similar situation comes up for an Or conditional. If you have A Or B, and you know that A is True, then you also know that the overall result is True, regardless of the value of B.

As a consequence, most languages look at the first Boolean condition, and then evaluate the second condition only if it affects the overall result. VB.NET adopts this same convention because it works with the Common Language Runtime, which is shared by other languages. So in VB.NET, you can't be sure the second part of the conditional gets evaluated. If the first part is False in an And operation, or if the first part is True in an Or operation, VB.NET ignores the second part. No action it contains takes place.

However, you shouldn't be putting actions in `If` conditionals in the first place. This is sloppy coding, and we already noted that VB.NET punishes sloppy coders. Here's a better way to do this code in a form that works properly in both VB6 and VB.NET:

```
Dim bRecordInitialized As Boolean
bRecordInitialized = InitializeRecord(sNewID)
If len(sID) = 0 And (bRecordInitialized) Then ...
```

Remove Implicit Object Instantiation

VB6 offers two ways to declare and instantiate an object. Here's the way most developers use:

```
Dim objMyObject As MyClass
Set objMyObject = New MyClass
```

This technique is used the most in VB6 because the second line immediately instantiates the object, thus removing any uncertainty about when the point of instantiation occurs.

Here's the second way to declare and instantiate an object in VB6:

```
Dim objSomeObject As New MyClass

' some intervening code goes here ...

' This is the first reference to a
' property or method of the object.
objSomeObject.SomeProperty = "A string value"
```

In this case, the object is actually not instantiated by the first line in VB6. The first time a member of the object is referenced, the object is instantiated before carrying out the operation. In this case, for VB6, the last line in the example instantiates the object.

VB.NET has a major difference in how objects are instantiated. If you declare an object with `Dim ... As New ...`, then the instantiation is immediate. The syntax above does not change for VB.NET, but `objSomeObject` will be instantiated on the first line instead of the last line. This is the preferred way to instantiate objects in VB.NET, and it is used in many examples in this book.

This difference between VB6 and VB.NET normally doesn't matter. There are a few exceptional cases, however, in which it does. For example, if the logic between the declaration and the property reference depends on the object *not* yet being instantiated – say if the object creates a file, but the logic assumes the file is not there yet – then the code will not work properly in VB.NET.

Candidates for Migration to Visual Basic.NET

Many current VB projects will be evaluated as candidates for converting to Visual Basic.NET to gain new functionality, particularly web functionality. Some will be good candidates, and others are probably not worth migration, but should instead be rewritten from scratch.

Even with well designed and well written applications, moving to VB.NET will not be a transparent conversion. But there are some things that can make it easier. Many of them are simply good design principles, but they are worth reiterating.

Any tiered design will transfer more easily to Visual Studio.NET. Fat VB clients, where all the business logic is mixed up with the UI code, will probably not be practical candidates for migration. This gives even more reasons for current projects to be undertaken with good multi-tiered design.

In general, classes and components will migrate more easily than user interface modules. The migration tool can convert VB forms to Windows Forms, but the capabilities of Windows Forms and the new .NET controls are not an exact one-to-one match with older forms and controls. This means manual work in migrating many VB forms applications, especially those that render sophisticated user interfaces or use third party controls extensively. It will be easier for many of these applications to simply redevelop the user interface from scratch in Windows Forms, or to leave the applications in VB6.

If the current project is being migrated to the web, the current user interface code in VB forms will be even less useful. For example, VB designs that depend heavily on code in control events will have significant problems in migration to the web. Events in Web Forms often require a server roundtrip, and there are some events used in VB forms that are simply not supported in Web Forms.

Limitations of the Visual Basic Migration Tool

Chapter 9 discussed the migration tool that Microsoft is including in Visual Studio.NET to migrate VB6 projects into VB.NET projects. It will convert code modules, making syntax changes as necessary, and will insert TODO: items if it thinks manual changes are needed. VB forms are also converted to WinForms, fixing the most common changes of control properties, and producing a class module for the form.

The MSDN Library contains an article called *Preparing Your Visual Basic 6.0 Applications for the Upgrade to Visual Basic.NET*, which can be found at:

http://msdn.microsoft.com/library/techart/vb6tovbdotnet.htm

However, here are some of the most important notes and recommendations from that article.

Dealing with DHTML pages and WebClasses

Both DHTML pages and WebClasses have been replaced in Visual Basic.NET with Web Forms. The migration tool will not upgrade DHTML pages, and Microsoft recommends that WebClasses be left in VB6. WebClasses can be upgraded to VB.NET, but will need some manual modifications before they will work.

Dealing with Data

VB.NET will still support the use of DAO, RDO, and older ADO object models for accessing data. (Using ADO in VB.NET was discussed in Chapter 9.) However, data binding to controls with DAO or RDO will not be supported. Such data binding will need to be changed to ADO to work in VB.NET.

Problems Converting Late-Bound Objects

The migration tool will have the intelligence to take care of many changes with object models. For example, when upgrading a form with a label, any references to a Caption property will be changed to a Text property.

However, for this to work, the migration tool must know that it is dealing with a label. If a label object reference is late bound, it is not able to tell this. For example, if the following code from a VB6 program is encountered:

```
Dim objLabel as Object
Set objLabel = Me.Label1
objLabel.Caption = "Text to appear in the label"
```

then the migration tool will be unable to identify `objLabel` as a label control, since it was declared as type `Object`. That means it won't know to change the `Caption` property in the third line to a `Text` property.

The recommendation to avoid this problem is to use early binding whenever possible. If this is not possible, manual changes will be necessary.

Use Intrinsic Named Constants Instead of Values

It is good programming practice to use VB's intrinsic constants for many settings. For example, this is good coding practice:

```
Me.WindowState = vbMaximized
```

This line could be coded with the actual value of the constant `vbMaximized`, which is 2. In that case, the line would be:

```
Me.WindowState = 2
```

The migration tool is not going to change either of these lines. However, in some cases the values of the intrinsic constants are changing in .NET. If the second coding technique is used, the value being used may no longer match the intent. If the intrinsic constant form is used, there will be no trouble in migration.

Another example is using `True` and `False` instead of –1 and 0. In VB.NET, `True` becomes 1 instead of –1, but `False` stays the same. The code migration tool will not fix logic that uses –1 explicitly for `True`.

Problems with Fixed Length Strings in Structures

Chapter 3 discussed the fact that fixed length strings are not a native type in .NET, and that a compatibility fix is available. The migration tool will apply this fix for types declared as fixed length strings.

However, the migration tool does not work for fixed length strings used in user-defined types (which are replaced by structures – see Chapter 3). It is not possible to put a fixed length string in a structure. That means such cases will require manual adjustment. For example, this user defined type:

```
Type Customer
    CustID As Integer
    CustPhone As String*20
    CustStatus As Boolean
End Type
```

would need to be converted to:

```
Structure Customer
    Public CustID As Integer
    Public CustPhone As String
    Public CustStatus As Boolean
End Structure
```

Then, at some point in the logic when an instance of this structure is created, the `CustPhone` member would need to explicitly have exactly `20` characters placed in it, like this:

```
Dim stcCustomer as Customer
stcCustomer.CustPhone = String$(20, " ")
```

It would be important to check the length of `stcCustomer.CustPhone` every time it is changed to keep it at twenty characters.

This is not going to be worth the trouble in most cases, so if it is at all possible to switch to a variable length string in the structure, by all means do so. Of course, one of the typical uses of a user defined type is to mimic a record layout that has fixed length fields in it, and this will be difficult to do with structures in VB.NET.

Getting a Conceptual Head Start

What else can you do to prepare for VB.NET? Certainly, programming on the public beta is a great start, and highly recommended. But there are also a couple of ways you can prepare using VB6.

Start using the SOAP Toolkit for Visual Studio 6

As previously mentioned, the SOAP protocol is a foundation technology of Microsoft.NET, and Web Services uses it as a protocol. Anyone expecting to remain current with leading-edge Internet-based systems should be very familiar with SOAP and systems based on it. Fortunately, that familiarity can be gained right now using VB6 plus the SOAP toolkit, which is available for download at:

http://msdn.microsoft.com/xml/general/toolkit_intro.asp

Visual Studio .NET will use SOAP extensively, and will hide a lot of the implementation details. The Visual Studio 6 SOAP toolkit requires a lot more manual work to get a distributed component working than will be needed in the .NET Framework. However, it's worth the effort to become knowledgeable about the capabilities and limitations of the XML Protocol.

Develop an Understanding of Inheritance and Related Object Concepts

Full inheritance and the concepts related to it, such as overriding and constructors, are very useful, and are some of the biggest additions to VB.NET. Once you learn to use these concepts, you'll wonder how you ever lived without them.

You should start working to understand these concepts now. Be aware that you can even simulate some of these concepts in VB6 today, and many VB books discuss inheritance simulation techniques. Those techniques are clumsy, and might have performance issues. However they're useful as a learning tool, and can help you start learning the design possibilities inherent in these advanced object concepts.

Resources

Microsoft has a rapidly growing volume of information about .NET and VB.NET online. Various other people and organizations have also contributed to the .NET knowledge base via web sites, sample applications and other resources.

Microsoft Resources

Web site	URL
Microsoft Visual Studio site	http://msdn.microsoft.com/vstudio/
.NET download site	http://msdn.microsoft.com/net
VB6 to VB.NET upgrade information	http://msdn.microsoft.com/library/techart/vb6tovbdotnet.htm
Remoting article	http://msdn.microsoft.com/library/techart/hawkremoting.htm

Other Resources

Web site	URL
DevX .NET Information (Massive index of .NET sites)	http://www.devx.com/dotnet
VB6 to VB.NET site	http://home.earthlink.net/~butlerbob/Port/PortVBNet.htm
General .NET information	http://www.gotdotnet.com/

Newsgroups and Email Lists

Web site	URL
Microsoft VB.NET	news://msnews.microsoft.com/microsoft.public.dotnet.languages.vb
Microsoft General .NET	news://msnews.microsoft.com/microsoft.public.dotnet.general
DevX VB7	news://news.devx.com/vb.vb7

General Acknowledgments

This book was a lot of fun to write. At times it was also very challenging, especially when faced with particularly difficult problems for which no documentation exists.

Whether they knew it or not, a lot of people helped out a great deal – often because of material they posted to various newsgroups or email lists. In an effort to give credit where credit is due, here are the names of some of the people whose newsgroup posts were of value:

- ❑ Jonathan Allen
- ❑ Chris Anderson
- ❑ David Bayley
- ❑ Mark Boulter
- ❑ Wally McClure

Thank you all – keep up the good posting!

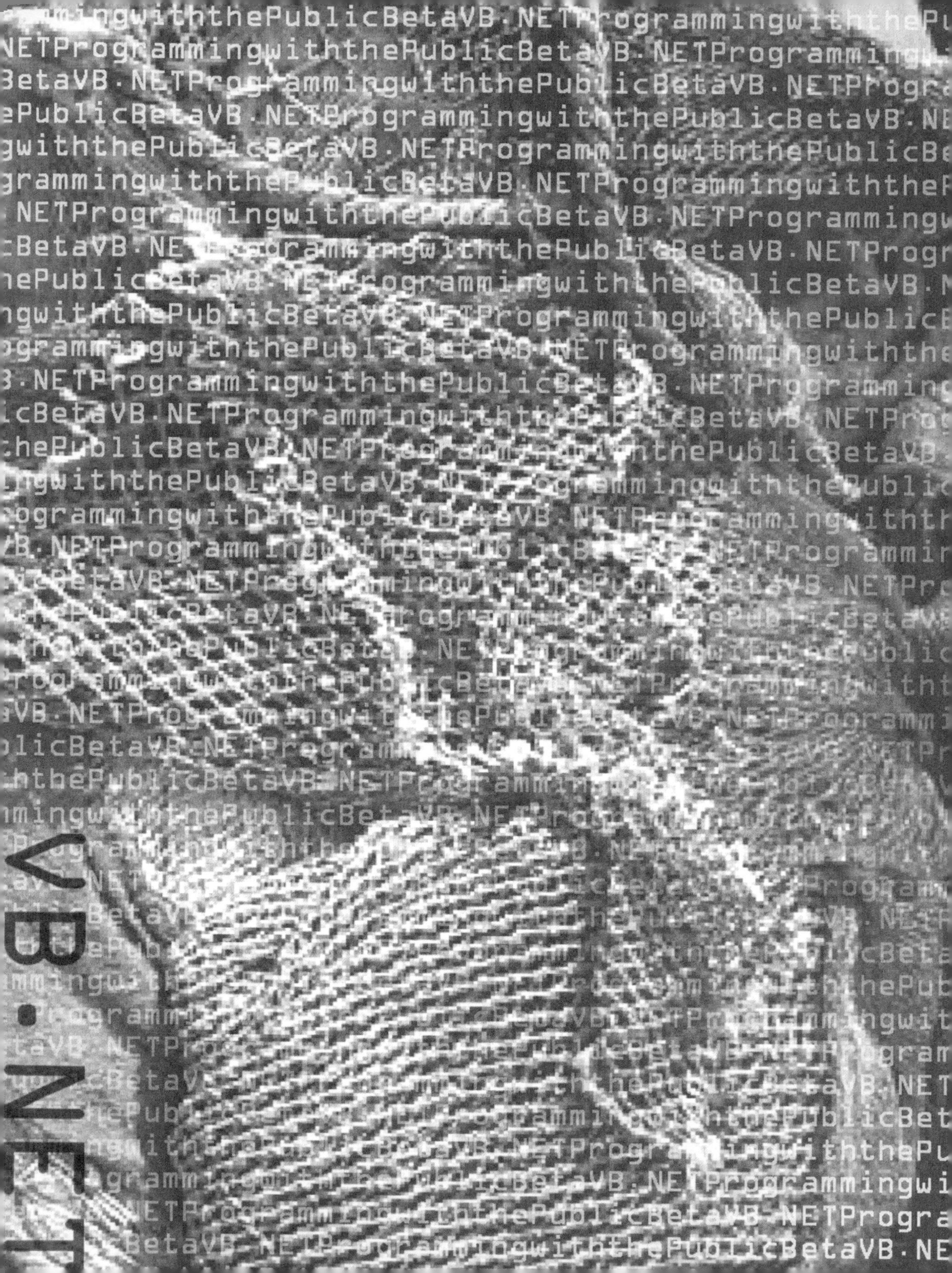
VB.NETProgrammingwiththePublicBeta
VB.NET

Index

A Guide to the Index

The index is arranged hierarchically, in alphabetical order, with symbols preceding the letter A. Most second-level entries and many third-level entries also occur as first-level entries. This is to ensure that users will find the information they require however they choose to search for it.

431

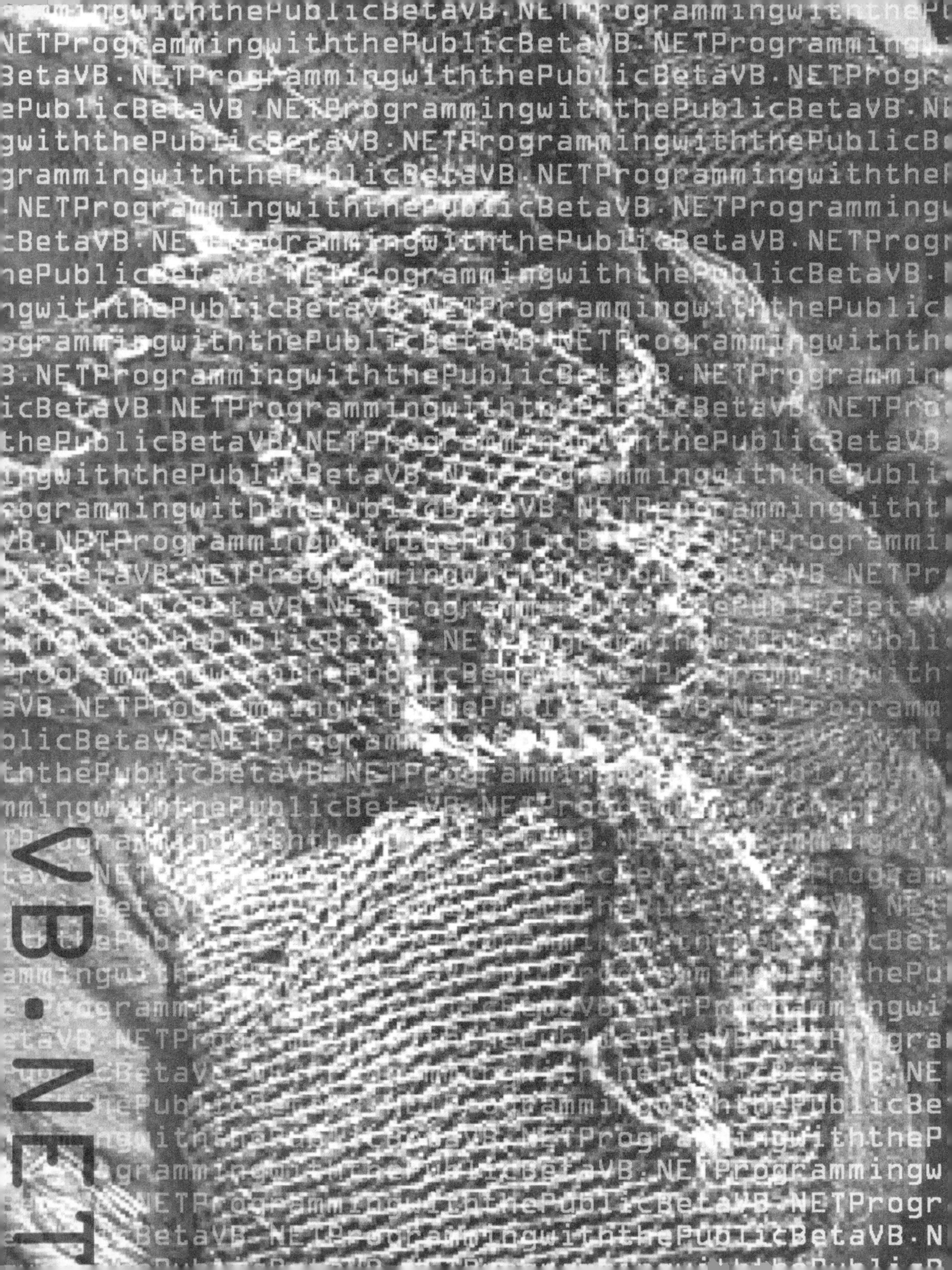
VB.NET
VB.NETProgrammingwiththePublicBeta

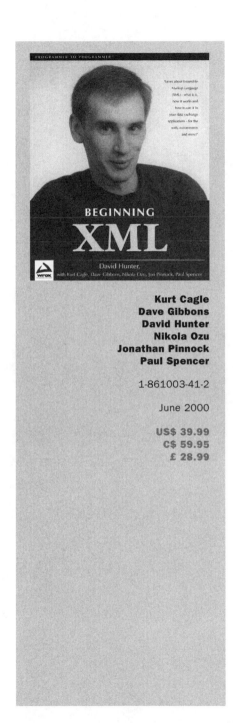

This book explains and demonstrates XML and related technologies. This is the exciting new way of marking up and manipulating data within your applications. XML is platform independent and versatile, meaning that it is rapidly becoming a major technology. Anywhere that data is exchanged between applications or tiers is a potential application for XML. This book will teach you how to use it in your data exchange applications – on the web, for e-commerce or in n-tier architectures – by explaining XML theory, reinforced with plenty of practical examples and real life solutions.

- XML syntax and writing well formed XML

- Using namespaces in XML

- Adding style with CSS and XSL

Summary of contents

Kurt Cagle
Dave Gibbons
David Hunter
Nikola Ozu
Jonathan Pinnock
Paul Spencer

1-861003-41-2

June 2000

US$ 39.99
C$ 59.95
£ 28.99

Stephen Mohr
Scott Woodgate

1-861003-29-3

January 2001

US$ 49.99
C$ 74.95
£ 38.99

The BizTalk™ Framework is an XML framework for application integration and electronic commerce. Microsoft's BizTalk Server 2000 runs on Windows 2000 Server and is capable of integrating with delimited and positional flat file formats, EDI documents, and XML. It allows you to perform the three tasks critical in enterprise application integration: design the flow of information through a system, use BizTalk and its interfaces as the glue to perform the actual integration, then track the flow of information through the resulting system. It does this by providing the integration code in a central server, removing the need for writing integration code into programs, and does much of this by configuration of the server, reducing the amount of time you need to spend programming the integration code. This book teaches you how to use BizTalk Server as an Enterprise Application Integration tool, to integrate applications into co-operating systems. It is especially suited to rapid deployment B2B and B2C e-commerce applications, where you need to integrate with legacy applications. This book is for programmers, familiar with developing Microsoft web solutions, who want to integrate existing applications to create enterprise systems.

● How to design the flow of data through an enterprise application

● How to use BizTalk Server to integrate applications

● How to translate between document formats

Summary of contents

Associated Titles
INTRODUCING .NET | wrox

.NET is Microsoft's vision of "software as a service", a development environment in which you can build, create, and deploy your applications and the next generation of components, termed Web Services. All of Microsoft's major flagship products from Visual Studio to Windows and eventually Office are gradually being integrated into the vision and they will all offer services that will allow greater integration between products. .NET will allow developers to develop in whatever language they are comfortable with, via the introduction of a common language runtime, whilst at the same time provide "building block services" to ease application development. Introducing .NET is designed to tell you exactly what you need to know, to cut through the fog and to bring you a clear picture of what .NET is, and what you can expect to be able to do using it.

● Examines the .NET Framework in detail

● Explains what is and isn't part of .NET

● Examines how the different parts fit together

Summary of contents

Chapter 1:   .NET Overview
Chapter 2:   Intro to the CLR
Chapter 3:   An Introduction to C#
Chapter 4:   What's New in Visual Basic.NET
Chapter 5:   New Features in Visual Studio.NET
Chapter 6:   .NET Class Framework
Chapter 7:   ASP.NET
Chapter 8:   Web Services
Chapter 9:   Windows Forms
Chapter 10:   Building .NET Components
Chapter 11:   ADO.NET
Chapter 12:   Enterprise Servers
Chapter 13:   ASP.NET Case Study

Appendix A: .NET Framework Reference
Appendix B: Using Classic COM Components in ASP.NET

James Conard
Patrick Dengler
Brian Francis
Jay Glynn
Burton Harvey
Billy Hollis
Rama Ramachandran
John Schenken
Scott Short
Chris Ullman

1-861004-89-3

January 2001

US$ 34.99
C$ 52.95
£ 26.99

Mark Chaffin
Brian Knight
Todd Robinson

1-861004-41-9

December 2000

US$ 49.99
C$ 74.95
£ 35.99

Professional SQL Server DTS provides a complete introduction to DTS fundamentals and architecture before exploring the more complex data transformations involved in moving data between different servers, applications, and providers. The book then focuses on DTS programming via the DTS object model, enabling developers to incorporate custom transformations and reporting capabilities into their applications. Advanced topics are explained including error handling, dynamic data loading, and data warehouses. With code and case studies this book gives the reader a complete picture of how to use DTS to its fullest potential. This book is principally aimed at database programmers and administrators who have a working knowledge of SQL Server, and who wish to take DTS beyond its most basic level and tailor it to their needs. It will also appeal to managers and project managers who want to gain an understanding of DTS and how it could benefit their businesses.

● A detailed explanation of the seventeen principal DTS tasks

● Connecting to, querying, and converting heterogeneous data

● Dynamic configuration of your DTS packages

Summary of contents

This book explores Application Center 2000, Microsoft's deployment and management tool for high-availability Web applications built on the Windows 2000 operating system. The book follows Wrox's Programmer to Programmer™ strategy, focusing on the product from the point of view of the developer rather than just the administrator. While it fully covers setup and administration issues, it is more than just a 'setting-up' book, addressing the issues involved in building and configuring applications on AC2K clusters - such as application design, component use, installation, session state management, and much more. This book is for any Web developer (Web sites or Web applications) that needs to achieve scalability through the use of a server farm or in a multi-server environment; this includes those looking for true 'enterprise-level' scalability.

- Simple-to-implement scalability, using multiple servers to 'scale-out'
- Automated high availability through load sharing and automatic fail-over
- Automatic synchronization of content and machine configuration across a cluster

Summary of contents

Chapter 1: Scalable Web Sites and Web Applications
Chapter 2: Creating and Managing Web Clusters
Chapter 3: Deploying Web Sites and Web Applications
Chapter 4: Managing Client State and Server Logs
Chapter 5: Component Load Balancing in Application Center
Chapter 6: Stress Testing Web Applications
Chapter 7: Using the Web Application Stress Tool
Chapter 8: Monitoring Server Clusters and Applications
Chapter 9: Creating Custom Monitors and Alerts in Application Center
Appendix A: WMI Events
Appendix B: Command Line Reference

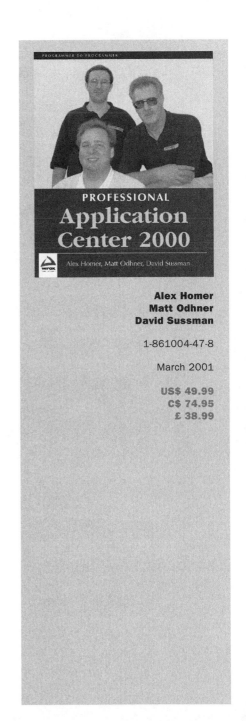

Alex Homer
Matt Odhner
David Sussman

1-861004-47-8

March 2001

US$ 49.99
C$ 74.95
£ 38.99

Rob Vieira

1-861004-48-6

December 2000

US$ 59.99
C$ 89.95
£ 45.99

SQL Server 2000 is the latest and most powerful version of Microsoft's data warehousing and relational database management system. This new release is tightly integrated with Windows 2000 and offers more support for XML, as well as improved Analysis Services for OLAP and data mining. Professional SQL Server 2000 provides a comprehensive guide to programming with SQL Server 2000, from a complete tutorial on Transact-SQL to an in-depth discussion of new features, such as indexed views, user-defined functions, and the wealth of new SQL Server features to support XML. Whether you're coming to SQL Server 2000 from another relational database management system, upgrading your existing system, or perhaps wanting to add programming skills to your DBA knowledge, you'll find what you need in this book to get to grips with SQL Server 2000 development.

- A complete introduction to Transact-SQL
- Creating and using views, stored procedures, and user defined functions
- Querying a SQL Server database using English Query and Full-Text Search

Summary of contents

If you're looking for a way to create attractive, intelligent web pages or, if you're just looking for a way to extend your HTML know-how, then ASP is an effective way to acheive your goals. With ASP, you can customize your web pages to be more dynamic, more efficient and more responsive to your users. It's not just a technology, though - to get the best out of ASP, you'll be using it in tandem with HTML, and with one or more of the web's simple scripting languages. The book will teach you everything you need to create useful real-world applications on the web.

- Teaches VBScript as an integral part of learning to use ASP

- Describes how to make your pages more dynamic with HTML and script code

- Covers writing and debugging script code

David Buser
Jon Duckett
Brian Francis
John Kauffman
Juan T Llibre
David Sussman
Chris Ullman

1-861003-38-2

December 1999

US$ 39.99
C$ 59.95
£ 28.99

Summary of contents

Burton Harvey
Simon Robinson
Julian Templeman
Karli Watson

1-861004-87-7

December 2000

US$ 34.99
C$ 52.95
£ 26.99

C# is a modern, object-oriented language that combines the simplicity of Visual Basic with the power and flexibility of C++. C# has been specifically designed by Microsoft to be the language of choice for writing applications for their new .NET platform - the first development platform designed from the ground up with the Internet in mind. As well as providing a tutorial to the C# language itself, A Preview of C# provides a great introduction to the .NET framework and will give the developer everything they need to orientate themselves in this exciting new environment and start building real-world applications. This book is for existing developers, probably with a C++, Java, or Visual Basic background who want an overview of C# and practical information on how they can develop in C# on the .NET platform. This book was written on the public beta release and while we can't guarantee that the final version will be identical, you can be sure that almost all of the concepts, examples and explanations will still be valid for the final release.

- Explains what C# is and how it fits into the .NET framework

- Writing Windows applications using C# and Visual Studio .NET

- Examples of how to achieve real-world programming tasks in C#

Summary of contents